Reflections of a Zen Buddhist Nun

Kim Iryŏp is shown in this photograph taking a break during the writing of "Path to Eternity: A Message to Journalists" (Chapter 17 of this volume). Early summer 1966. *Photo courtesy of* Hwanhŭidae.

KOREAN CLASSICS LIBRARY: PHILOSOPHY AND RELIGION

Reflections of a Zen Buddhist Nun

Kim Iryŏp

translated and with an introduction by
Jin Y. Park

University of Hawai'i Press/Honolulu
Korean Classics Library

19 18 17 16 15 14   6 5 4 3 2 1

Library of Congress Cataloging-in-Publication Data

Kim, Ir-yop, 1896–1971, author.
  [Onu sudoin ui hoesang. English]
  Reflections of a Zen Buddhist nun / essays by Zen Master Kim Iryop ; translated and with
an introduction by Jin Y. Park.
    pages cm—(Korean classics library. Philosophy and religion)
  Includes bibliographical references and index.
  ISBN 978-0-8248-3878-2 (cloth : alk. paper)
  1. Zen Buddhism.   2. Self.   3. Conduct of life.   4. Kim, Ir-yop, 1896–1971.   I. Park, Jin Y.,
translator.   II. Title.   III. Series: Korean classics library. Philosophy and religion.
  BQ9266.K5713 2014
  294.3'927—dc23
                            2013037984

*Translations in this series have been funded by a generous grant from the Academy of Korean Studies,
Seongnam, Republic of Korea.*

University of Hawai'i Press books are printed on acid-free paper and meet the guidelines for
permanence and durability of the Council on Library Resources.

Design and composition by Wanda China
Printed by Integrated Book Technology, Inc.

To the nuns at Hwanhŭidae and Kyŏnsŏngam

Contents

Acknowledgments

I am indebted to many people whose contributions, support, and assistance made this book possible. I would like first to thank Robert E. Buswell for including Kim Iryŏp's works in the Korean Classics Library series and for offering me guidance throughout the process of translating and producing this book. Without his determination this book would not have seen the light of day. Jennifer Jung-Kim aided me in many ways during the translation process, and I greatly appreciate her help. I thank the two anonymous readers for their valuable comments on an earlier version of the translation. I also offer my sincere appreciation to Patricia Crosby for her insightful, meticulous, and thoughtful copyediting of the manuscript and to Wanda China for her help in its production. I am grateful to the Academy of Korean Studies for funding the translation.

Kim Iryŏp's disciples at Hwanhŭidae always welcomed me when I visited them to look for unknown materials associated with Kim Iryŏp or to get a sense of Kim Iryŏp at the place where she lived and practiced. I am thankful for and humbled by their warm reception. I want especially to express my boundless appreciation to Wŏlsong sŭnim for her generous support of this book's publication. I also thank her for allowing me to interview her and thereby gain a better understanding of Iryŏp no sŭnim (or Great Master Iryŏp) from the perspective of someone who practiced under her. I would like to express my gratitude to Kyŏngwan sŭnim, who helped me in various ways over the years, facilitating my visits to Hwanhŭidae and interviews with the nuns there as well as helping me locate materials on Iryŏp sŭnim. Thanks go to Tanho sŭnim for helping me understand the life at Hwanhŭidae and Kyŏnsŏngam and to Namo sŭnim, who took the time to reproduce the picture of Iryŏp sŭnim that appears as the frontispiece of this book. The College of Arts and Sciences at American University helped me in a number of ways throughout the process of this translation, for which I am thankful. Graduate students Andrew Sonntag, Maegan Reese, and Jeoffrey Pucci helped with the preparation of the index and with proofreading; I thank them for taking the time to assist me.

Translator's Introduction
Kim Iryŏp, Her Life and Thought

Kim Iryŏp (1896–1971) was a writer, new woman, and Zen Buddhist nun whose life offers us a panorama of modern Korean society. Modernity as a global phenomenon has brought changes in the way people understand the world and create values. Rationality, secularism, freedom, equality, and civil society are some of modernity's major characteristics. To understand modernity in East Asia, however, it is necessary to recognize that, along with these universal tenets, modernity brought with it a wholesale encounter with the West that transformed East Asian societies and their intellectual environments. The scale and nature of this transformation cannot be overemphasized. Kim Iryŏp's life and writings bear witness to the disruptive forces set loose when traditional and modern Korea collided.

There has been until recently limited scholarship on Kim Iryŏp. Early studies examine her writings in the context of the formation of modern Korean literature,[1] or compare her with Higuchi Ichiyō (1872–1896), the most well-known female writer of the Meiji period (1868–1912) in Japan.[2] Beginning in the late 1990s, along with the increased interest in modernity and gender in Korea, Kim Iryŏp's activities as a new woman and her influence on the identity and life choices of women in modern Korea began to attract attention.[3] Publications on modernity and gender in Korea almost always mention Kim Iryŏp, and the issues with which her name is associated are diverse, ranging from her views on the modernization of women's clothing to female sexuality and chastity, marriage, divorce, women's education, parenting, and the role of the journal *New Women*.[4] The influence of Christianity on Iryŏp has also recently become a topic of research.[5] Nevertheless, Kim Iryŏp as a Buddhist nun and her Buddhist writings have rarely been explored.[6] On the surface Kim Iryŏp appears to have lived two distinct lives. During the 1920s she was a public figure, an exemplar of Korea's new woman; from the mid-1930s until her death in 1971, she lived as a Buddhist nun, confining her activities primarily to the religious domain. The conclusion of some is that there was a bifurcation of Iryŏp's life, the line of demarcation being her tonsure.[7] Recent scholarship, however, has begun to see more continuity between the two periods of her life.[8]

Iryŏp published throughout her life. Her literary publications before she took Buddhist vows took the form of poems, short stories, and autobiographical essays in which she focused on women's identity, the meaning of religious practice, and existential loneliness as she faced the death of family members.[9] In the period when she identified herself as a new woman, she dedicated herself to gender issues, trying to understand women's existence within a social milieu. Once she became a Buddhist and then a Buddhist nun, she fully embraced Buddhist teachings, interpreting human existence through a religious worldview.

Reflections of a Zen Buddhist Nun, titled in Korean *Ŏnŭ sudoin ŭi hoesang* (Memoir of a practitioner), was published when Iryŏp was in her sixties and is a combination of the diverse aspects of her life, a life that may properly be characterized as a space wherein traditional and modern values contend and co-exist. When she wanted to move forward, tradition held her back; when she felt disillusioned with the new values because of the limitations of society's capacity to embrace them, traditional values offered her a new vision. In turn, Iryŏp's religious understanding offered a new path for Buddhist tradition through her own creative interpretations. Iryŏp's life also reflects the encounter of two major religions: Christianity and Buddhism. Through her reflections on them, Iryŏp ponders the meaning of religion and religious practice in the modern secularized world and offers a way that these two religions might understand each other.

Iryŏp addresses a variety of questions in her book: How does one come to terms with one's identity? What is society's role in the construction of identity? What is the meaning of rebellion and what are its limitations? What does it mean to be in love and what are its different dimensions? How do we philosophize that experience and how do we do so in the context of Buddhist teachings? What is the meaning of religion? How do we live as religious practitioners? How do we understand God and the relationship between good and evil? What and how does Buddhism teach us about all of these issues? What is the ultimate meaning of Buddhist practice? Iryŏp shares these and other concerns with her readers as she reflects on her life experiences. All of these questions coalesce for her around one issue: How to be a real human being. Her creative activities as a writer, social rebellion as a new woman, and religious practice as a Zen Buddhist nun were paths toward the single goal of how to be fully human and thus to live as an absolutely free being with unlimited capacity.

A Pastor's Daughter Grows Up to Be a New Woman

Kim Wŏnju, as she was known before she took the pen name Iryŏp, was born in the northern part of Korea, the first child of a Christian pastor and his wife. According to her book, her father was from a learned family and her grandfather, the headmaster of a public school, was well respected by the people of his village.[10] Her mother was the second wife of her father, whose first wife had died. Iryŏp's mother was not a traditional woman by Korean standards of the time and was not interested in traditional women's work. Iryŏp remembers that her mother wanted to educate her daughter just as boys were educated so that Iryŏp would have the same opportunities as men and not be destined to live the life of a traditional woman.[11] Her parents had an unusual zeal for the education of their first child. Bhikṣuṇī (Buddhist nun) Wŏlsong, a disciple of Kim Iryŏp who served her during the last years of Iryŏp's life until her death in 1971, mentioned that Iryŏp's mother's non-traditional concept of gender must have been a significant influence on Iryŏp's worldview.[12] However, Iryŏp rarely discusses in her own writings her relationship with her mother or her mother's influence on her. By contrast, Iryŏp had an unusually close relationship with her father, and in several of her later works she reflects on the influence of her father's Christian beliefs on the formation of her own thought.

Iryŏp describes her father as "the most devoted Christian" in Korea.[13] Her father's religious devotion inspired young Iryŏp to envision her future as a Christian missionary spreading the word of God.[14] Iryŏp's faith in Christianity, however, slowly declined as she went through adolescence and began questioning certain aspects of life, including some Christian doctrines. By the year 1918 she had almost completely lost her faith. Even so, she did not publically discuss her relationship to Christianity at that time or for many years thereafter. Her thoughts about Christianity appear only in her later works, and *Reflections of a Zen Buddhist Nun* was the first venue in which she seriously engaged with the subject. One of the reasons for her delayed reflection on Christianity seems to be her relationship with her father. It would have been difficult for her to challenge her father's deeply held religious beliefs and his life as a Christian minister.

Iryŏp credits Christianity for her parents' ideas about educating female children. She was allowed, after completing her education in her hometown, to move to Seoul to attend Ewha[15] Hakdang (1913–1915), where she received today's equivalent of a high school education, and continued on at Ewha Chŏnmun (1915–1918), an institution of women's

higher education. In 1918 Iryŏp married Yi Noik, a biology professor at
Yŏnhui Chŏnmun (today's Yonsei University). Iryŏp has little to say about
him, but we know that she met him through the owner of the rooming
house where Yi was staying at the time. Yi, who was almost forty years
old when they met,[16] offered Iryŏp both financial security and support for
her aspirations to become a writer. In 1919 Iryŏp expressed her desire to
go to Japan for further studies, which her husband also supported. During her stay in Japan from 1919 to 1920, she met Korean intellectuals in
Tokyo, including Yi Kwangsu (1892–1950) and Na Hyesŏk (1896–1948).
Yi Kwangsu was a well-known writer, poet, literary critic, and intellectual
who left a visible mark on the history of modern Korean literature. Yi
gave the pen name "Iryŏp" to Kim Wŏnju, encouraging her to become the
Higuchi Ichiyō of Korea.[17] The name "Iryŏp" is the Korean pronunciation
of the same Chinese characters that are read as "Ichiyō" in Japanese. Na
Hyesŏk is known as the first female to paint in the Western style in Korea.
Na went to Japan in 1913 to study painting. In her essay "Ideal Women"
(Isangjŏk puin), published in 1914, Na mentions Hiratsuka Raichō (1886–
1971), a leading Japanese writer and activist of women's issues at the time,
as someone whose life and thought were close to what she considered
those of an ideal woman. This indicates that Na must have been familiar
with the women's movement in Japan. This suggests as well that, in addition to Iryŏp's own exposure to women's movements in Japan, Na influenced Iryŏp's ideas about the women's movement. Iryŏp and Na would
share their intellectual lives for years to come through their activities as
writers and new women.

Iryŏp returned to Korea in 1920 and launched a journal titled *New
Women* (*Sinyŏja*). The journal was credited as the first to be published in
Korea by a woman for the promotion of women's issues.[18] During this period, Iryŏp also organized a forum called the Blue Tower Society (Ch'ŏng-
t'aphoe), providing further evidence that she was aware of and influenced
by the Japanese women's journal *Bluestockings* (*Seitō*), published by the
Seitōsha (Association for Bluestockings), which was run by Hiratsuka
Raichō and other female intellectuals in Japan.[19] *New Women* had a short
life. Its inaugural issue was published in March 1920 and the fourth and
last issue was published in June of the same year.[20] Iryŏp nowhere explicitly mentions the financing of the journal, but it has been proposed that
the cost of its publication was exclusively borne by her husband; the short
life of the journal was therefore likely due to financial difficulties.[21]

The publication of *New Women* marked one of the turning points in
Kim Iryŏp's life because it was the first venue in which her writings became known to the public. As the journal's editor-in-chief, Iryŏp found

her own voice and began to secure her position within Korea's intellectual circle. For about a decade following the publication of the journal, Iryŏp demonstrated her talent as a writer and proved herself a passionate public speaker on behalf of women's issues and social change. The publication of New Women was an essential factor in the formation of the identity of the new women as a group in Korea. It has been noted that the emergence of this group was visible by 1920, but it had not developed a clear group identity until the publication of New Women.[22]

Closely related to the emergence of the new women is the introduction of a public education system for women in Korea. Ewha Hakdang, the first modern women's educational institution in Korea, was established in 1886, but it took time for the idea of educating women to catch on. In Confucian Korean society, a woman's role was limited to working in the home, and the idea of allowing a female child to receive a public education was new. Only one student enrolled at Ewha Hakdang in its first year.[23] The trend gradually changed, and the number of students attending the school grew from a single individual in 1886 to 47 in 1899, and 174 within the next ten years.[24] By the 1920s it was not unusual to see female students on the streets of Seoul.[25] This new generation of women, with their formal, modern-style education, more often than not was awakened to gender issues and demanded changes to the traditional roles and positions of women in their society. In contrast to the traditional image of women, the new women envisioned life above and beyond traditional domestic roles. Yi Paeyong proposed the following five traits as characteristics of the new women: "first, economic independence; second, rationalization and simplification of the family system; third, rejection of male-dominated traditional thought; fourth, a call for a stronger awareness of women's responsibilities and duties; fifth, campaigns by women's organizations and female students for 'old women' so that they can become aware of various women's issues including health and child education."[26]

Despite these general commonalities, the new women were not an entirely homogeneous group, and all kinds of ideas shaped the evolving concept of the new women.[27] Kim Iryŏp and Na Hyesŏk were often categorized as "liberal new women" who emphasized sexual freedom as a ground for women's liberation.[28]

Iryŏp's writings during the 1920s and early 1930s can be grouped into three types: writings on women's issues, autobiographical essays, and religious essays. Over this ten-year period, Iryŏp's perspective and major concerns about women's issues changed. From 1920, when she first published in New Women, until around 1924, her approach to women's issues was modest, focusing on education and emphasizing the importance of women's self-awakening. In the inaugural issue of *New Women,* Iryŏp urged her fellow new women to be discreet in action and cautioned that any individual inappropriate displays would lead to a negative judgment of the entire group.[29] Iryŏp also emphasized the importance of new women's responsibility in bringing about changes to their society.[30]

In July 1924 Iryŏp published an essay entitled "Our Ideals" (Uri ŭi isang) in which she proposed three new ideals for women: 1) a new theory of chastity (*sin chŏngjo ron*), 2) a new individualism (*sin kaein juŭi*), and 3) the exercise of discretion in choosing a spouse. This is the first time Iryŏp spells out what is known as her "new theory of chastity."

"Our Ideals" begins by declaring that if women wish to lead a new life, they should rigorously challenge traditional morality regarding female sexuality. In this context Iryŏp singles out the issue of chastity. As traditionally conceived, chastity was exclusively a woman's virtue, a moral principle that dictated that a woman should be faithful to one man. Challenging this definition, Iryŏp claims that chastity is not a moral concept but should be understood as a measure of one's affection for one's lover.[31] Her purpose here is twofold: She first reveals the traditional concept to be a moralistic mechanism for controlling women and, second, claims equal acknowledgment of women's sexuality with that of men in Korean society. Iryŏp supports her point by arguing that controlling women by making their chastity into a moral principle negates their individual identity. In the 1927 essay "My View on Chastity" (Na ŭi chŏngjo kwan), Iryŏp repeats this argument and reinforces her philosophical reasoning on the relationship between the new concept of chastity and the recognition of individual identity, in this case with the individual meant to include both sexes. In asserting chastity as the highest expression of one's love and thereby of one's individual being, she hoped to connect it as intrinsic to the creation of a new world and new values.[32]

Iryŏp was not alone in challenging the traditional conceptions of female sexuality and chastity as the ground for gender suppression and thereby establishing their reconceptualization as a first step for women's liberation. Writings by Japanese new women foreshadowed Iryŏp's, as can be seen in Raichō's 1915 essay "The Value of Virginity" (J. Shojo no shinka) in which she criticizes the traditional morality related to women's virginity in a way similar to Iryŏp's.[33] Raichō was preceded by a Swedish thinker, Ellen Key (1849–1926), who published extensively on the issue of women's liberation in connection with love, marriage, and sexuality. Key is not widely familiar to feminists today, but she had a strong influence on the new women in the beginning of the twentieth century in America and Japan as well as Korea.[34]

Iryŏp's view on chastity might have been the most well-known aspect of her thought as a new woman, but it was not the only theme that occupied her during this period. Iryŏp's other publications deserve equal attention because, unlike the subject of chastity, which faded from her writings after 1927, the issues dealt with in other of her works during this time appear repeatedly with some variation in her later works. One such theme is Iryŏp's reflection on religion and religious practice, which is a major theme of the short story "Revelation" (Kyesi), published in the inaugural issue of *New Women*. Iryŏp here reflects on the function of religion through the story of a mother who blindly attaches herself first to shamanism and then Christianity to save her dying sons, all to no avail. The story begins three days after the protagonist's second son suddenly falls ill. The protagonist, Mrs. Kim, is in despair, having lost her eldest son three years earlier when he was only seven years old. Despite her extreme distress, Mrs. Kim does not go to a shaman this time, as she had when her eldest son was dying; she is by now a faithful Christian. But, despite her desperate prayers and those of other church members, the son dies. The boy's last wish was to have a Bible with gold-embossed letters on the cover like that of a classmate. The story ends with an allusion to the indifference of the environment surrounding this tragedy, the continuation of everyday routine even as the mother drowns in her sorrow. It is easy to comprehend in this story Iryŏp's struggle to understand the meaning of religion and the individual's relationship to faith. The gloomy conclusion is no doubt suggestive of her attitude toward these matters at the time. Thirty years later, in the essays contained in *Reflections of a Zen Buddhist Nun,* Iryŏp will offer, among other things, full-fledged reflections on the meaning of faith, religion, and religious education, as well as her relationship to and understanding of Christianity and Buddhism.

In another of her short stories, "Awakening" (Chagak, 1926), Iryŏp tells of a young wife named Sunsil whose husband cheated on her while in Japan for his studies. Unlike the traditional woman, who would be a steadfast wife despite her husband's unfaithfulness, Iryŏp's heroine boldly leaves his family, with whom she had been living, even giving up her newborn child to pursue an education and become independent. The story ends with Sunsil's self-affirmation: "Now that I have escaped a life of cruel slavery, I have the choice to be a full human being, leading a worthy and meaningful life. And I am going to look for a person who will take me as such."[35] In this story, published a year before the publication of "My View on Chastity," Iryŏp portrays Sunsil as a new woman who bravely faces the perennial issue of the unfaithful husband, not by subjecting herself to the fate of the traditional woman but by turning the situation into an occasion for self-development.

Iryŏp's autobiographical essays frequently express her loneliness at being the only surviving member of her family. The death of her sister in 1907 is the occasion of the poem "Death of a Sister" (Tongsaeng ŭi chugŏm). Her mother died in 1909 in childbirth, with the newborn baby, a boy, succumbing several days later. In her essay "Mother's Graveyard" (Ŏmŏni ŭi mudŏm, 1920), she remembers how her mother desperately prayed for Iryŏp when she was sick as a child. In 1915 her father died; she was nineteen.[36] Her half-sister, Iryŏp's only immediate family member left after the death of her father, died in 1919. The occasion is described in her essay "Death of a Sister" (Tongsaeng ŭi chugŏm, 1920). In "Before My Father's Soul" (Abŏnim yŏngjŏn e, 1925), Iryŏp asks her dead father for advice about how to get through the difficulties she was facing at the time. "Hometown Hill Where My Siblings Were Buried" (Tonsaeng mudŭn twit tongsan, 1933) contains Iryŏp's recollection of playing with her sisters as a child and her mourning that they are all gone. Her autobiographical essays during this period are charged with dialogues with her dead family members, reflecting her sense of loss and loneliness. In the background of Iryŏp's solitude we find existential questions that will soon be expressed more explicitly in her writings and her life. From 1930, when she published her first essay about Buddhism, "The Second Anniversary of Being a Buddhist" (Pulmun t'ujok i chunyŏn e), until the publication of "Practicing Buddhism" (Puldo rŭl taggŭmyŏ) in 1935, Buddhism became one of the major themes of Iryŏp's writings.

In the World of the Buddha

Kim Iryŏp's introduction to Buddhism took place around 1927, when she became involved with the journal *Buddhism* (*Pulgyo*).[37] She began contributing to the journal in 1927 and continued until 1932, just before she joined a monastery in 1933. According to one source, Iryŏp was deeply impressed by a dharma talk given by Zen Master Man'gong as early as 1923.[38] Nevertheless, she did not seem familiar with Buddhism when her first writings appeared in *Buddhism*. Recalling those days, Iryŏp confessed that at that time she was not interested in Buddhism and did not bother to read those sections of the journal that covered Buddhist doctrine.[39] In other words, Kim Iryŏp's involvement with the journal *Buddhism* was not initiated by her interest in Buddhism. It was rather through the offices of Pang In'gŭn (1899–1975), a Korean writer and the husband of a friend from Ewha Hakdang, that Iryŏp was introduced to the journal as an outlet for her literary works. As has been pointed out by Pang Minho, a scholar of

Korean literature, the fact that a Buddhist journal welcomed contributions from a non-Buddhist writer like Iryŏp demonstrates the efforts that modern Korean Buddhism made to connect with the general public.[40] Not only was Iryŏp not familiar with Buddhism around 1927, her upbringing as a Christian gave her the impression that Buddhism was a superstition and Buddhists immoral people. But when Iryŏp actually met the Buddhists involved with the journal, she realized that Buddhism was far different from what she had been led to believe. She found Buddhist ceremonies solemn, sacred, and peaceful. She also noticed that, contrary to what she had heard about Buddhist monks being wanton, the people working for the journal *Buddhism* were modest and reasonable. Her understanding of Buddhist doctrine probably began through her efforts to improve her knowledge of literary Chinese (*hanmun*). It was in that context that she began reading Buddhist scriptures with a Buddhist scholar, Kwŏn Sangno (1879–1965).

Kwŏn Sangno was the editor of *Buddhism* from its inaugural issue, published on July 15, 1924, until October 1931, after which Manhae Han Yongun (1879–1944) was the editor until February 1937. Since Iryŏp was a regular contributor until 1932, she must have been in frequent contact with Kwŏn, even though no reference to him appears in her writings. However, she does not even mention him in her essay describing her initial encounter with Buddhist thought, other than to say that she studied scriptures with him. She does not tell which scriptures she studied. What we do know is that from her first exposure to Buddhism, Iryŏp had a favorable impression of the religion.

> I cannot say that at that time I understood Buddhist teachings, which are both ordinary and profound, but I could at least feel clearly that it was definitely good. I also believed Buddhist teaching to be something big that could save not only me as an individual but the entire world, and the entire universe as well. My heart was filled with a desire to learn, but I was not even sure what I should know or what I wanted to know. I did not know whom I should ask or even what to ask regarding Buddhism, yet the idea that I should let other people learn about Buddhism became urgent.[41]

Iryŏp seems not to have known much about the situation of Korean Buddhism at the time other than what she describes above through her experience with the people associated with the journal. Like other East Asian countries, Korea opened its door to foreign powers at the end of the nineteenth century, a situation that presented Buddhism with new and challenging social influences. Korean Buddhist efforts to meet the challenges of the changing environment appeared in two major forms. The first was Buddhism's attempts at renovation to prove its relevance to modern society; the second involved the resurgence of Zen (Sŏn) Buddhism through the revival of the monastic tradition and meditation training.[42] By the 1920s, Korean Buddhist reformists were aware of the importance of bringing Buddhism down to the public from the secluded mountainside. They emphasized popularization as one of the most urgent tasks for the survival of Buddhism in the changing environment of the time. A series of essays demanding the reformation and revitalization of Korean Buddhism appeared from the 1910s to the 1930s. Kwŏn Sangno's "Treatise on the Reformation of Korean Buddhism" (Chosŏn Pulgyo kaehyŏngnon, 1912–1913) was the first to appear in this context. Kwŏn here emphasizes the importance of education for the reform of Buddhism. Following Kwŏn's treatise was Han Yongun's "Treatise on the Revitalization of Korean Buddhism" (Chosŏn Pulgyo yusillon, 1913), which became the most well known of this group of writings. There is no indication in Iryŏp's writings of whether she had read any of these treatises,[43] and her analysis of Buddhism at the time seems to be based more on her own experience as a Christian. She, for example, wondered why Buddhists were not actively involved with proselytizing, whereas the voice of Christianity was growing louder and its zeal for proselytizing stronger. Iryŏp worried about low attendance at Buddhist temples and questioned whether the women who did go to temples actually knew anything about Buddhism. She was also concerned about the lack of networking among Buddhists and expressed the need for a sense of engagement among members of the Buddhist tradition. Iryŏp wanted to improve this situation and wrote of her intention to propose a scripture reading group as well as a Buddhist study group to several other people in a youth committee with which she seems to have gotten involved. She also expressed her wish to spread Buddhism to those with no opportunity to encounter this teaching.[44] Whether she actually submitted such a proposal and, if so, whether the study group achieved the goal she had set, is not known. Regardless, her observations about Buddhism during her two years of exposure to the religion were quite accurate and address issues with which Korean Buddhism would long struggle.

From her initial encounter with Buddhism around 1927 until 1933, when she joined the monastery, Iryŏp continued her diverse ways of studying and practicing Buddhism. She divorced in 1921 and in 1929 remarried a non-celibate Buddhist monk named Ha Yunsil, who was also involved with the journal *Buddhism*.[45] During this period Iryŏp apparently followed the path of a lay Buddhist practitioner and, together with her non-celibate monk-husband, led a secular life. In her essay "Buddhist Practice and My Family" (Sin Pul kwa na ŭi kajŏng) published in 1931, Iryŏp describes her life with Ha Yunsil as an acceptable way to practice Buddhism. She regrets the waste of the ten-something years before she became a Buddhist when she was ignorant of the Buddha's teaching. She notes that she had considered joining the monastery when she first became a Buddhist but realized that she would not be able to completely extinguish desires and feelings of affection and thus decided to remain a lay practitioner. She married a non-celibate monk, she explains, in order to secure her Buddhist practice far into the future.[46] Although she does not perform Buddhist rituals, she claims that, whenever she has time, she practices chanting to develop concentration (yŏmbul sammae); she also reads introductory books on Buddhism.[47] She ends the essay by expressing her wish that, later in life, she will be able to practice meditation.[48]

Her commitment to the life of a lay practitioner eventually changed, and in 1933 she joined the monastery. She was thirty-eight years old. After this point her activities as a writer diminished, and in 1935 she completely stopped publishing her writings.[49] "Practicing Buddhism" (Puldo rŭl taggŭmyŏ), which appeared in the journal Three Thousand Li (Samch'ŏlli) in January 1935, was almost her last publication until other of her works appeared in the late 1950s. In "Practicing Buddhism," Iryŏp tells how her teacher, Zen Master Man'gong, advised her not to write poems or fiction,[50] and she declares that she would faithfully follow that dictum for the next two decades. In an essay written on the anniversary of Man'gong's death that appears in Reflections, Iryŏp reminds herself of her teacher's comment on her literary activities. When he admonished her that a bowl that is full cannot be refilled, Iryŏp responded that she had already emptied her bowl, meaning that she had left behind her practice of writing and reading.[51] Since then, she avows, she has devoted herself only to practice, never going to bed before ten o'clock in the evening and never failing to rise before two o'clock in the morning. In the 1960 edition of her essay "In Memory of Great Master Man'gong" (Man'gong taehwasang ŭl ch'ŭmo hayŏ), Iryŏp records that she had stopped reading and writing "for more than ten years" after the master advised her to do so.[52] In the 1962 version of the same essay, which appeared in Having Burned Away My Youth (Ch'ŏngch'un ŭl pulsarŭgo), she is more specific about the dates, stating that "for eighteen years," she stopped reading and writing.[53] During the 1950s she gradually resumed publishing her writings. In 1960 her first book, Reflections of a Zen Buddhist Nun, came out.

Iryŏp entered the monastery of Sŏbongam on Mount Kŭmgang in June 1933. Zen Master Man'gong was her dharma teacher. In 1934 she received a dharma teaching from Man'gong that states, "Only after the nature [of your mind] becomes pure like a lotus flower should you go out from this mountain."[54] She also received from Master Man'gong her dharma name, Hayŏp, meaning Lotus Petal. From the time when she first joined the monastery until she settled down in Kyŏnsŏng Hermitage (Kyŏnsŏngam) in 1936,[55] Iryŏp practiced in several different places. She began practicing at Chikchi Monastery (Chikchisa) in Kimch'ŏn, Kyŏngbuk Province, and then at Sŏbongam and Mahayŏn on Mount Kŭmgang; she then moved to Sŏnhakwŏn in Seoul. She practiced in each place for about three months before moving on to the next.[56] She did a winter retreat at Sudŏk Monastery (Sudŏksa) in 1936[57] and remained there for the rest of her life.

Generally speaking, Buddhist nuns in contemporary Korea are trained in two ways. Basic doctrinal education is received in a seminary (*kangwŏn*), and meditation is practiced in a meditation hall (*sŏnwŏn*). This tradition had not, however, been fully established at the time Iryŏp joined the monastery. The first meditation hall for nuns opened at Kyŏnsŏng Hermitage at Sudŏk Monastery at the beginning of the twentieth century.[58] Immediately after its opening Kyŏnsŏng Hermitage became a major force in revitalizing the Zen tradition for Korean nuns, and today it continues to play a central role as a place for nuns' practice in Korea. Iryŏp was one of the first generation of nuns in modern Korean Buddhism to pursue their practice at Kyŏnsŏng Hermitage, where she stayed until her death in 1971 except for a short period when she stayed at Hwanhŭidae for health reasons. Iryŏp's teacher, Zen Master Man'gong, is one of the most well-known Zen masters in modern Korean Buddhism. He is also known for his dedication to the training of nuns. Myori Pŏphui (1887–1975), who is considered the revitalizer of Zen meditation practice for nuns in modern Korea, also practiced under Master Man'gong and eventually earned recognition for her awakening from him.

Around 1966, due to age-related health problems, Iryŏp moved to a structure called Hwanhŭidae (Delightful Terrace). At that time, Hwanhŭidae was a small house, which had been renovated into a place of practice by Wŏlsong, one of Iryŏp's disciples. Daily life at Kyŏnsŏng Hermitage and Hwanhŭidae during Iryŏp's time there was undoubtedly not exactly the same as now, but the daily routine of these places today gives us a sense of Iryŏp's life.[59] Practitioners get up at 3:00 a.m.; morning prayers and meditation follow. Breakfast is served at 6:00 a.m. After the morning meal, practitioners do cleaning and have free time for about an hour. At Kyŏnsŏng Hermitage, practitioners meditate between 7:00 and 8:00 a.m. At 10:00 a.m., morning offerings to the Buddha (*sasi maji*) are performed, a ritual that includes about an hour of prayer. Lunch is served at 11:00 a.m. and dinner at 5:00 p.m. In between, practitioners are free to devote time to study, practice, or doing chores around the temple. At 6:30 p.m., the evening service is performed for about half an hour. After the service, some might continue prayers to the Buddha until about 7:30 p.m. During the evening study time, practitioners are on their own either to meditate, study Buddhist texts, or engage in other practices. Bedtime is between 9:00 and 10:00 p.m. The time between waking and retiring at Kyŏnsŏng Hermitage is devoted to meditation, whereas at Hwanhŭidae the time is divided among meditation, sūtra studying, and various chores and errands for the management of the place. Iryŏp moved back to Kyŏnsŏng Hermitage from Hwanhŭidae in 1970, expressing her wish to spend her final days with other practitioners.

Iryŏp's Buddhist practice was mainly focused on meditation, and the form of meditation she practiced is known as *hwadu* (Ch. *huatou*, or "critical phrase") meditation. In November 1934 Iryŏp was interviewed by the literary journal *Opening of the World* (*Kaebyŏk*). Her first interview after her tonsure in June 1933, it appeared in the January 1935 issue. The reporter who conducted the interview asked Iryŏp whether Iryŏp was studying Buddhist scriptures, to which Iryŏp responded in the negative. Iryŏp confirmed that she exclusively practiced *hwadu* and described *hwadu* practice as being like "resolving one big doubt." She added, "This is a practice of focusing one's mind on a single thought."[60]

Hwadu meditation is a Zen Buddhist practice originally developed by the twelfth-century Chinese Chan master Dahui Zhonggao (1089–1163).[61] Pojo Chinul (1158–1210)[62] first introduced this style of meditation in the thirteenth century; it was fully integrated into Zen practice by his successor Hyesim (1178–1234).[63] Since then, *hwadu* meditation has been the dominant form of Zen Buddhist practice in Korea. *Hwadu* meditation developed out of *gongan* (better known in the English-speaking world by its Japanese pronunciation *kōan*) tradition. A *gongan* (or a *kōan*) in general refers to a dialogue between a Zen master and a student. *Hwadu* meditation takes a "critical phrase" (*hwadu*) from a *gongan* dialogue and utilizes that phrase in meditation. In the case of Iryŏp, Master Man'gong gave her the well-known *hwadu* "Ten thousand things return to one; to where does the one return?"[64] The fundamental idea of *hwadu* meditation is to liberate oneself from a habitual mode of thinking. The Buddhist worldview is known as "dependent co-arising" (*yŏn'gi*). It teaches that nothing exists as an unchanging, independent essence; instead Buddhism claims that things exist through the cooperative functioning of different constituents, which are subject to interactive movements of causes and conditions. This idea applied to the individual self is the Buddhist theory of non-self (*mua*). The self is non-self in the sense that what we think of as self is contingent and provisional. What we call self is constituted through the combination and co-working of different factors and nobody possesses an unchanging and permanent essence that could be called one's core self.

Iryŏp understood these Buddhist ideas as a fundamental source of freedom and equality. Reflecting on the time when she joined the monastery, she states that she felt a sense of urgency, describing this urgency as a "need to survive." This was the topic of the dharma talk Man'gong gave to her when she became his disciple: "When one leaves the secular world and joins a monastery, the study for the person is 'to survive.'"[65] The existential urgency expressed by Man'gong as grounds for Buddhist practice becomes a major theme of Iryŏp's Buddhism. Iryŏp explains this awareness of existential reality as a desperate desire to become a "human being."[66] To become a human being, to her, is to find the real self, the real "I."

In the preface to *Reflections of a Zen Buddhist Nun*, Iryŏp diagnoses the period in which she was living as a time of the lost self. Individuals in her time, she proposes, have lost themselves but are unaware of that fact. The time of the lost self, from Iryŏp's perspective, is characterized by life lived in a bound state, a constrained life that inevitably results in dissatisfaction and discontent. The purpose of Buddhist practice for Iryŏp is to enable the self to realize its true nature and thus liberate itself from its bound state. Iryŏp asserts that this realization is absolutely necessary for at least two reasons. First, without this realization of the Buddhist teachings, we believe that our being is limited to the boundary of our physical reality when in truth we are unbound beings with limitless capacity. Our existence is constrained by the limits created not only by our physical reality but also by our limited mental capacity. Second, without this realization, we cannot recognize the source of our suffering. Iryŏp tells us that suffering in this life is caused by a failure to see the reality of one's self, which then becomes the cause for further suffering in future lives in the cycle of transmigration. With the realization of the limitless capacity of oneself comes the freedom of an open self. Iryŏp calls this self the "great self" (*taea*).

In contrast to this great self, people tend to prefer the boundaries inherent in the worldly idea of the self, which allows them to remain within their comfort zone. The self that insists on staying within its shell is what Iryŏp calls the "small self" (*soa*). One who has achieved the state of the great self and is capable of generating the values of its own existence Iryŏp calls a "person of culture" (*munhwain*). In the chapter entitled "Buddhism and Culture" (Pulgyo wa munhwa) in *Reflections*, Iryŏp characterizes the

Buddha as a great person of culture and professes that she joined the monastery because she recognized that to become such a person meant practicing Buddhism.

The capacity attained by liberating oneself from the boundaries of the small self and embracing the freedom of the great self is what Iryŏp calls "creativity" (ch'angjosŏng). This creativity is for Iryŏp each individual's original mind (pon maŭm), a mind that is absolutely open and the source of one's existence. An individual who realizes original mind becomes a "complete being" (wanin), a being whose existence embraces the entire universe. Unlike the religious commonplace that confers on a religious leader entirely positive attributes, Iryŏp claims that the Buddha unifies within himself the qualities of both a buddha and a demon. The world, then, is envisioned as being inclusive by virtue of the existential reality of Buddhism, which is that no being exists as an independent entity. The idea that the Buddha encompasses both positive and negative qualities is not an endorsement of evil but an understanding that any binary construction, including that of good and evil, is mutually indebted for its existence. This world of mutually indebted genesis is one of absolute equality wherein a broken piece of a tile and the Buddha share the same logic of existence.

In her later life, Iryŏp's ideas of the great self, creativity, and original mind evolve into a philosophy of "life" or of "life force" (saengmyŏng). She briefly discusses this concept at the beginning of *Reflections,* and the idea constitutes a major theme of her last book, *In Between Happiness and Misfortune* (Haengbok kwa pulhaeng ŭi kalp'i esŏ), published in 1964. She submits in this book that the state of life is a state of oneness and this oneness is the source of all existence. This oneness is not "the one" in the sense of being the first or the most precious; it is the one in the sense that there are no other numbers, nothing is outside of this one; it is the all-inclusive one. The sensory world is the material world, and for Iryŏp, the ground of this visible and tangible world is life or life energy. Life energy itself is one, it being a state before division. Since it is one without division, it is absolute. The goal of Buddhist practice for Iryŏp is to realize this one and absolute state of existence. It is this realization that allows us to begin to take down the boundaries of the small self and attain freedom.

With her philosophy of life, Iryŏp's journey had taken her to the most fundamental ground of existence. It began when she challenged the socially constructed identity of a woman. She rebelled against this externally imposed identity and value system by critically evaluating women's role in society and society's concept of the female virtue of chastity. After joining the monastery, her search for identity extended to the terrain of the nature of freedom and equality. As a new woman, her challenge was directed outward to identifying the source of constraints imposed by society on her as a female. As a Buddhist practitioner, Iryŏp examined the nature of the self; the direction of her search for freedom and the meaning of existence turned inward. The social criticism of her early period gave way to the spiritual and religious search for the fundamental nature of existence itself. It was Buddhism that offered the foundational teaching for Iryŏp's journey into her self.

Kim Iryŏp and Her Readers

Kim Iryŏp led a multifaceted life that sometimes embraced conflicting ideas and ideals. She was a born Christian who became a Buddhist nun; known for her demand for sexual liberalism, she came to live as a celibate nun; she was a writer who intentionally and willingly suspended writing (or suspended the publication of her writing) for nearly two decades. These different aspects of Iryŏp's life raise questions about her life story. Among the most frequently asked are: Why did Iryŏp give up Christianity and become a Buddhist nun? Why did she decide to publish her writings after twenty years of silence? And what happened to her feminist ideas after she joined the monastery?

Iryŏp was a Christian from birth. At the young age of eight, she imagined her future as a Christian missionary delivering God's word to nonbelievers. She remembered her father as the most devout Christian in Korea, someone whose faith never faltered. He taught his daughter in exactly the same way he taught his other fellow Christians, which meant that he did not allow any questions or misgivings about God's message and intentions. When Iryŏp expressed faint doubts about God and wanted to ask questions about the meaning of certain Christian doctrines, her father admonished her that prayer and faith alone provided the answers. In the essay "Having Burned Away My Youth: A Letter to Mr. B.," Iryŏp describes how her father responded with "let's pray and repent" whenever she voiced doubts about her beliefs.

The strict evangelicalism of Iryŏp's father took a toll on his daughter during her young adulthood, as she seriously questioned diverse aspects of life, including certain Christian doctrines. Iryŏp's father died in 1915 when Iryŏp was nineteen years of age and before he could know the course his daughter's religious life would take. Iryŏp herself would not address her questions about Christianity until later in life, as we read in several chapters of *Reflections*. Published when she was in her sixties, this work is the first in which Iryŏp publicly discusses her relationship with Christianity. Iryŏp expresses in some of her essays that she was exceptionally close to her father, which must have added to the difficulty of looking back at her relationship with Christianity and openly discussing Christian doctrine. Iryŏp asserts that her father's strict Christianity and discouragement of religious doubt backfired, eventually causing her to lose her faith. It was not against Christianity itself that Iryŏp rebelled but rather a certain way that Christianity was taught and that Christian doctrines were interpreted. It is not entirely clear when she turned her back on Christianity, but by the time she completed her studies at Ewha Hakdang in 1918, she already considered herself a non-believer.

Recollecting the time when her belief in Christianity was shaken, Iryŏp points to the issue of good and evil as one of the questions that disturbed her in her relationship with Christianity. If God were the creator of all beings, Iryŏp reasons, God must be the source of both good and evil and should thus be held responsible for the fall of Adam and Eve. It was God who created Adam and Eve, Iryŏp argues, and it was God who gave them the freedom to violate His laws. The ultimate responsibility for their transgression should then lie with God, not with humankind. Behind this reasoning lay her doubts about the binary structure that Iryŏp understood to undergird the Christian worldview as well as secular logic. Iryŏp argues that the binary logic that makes a clear distinction between God and humans, the creator and the created, together with the binary value system of good and evil, has limitations that ultimately render it untenable. The dividing line between good and evil, she came to see, is not as solid as binary logic assumes it to be. For Iryŏp, all of life is ultimately one, and binary logic fails to recognize this fundamental nature of existence. The Buddha, as the representative of the Buddhist worldview, is the source of both good and evil, humans and devils, medicine and poison. The binary opposites and the accompanying value judgments arise, from Iryŏp's perspective, when the oneness of life is misunderstood as consisting of fragments. A being understood through binary logic is an isolated entity whose capacity is limited. Iryŏp regards this misapprehension as the fundamental source of constraints on individuals' freedom.

Although Iryŏp had doubts about certain Christian doctrines, she did not consider religious practice objectionable in and of itself. In *Reflections,* she suggests that had she understood the concept of God as a vehicle of skillful means to uplift people, she would not have lost what she referred to as the jewel of faith.[67] Iryŏp emphasizes the importance of religious education, which she distinguishes from the mere accumulation of knowledge, because religious education teaches people how to live. Through her reflections on the meaning of religion, religious practice, and God, Iryŏp eventually concludes that "the Buddha and God at their origin are from the same seed."[68] Iryŏp reasons that the Buddha reached the realization that the bound state is not permanent, that one's capacity is limitless and thus we are capable of embodying freedom. The same holds true for God, Iryŏp believes. God is a being capable of fully utilizing the unlimited capacity with which each being is endowed. The idea that God is a creator means, for Iryŏp, that God embodies the creativity inborn in each of us. To claim that God created the world is not only wrong but actually diminishes God, since in that case God would be responsible for all of the evil that exists in the world.[69] In this way Iryŏp reconciled with Christianity instead of completely disavowing it in favor of Buddhism. The concept of God she proposes here is obviously different from the God she learned from her father when she was a child. Whether or not Christians would agree with Iryŏp's understanding of God is a different issue. It can at least be assumed that Iryŏp herself believed that she was not completely denouncing Christian teachings; she simply disapproved of and challenged certain ways that Christianity was understood, interpreted, and practiced.

Reflections of a Zen Buddhist Nun is Iryŏp's first book and her first major publication after she suspended publishing in 1935. In 1962 her second book, *Having Burned Away My Youth*, was published; two years later, her last book, *In Between Happiness and Misfortune,* appeared. Why had she decided to break her silence and return to writing? In the introduction to *Reflections*, Iryŏp makes clear that the book is written for the purpose of proselytization. She regretted the general lack of concern among her contemporaries about serious questions such as the meaning of existence. Her response to that situation was to adopt a method that combined philosophical issues with stories from her own life, thereby making accessible a serious examination of the meaning of existence and the practice of Buddhism. In *Reflections* Iryŏp characterizes her writings as like "sugar-coated medicine for little children," in which she mixes Buddhist teachings with "the dreams of my old days." She thus declares the goal of her book as being to "help readers come to the realization that, as we all have lost ourselves, we need to find our true selves if we are to become real human beings."[70] Iryŏp rarely adopted the Zen style of writing that uses cryptic expressions. According to Bhikṣuṇī Kyŏngwan, a second-generation disciple of Kim Iryŏp, this is because Iryŏp wanted to communicate with ordinary people. Kyŏngwan writes, "In the Zen writings of Zen Master Iryŏp, there is minimal discussion of Kanhua Zen [*hwadu* meditation], and most writings focus on Buddhist doctrine. That is because the purpose of her writings was to spread Buddhist teachings to the general public."[71]

If the desire to proselytize was the immediate inspiration for Iryŏp taking up writing again, behind that can be seen a deeper relationship between Iryŏp and her writing. Even though Iryŏp stopped writing for almost two decades, it does not seem that this suspension was ever meant to be a permanent and complete abandonment of the act of writing. In the aforementioned interview with the journal *Opening of the World*, the reporter asked Iryŏp whether she would resume her writing at some point in the future and Iryŏp responded positively. She proposed that for writing to have meaning the one writing must be a fully functioning human being, by which Iryŏp implied something far deeper than the common-sense understanding of what it meant to be a human being. In an essay published in January 1935, she reaffirms this idea when she writes, "If I wish to be a great writer, I believe that I should learn all about the life and the universe and only then should I begin to write again. Looking back, I am ashamed of all the writings I have done in the past."[72] Writing for Iryŏp is not at bottom something that contradicts Buddhist practice. Zen tradition frequently characterizes itself as "a special transmission outside scriptures/ Without relying on words or letters/ Directly pointing at the mind/ Looking at the nature [of the human mind] and attaining buddhahood."[73] This definition of Zen does not mean that Zen does not rely on words or that it rejects the use of language. It is rather a warning against being enslaved by stock expressions and stagnant modes of thinking. When Master Man'gong told Iryŏp not to read or write, he could not have intended that she should stay away from the literary world entirely; abstaining from writing or reading is only a temporary measure in the process of practice, which facilitates a state in which the practitioner experiences self-transformation.

At a deeper level, resuming writing for Iryŏp was a way to reconcile herself with various stages of her life and to give herself an opportunity to reinterpret her life stories. All three books published in the 1960s take the form of autobiographical essays in which some of the major events in her life are interpreted from a Buddhist perspective. This reconciliation takes various forms: reconciliation with Christianity, reconciliation with her parents and family members who all died when she was still young, reconciliations with her ex-lovers, and eventually reconciliation with life itself.

Finally, but not least importantly, we have to ask what happened to her feminist ideals after she joined the monastery. After becoming a nun, Iryŏp did not explicitly engage in activities related to women's movements. Nor do her writings deal with the issues of gender discrimination or women's liberation. When the interviewer from the journal *Opening of the World* asked Iryŏp what would happen to her involvement with women's movements now that she had entered the monastery, she responded, "They are nothing but temporary emergency measures. They cannot be eternal and unchanging truth."[74] Neither the reporter nor Iryŏp further elaborated on the issue, but Iryŏp's response was apparently sufficient to draw criticism, some quite severe, from the later generation of feminists.[75] As a new woman, she challenged the socially constructed forms of suppression. When she became a Buddhist practitioner and then a Buddhist nun, Iryŏp's attention gradually shifted from social conditions to existential reality. Her focus changed to religious and spiritual concerns, where it remained until her death. One might approach the issue of Iryŏp's involvement in women's movements from two different but related perspectives. The first is to understand her feminism in the context of her life; the second is to consider the issue in the broader context of religion's social engagement.

As I have discussed elsewhere,[76] Iryŏp's lives as a new woman and as a Buddhist nun are both based on the same value: to live as a being who is free and who is creative. The former is the condition for the latter. A being that is bound cannot be creative, and a being whose creative power is suppressed by externally imposed norms cannot be a fully functioning human being. As a new woman, Iryŏp pursued this value at a societal level; as a Buddhist nun, her focus was changed to the existential level. Her discussion of love, which appears in her last book, *In Between Happiness and Misfortune,* well demonstrates this evolution in Iryŏp's thought. In it, she examines love as a fundamental capacity that both sentient and insentient beings possess. This is unlike her outlook during her pre-monastic period, when love was understood in the context of female sexuality, in regard to heterosexual love, and also for the purpose of women's liberation. After she joined the monastery, heterosexual love was no longer her major concern. Does this indicate that consideration of one's existential reality necessarily excludes a social consciousness? This need not be the case; there are instances in Western intellectual history where the opposite was actually true, times, for example, when intellectuals espousing existentialism were among the most socially engaged. This leads to a broader question that Iryŏp's life raises with regard to her position on gender: That is, is religious practice in general and Zen practice in particular compatible with social activism? Recent Western-language Buddhist scholarship has generally been critical of Zen Buddhism's failure to translate individual practice into social engagement.[77] In her silence on gender issues, Iryŏp might be subject to the same type of criticism. Iryŏp, however, did not retreat into a solipsistic world after she entered the monastery. During her time as a monastic, she remained engaged, but the form of engagement changed. She held the position of head nun of the meditation hall (*ipsŭng*) for almost thirty years. In other words, she played a role in the monastic community of which she was a part. She reached outside the monastic community to engage with the general public by publishing her writings. This time, however, the scope of her writings was not limited to gender issues. It could be argued that in order for her to be faithful to her stance on gender equality, which she had advocated as an activist for women's liberation, her engagement as a Buddhist nun would have had to include a more active promotion of gender issues. In that case, her Buddhism could have taken a form similar to the various types of socially engaged Buddhism, such as Minjung Buddhism, that were current in the 1970s and 1980s in Korea.[78] Iryŏp chose otherwise and cannot justly be blamed for changing her priorities from that of social engagement to dedication to the religious life.

The inaugural issue of *New Women* contains an essay titled "On the New Women's Social Responsibilities" (Sinyŏsŏng ŭi sahoe e taehan ch'agim ŭl nonham) in which Iryŏp explains that the name of the journal was chosen in order to emphasize the new women's responsibilities for social change and women's liberation.[79] That was in May of 1920. Later in her life, as a Buddhist nun, Iryŏp points to a different type of responsibility. In her Buddhist writings she repeatedly emphasizes that it is each person's responsibility to find him- or herself, and for her that meant to realize that we are beings with infinite capacity. The question that she does not address in her writings in this context is whether it is possible to carry out that responsibility without actually changing social structures, or whether an individual's mental transformation through religious practice is sufficient.

The Text

What follows is a translation of *Ŏnŭ sudoin ŭi hoesang*, or as I have titled it *Reflections of a Zen Buddhist Nun*, which was published in 1960. The complete Korean original consists of fifteen chapters. With the exception of two chapters, omitted because the ideas presented there are found elsewhere in *Reflections*, the complete work is included here in Part One. Part Two contains translations of four essays by Iryŏp on Buddhism that were published in other venues.

The combination of Buddhist teachings with Iryŏp's life story in the essays in *Reflections* offers the reader the core of her understanding of Buddhism and as well as its personal meaning to her. The autobiographical style of the book is uniquely her own. The internal structure itself speaks to the meaning of the work to Iryŏp at this time of her life. In "Preface" (Chapter 1) Iryŏp declares the goal of the book as being to proselytize. The next two chapters, "Life" (Chapter 2) and "Buddhism and Culture" (Chapter 3), consist exclusively of a highly philosophical and theoretical discussion of Buddhism. The style of these two chapters is unusual for Iryŏp's writing, which typically employs a confessional style, in that they contain nothing of her life story.

In both "Life" and "Buddhism and Culture" Iryŏp writes about Buddhism in the context of the equality of all existence. All beings, she explains, are equal in the sense that they have an inborn spirit that is universal. This absolute equality anchored in a universal spirit applies not only to sentient beings but also to insentient beings such as sand and rocks. Iryŏp does not explicitly define her concept of "universal spirit," that is, the spirit universally shared by all beings. Universal spirit is also characterized by Iryŏp as "creativity" and eventually the source of one's freedom. The two expressions "creativity" and "freedom" are interchangeable in Iryŏp's discussion of Buddhism with the expressions "Buddha" and "culture." It is these four words—freedom, creativity, Buddha, and culture—that most aptly characterize Iryop's Buddhist thought.

Iryŏp's use of the expression "culture" is unique in her discussion of Buddhism. Culture to her is an expression of the totality of human beings' creative activities. Totality indicates all-inclusiveness and absolute openness. Creativity is a function of human beings; it is expressed when a person is not attached to a phenomenon as a fragmented entity but rather understands it as a flexible reality with open-ended possibility. Iryŏp, for whom the Buddha is the "ultimate person of culture" (*tae munhwain*), defines people of culture as "those who have found the mind of human beings."[80] "Buddhism and Culture" talks about a person of culture as someone who has relieved herself or himself from the constraints of karma and who is thus the controller of her or his original mind.[81]

Following the two philosophical essays are two essays written in observation of anniversaries. "In Memory of Zen Master Man'gong" (Chapter 4) observes the fifteenth anniversary of Man'gong's death;[82] the essay "On New Year's Day of the Twenty-Fifth Year after Joining the Monastery" (Chapter 5) marks her twenty-fifth year as a Buddhist nun. The former tells how she came to join the monastery and how she learned her practice from Master Man'gong. The latter recapitulates for both her reader and herself what she accomplished in her twenty-five years of practice. Iryŏp never openly claimed that she had attained enlightenment, but in this essay, she seems comfortable in saying that in that quarter century she had reached a certain level in her practice.

In Chapters 6 and 7, we read about Iryŏp's position on social issues. In her letter to the organizer of the World Fellowship of Buddhists (Chapter 6), she insists on the necessity of Buddhist practice for the construction of a better world. In Chapter 7 she offers her reflection on the purification movement in Korean Buddhism that took place during the 1950s. Iryŏp rationalizes the necessity of the movement by pointing to the impure elements that existed in Korean Buddhism at the time. Dealing with social issues is not the strong suit of Iryŏp's Buddhism, and in both essays, readers might find her discussion on the topic unsatisfactory. Her proposals for the construction of world peace lack concrete plans and her support for the purification movement contradicts the fundamental thesis of her Buddhist thought, which is non-dualism. If even the Buddha manifests both good and evil, in what sense would the purification movement, which tries to eliminate impure aspects of Buddhism, be justified? Iryŏp does not address this question.

Chapters 8 and 9 deal with religion and faith in the form of responses to the conversion to Catholicism of a Mr. C. and to a letter from a childhood friend, respectively.

Mr. C. in Chapter 8 refers to the historian and writer Ch'oe Namsŏn (1890–1957), who had been an acquaintance of Iryŏp's for a long time before she joined the monastery. Ch'oe was one of the leading intellectuals in Korea during the first half of the twentieth century. His poem "From the Sea to a Boy" (Hae ege sŏ sonyŏn ege) is credited as the first modern-style poem in Korea. It appeared in November 1908 in the inaugural issue of the journal *Youth* (*Sonyŏn*), which is also considered Korea's first modern-style literary journal. Ch'oe Namsŏn was the editor of another literary journal, *Eastern Light* (*Tongmyŏng*, 1922–1923), to which Iryŏp contributed her writings. On November 17, 1955, Ch'oe declared his conversion to Catholicism; on the occasion, he contributed a short piece, "Life and Religion: Why I Have Converted to Catholicism" (Insaeng kwa chonggyo: Na nŭn oe k'at'orik ero kaejong haennŭn'ga?), to the *Korea Daily News* (*Han'guk ilbo*) and, in addition, read his declaration on the radio.

Before his conversion, not only was Ch'oe a Buddhist, but he published essays on Buddhism that would later have a significant influence on modern Korean Buddhist scholarship. Ch'oe's essay, "Korean Buddhism: Its Place in Oriental Cultural History" (Chosŏn Pulgyo: Tongbang munhwasa sang e innŭn kŭ chiwi), was published in 1930 in the journal *Buddhism*.[83] In it, Ch'oe emphasized the superiority of Korean Buddhism. He identified Wŏnhyo's (617–686) Buddhism as ecumenical Buddhism (*t'ong Pulgyo*) and promoted ecumenism as a characteristic feature of Korean Buddhism.

Religion for Iryŏp is a way to find one's original existential and ontological state, a state characterized by the wholeness of each individual being. Like the Huayan Buddhist vision in which a particle of dust contains the entire universe, Iryŏp believes that each being—both sentient and insentient—represents the entirety of the universe. Buddhist awakening is when the individual comes to realize the wholeness of his or her existence. This idea is clearly related to the Buddhist doctrine of dependent co-arising, although Iryŏp rarely uses this expression in her writings.

On the surface, religious practice encompasses two domains: one being the practitioner who has faith and the other being the object in which the practitioner believes. In the case of Buddhism there are practitioners and the Buddha; in Christianity there is God the creator and the believer in God. In some religious traditions the relationship between the two domains is dualistic (as in the case of Christianity); in others (as in some schools of Buddhism) they are non-dual. Because Iryŏp's Buddhist philosophy is based on absolute non-duality between the two, she reinterprets the Christian God in this light in this and several other essays in this volume. For Iryŏp, God is not a supreme being completely separated from humans, those whom He has created. Rather, like the Buddha, God is one who has realized the wholeness of His being; thus Iryŏp's God is not an object of worship but rather a model or evidence that a being is ultimately a whole and that religion is an education in that wholeness. Iryŏp in this essay reasons with Ch'oe that since the goal of religious practice is to become like the object of one's faith (God or the Buddha), it makes little sense to change religions, since changing the object of one's faith does not change the meaning of religious practice.

Chapters 10 and 11 are the most intimate in nature. They take the form of letters written to two men with whom Iryŏp had relationships before she entered the monastery. Chapter 10 is a letter to a writer named Im Nowŏl (Rim Nowŏl, act. 1920–1925), with whom she had an affair sometime between the fall of 1920 and 1923.[84] By the time she met Im in Japan, he was known as the "poet of the devil" because his writing style followed the literary tradition of art for art's sake. Im had a short career as a writer and, forgotten by critics and readers for many years, but he has recently been rediscovered and re-evaluated, gaining recognition as a talented, original writer of modern Korean literature.[85] In this period of Iryŏp's life, exact knowledge of dates and her whereabouts have not been verified. What is known is that the relationship began during Iryŏp's second trip to Japan and cost her her first marriage. As the relationship with Im became serious, Iryŏp demanded a divorce from her husband, Yi Noik. But the relationship with Im soon came to an end when Iryŏp found out that Im already had a wife and a child in his hometown in the northern part of Korea. Chapter 10 details Im's dramatic suggestion that he and Iryŏp resolve the problem of his marital status by committing double suicide. As Iryŏp reflects back, she reinterprets their time together in the context of the Buddhist teachings.

Iryŏp spent an even shorter time with Paek Sŏnguk (1897–1981), the recipient of the letter in Chapter 11, and yet his influence on her cannot be overemphasized. Iryŏp met Paek in 1927 when she began to contribute to the journal *Buddhism.* Paek briefly served as president of the company that published the journal. In 1928, Paek resigned the position and went to Mount Kŭmgang to do Buddhist practice, thus ending their relationship of less than a year. Chapter 11 offers a detailed description of the relationship and the Buddhist philosophy that Iryŏp learned through Paek. Paek is a unique figure in Korean Buddhism of the colonial period. Unlike most major figures of the time, who studied Buddhism in Japan to learn how to reform Korean Buddhism, Paek studied philosophy in Germany, drawing on that education to try to create a new Buddhist philosophy. He wrote a doctoral thesis entitled "Buddhistische Metaphysik" (Buddhist metaphysics). After returning to Korea, he translated it into Korean as "Buddhist Pure Philosophy" (Pulgyo sunjŏn ch'ŏrhak) and published it as a series in *Buddhism.* "Buddhist Pure Philosophy" offers a succinct discussion of Buddhist logic and epistemology by clarifying the similarities and differences between Buddhist philosophy and the major tenets of European philosophy.[86] In the first half of Chapter 11 Iryŏp offers a detailed record of her relationship with Paek, looking back on it nearly twenty years after the affair ended. In the second half of the chapter, she reflects on the meaning of the affair from a Buddhist perspective.

Chapters 12 and 13 are letters written to or for Iryŏp. Chapter 12 is a letter by Paek, and Chapter 13 consists of a letter of appreciation from Bhikṣuṇī Wŏlsong, who tended Iryŏp during her last years until her death and helped Iryŏp prepare the manuscript of *Reflections* for publication.

The four essays selected for Part Two convey the various dimensions of Iryŏp's Buddhist philosophy and practice as well as their social dimensions. "Return to Emptiness" (Chapter 14), which originally appeared in *In Between Happiness and Misfortune,* reveals the final evolution of Iryŏp's Buddhist philosophy. Reflections on the meaning of "I," the generation of the "lost self," and other themes of her earlier Buddhist thought reappear in this essay. Here, though, Iryŏp stresses the importance of being aware of life (*saengmaeng*), or life force, which we can connect with her discussion of the universal spirit discussed in "Life" (Chapter 2). Chapters 15, 16, and 17 are selections from dharma talks posthumously published in *Until the Future World Comes to an End and Even Afterward* (*Miraese ka tahago namdorok*). In Chapters 15 and 16 Iryŏp discusses the importance of meditation, prayer, and chanting in Buddhist practice. Chapter 17 is a recorded dharma talk delivered on June 23, 1966 (May 5, 1966, according to the lunar calendar). This essay succinctly summarizes Iryŏp's core Buddhist thought as conveyed to journalists, emphasizing their role in and responsibility to society.

The original Korean edition of *Reflections of a Zen Buddhist Nun* contains a number of typographical errors, likely due to the unsophisticated copyediting and printing skills in Korea at the time. Most of the essays in *Reflections* were reprinted in Iryŏp's 1962 book, *Having Burned Away My Youth*. While translating the 1960 version of *Reflections,* I consulted the reprinted essays and sometimes followed this 1962 version, which reflects Iryŏp's corrections of some of the typos in the 1960 version and some stylistic modifications. Still, as I point out in the endnotes, the meaning of some passages remains unclear in the original Korean. In those cases, I have provided literal translations, even though their meaning is obscure in English.

For some of the essays reprinted in 1962, Iryŏp changed the titles to better reflect the content. For example, the essay "Contemplation upon Reading a Letter from My Friend M." in the 1960 version is entitled "What Is Faith? Contemplation upon Reading a Letter from My Friend M." in *Having Burned Away My Youth*. The 1960 "To Mr. B." essay appears as "Having Burned Away My Youth: To Mr. B." in the 1962 publication. I have adopted the titles used in the 1962 publication when they better reflect the essays' content.

Several essays in *Reflections* were written or appeared publicly, mostly during the 1950s, before they were collected into a single volume. "In Memory of Zen Master Man'gong" was dated October 20, 1956; "On New Year's Day of the Twenty-Fifth Year after Joining the Monastery," December 31, 1957; "To Mr. R.," August 1958; and the letter to the World Fellowship of Buddhists in Bangkok was dated 1958, when the meeting was held. The opening essay, "Life," was a revised version of an essay originally published in the *Choson Daily News* (*Chosŏn ilbo*) in the 1950s, according to *Until the Future World Comes to an End and Even Afterward.*[87]

All endnotes are mine. (No notes appear in the original Korean text.) All parenthetical insertions in the main text are Iryŏp's own, except where I have provided the corresponding Korean version of a word or phrase.

Part One

CHAPTER 1

Preface

The value of one's existence is measured by whether one stands as an independent being, leading one's life according to one's own will. When we say "I," this "I" has meaning only when we are fully in charge of ourselves. When we are free to do everything our own way, there is no reason for complaint or discontentment. Freedom and peace cannot be attained outside of oneself because they are the very self of each and every existence. Everything that happens in our lives is a reflection of our own self.

It is a universally accepted truth that humans occupy the highest position among beings in whom the standard of the value of existence also resides.[1] Why then do humans, who are the most precious beings among beings and who should naturally be the masters of their own lives, feel so constrained? Why do they have so many complaints and causes for discontentment? This seems the very proof that humans in fact have lost their selves, that they have lost their original minds. People have turned into beings who are imprisoned by a mirror which reflects only themselves.

After I joined the monastery, three things greatly astounded me. First, I was shocked when I realized that I had lost my own self. Second, I was astonished to realize that the entire world consists of people who have lost their selves. And third, I was stunned to realize that even though the entire world is populated by people who have lost their selves, they are not aware of it and instead delude themselves that they are smart and pretend to know everything. People act, but they do not even try to think about what it is that makes them act. This last point shocked me even more.

That which cannot be utilized according to one's own will is not one's own. Why are people not aware of this? If one were aware, one would naturally wonder whether the self that is not capable of doing things in accordance with one's own will could still be considered one's own self. If one is attentive, it is not difficult to learn that one cannot use things that do not belong to oneself; one who cannot control one's own self cannot be the owner of one's self. This idea should lead to the realization that one should first know one's own self. But people fail to see this, and that is because they have lost their selves, lost themselves.

The "I" that we think of as "I" is not "I."

The "I" that is not verbalized, the "I" before thought arises, is the real "I."

The "I" that is verbalized (the reality after thoughts have arisen) is the "I" that is the object of others. Since things cannot co-exist, the "I" that is verbalized should be cast off to make way for the whole "I" that exists before and after a thought arises. We must give up everything in order to possess everything. This is the principle of the universe. Therefore, when the self and others become one, when a demon and the Buddha become unified, when time, space, inside, and outside make a unity, this self is the complete "myself." Unless everything becomes one's self, one cannot control one's own life, and when one is not the master of one's life, there cannot be freedom or peace.[2]

From beginning to end, the only real answer to all problems is to live as a human being. When we learn how to live as human beings, no problem remains unsolved. How, then, do we find the complete self? This is the big issue. Only when this urgent issue is resolved do we finally become human beings; only when we become human beings does the life of a human being begin; and only then will we be able to think about family life, social responsibilities, and so on.

A human being is a being that has attained perfection, that is, has closed the circle. Be it the earth, a thought, or a self, all are round and thus ultimately end where they began. There is the thought that enables us to cut off other thoughts that arise one after another; this thought is the complete wholeness of time and space. Only when one is capable of fully grasping and using this one thought can he become the master of his own life. Just as we generate thousands of different beings with our thoughts—thoughts that function in thousands of different ways—so are there thousands of different ways to find one's own self. I explain this concept in the simplest way possible in this book. Feeling it urgent to let people know that there is existence before this life, I hurried to pick up my pen.

There is the "I" before a thought arises, and there is the "I" after a thought arises. Whether it is the "I" before or after a thought arises, one always lives as an "I." It might be difficult to think about the "I" that unifies the "I" before a thought arises and the "I" after a thought arises, but since it is true that "I" exists, if we are to make plans and prepare a budget for life, we need a clear understanding of what happens before and after this physical existence. That is, we should seriously ask ourselves about what happened before our birth and what will happen after death. However, not only are people unaware of this issue, anyone who brings it up is treated as a mad person. Such is the intellectual level of people today. When people think about the afterlife, they stop at the idea of heaven or nirvana, which is only one chapter of eternal life. In this circumstance, even when they are aware of the principle of the endless repetition of life and death, people cannot talk about it in our society.

That being our situation, I have collected and come to publish my writings in the manner of using sugar-coated medicine for little children. What I've written could be likened to a bowl of rice with mixed vegetables, wherein the Buddhist teachings, the solution for all problems (the first principle of the universe), are explained in the context of dreams of my old days and within the context of a story of human feelings. Several chapters in this book deal with more or less the same topics. This is intentional in order to reach out to those who are not readers of books and who, out of boredom, will stop reading after a single chapter. This book is a subtle attempt at proselytizing Buddhist teachings to help readers come to the realization that, having lost ourselves, we need to find and know our real selves so that we can become real human beings. Some people will lose interest just reading the word "proselytizing," but that is because they do not know what religion means. Religious education is a comprehensive path to all of education; it offers the ultimate solution for all problems. Only those who have completed religious education can be considered to know the values of existence.

This life is at best a hundred years long, and people consider it a big job to live just this life. What is there to say about life without end? What a serious business it would be to prepare oneself for this life that will continue for eons of time. To prepare for life is to prepare for death. A solid preparation for death promises a life without danger. What prepares one for death is original mind, the mind that is infinite and profound and unmoving. A being who anchors herself by this unmoving mind earns a place in the security zone, which never changes. No intruder would dare set foot in this secure space.

It is urgent that all living beings make it their priority to resolve the dilemma inherent in both this life and the afterlife. This book offers the solution. Since I have not yet fully embodied the correct teachings myself, I admit that there are numerous places in this book that do not perfectly represent the teachings, and I feel a sense of shame at that. In order to become a human being, it is urgent that we recover original mind, which is the power of action of existence before a thought arises. I believe that this book will at least generate a sense of urgency for the recovery of that original mind and thus will serve as a reference for those who would like to plan for the thousands of years of lives to come.

> Kyŏnsŏng Hermitage, Sudŏk Monastery
> Tŏksung Mountain
> The Author

CHAPTER 2

Life

Because life (*insaeng*) concerns everyone, different people take different positions, propose different perspectives, and argue against one another. However, before discussing issues related to the life of a human being, we should first ask whether we are living as a human being. I would say that living as a human being is the beginning and end of all questions. All problems are solved once we know that we are leading such a life, whereas many questions arise when we do not know the meaning of life. The standards regarding the values of existence are determined according to whether we are beings capable of controlling our own lives. A being who lives an independent life is one whose life is of utmost value. Who, then, is this being, the being we call "I"? One cannot have a doubt about the fact that this "I" refers to a human being, which is universally confirmed to be the most valuable of all beings existing in the world.

When we say "I," this "I" has meaning only when the "I" is capable of being completely in charge of his or her life. By the same token, only the "I" who is free to handle life can be considered to be living the "life of a human being." In our lives, however, the "I," or the self, is far from free. Why, then, do we still refer to "I" and pretend that that "I" belongs to us? The answer does not require any investigation into the meaning of the expressions "I" or "myself." Even a child knows that to say something is "mine" means that I am in charge of that thing. If we are not the owners of our lives, can we still be considered to be living as a human being? Can we still say that we have the mind of a human in such a life? Because we are alive, we desperately claim freedom and peace as absolute necessities. If we are really free beings, how can there be any complaints or dissatisfaction? Freedom and peace belong to us as individuals; so why do we try to find them in something external to us?

Moreover, if we are free beings, we should be free from the boundaries called the universe, the numbers called time, and the limits called space. Why are we still bound by time and space and unable to free ourselves from the birth and death of this body? It is because, even though we define ourselves as human beings, we have lost the original mind of human beings; this original mind is creativity equipped with all kinds of qualities. Since we have lost our original mind, we fail to ask the fundamental questions about our existence. That is, we fail to ask why we still call this "I" our own when we cannot take charge of our lives.

Human beings primarily consist of the material mind that senses joy and sorrow.[1] We are beings controlled by a thought that is thinking of thought. Only when we live according to the "mind of nothingness" (*mujŏk chŏngsin*), which is the thought before a thought arises, does life as a human being begin. Only when each of us finds the original mind of a human being, which is the "existence of nothingness" (*mujŏk chonjae*), and are capable of putting it at our own disposal, does the human being's life open up. When that happens, we become independent beings no longer susceptible to being manipulated by the environment. Once a person reaches this state, whenever, wherever, and whatever kind of life he leads, no matter the shape of his body, he finds nirvana.

For those who have lost their minds, the first step to recover from that illness is to realize that they have lost their minds. Likewise, as soon as we realize that we are not yet leading the life of a human being, a path to become a human being opens up. Problems of life will not be resolved until we realize the meaning of being human. Sentient beings on this earth look at other sentient beings and think that things are the way they should be, never investigating what it really means to be human. Since we are unsure about the meaning of life as a human, we are not concerned about how to control our minds. The problem is posed in the following question: What will happen in the innumerable lives to come if we do not learn how to cultivate our minds now? Anyone who does not make the effort through cultivation of mind and body might not be reborn as a human being—even the lowest of humans—in the next life. This is a serious issue.

If you want to become a human being, you should have at least basic knowledge about life. That is, you should know that since life is long, your efforts in life should also have duration. You should be clear as well that responsibility for your life is exclusively your own. You cannot say "My parents will take care of it" or "My friends will help me with that." The mentality that there is such a thing as a free ride is derived from a logic of life based on an exchange value. But when it comes to one's responsibility in life, such logic does not apply. Neither does love or compassion. When we look inside the mind of a person in love, we find that self-interest is hidden behind that love. God or the Buddha loves people for themselves.

The universe exists through a polarization of arising and ceasing, and the repetition of construction and destruction is unending. Existence is a continuation of the dual movements of union and diffusion that will last for innumerable eons of time. This means that the duration of our body and mind is uncountable; they are eternal. But not only have we not yet even begun to think about the most fundamental issue of this life, we tend to regard being reborn in heaven as life's final point. Then there are people who do not believe in heaven[2] and thus deny the existence of the next life. Nevertheless, the next life will surely be their reality in the future. This life is only one short chapter in the innumerable chapters that are the lives and deaths to come. There are endless garments called life that need to be changed [through transmigration]. There are those who think that there is only one life and one death and that this one death is the end. Such people are like dolls that lack the mind of a human. In facing death, they tremble like a goldfish that feels fear when the water in its tank is changed. Such people live a life as transient as that of a maw worm. When a friend says "I will see you tomorrow," these people reply, "There is no tomorrow. You are a fake. I am done with you." For those who believe only in this physical body, life is transient, which results in a life without faith. The tick-tocking of a clock is the sound of the footsteps of a killer demon called impermanence that comes after us to take us to our death. We breathe in, and if we fail to breathe out the next moment, that is the end of this life. What will you do if you have not prepared yourself for death? This is the first and the most significant issue for us, as sentient beings, to resolve.

Our future lives are the extension of the mind we presently have. Setting this mind firmly right now is the way to prepare for death. A firm mind means an existential and proper mind. Since such a mind is in accord with the principles of the universe, when we make our mind firm, we achieve comfort. This comfort is the nucleus of life. If we do not attain this state, what would be the point of having all the other things? Once we resolve the issue of existence itself, we resolve all other life-related issues, and once those are resolved, we attain great comfort. This great comfort, however, cannot be achieved in a state where a being is bound and there exists the dualism of subject and object.

The root of all existence is "one," and this "one" is just a name that we assign out of necessity. Once we talk about "one," "two" will emerge. When we claim this root (*ppuri*)[3] [of existence] and that root [of existence], different roots will create a distinction between "my" root and "your" root. Establishment of "one" becomes the cause of conflict. This root I call "oneness" is the root of non-being (*mujŏk ppuri*), the state of existence that comes before we call the name of the Buddha or God and before the creation of the universe. A being that maintains the root called non-being attains comfort, whereas a being that separates itself from this root and leads a life like a fallen leaf suffers from deracination. Such a being is like a fish taken out of water. This is why we need to take refuge in the Buddha (which means to take refuge in one's own self).

In order for a small tree to grow big, the small tree must be extinguished so that in the union of the big and small trees, the small tree becomes a big tree. This illustrates the principle that only by dispossessing everything can one attain everything. The problems of life can be easily resolved if everyone unfailingly makes the effort to find his or her original ground of existence, which is creativity, and continues to pursue that path. Discord comes from people stubbornly holding onto their own theories. Any theory is a combination of logic and contradiction. Theoretical debates are like water and ice: When water freezes, it becomes ice; when ice melts, it becomes water. How, then, could anyone gain a result by having a theoretical debate, even if it continues for eternity?

Believers or scholars who argue against each other over religious doctrines or scholarly theories do nothing but move back and forth. As a new scholar appears, the old scholar retreats. What we need to discover is the fundamental foundation of water and ice. A systematic theory, or the law of logic, is nothing but an empty shell. Problems cannot be resolved with shells. Finding a solution means getting to the crux of the logic and making that realization happen in life. The Buddha delivered his teachings for forty-nine years. The topics of his teachings included all sorts of ideas, even one about how bones are generated out of thin air. However, at the end of his life, the Buddha negated everything he had said.[4] That was because truth cannot be verbalized.

Even so, humans can be moved by what they hear, and by being moved, come to discover (be awakened to) themselves. The self, creativity, original mind (*pon chŏngsin*), Buddha Nature, truth, original heart (*pon maŭm*), equality—all are synonyms, nouns that represent, at their root, the original identity of all beings in their existential and pre-existential state, which can be expressed neither pictorially nor linguistically. All beings are alter egos of this original existence. What is known as heaven or hell, buddha or demon, human or beast, suffering or pleasure, big or small, spacious or cramped, are all functions of this original existence.

Original existence, which is one's original mind, creates things and makes them function. It also creates God, the Buddha, and sentient and insentient beings; it is the creator. "In the entire world, only I am precious," In this statement Śakyamuni Buddha addresses this omnipotent self, the no-self in which self and others become one. The idea of "attaining one's self" or of "becoming a human" needs to be understood in the same way.

This "one's self" refers to the condensation of the capacity of one's mind. Only someone living as "I" can be said to live the life of a human. Only when one has a firm conviction of the need to be "a human" can one know the direction of one's thoughts and lay out the details of how to pursue this project of being a human. The person will then be sure to be aware that she is fully responsible for her life, which enables her to predict the hardships she is sure to face in the future. And this will also make her capable of facing present difficulties. When such a person becomes a leader of a nation or a society, her leadership will allow all people to live safely and productively and make everything possible for those who make the effort.

It is a misunderstanding to think that God or the Buddha is the creator. They are the ones who were aware of their own creativity and utilized it; they are the great people of culture (*taemunhwain*) capable of creating a work of art out of their bodies and minds as well as of others. To live as a creator, one must practice religion (which is a comprehensive education). Śakyamuni Buddha, who is in charge of this secular world[5] where we live, makes all other buddhas transcend the universe in their state of no-self and non-abiding and travel through different realms of heaven, of humans, of animals, or of hell,[6] according to causes and conditions in whatever form of body they happen to be. This earth, which belongs to the realm of sentient beings, is at the center of innumerable constellations. It is occupied by humans who, though born into the human realm, live more like [unthinking] dolls. Below the human realm lies the non-cultural realm, where insentient beings live. Above the earth is the realm of utmost culture, whose inhabitants all have the title "god."[7] The religions that worship these gods are called the "religions of humans and gods" (*inch'ŏn kyo*).[8] It is said that there exist some two hundred different religions, each with a large number of followers. These religions are based on faith in this self-reliant heaven, which is the highest heaven in the desire realm.[9]

Buddhism belonged to the "religions of humans and gods" in its initial stage. In terms of its doctrine, Buddhism evolved through innumerable stages and moved beyond the concept of heaven, transcended true voidness, and finally grasped the original source, which is without beginning or end, which defies any genealogy, and to which even the name "true voidness" cannot be applied. Buddhism teaches that grasping this original source and fully utilizing it is the foundation for eternal life. When one has finished all that needs to be done, up to the very last thing, as a human, as a sentient and non-sentient being in the realms of the non-human, of desire, form, and true voidness so that one becomes completely self-reliant regarding both noumenon and phenomena, then one comes to see one's nature and attains buddhahood. Buddhism recognizes such a person as a complete person (*wanin*).

A complete being is an all-inclusive whole (*wanjŏn*) or the self-embodiment of the entire universe. This complete body lacks nothing; even a piece of dung or a handful of earth could not be excluded. Since each entity is a complete being, even a particle of sand is a universal unit. A complete being, therefore, identifies himself with a particle of sand or with any other object—be it food, tools, animals, plants, mountains, water, the land, and so on. A grain of sand has its own thought as a grain of sand. The phenomenon of a grain of sand shows only the arising of thought (*sanggi*), but in reality a particle of sand encompasses both arising and ceasing, the unity of the mind; hence, the sand is the very unity composing the entire body of the universe. By the same token, there will be a day when a particle of sand becomes a complete human being, which is the whole of the embodiment of the universe.[10] The Buddha employed religious ideas, including humans and gods for those who are ignorant, but he did not exclusively emphasize ultimate reliance on faith as do today's Protestantism or Catholicism. The Buddha taught the law of causality, the understanding of which leads one to the path of independence.

There is no being that does not have thought. Any being who tries to find a unity between what comes before and after a thought arises and applies this unity to daily life will notice that consciousness influences every aspect of life. Anyone capable of being aware of what comes before and after a thought and utilizes this awareness in daily life will be able to create things. However, the person who tries to use his or her thought before it is unified into a totality will not be able to accomplish the original goal, which is the discovery of self (enlightenment). As such, premature use of one's thoughts is prohibited on the path of Buddhist practice.

Without an object, there is no shadow and the arousal of thought is like a shell. As there is an object inside a shell, ideas, whatever they might be, can surely be actualized. Think about this: Scenes of past events, our projections on the future—all co-exist in present reality without temporal or spatial distance.[11] Thoughts are reality, but reality changes. In the midst of this, we are barely free to act because we are not capable of turning ourselves around and realizing the origin of our thoughts. This original thought is the thought that is the other side of our thought.[12] Action is the other side of thought; this action is the thought before a thought arises. Since the physical body, karma body, and teaching body have not been unified, we are not free in our actions.[13] Action is "thought," which is the "I"; once one embodies all thoughts (that is, the thought of the physical, karmic, and teaching bodies) as "me," time and space become "I" at this moment right here; time and space are "me."[14] Those people (buddhas and bodhisattvas) in whom time and space in the universe become embodied do not need to travel to talk to each other; they communicate right where they are. Since the "I" in this case is no longer a limited being who is the property of "I," one can freely utilize one's self.

People in our time do not know that thoughts and words are expressions; that is, they are shells inside of which there exists the core, the formless dharma body. How can people who do not understand this simple logic talk about science? To do so is quite unscientific and irresponsible. Ignorance is to blame. Tolstoy was a sage who earned the name "prince of the intellectual world." But he misunderstood the Buddha's teaching, saying that Buddhism denies reality and that only through denial can the Buddhist earn nirvana. Buddhism is a teaching that completely sees through reality to its inner essence, and by doing so fully puts that realization into use. In Tolstoy's understanding of Buddhism, the compass that should show the right directions is turned upside down.[15] Don't we need to have a full understanding of reality in order to discover a correct path for life? We will feel relief only by finding the path that leaves no doubt, even when God or the Buddha denies the path. Only then can we make a plan about how to deal with the decomposition of this body and soul.

It is important to have a teacher who guides according to the true teaching. Once you find such a teacher you should give up egoist attachments and follow the teaching with absolute faith. The true principle (chŏngbŏp) of Buddhism encompasses all existence where dualistic oppositions cease to exist; it is a principle without beginning or end that transcends the limits of numbers, called time, and boundaries, called space. Each being's life is an eternity in this principle, which is the original source of life. Only when your practice is endless will there be no backsliding.

People in our time think it is possible to attain anything and everything relying solely on reason. However, contradiction is rational. Since any theory can rationally be justified, a believer who relies only on reason and logic fails to see the complete solution that exists beyond the boundary of theorization. That is why in the authentic Buddhist tradition those who study Buddhist scriptures are criticized as heretics and seen as wasting time. Even though they contain the teaching directly given by the Buddha himself, scriptures include theories that justify even the idea of transforming fire into water.[16] A person who wishes to study theories, including the theory of life and death, would be advised to attend school. No problems, especially those related to life, can be resolved with theoretical articulations based on the principle of dualistic oppositions. In fact, this is why there is no difference between Marx's materialist dialectics and

Tolstoy's idealistic theory of love. Both remain within the boundary of the imaginable theories of relativism. Marx confused people with his theory justifying contradiction, and, further, he made a great mistake in denying religious education, which is the ultimate guide for one's journey in life. Tolstoy might have offered minor benefits to people through his ideas based on causality. Such ideas could possibly be the best teaching in the secular world, but Tolstoy was as much in error as Marx in that he misplaced the compass for those seeking the path to eternity.[17] It could be said that Marx chose the worst part from the skin of truth, and Tolstoy took some good parts from it. However, Marx and Tolstoy are not much different in that both failed to grasp the marrow under the skin. Once we say that contradiction is rational, and that what is rational is contradictory, we might not be entirely wrong to develop a rational solution based on the context of the reality we face. However, unless we transcend the theoretical, there is no way to completely grasp the true reality upon which theory itself is based.

Religious leaders, scholars, and thinkers in our time tend to have God or some idealized entity such as the Idea or the One as the object of their faith. They seek solutions within the boundaries of what is called truth, scholarly theory, or contemplation, all of which are based on thinking. However, the object of faith must be cast off at the entrance to the world of salvation or the object of faith itself will block the way. All the object of our faith can do is to show us the path to salvation; we attain salvation by ourselves. I would advise scholars and thinkers that, once their thought and theories are fully developed and they have reached the ultimate stage in the arising of thought, they should exercise radical courage and jump into the stage of no-thought, the stage of the cessation of thought. It will be there that they will be able to attain awakening.

Faith, research, and thinking are all based on thought; existence is thought in its entirety. The state before existence, which is also the state before thinking, is the true identity of existence. To be a complete being means to be awakened to this reality of existence and to utilize it. By so doing, the complete being attains the great comfort that is a combination of freedom and peace. Once a thought arises, one ripple generates ten thousand ripples and thus creates the entire universe and all the beings in it. The countless numbers of sentient beings who exist in the world that we create are all another "me," each with a life different from others. Once one thought is removed, all of existence is right now and right here. However, as if we are afflicted with amnesia, we forget this fact and are blind to reality. What afflicts us is not mere amnesia. Being attached to the fragments of our own thoughts, we have lost the universal "I" and mistake the "I" that is as small as a particle of dust for the great "I." It is this attachment to the small "I" that causes us to forget our own self.

On the other side of the fragments of that unthinkable thought exists the self's true identity, the self-nature that is the essence of the universe. Identifying the universe as the self points to the reality that the individual self is itself the universe. This identification recognizes that individual beings possess the complete mind within, the state of non-thought to which one is awakened. We cannot accomplish anything without experiencing nothingness (*mu*), even for a moment, through non-thought. Without realizing this secret, we are not qualified to begin cultivating the discovery of ourselves as human beings. There is a place where that which is free from time and space has become part of the temporal and spatial world; from there we need to take an additional step if we are to find (or be awakened to) our true nature as human beings in concrete reality. We must first realize that a being that thinks is a shell or a shadow. When we reach this point we are ready to examine the true self-identity of the individual that resides within the shell.

Since sentient beings rely on their shadows, their alter egos, or fragmentary thoughts, what they hear, see, and learn is extremely limited. Consequently, their lives are not free; they are constrained. Even a drop of water, which is a fragment of one's thought, is equipped with all the elements of existence. There is no moment in which an individual is free from thoughts. The moment she is capable of grasping the other side of the thought, which is just prior to its arising, she can discover the inexhaustible source of her identity. Once an individual is capable of uniting her own thoughts and their opposites and her actions are in accord with this unity of opposites, she is fully in charge of a change in her body. She will realize that this body is akin to clothes, which can be worn as long as she desires and taken off as soon as the wish to change arises. Anyone desirous of achieving such a state in this life should join a monastery, or, if that is not possible, one should practice concentration to attain the total power of the mind. Only then will that person be free in her own actions; only when free in her own actions can she feel secure and able to control her life.

Actions do not always reveal whether or not the actor is a complete human being. It is much easier for those wise godly spirits who do not possess bodies than it is for humans to attain supernormal powers. Among all beings, the godly spirits possess the most forceful supernatural powers. There exist eight types of good godly spirits.[18] They practice and protect the Buddha's teachings, but since godly spirits do not have perfectly formed bodies, humans do not aspire to be gods. Members of the army of demons, heretics, or godly beings who endure over several eons of time are able to exercise their five supernatural powers (*o sint'ong*) at will.[19] Even the spirits of stones or trees can exercise supernatural powers. The point is that the capacity to exercise supernatural powers should not be used to make a distinction between sages and normal beings. Should the practitioner become preoccupied with the supernatural powers that attend a certain state of mental maturity, those powers themselves become an obstacle to practice. Even when the practitioner is close to sagehood, until buddhahood is attained he cannot be sure of himself; a moment's distraction will allow a demon or the spirits to tempt him to use those powers and become prideful. Pride prevents us from concentrating on practice, which eventually causes backsliding.

Since "I" am not originally "I," the "I" has a teacher; that is, as long as others exist, "I" am not the only one who is "I" and, thus, others are my teachers.[20] In advancing on the path to becoming a human being, all thoughts should be cut off and all obstacles removed and an attitude of non-reliance on others firmly maintained. At the same time, we should be aware that time and space are all "me"[21] and that evil thoughts are delusions created by the self.

Humans are beings with thoughts that are constantly arising and ceasing. The arising of thoughts constitutes the factual reality, whereas the cessation of thoughts constitutes the inner reality of the self, which is creativity. The "I" refers to the unity of these two. The being that is born from the arising of a thought is a demon, the constructor. When this constructor takes charge of all activities related to good and evil, he becomes the demon king, the vastness and absolute nature of whose project sentient beings cannot even imagine. In charge of the material causation of truth and beauty, the demon king Pāpīyan is the lord of the heavenly realm, which is located in a higher place than the inner palace of the Tuṣita heaven, a place of rest for all bodhisattvas. The practitioner must vigorously struggle with the demon king because the demon's purpose is material expansion, whereas the practice of the mind is its opposite, that is, in decreasing materiality. The Buddha as the completed "I" unifies within himself both a demon and a buddha. Since the entire universe is contained within the self—whatever shape an individual takes, whatever type of being he encounters, regardless of when and where that encounter takes place—mind will meet mind and harmony will be maintained. Heaven is not distinguished from hell; only in following conditions and causes does an individual lead the life of a sentient being. Attaining buddhahood means attaining humanhood. When we think about the heavenly sage (*sinsŏn*), we imagine the epitome of goodness and beauty, one who leads the most splendid life. But heavenly sages refer to those who have attained comfort in their minds and thus have freed themselves from suffering. The Buddha is the unchanging heavenly sage who has attained eternal comfort among comforts. The Buddha is a being in whom you and I, the people of heaven and the people of hell, and the self and others, attain comfort all at once; the Buddha is an individual in whom the universe becomes embodied in its stable form.

Śakyamuni Buddha mentioned the four main things that are difficult to attain: to be born as a human, to be born as a man, to be granted the opportunity of joining a monastery, and to encounter the teachings of the Buddha. Leaving the life of a householder (*ch'ulga*) does not simply mean joining a monastery and pursuing a practice. Any individual who, within her own situation and relying on the guidance of teachers, solely dedicates herself to the practice of unifying mind and body and thus bases her activities on efforts to remove material desire and the egoistic mind can be a household monastic (*chaega ch'ulga*), just as if she had left the household life. We all have managed to be born in the human realm; if we maintain the mind as it is and hold onto the teachings for the lives to come, we can at least lead a stable life. The extension of this mind continues in the lives to come. If we do not have a firm belief about this mind, what will happen to our lives in the innumerable eons to come? This is the problem.

It is not easy to overcome the issue of life and death. Even so, an individual can at least be in charge of the body's transmigration. Being sentient beings, we face the utmost pain when we encounter death; that is the reason why it is so difficult to remain alert at the time of death. A sentient being's most urgent concern should be to maintain the spirit that enables him or her to pursue the right path in life and by doing so to prepare for death. It is the principle of the universe that beings cannot avoid existence. If existence is to continue, comfort should be a part of it. Since existence cannot be avoided, life's continuation without the accompaniment of comfort entails suffering: This is the reality we face.

All beings naturally desire comfort. When hungry, beings need to eat to be comfortable; if the desire to do something arises, the desirable action must be taken in order to be comfortable. A place of great comfort is a place where all desires have been satisfied, a world in which nothing more is desired. Comfort is invaluable; it is not something that can be bought through material means. Only through cultivation and effort does comfort become possible. If you wish to be fed three times a day, you should prepare food three times a day; likewise, if you want to continue to live, you must continue to seek out this invaluable comfort. The attainment of invaluable comfort requires continuous cultivation and effort. If we are to lead a life without a beginning or an end, we cannot be bound by the limits of time or space; we should continue to practice concentration of the mind. In order to pay for our existence, a life as a human with body and mind,[22] our efforts should be simultaneously internal and external. This is the way to become and live as a human being.

This is what we should do, and what we can do. Why do we complain that ten thousand years or a hundred thousand years is too long? By virtue of being born as humans, we are in the human realm and thus equipped with creativity, that all-encompassing capacity. Wherever and whenever, whether our position is high or low, the great teacher, the Buddha, will guide us by means of the law of non-discrimination. This, however, happens only if we seek the Buddha with a mind of utmost sincerity.

The Buddha is eternal. He teaches us the seed of infinity that enables us to live in freedom. This is possible by realizing the absolute "I"; this is what the Buddha meant when he declared when he was born into this world: "In the entire world, only I am precious."

CHAPTER 3

Buddhism and Culture

The Buddha is the pronoun for all existence, an alias for the universe as well as the real name for each of us. Each and every thing in the entire world, both inside and outside, can be represented by this one letter, Buddha (Pul). Phenomenal reality, within the limits of human speculation and divided sensory capacities, is the external aspect of the Buddha. Its internal aspect is existence before a thought arises, before even the name of God or the Buddha begins to appear. The Buddha is the omnipotent self of all beings, equipped, as part of its internal nature, with creativity and all the necessary elements in the universe. This self is the truth, which cannot be verbalized.[1] Since the self is the creator and without a separate identity, it is not a thought, nor does it have a shape. Nonetheless, it creates all beings and completes numerous functions. The world, the external aspect of the Buddha, repeats the historical cycle of prosperity and deterioration. When Buddhism flourishes most, the period can be called a sacred age, a time when intellectual levels are at their highest and the world prospers. When Buddhism deteriorates, the universe declines, the level of humans falls to the lowest point, and the world is weakened. Compare the life of people today, when the Buddha's teaching is declining, with the normal, peaceful, prosperous life of our ancestors less than a thousand years ago, when the Buddha's teachings were prospering.

The standard value for existence lies in how we each grasp and utilize our self, which is the original mind of the self, the mind of which one is the commander. A person who understands and utilizes his self enjoys the happiness of nirvana (which means to attain spiritual peace) in whatever form he may be, whatever he does, and wherever and whenever he does it. That is because such a person has regained the absolute existential equality of life. Each entity is individually the entire universe, whether the entity is sentient or non-sentient, big or small, strong or weak. When universal mind is attained, a being enjoys freedom and peace, whether the being is a grain of sand rolling around in some nameless place or a blade of grass blowing in the wind. Individualized absolute freedom exists even in an insect. A knife that is sharp enough to slice off the blue sky cannot disturb the free movements of this being. Those of us who are not aware of our rights to this absolute and inborn freedom degrade ourselves in the same way that we despise an insect, and by so doing, devalue ourselves. When that happens, we fear the Buddha and God as if they were beings we dare not look up to. Only those who have a balanced mind can realize that there are no beings below us to despise and none above us to admire; only such individuals can be said to be human beings.

God gave Adam and Eve the forbidden fruit so that He could plant the seed of faith in them and make them part of Him. But they betrayed God and became sinners. Followers of God say that He allowed freedom to Adam and Eve. That argument, however, lacks common sense: Even if God had actually wanted to give Adam and Eve freedom, he must have known that humans, with their greed, would undoubtedly eat the fruit.[2] Humans are considered the highest among beings because humans are capable of leading their lives independently, free of the influence of external causes. It is easy to say "Everything depends on me" or "All I need to do is change my mind and everything will change," but people are not capable of living independently. We use the expression "I," but this "I" is possible only when each of us is in charge of ourselves. Even a child knows that she is in charge of things in her possession. We live like someone who is not the owner of the "I," yet remain ignorant of this fact. Confused, we do not even try to search for the "I" of which "I" am the owner and which exists within each of us. This is the very reason that Buddhist culture, which is the study of finding the unbound "I," is required in our time.

The universe repeats the four stages of formation, sustenance, decay, and disappearance; existence repeats the cycle of birth, aging, sickness, and death. All beings are subject to this fourfold great principle and repeat life and death endlessly. Since the earth was created two billion years ago, the energy of the universe has gradually deteriorated. As the energy of the universe became weaker, the mind of the individual declined and became obscured. Humans are obliged to enlighten all beings in the world, regardless of whether they are sentient or insentient, whether they are in heaven or in the *asura* [titans] realm or in hell. Despite their role, humans have lost their original minds and become like dolls. They have become controlled by physical reality, the result of previous karma that accumulates and extends delusory habitual energy. One acts, but has lost the capacity to ask the true identity of that which makes one act. Hence, humans on this earth have lost their selves. Having lost one's self, one fails to understand that self and others are not different; one fails to realize that everything is in fact one's own self. This failure is also the cause of the great tragedy of human beings, which is to continue to hurt one another. Before a thought arises, there exists only "one." Once a thought arises, along with the division of self and other, the division of "this" and "that" arises as well. Conflicts emerge, and exploiting others for one's own benefit is inevitable. Phenomenal reality is without doubt our reality, but it is also a dream. As soon as there is birth, death comes; as soon as there is day, there comes night. Only if we realize that this reality is a dream, the real meaning of which we might never know, do we come to understand that killing is part of an exchange process performed to feed ourselves. It is an existential conflict for survival, and both self and others go through the painful process of life and death. However, even at war, we should act without evil intention toward others.[3]

Incessant transformations take place in dreams. Good things happen in dreams and then come to an end; bad things happen in dreams and also come to an end. If one is aware that all are dreams and that we bring good and bad on ourselves by ourselves, such situations will cause no pain. Buddhism teaches that dreams and awakened reality are the same. Dreams are reality, and reality is dreams: They are one. The being busy with life's struggles and the being lost in a dream from which he seems unable to awaken, both are the self. Once we are able to be the controller of our behavior we can lead a balanced life regardless of suffering or pleasure.

This "I" is a being of absolute freedom in whom the self and others are one and who does not need an idol, be it the Buddha or God, or an institution called Buddhism or Christianity. The Buddhist meditation center is a place for the highest level of education where an individual is trained in mental concentration and earns a certificate of being a human. It is the order of things that one should first earn a degree to be a human in order to enter a human community.

When an individual's life is at her or his disposal, there is no cause for complaint or discontent. That is because the person now has become free and peaceful. Freedom and peace are different names for one's own self. Searching for freedom and peace outside ourselves is like fire making a journey in search of fire. Likewise, we humans travel to the mountains and the fields in search for our selves, pursuing our selves, while all along leaving our own selves behind. Man and man's voice are the same, even though they do not see each other. This self does not have a shape, and thus we do not see it; but we at the same time notice that others (other buddhas) see and utilize this "self." A human being should at least realize that, unless he knows the Buddha, he is yet to be awakened to his own self. There are, however, people, even among those who consider themselves leaders, who are not aware that the Buddhist teachings mean one's own self; nor do they realize that Buddhism trains people to regain their lost selves. With utmost confidence and effort, even common people can realize the most unimaginable ideas. People in our time devalue themselves and make no effort to find themselves. To such people, the thought of learning about their own all-powerful selves is remote because they are unaware that there is nothing that cannot be accomplished if one only tries.

Becoming attached to the Buddha is not Buddhism. In modern times, as people become acknowledged as great sages, the word "buddha," or attaining buddhahood, comes to represent the perfect and highest state of existence. To understand the word "buddha" as inclusively signifying all principles is a supreme example of culture.[4] Buddhist teachings are the unity of culture and non-culture. Material culture, which emerges with the arising of thoughts, is also culture, but since it does not have the capacity to overcome nature, it cannot be a peaceful culture. Only the culture before the arising of a thought can be the supreme and great peaceful material culture, because this culture is based on the creativity of material things.

The most civilized realm of existence is heaven, but it is also a realm in which beings are attached to supreme good and supreme beauty. As long as beings are entranced by supreme pleasure—which also offers an opportunity to cultivate the mind—the remnants of defilement plant the seeds of defilement. Eventually beings come to experience the suffering of hell similar to the tragedy of a wealthy person going through bankruptcy. In the world of Buddhist teachings, where both good and evil are discarded, there exists only the great peace without defilements—nirvana.

Monks and nuns in our time live by selling the Buddha's teachings; likewise, the people of culture live by selling culture. The person of culture is one who is not attached to an individualistic or private life but who rather voices the balanced mind. A person of culture means a complete person (wanin); an artist is someone who has made herself part of a family with the universe. During the time when the Buddha's teaching is at its apex, the "great person of culture" who has made herself or himself one with time and space is called a "person of the Way" (toin) rather than "a person of culture" or "an artist." The "person of the Way" was a generic expression for the complete person. The person of culture is like an actor capable of playing different roles with the same body; the person of culture is a creator who constructs all forms of existence. The person of culture first becomes aware of her own creativity, which is equipped with all the cultural assets needed to attain power for creative activities (which is to attain awakening).[5]

During the Three Kingdoms period (which was Korea's highest cultural period, when Buddhism was at its peak), in order to study with the greatest singer of the time, a master of the original sound known as "pure sound" (*chitsori*),[6] one had to have trained himself to concentrate on sounds. This person had to go through a test to determine whether he could recognize the voice of his teacher from hundreds of miles away. Similarly, in order to qualify as a student of a great painter, one had to be able to make ink of a certain density using an ink stick. When a drop of that ink was put in water, it should not become diffused. What is called Buddhist culture, or culture, indicates the mind that is all-capable.

Muyŏngtap (Pagoda without a Shadow) that stands at Pulguk Monastery in Kyŏngju was built by a mason from Tang China (who was originally a monk).[7] This mason once created a stone chicken and placed it amid dozens of real chickens in the village in an attempt to test his artistry. Chickens are usually sensitive about defending their territory, and when they saw this intruder, they attacked. The stone chicken stood firm against the attackers. Witnessing this phenomenon, the mason gained confidence in his work. It is said that Su Dongpo [Su Shi, 1037–1101] of Song China was told by his father to read the same text for ten years, but because his mother distracted him, he read it for only eight years. As a result, he understood the meaning of the text but failed to grasp its spirit (the Way). Later, he resumed the practice and eventually mastered both the meaning and the spirit of the text.[8]

Roman and Greek cultures are also part of Buddhist culture. One can find historical evidence that, two hundred years after the passing of the Buddha, Buddhism was introduced from India to the distant Roman Empire. The process took approximately ten years, between the reigns of King Aśoka and King Kaniṣka. This claim is based on the chronological chart of the introduction of Buddhism to other regions that appears in the history of Indian Buddhism.[9] One might ask whether Catholicism (which belongs to the category of religions of gods and humans, that is, the initial stage of Buddhism), whose head is the pope in Rome, is the religious organization that developed from the remnants of Buddhism after its decline in that region. The evidence for this might be found in the similarity of some Catholic rituals to Buddhist rituals: They both refer to their temples as monasteries and the members of their religious organizations as monks. It has been almost three thousand years since the Buddha entered nirvana, and, although the Buddhist teachings have generally declined, Korean Buddhists who follow doctrinal Buddhism still say that Korean Buddhist practitioners are rigorous. There is an emerging intellectual trend, even in the West, among the cultural avant-garde who are tired and discontented with material culture to convert to Buddhism.

Ours is a time when all of the authentic cultures have disappeared. But at least in Korea, there remain a few true persons of culture who embody the Buddhist teachings and who can reconstruct the true identity of culture. Anyone who yearns for knowledge of true culture should learn to embody Buddhist teachings, the essence of culture. This is why Zen Master Man'gong always said that Asian and Korean Buddhism should not miss the opportunity to engage Western culture, which, tired of its old materialism, is turning toward the East. A true culture will thus be created through Buddhism by combining the East and the West.

It is common sense that life means movement, yet those who claim to be people of culture in our time are satisfied with a work of art that only appears to be alive. They are not aware that a true work of art should be imbued with the life energy that is the essence of culture; they do not know that the essence of culture is one's own mind, which is the marrow of the Buddhist teachings and the true identity of the universe. Moreover, since they do not know that the true identity of the universe, its existential self-nature, is the being before thought arises, they believe that an expression like "man is a thinking being" is a philosophical statement. They believe that the expression "life is short, art is long" comes from a great artist. A thought or work of art is a shadow of the artist. People deny the creator—that is, deny their own self—and come to think that a shadow exists without its object. It is they who have lost their minds and believe the ideas of those who have also lost their minds and pretend to be persons of culture.

In our time, even those who claim to be people of culture have lost their minds. They write about a Buddhist nun who examines cultural capability and cultural products in order to be a person of culture and criticize her as someone who is lost even by the standards of the secular world. Such writing is read by others who call themselves people of culture.[10] Such is the state of the person of culture in our times. If one wants to be a person of culture, a person who has regained her own mind and thus become a human being, the person must be aware that the sole standard of value underlying the identity of culture is Buddhism. One does not need to use the expression "Buddhism," since Buddhism here indicates the concrete entity of culture that is the product of creativity. It might not be easy to find someone who has eyes to recognize the concrete expressions of culture today because the person of culture is so rare. Yet, if we look more closely, there must exist many objects of Buddhist culture in the world.

On Tŏksung Mountain there is a cultural object, the great dharma hall of Sudŏk Monastery, constructed during the time of the Kingdom of Paekche. Archaeologists claim that, among the world's wooden structures, this dharma hall distinguishes itself as an architectural work. An American archaeologist once said that the dharma hall was more valuable than all of the national treasures at Pulguk Monastery in Kyŏngju. He added that there might be someone who could create a buddha statue (like the one in Sŏkgulam stone caves), but no one today could imitate the great dharma hall of Sudŏk Monastery.

When we say oneness, concreteness, or representation, we are referring to the actual, concrete reality that is one's own self, the self that does not have an outside.[11] When one owns something, one uses it within its limitations; when one says "I," this "I" is a concrete reality, the reality one is fully in charge of.[12] Since the creator and the created are not two different entities, this great dharma hall, which is a work of art by a person of the Way, is the creation of someone fully in charge of himself.[13] The creator can create a mountain or water and he can make them come or go. This is possible because the subject and object become one when the subject "I" is completely free. The state of one's mental maturity determines whether a certain epoch or being represents culture or non-culture.

Within earth's same planetary system there exist eight planets, including Mercury, Venus, Mars, Jupiter, Saturn, Neptune, and another.[14] These planets control good and bad luck, the disaster and fortune of humans. The eight planets belong to the world of non-culture, and there exist innumerable constellations of stars that barely belong to the world of culture. But still flying saucers and wireless radio are received from them.[15] At our present level of culture we are unable to examine, even with a telescope, the state of the star located closest to us. Launching a satellite is the only way to make a journey to the world of stars. Still, people already are fantasizing that science can solve all problems, which is like trying to wag a toad's tail. It is characteristic of the mind of the "small I" (soa).[16] One's position in real life is equivalent to one's level of mental maturity. The world of the stars exists at the center of the universe , which is the most non-cultural world where non-humans exist. Above this non-cultural world is the realm of refined cultural people, which extends up to the realm of non-form, by which I mean true goodness and beauty. The most refined cultural world is heaven, but since this world is the opposite of hell, it will eventually come to an end.

The true realization of culture is a balanced life in which heaven and hell are not two and good and evil, beauty and ugliness, are one. The true cultural life means being at the level of mental maturity where one can find great comfort. If we attain such a state, we will not lose peace of mind even in the midst of war. We will not worry even when we find ourselves under a bridge that is about to crumble. The person of culture is one who has freed herself from material constraints and attained liberation. The great comfort she experiences is unchanging; it enables her to lead a normal life, whatever the circumstances she finds herself in, because she has already attained the complete mind that is the key to freedom and peace, and by so doing, has earned the "living expenses" that will guarantee a satisfactory life for eternity.

The Buddha is a great person of culture. But since the aspiring person of culture in our time does not even recognize his own teacher (the Buddha), who is there to teach that person how to appreciate cultural capability of an individual and cultural creations? When the Buddha had to play a role in a historical context, he took the role of a good person who would have a positive influence on others; but, all the same, he demonstrated his capacity as a great person of culture who encompassed both tragedy and comedy, good and evil. The sermons he delivered over a period of forty-nine years are a great work of art, an unsurpassed magnum opus. To call him "teacher" makes him seem too aloof from us. The Buddha is the original identity of each being, and without knowledge of that we lead our lives like a tree that has lost its roots. That is why we must take refuge in the Buddha (which is the same as taking refuge in one's self) if we are to overcome this deracination. The Buddha is concerned about other people not because he has great compassion but because all of existence is part of him; so far as one does not deny the Buddha, the Buddha will make efforts to encompass all beings within his own being. Even non-believers who adamantly wish to remain in the ignorant land of individuality and protect themselves from the bright wisdom of the Buddha live within the realm where they can be influenced by the Buddha. The ignorant ones who deny the Buddha are called persons of non-culture. The wise ones, like Great King Sejo [r. 1455–1468], support Buddhism, whereas cruel persons of non-culture, like Yŏnsan-kun [r. 1494–1506], suppress the religion. People of secular culture who possess intellectual minds (the faculty of judgment in the secular world) are still, compared to secular people of non-culture, able to separate themselves from material greed and the egoistic mind.[17] If they are able to follow the direction of their teacher, the Buddha, they will become true people of culture. One needs a teacher even to make a pair of straw shoes. How could anyone who wishes to transform his mind — which is a cultural asset in itself — but does not know how to respect his own teacher become a person of culture?

To become a great person of culture, one must first remove those inner elements that do not accord with culture and by so doing become united with the "great I" (*taea*). In the process, one should be able to separate, while still alive, from one's body and then completely let go of even one's spirit, which is consciousness. Only when we are able to let go of everything can we earn everything. The realm of unity, in which all the boundaries are broken down, is the place of no-thought where both self and others disappear. If we are willing to move a step further, we find (or are awakened to) the "great I" (the great person of culture) in which the self and others are one. When that happens, we become the omnipotent creator who has earned creativity from the totality of life. There is no being who does not have thought, but this creativity, which I have identified as the cultural capability of each individual, is the other side of thought. People in our time are unaware of the real meaning of culture and try to learn to think through the manipulation of material objects. By so doing, they fail to produce a work of art that is alive. People comment, "This bird looks like it's alive, like it's about to fly," when that is not really the case. Sculptors whose sculptures are as lifeless as dolls and writers whose writings at best play with adolescent girls' sentiments claim that they have become masters of their art. This is the situation of world of culture in our time. People claim to be persons of culture when they do not know that to be a master in the arts means to be one with the universe. For a creative writer, the most effective creativity is not one hundred years' thinking about the structure of one's writing or a thousand years of writing practice; it is a one-minute experience of no-thought.

In the East, where not long ago Buddhist culture still prospered, there are still people who are aware of the principle, the fundamental Buddhist teaching, that only when one frees oneself from all bondage does one acquire everything. Such people must maintain sexual abstinence, cut off all thoughts, and try to grasp no-thought, if they want to attain even one goal. No-thought is the state of both fullness and emptiness and also the state of absolute completeness. The world of culture attained in that state is the true world of culture, a state of oneness of the object and the mind; this is a state of peace where culture and non-culture become one. When this happens, the entire world is the majestic body of the Buddha, the real world of culture, in which the illiterate become civilized and the civilized earn the wisdom of Buddhism. Mosquitoes and bugs become beings of culture, and a piece of stone or a clod of earth becomes a work of art.

If you conceive that a specific object represents the Buddha, that object cannot be the Buddha. That is because the world of the Buddha is the world of absolute equality in which even a piece of broken tile has the right to claim that it is the Buddha. This is also why Buddhism does not exist apart from culture as conceived by human beings, who are the highest among beings. But people in our time are like those who suffer from amnesia. To regain the lost mind, we need to enter into the world of Buddhism, since there are among Buddhists people who still maintain the original mind. Our conscious mind is created through our original mind. People understand life to be constituted only by this conscious mind, which eventually comes to an end. Their lives are therefore controlled by the conscious mind, which is the karma body that is constructed through delusion and accumulation of habitual energy. The determination to be a person of culture means to be a free individual relieved of the constraints of karma, living as the controller of her original mind, of which she is the master.

All entities and their functions exist because of activities of what we call the "I" or the "mind" that existed before the birth of the "I" and the construction of "cultural entities." These activities are called life. There is no way to stop living, so, whether life has meaning or not, we cannot help but continue to live. If we are to live with courage and will and without worries, we must be fully ready for this life, for which we are solely responsible. This is the problem. Cultural entities are, after all, the work of humans, whether they are based on Buddhism or another cultural condition. As time goes on, their true spirit and inner light[18] deteriorate and they become history. They turn into dead artifacts and eventually, like other dead objects, disappear. Witnessing the disappearance of all other entities, we also know that it is inevitable that we, too, will disappear. Instead of holding on to the name "person of culture" in a world in which culture is disappearing, we should try to make firm our cultural mind, which is our life code. This life code is eternal and the fundamental entity of all the cultural assets that comprise cultural identity; it is the true identity of one's self and the creativity of all beings. Life and death are grave issues for sentient beings, and we should always be ready for death. We come in and go out of life and death on the endless path of transmigration, and if we make sure not to lose the cultural mind that prepares us for death, we will ultimately attain all cultural assets and become the creator of a great buddha-fied culture. A creator is the one who unifies culture and non-culture.

In Memory of the Great Master Man'gong on the Fifteenth Anniversary of His Death

It is already becoming part of the past. Fifteen years have gone by since the master entered nirvana, quietly, as if the entire world had died away, on an unusually warm early winter day. Why did he keep himself so busy, trying to save sentient beings who are leading lives of naïveté amidst the greatness of nature, where birds sing timeless songs under white clouds and on green mountains? What was he trying to show us through the dramatic last moments of his life as he entered nirvana? Once the work of busy spring days is finished, autumn will arrive and discolored leaves will fall from the trees. This is as it must be, the law of nature.

What we consider major events in life — such as birth, aging, sickness, and death — and feelings — such as pleasure, anger, sorrow, and joy — are the manifestations and extensions of the accumulated habitual nature generated throughout our previous lives. In that sense, to live this life is nothing more than to engage in the activities of sleepwalkers. Once this life is over another life will take hold of us in a moment, like scenes in a movie that continuously appear one after another. Once this body's life span comes to an end, we will move on in accordance with good or bad karma to the next scene of our lives, over and over again. There is no way to stop this continuity, so how could a buddha or a sentient being not be concerned about this [process of rebirth]?

We cannot simply give up on living. Whether the result of delusions generated in the eternal journey of suffering and pleasure or like a sleepwalker's movements, this life must continue eternally into the future. This is the principle of the universe.[1] Hence, Master Man'gong composed the following poem as he reached Piro Peak on Kŭmgang Mountain.

This body is in the blue sky; Below my feet is Piro Peak;
Inside my eyes is the Eastern Ocean; Washing the eyes and washing
    the feet;
Is this not suffering?[2]

The spirit can be detached, but the individual can never avoid reality. This reality, however, is a shell or a shadow, which is why it cannot be trusted, nor is it self-sufficient. In this world, birth is followed by death, day by night, union separation. Good soon turns back into evil.

A shell, however, encases certain contents, and behind a shadow there is the object that casts that shadow. Similarly, behind what we perceive as reality, which is no more than a painting, "real identity" exists as the source of life and creativity. Real identity does indeed exist and is the perfect being without expression; it is "existence among non-existence" (*mujungyu*), which does not reveal its name even as it performs all of its activities. Each of these visible activities is a function of the existence of non-existence. Only by learning and embodying the activities of non-existence (*mu*) can an individual become an independent being free from the control of his environment and thereby lead a life that is free, unbound from the cycle of life and death, suffering and pleasure. A life of freedom is a life without complaints.

Each of us is freedom and peace just as we are, and freedom and peace are the very embodiment of Buddhist teachings. All beings desire peace, but until Buddhist teachings are embodied, peace cannot be realized. At a time when the Buddhist teachings were sleeping — and as a result, plaintive cries and a lack of freedom echoed around the world — Master Man'gong appeared on Tŏksung Mountain and led the effort to revive Buddhism. He was one of the leaders of the purification movement of Buddhism. (He initiated the Buddhist purification movement that took place thirty years ago.)[3] Over a period of forty-five years, he launched from his base on Tŏksung Mountain a number of Buddhist activities, transmitting the core of Buddhism nationwide. Countless numbers of his disciples, dharma students, and lay followers received his dharma transmission.

The major figures in Korean Buddhism today are either disciples who studied under him, followers who learned from him or those influenced by the master's teachings who devote themselves to Buddhist activities. In spite of these followers, the current Buddhist purification movement lacks dedicated devotees, which is why, in spite of continued efforts, a thorough cleansing of the remnants of impurity has been delayed. This shows that the number of people who were influenced by Master Man'gong were many but not sufficient. Because he did not have the opportunity to meet many with whom he shared a dharma connection, he was unable before he died to fully exercise his power and influence people with his Buddhist teachings. There are only a few among the general public who are aware that this extremely precious great teacher, who could teach them the "correct path in life," lived among them. The quality of human beings degrades as time passes, and we live in a period when we are falling into the eons of time of nothingness (*konggŏp*).[4] People in such a world cannot distinguish the sage from the commoner.

Ignorant people tend to trample on the most precious treasure while wholeheartedly embracing that which damages them and refuses to let them go. Aware of this human tendency, the master decided not to waste his dharma power and instead quietly allowed himself to transform [accepting death]. What I have said thus far should suffice as a general description of the master's life in this world and the way I felt about it. However, in the hope of using this occasion to lead readers to the Buddha's teaching by describing several more aspects of the master's life, and because of the human dimension implied in an essay "in memory of" the master, I would like to offer further details as to how I felt about him.

Master Man'gong was fully in charge of his life. However, even we who studied under him were not fully aware of the capacity of his dharma power when he was alive. Only those with the mental power to be free in their own lives can be fully in charge of their destiny. Such an individual would be like water facing water and fire facing fire. Only after Master Man'gong changed his dharma body[5] did we realize that he was one of those people who could control his destiny at will.

The master could protect others by taking responsibility for their destinies. I was fortunate to be able to entrust my destiny to him. The power of my karma nevertheless remains so strong that I have yet to attain the state of faith needed to completely let go of my destiny, that is, attain the state of no-self. Only a thin thread of faith (that life cord) sustains the center of my life and prevents me from losing the master's teachings.

Master Man'gong prepared himself for life and death over the course of past lives, which is why he possessed nearly superhuman powers in his courage and will to live. He proved just how spiritually affluent he was by his command of the essentials of life. All of his actions demonstrated how the all-powerful self, which creates things and makes them work, can be grasped and utilized. He exercised the same courage in both favorable and unfavorable situations and responded accordingly, whether facing life's tragedies or comedies. Even in his eighties he seemed like a young, lively, generous, and leisurely person. He acted and lived, accepting each situation he encountered as it was, humanizing each. There seemed to be no separation between him and life.

We, his disciples, had yet to see clearly through phenomenal reality. Even as Master Man'gong grew older, we had no doubt that the harmonious ambience of our communal life would continue; we naïvely believed that, as the days and months went by, our master would always be there offering the endless water of life to all men and women of belief who came to study under him. For such a teacher (a teacher who has mastered all of the principles) to be born on this earth is in itself an unusual phenomenon, but to be alive at the same time as such a teacher is an extreme privilege. Only after Master Man'gong passed away did I realize so keenly how fortunate I had been to study under him for fourteen years. My gratitude has only deepened with time.

As I mentioned earlier, it was fifteen years ago today, on October 19 according to the lunar calendar, in the early morning of one of the clearest days of the season. The atmosphere made one feel as though the entire world would be subsumed in silence. Master Man'gong took a deep breath and never resumed breathing. Given the condition of the master's health, his death was not unexpected. Still, since we knew that our teacher had demonstrated unsurpassed teachings, each of us understood the meaning of the incident in his or her own way. Moreover, as we witnessed Master Man'gong put aside his body as if he were changing his clothes, we became keenly aware that he must have been preparing for death before the actual death took place.

In the spring before he passed away, Master Man'gong had said, "Since this world does not need a teacher, I'd better depart..." and just like that, he began preparing himself. One day he brought me a tattered traditional Korean topcoat and asked me to alter it to fit him. He said, "A monk in tattered clothes needs to return in tattered clothes." The master's words were fully charged, but we were still far from fathoming their meaning. Throughout that year, he delivered dharma talks at every opportunity and even created opportunities to give them, delivering them with the utmost sincerity.

Master Man'gong always met people with humor regardless of who they might be, and wherever he was there was laughter. But in the midst of it, he was always closely observing whether or not his students fully devoted themselves to their practice. If he happened to come across a practitioner who was wasting time, the master harshly admonished the individual, telling him that he was a machine-like being, totally mindless of his own situation. Wherever and whenever, be it in the yard, on the road, or while lying down for a rest, he gave dharma talks to men and women of faith or the disciples who happened to be at his side at the time, saying, "Before I die, both ordained and lay practitioners who have studied under me should be able to enter the path of practice…It is not something that one can attain by going far away; all you have to do is have a serious question: What is this mind that you use each and every day? When the question becomes sincere enough, you will already have earned entry into the practice! If this were something that I could place inside of you by making a hole in your body with a chisel, I would do that, but this is not the case. Regardless of how desperately I want to teach it to you and how desperately you would like to learn it, it is not possible because your mind has been contaminated by the world of the five impurities (*ot'ak akse*).[6] What should we do? Should we grab each other and wail? There is no solution. How lamentable!" Master Man'gong deplored. "To live this one life is a great concern. How will you deal with the lives to come if you fail to deal with the problem of the contaminated mind in this life? How will you encounter this unsurpassable teaching in a future life?"

Dull-witted, we were unable to clearly comprehend the teachings that our teacher offered us from the depth of his heart, and in the meantime, a year, with all of its days, had come and gone until the twentieth day of October 1946 arrived. Earlier that spring, the master had said, "Around October, the harvest will have been completed and people will have some leisure time. That would be a less burdensome time for people to deal with a funeral…" In fact, he ended up passing away in October, as he had wished. By then he had already disposed of all of his clothes and the few bowls and possessions he had used. I wonder now whether he has simply moved into a different temporal zone, or whether he has moved into a different space as well, and whether he would never return to this world again. At any rate, his venerable body has decomposed.

Twenty-eight years ago, when I began to study under the master, I felt great joy, which I imagine must have been the feeling that Śākyamuni Buddha experienced when he left his palace. I was not a very useful being in the secular world, a lone woman with no close relatives. Who would make a big deal if a woman like me quietly withdrew from that vast world? I became convinced that I had become a completely different person, even biologically, someone who would not be disturbed even if the greatest man in the world were to kneel down before me and offer me the greatest conditions for love, even if I were in the arms of the handsomest man in the world. I felt that I had rid myself of all material desires and that I could soar toward the world up there, a feeling I had discovered all by myself and had never before experienced. That was how I felt about joining the monastery. At the entrance into this mountain, I felt as though even the mountains and the trees were welcoming me.

At the time, I saw myself as a young, healthy woman who possessed uncommon knowledge. I considered myself to be a pure virgin. This notion was based on my idea that if a woman has sufficient mental power to clear from her mind even the shadow of a man from her past, she is a virgin.[7] I thought I had chosen the path of a courageous woman, and I believed that if I could be satisfied with my inner life, I would not care what others might think about the path I had chosen. I was quite proud of myself, and at the meeting with Master Man'gong I expressed these thoughts to him without the slightest hesitation. I told him,[8]

> When I was a child, I was a follower of Jesus Christ, but I retreated from faith and even reached the point where I denied the theory of heaven and hell. I behaved liberally and concentrated on literature. Then I became a Buddhist and thought that the entirety of this life—that is, birth, aging, sickness, and death, pleasure, anger, sorrow and joy—is nothing but the accumulation and extension of the habitual nature of delusions that one has earned through repeated previous lives. Life has no meaning as such. But just to idle away and die is not the solution. I was aware that problems would reappear and that only the Buddhist teachings could solve them. So I came to see you to learn Buddhist teachings and then teach them to others. In other words, this life continues through infinite eons of time. Whether or not it has meaning, we cannot die even if we wish to. Each individual will continue to live throughout the never-ending future in the form of a karma body, which is the spirit, be it great or small, strong or weak, superior or inferior. This is what I have learned at the temple as a follower of Buddhism. Anyway, based on the size, strength, and superiority of your spirit, your personality will be formed; if you want to perfect your personality, the spirit, or what we could call spiritual income, should be sufficient to build mental power. You should be the perfect person and use this mental power so that you are constantly in control of your life, making it the way you wish it to be. I know that the income, or capacity of one's mental power, can be earned only through meditation, and that is why I have come to see you, a scholar of meditation.

I continued ranting on in this way. The master was responding to my tirade with good-natured laughter, which made me feel that he was welcoming me enthusiastically. Feeling that way, I was able to talk to the master without much difficulty, saying whatever came to my mind. I do not recall all that I said that day, but I remember that I did talk a lot. The master seemed to approve of my proudly chattering on about myself, although he did let me know that I needed faith. As I retreated from the meeting, I felt somewhat disappointed; but at the same time, the ambience made me once again reflect on myself.

At the time Master Man'gong said, as if talking to himself, "In the secular world, you could be quite a woman, but..." He gave me a gentle glance and continued.

> Meditation is not something special. It is a way of learning and earning the mind of the mind that wishes to do meditation. This mind of the mind is the creator of all, which is the Buddha. People in the world are not at all aware that they have lost their selves, and that is because they do not even try to understand what the Buddha means. The expression "the Buddha" is a pronoun for everything; if it is the pronoun, then it does not even have to be called the Buddha. Spirit, truth, the Dao, self, the heart, thought, and so on — any name will work. This "small I," that fragmentary being that is the object of all the beings, the alter ego of the Buddha, needs to be extinguished for it to be united with the Buddha of the "great I," which is the real essence. This is how you become the unified Buddha. To take refuge in the Buddha means to take refuge in one's self. To be born as a human is extremely difficult, and if we are to maintain this status, we should try to follow this teaching. The mind that makes efforts to follow this teaching is called the religious mind, without which we are like a tree that is uprooted: We lose our hold on the existential life code. The religious mind is not limited to the belief in God or in the Buddha. Whoever it might be, if one sincerely serves the person as one's teacher, or whatever one might do, if one does it, devoting all one's mind and body, that is what is called the religious mind. This is religious practice. However, our human mind is so weak that if the object of belief is not good enough or if we encounter difficulties on the path of our work, we lose our conviction, doubts arise, and crossroads emerge. This is why we should find as our timeless and spaceless teacher one who, like buddhas or patriarchs, is a perfect being who has learned and earned the unified mind, and then rigorously move forward. If one achieves buddhahood, which is the all-capable mind, by so doing, one becomes unified with time and space: the person is one with them.
>
> If one achieves such a state, and if that person works as a housemaid, the bowl of rice she prepares would be food in which mind and body have become one. If the person serves that bowl of cooked rice

to the Buddha, it would be a delicious meal not only for the Buddha but for God, humans, strangers, and beggars. It is a unified bowl of rice. It would be like offering a feast to the innumerable people from everywhere in the world (above and below, in all four directions, and from in between the four directions). Suppose there is a soldier who is fully equipped with soldierly courage and who convinces himself that if he had a thousand or ten thousand lives, he would not save even one for himself but devote all to his cause. A soldier with this mindset who pulls the trigger while pointing the gun at an enemy has the power to handle as many as a thousand or ten thousand enemies. In the same way, one deals with a given situation, faithfully devoting both mind and body, and practices meditation to control the mind of the mind. This is called a dual practice, a way to set a direction for one's thinking and at the same time set a goal for one's action. The mind of the sentient being, though it is a fragment of the original mind, has all the elements of the original mind. That means that if one fully utilizes this mind and carries out one's duties, from the beginning till the end, great work can be accomplished....

The master further said,

One becomes a perfect person through the accomplishment of one's work. Since this life is long, what should be carried out in this life is long as well.[9] All beings exist eternally, and in order to sustain themselves, they cannot but carry out, for infinite eons of time, dual activities: For self-preservation, we need to cultivate the mind through the practice of no-form and no-thought, and at the same time we should make continued efforts to advance in our work fully utilizing our spirit and body.[10] Pursuing this dual path is the rule, which is without beginning or end; this is the formless law. This is the law that enables us to make an effort to be in accord with, embody, and transform ourselves so that we can attain buddhahood (be a complete person). This dual activity should be understood as the permanent and natural path of human existence, and if we practice dual activity with this in mind, we will ultimately earn unchanging security and, along with it, infinite life power. When that happens, whenever, wherever, in whatever form we live, doing whatever work, we will not deviate from the path.

Now, if we are to devote ourselves to earning the means to live this endless life, we should first contemplate a plan for our current life. To make a plan for this life, we should consider the following questions: Since it is true that we exist now, does that mean that each of us existed before the current existence? What will happen after this existence? Such doubts should occur, and if they are resolved, we will gradually have doubts about what happened before the creation of the universe. Only then will we realize that we have lived without knowing our own true reality. This should awaken us to the reality that the life we have been leading is not that of a human being. This is the very beginning stage of recovering one's mind. This is the path leading to sagehood...[11]

People in modern times lead disorderly lives without thinking about what comes first and what later. This is why it is difficult for them to have peace in body and spirit.[12]

Having heard the master's dharma talk, I retreated from his meditation room. Afterward, I sat motionless and began to have doubts about what the thought of my thought meant. The power of my karma kept me from advancing with this practice, so I realized I had to make a great effort. Still, I was already happy knowing that by studying under a teacher who had resolved all these problems, I would be able to resolve my own. My satisfaction was boundless.

Master Man'gong was not overly bound up in the formalities of Buddhist teaching. He was a multifaceted person of culture who embodied both principle and phenomenon. He was also a great artist who could make each scene of daily life into a live tragedy or comedy. Moreover, he made any situation in which he found himself into a stage, playing all the roles himself. He could play a man, a woman, a boy, or an old man; he could cry, laugh, sing, or dance. It was his way of buddha-fying life. He was an excellent performer of the notoriously difficult "pure sound" (*chitsori*, the sound coming from the belly), the sound of heaven filled with the universal spirit;[13] he inherited this skill from the national master Chin'gwang. Master Man'gong was also a great performer of the monk's dance, which is considered a perfect representation of Buddhist teachings. He had found an artistic métier unique to him, and he performed it in a hundred or thousand different ways. He both directed everyone and could execute everyone's performance.

One of his direct disciples said that Master Man'gong was not only a great performer, he was also a great poet, calligrapher, martial arts practitioner, and artist of flower arranging: He was known as an omni-talented person. The fact that he was also a talented sculptor is evidenced by the fact that the first time he tried his hand at sculpture he made quite a handsome statue of the Buddha, which he had installed at Kŭmsŏndae, where he was staying at the time. He had supernatural powers. He hid them most of the time, and exercised them only when he had to.

When he solemnly sat as a dharma teacher, his appearance compelled those who were present to lower even the sound of their breathing; but when he was casually chatting, he adapted himself to whatever situation he found himself in. Such an open attitude made everybody feel free to socialize with him. Being skillful in responding properly to any situation, he could converse pleasantly with people so as to soothe their minds; at the same time, he could deliver edifying lessons in plain language to lead them to an awakening. Even in daily conversation he always made those around him laugh.

Once when female audience members were flooding into a theater entrance, Master Man'gong said, "All these housewives! So many of them!" A woman who overheard this remark responded, "Housewives, you say? Am I your housewife?" He retorted, "Am I your husband? Why are you nagging me?" I still cannot help laughing when I think back on that scene. Every morning, as soon as he got up he would give a loud cough and ask us whether anybody understood what it meant. His point was that only those who have completely mastered the study of meditation would understand the meaning of the cough.

Let me relate another teaching that the master regularly gave us. He taught that the study of meditation is to learn and earn our own selves so as to be able to live for eternity as the leaders of our own minds. He said that self-knowledge leads to knowledge of others. Many people came to see him, he said, but since people do not know themselves, all they saw in him was his appearance—his clothes, for example—and failed to see the real him. People heard what he said, he added, but they did not understand what they heard. He also said,

> The most precious achievement in life is to lead one's life as its master. People in the world do act, but they do not know what makes them act, and thus they live like animals, attached to food and sex. You cannot own what is not at your disposal, so it follows that if "I" do not have the capacity to control "myself," "I" cannot be "my own." In order to know yourself, you need to control your own mind. If you are aware of this fact, how can you not devote to this practice? If you know that you have lost your own mind, what is there to hold you back?
>
> The root of all existence (inner essence, which is the source of life) is one. People in our time have various thoughts and differing theories that allow them to observe from different perspectives. They debate among themselves about the meaning of life, but they do so because they have lost themselves. The root is one, but at the phenomenal level, there exist divisions between you and me, between this and that, that

inevitably cause conflicts between the self and others. Each of us inevitably views things from a different perspective. But shouldn't thoughts be directed toward shared aspects and the internal world reveal the universe of peaceful unification?

However, people are not aware that all existence shares the same bloodline, and so diverse religious schools, various systems of thought and fields of scholarship, manifold forms of art, and disparate events generate extreme confusion, and there is not a day of peace for any living soul. Moreover, since few people nowadays embody the oneness of the self and others, they do not recognize that others are in fact the same as themselves and that foreign countries are all their own countries. That being the case, an individual sustains his own well-being by causing harm to others one nation benefits itself by invading other nations. Amidst such an atmosphere, human cruelty has reached a level where kinsmen hurt one another.

If a person is already aware of such situations and has joined a monastery to practice meditation, she should eradicate all intellectual knowledge and whatever comes to mind before and after and solely devote herself to the practice of the mind, which should begin in the state of a blank piece of paper. Can you practice with such a spirit or not? That is the only significant question. This teaching of Buddhism is not something that can be learned through the conscious mind. While you are alive, you should try to separate from your physical body and wipe out your spirit, which is your conscious mind. If there lingers in your mind the desire for something material, however precious that something is, you are not qualified to practice meditation.

Master Man'gong further said to me, "I know you were known as a female poet in the secular world. The poems you have written so far are nothing but a bird's singing. Poesy by a human can be written only after he or she has become a human being. It is true, though, that you write poetry and other literary works because you were trained in that field over many previous lives. It would be very difficult to eradicate that karma. Do you think you can completely give up reading and writing? One cannot fill a bowl if the bowl is already full." I responded, "I have already emptied my bowl." After that, for ten-some years,[14] I did not read nor did I have any intention of doing any writing. Hoping that I would soon awaken to my nature and attain buddhahood, I never went to bed before ten o'clock in the evening and never failed to get up before two o'clock in the morning. The master had noticed that I possessed substantial intelligence and was able to find solutions to some trivial problems, so he thought that I would easily attain awakening. However, he came to realize that I was a woman lacking an understanding of reality. He told me, "You are not an easy person to teach. If not me, who would be able to teach you?" Thinking of this, I have no doubt of the deep debt I owe my teacher, Man'gong. I cannot but bow once again to him and shed tears of gratitude.

When I first began to study with the master, he said to me,

> Who is the Buddha, and who are you? Both the Buddha and you possess the same quality, so why would you not be able to attain awakening? Three days would be too long and seven days would be too long to attain awakening.[15] The Buddha is the complete person who unifies the "I" who is thinking and the "I" before thinking, which is creativity. This creativity is the other side of thinking, which is no-thinking, because it is what is earned when one completely transforms thinking.
>
> Once a lecturer (a great Buddhist scholar) went to see a Buddhist teacher and asked him about the Dao. The teacher said, "What was it that did the lecturing?" "My mind did it." "That cannot be. Do you mean that the empty space did the lecture?" "That should be the case." The lecturer did not give in and was leaving to go back. And at that moment, the teacher called out to the lecturer by his name. The lecturer turned around, at which moment, the teacher asked, "What is it that has turned around?" At the question, the lecturer suddenly attained a great awakening. He came back to the teacher and gave him a full bow. The teacher said, "What's the point of receiving a bow from a blockhead like you?"

Having heard this story from the master, I considered myself among the dullest of students and thought that I would need about three months' practice.[16] Facing the wall, I tried to get into the "*samadhi* of the doubting mind" (*ŭisim sammae*)[17] by meditating on the teacher's question: "All things return to one, what is this one?" A full three years passed, and I was able to enter the state of the "*samadhi* of the doubting mind" (which is the nothingness that is not bound by time or space) quite a number of times. My wisdom increased, and from time to time I was able to answer the master's dharma questions. That diminished my doubts, but whenever I gave an answer with confidence, the master reproached me. Contrary to my expectations, I was not to quickly attain buddhahood. Meanwhile, time flowed by ceaselessly, and restlessness overwhelmed me. Attaining buddhahood is a must for setting a plan and calculating a budget for life, that is, traveling the right path in life. It did not seem, however, that I would be able to attain that buddhahood. What would happen if time passed by like this, with no preparation for death, and suddenly death were to happen! The future looked so hopeless, and that hopelessness was truly terrifying!

I wished I could dismiss the whole thing and say, "To hell with buddhahood!" And I wished I knew how to just put an end to my life. When I was in the secular world, I had thought that there was a final destination: the escape called death. However, I came to learn that there was no way to evade life and that however we might wish, we could not put an end to life. That there is no end of life is the principle of the universe.[18] Because attaining buddhahood did not look like it would happen in the foreseeable future, my despair reached its apex. I do not recall ever despairing that deeply when I was in the secular world. I had thought that there were no tears in the life of a nun; I had no idea that I would be in a situation as a nun where I would shed tears without end.

Nevertheless, I realized that had I never encountered this unsurpassable teaching of discovering one's nature and thus attaining buddhahood, I would have completely wasted this precious life of being a human. If I wasted this life, what would happen in my future lives, which are extensions of my current life and do not have an end? This thought frightened me and convinced me that I should lift myself out of the abyss of despair. I had to rise again with the agonizing courage for life, like a sprout that is covered with ice and squeezed in between two rocks.

However weak my power might be, I had to make desperate and endless efforts to push myself forward. At that time, the master's dharma talk was nourishment to my withered soul, like sweet dew is to plants. The master repeatedly invoked his motto, "Throughout the lives to come, all you need to do is meditate." Meditation serves to unify the noumenon and the phenomenon. Given that this life is long, practice also takes a long time to complete.[19] As Master Man'gong said,

Is it not true that you have innumerable lives, an infinite amount of time, and that you have universal capability, that is, you are equipped with everything you need? Is it not the case that I, Man'gong, am here in front of this gathered assembly as real evidence of awakening, as a guide for you? No matter what, you will have to find yourself; it is your job to find your own self. Why, then, would you try to find yourself from outside, from others? Each of you should find it directly from your own real existence, which should be the easiest way.

The *sūtra* says, "How would you wait for another life to save this body?" The essential meaning of this passage is what I have tried to teach through various skillful means: That is, the only thing that matters is this moment, which is the unity of time and space; consequently, you should completely grasp the meaning of this moment. However, the moment when a thought arises is a moment of time that comes and goes. It is the aspect of nothingness that does not stay even for a second; it is the existence in thought.

Thoughts always remain. They are material realities that, during the day, persist as thoughts, at night, as dreams, and after death, they float as spirits. The same material reality arises and persists in different ways according to whether one is happy or angry. These realities are also different when one is alive and when one is dead. Thoughts arise in fragments, one moment after another, in sequence. The fragmentation occurs because the existential original mind of these thoughts, which is the original essence of the three thoughts (day, night, and postmortem), has been lost. People only understand spirits in their three different forms. Even believers think that there is a separate spirit after death. They call it the "soul," which is separate from thoughts in this life. The three realities—body, dreams, and spirits[20]—are one reality that exists with the arising of thoughts. One needs to understand the original body, which exists before the arising of thoughts, and embody this concept in order to become a human being. The physical body exists after the arising of thought; the karma body exists with the arising of thought; and the dharma body is creativity. When these three bodies become unified in one's activities, the human being is in control of his or her own life. The only goal should be to become a human being. This is not impossible. However, if you torture yourself with this idea, you are merely devaluating your own capacity and damaging yourself throughout the time you are agonizing.

When I joined the monastery I was confident about my abilities. But as I realized that I had not naturally questioned the things I should have as a human being, I was dumbfounded and lost my confidence. I know now that I could not have evaded these questions. I recovered my courage and raised my questioning mind, never once lying down for days at a time. One day a thought came to my mind that made me write the following poem, which I took to the master:

> I let myself alone,
> While wandering around, searching for others;
> Like a man and his sound,
> They failed to see each other,
> There exist no forms to see each other,
> But no way to lose each other either.

Without reading the poem the master slid it under his knee and offered me his hand, which I held respectfully with both of my hands. Without saying a word the master then took out the poem. After reading it he said, "You need one more line here!"

The following year, after the master passed away, I reread the poem and revised it as follows:

> I let myself alone,
> While wandering around, searching for others;
> Like a man and his sound,
> They failed to see each other,
> There exist no forms to see each other,
> But life is self-reliant.

I am confident that the revised phrasing suggests finally having earned a glimpse of self-nature, also called the Dao of self. In the following paragraph I offer my interpretation of what I have learned from Master Man'gong.

All human beings, including myself, the master, and the Buddha, as well as non-human beings, including various gods of good and evil, animals, and non-sentient beings, exist in this phenomenal world as individual beings. However, in terms of the mind, only the "I" exists. This mind is the root of all existing beings. This is not just a theoretical issue.

One should first grasp this mind, which is the root. The master was someone who realized this, and he lived accordingly. I believe that even though the master's body no longer exists, his mind, in whatever form it takes now, continues his practice in its own way. What enables me to pursue for myself the life my teacher lived, what enables my eyes to see the realization of the master's life, is faith.[21] Only through faith—the faith of non-self, which is possible when we completely frees ourselves of all possessions—are we capable of seeing.

I was not able to reach the faith of non-self; therefore, I am aware that I could not see the master in his entirety. Among the gathered assembly, there were people whose faith was stronger than mine; they were able to become like the master. There also must be monks and nuns whose faith was weaker than mine, but by virtue of causal conditions, they lived lives very like that of the master. We accomplish ourselves in direct proportion to our faith. Because people in the secular world do not have faith, Master Man'gong left the secular world behind.[22] The buddhas and bodhisattvas hide themselves, waiting for their time to come. Faith serves only as the foundation. There must be construction on the foundation, and this construction constitutes the "I," which is the quintessence of nothingness. Only when we reach the "place of no-thought," or calmness, can we turn everything into this "I."[23] Calmness is defined as one's own unrivaled sphere of activity. Only when one becomes capable of embodying all of the different aspects of sentient beings can everything be turned into this "I."

If we want to make all sentient beings "my-selves," we should understand the mind, the all-capable self that creates all sentient beings. It is called the "place of no-thought" because the mind here is not the same mind that is aware of itself. Our thoughts are fragmentary, but since they are not completely separate from no-thought which is equipped with all the necessary elements for awakening. As far as we grasp the meaning of the idea that time and space are the beginning and the end, this would allow us to control all of our thoughts.[24] If this place where the continuity of previous and next thoughts is cut, the place that is free from the constraints of time and space, becomes completely "my-self," we will be able to act accordingly. The person whose mind denies the realization of the power of this mind and instead attributes certain events to the work of miracles or mysteries, such a person is no different from a doll, and such a mind could not be reborn as a human being in the next life. For the person capable of controlling time and space, all the beings in the world become "my-self"; in such a state, one can, at will, access all the capacities of all beings at will.[25]

People say that nothing is impossible for human beings, and this is 100 percent true. The idea that the universe is "my-self" is also perfectly realizable. Imperfect realization happens because one continues to hold onto individualist elements, if not physically, then mentally. Once we are capable of reaching the state of no-self, the place where the self is completely removed, we become one with others; we take ownership of the entirety of existence and non-existence. This is the law of gaining everything by getting rid of everything. Such a state of "forgetting thinking" could generate a poem of "forgetting thought" like the following:

> Time comes and goes by itself, as space spins by itself;
> Time and space being within my own boundary, they are politely
>   protective;
> All that is heard is the laughter of unity coming from outside of the
>   eons of time.

I have struggled for a long time and heard many dharma talks that were not greatly beneficial to me. But as I became capable of gauging the level of my faith, the master's teaching has reconfirmed what I have realized. I came to understand that if I found something to be the object of my faith I should devote all my life and soul to reaching unity with that object. There is a story about a monk named Myŏngghak. He had faith in his disciple, a mature practitioner, and faced death. He had faith, but because of his excessive greed, he came back as a huge snake. The snake was guarding a barn that Myŏngghak had coveted when he was alive. At the ceremony on the forty-ninth day after the monk's death, the disciple offered the snake a jar of soup. As the snake finished the soup, the disciple urged it to bash its head against a rock so that it could be reborn as a human being. The snake did nothing but shed tears, obviously repulsed by the idea of facing another death. The disciple pushed the snake harder. Having no other choice, the snake hit its head against the rock, as it was told to do, and died. Causal conditions guided it to a womb where it grew for ten months and it was born as a human. When the child reached the age of five, he was taken to a hermitage to be educated and there attained awakening. The name of the hermitage, the Hermitage of Five-Year-Olds (Oseam), comes from the story that the child earned awakening at the age of five.[26] Even born as a snake, his faith remained. My faith has yet to reach the state of absolute confirmation. That makes me gloomy, but at least I have faith that if I were to die now my master would save me, even though my mental power is as yet not fully mature. This means that I am not completely in darkness. This is why the master used to tell us that we should say, if only for the saying's sake, "I am a disciple of Man'gong" so that we will not forget. We should use our time while alive to practice and enhance our power to practice. I know this should be the case, since I know that, for those of us who live in the age of declining dharma, to enhance the power to practice is to strengthen our faith. I am telling you again: We already have eternal time, the all-capable self, and we also have our teacher, who will guarantee our path on the journey without end. We can make it if only we try; we cannot not do this. Why do we complain that years of practice are too long or that ten thousand years of practice are too tedious?

The master said that as sentient beings living in the age of declining dharma, we have only accumulated ignorance. We have experienced extreme suffering for a long time, which made the weight of our mental state heavier and more difficult to overcome.[27] The master also said that even if we take a wrong path in our practice and are brought before the king of death, if we remember to say "I am a person who practices meditation," we will not fall into evil ways but will be born as a human being again so that we can continue to practice. Truthfully, there should be nothing to worry about so long as we do not forget about meditation and proceed on its endless path.

This is why I selected five teachings from among those given by the master and vowed to follow these special teachings so that, for the lives to come, I will not deviate from my teacher and meditation practice. Just as a living being has to eat three meals a day, meditation is a meal for an eternal being. The person who is aware of his existential state should not forget this. Only after I studied with the master did I learn the meaning of the teacher-disciple relationship. I learned that if you are to be a teacher yourself, you must be confident that you have the capacity to fundamentally change the student and to take responsibility for her from the beginning until the final stage of her journey. The student, in turn, should so respect and trust the teacher as to be happy to devote to the teacher a thousand or ten thousand of her lives. The student should follow the orders of the teacher without regard for any danger to herself.

Master Man'gong thus said that the degree of accomplishment of a student's practice depends on the degree of the student's faith in his or her teacher. I have not left this mountain for the past twenty-eight years, even for events that required me to leave, because Master Man'gong told me that "Only when you are confident that your nature will be free from contamination and remain pure like a white lotus should you consider going down this mountain."[28] I cannot yet fully control my mind (and thus would not be able to fully follow his teaching on the mind), so I must strictly follow his teaching concerning my actions. It is true that anywhere in the world can serve as a place to practice the Buddha's teachings. However, it is also true that the spiritual power of a place declines over time. I need to benefit from the influence of this place, Tŏksung Mountain, where a living buddha has practiced. I knew that the master was fully qualified to be a teacher, but I was not ready to be a student because I was unable to put into action even one-tenth of his teachings. I was, however, confident that I would become disciplined.

I would be endlessly thankful if there was someone to take care of me in this life, where I have to live in my current physical body. How much more gratified I was when I realized that I had met the teacher who would take care of me for the eternal life to come! If only I devoted this "small I," the teacher would exchange it for me with a "complete I." I also advised others to become followers of Master Man'gong. Once they decided to follow the master's teachings and met with him, their habitual worries melted away in the warm and supportive atmosphere surrounding him, his spiritual power. Even those who came with enmity were disarmed in spite of themselves when they met the master, ending up becoming his followers. For more than forty years, Master Man'gong edified numerous people according to their capacities and guided them to find their own minds.

Frequently people who had come to meet the master with tears in their eyes left his room with a smile, saying, "I won't ever cry again." In this essay of mourning, I will not talk about how he discussed the highest level of Buddhist teachings or how he elevated Buddhism. Since I am far from fully understanding the master's teachings, any attempt to present his thoughts might do damage to them. That is also why I have omitted in this essay many of his impromptu poems or his songs of awakening as well as passages from his transmission of the Buddhist teachings.

An elderly "new woman" became a student of the master through my introduction. Because of her personal situation she was not able to continue her practice at home and missed many opportunities to listen to the master's dharma talks. She sighed at her situation and wrote the following poem, which she sent to Master Man'gong.

Yesterday had its own worries,
Today there is other work to attend to;
Another day is passing by,
While opportunities to address my own work are delayed,
I am not regretting
That I was not able to hold the sun setting in the West;
My busy schedule
Prevents me from visiting Kyŏnsŏng Hermitage for practice.
Tick, tock, a clock is ticking.
That is the sound of the killer called impermanence.
What should I do with my future,
Which stretches out ten thousand, a hundred thousand miles?

The master responded with a single sentence: "A hundred blades of grass are mothers of the Buddha." Upon reading the master's response, the woman came to realize the inner truth of the Buddhist teachings, which is that the Buddha is this world. She finally was able to live in lasting peace. Only when we are able to carry out the transformation of the mind so that not even a single strand of hair is excluded is everything accomplished. Should we be unable to reach that final state, still we should be able to gain the courage and foresight for judgment daily life if we have faith in the master and listen to his dharma teaching. The master is an inexhaustible source that enables us to practice the Buddhist teachings in daily life; his example helps us revive our sense of responsibility that so easily becomes paralyzed and encourages us to ameliorate our lives which easily become degraded.

Under the influence of the master's teachings, believers and disciples come to understand that since this life, which is the mind, is long, the path of practice is long as well. The realization makes them work to earn "spiritual income" by devoting themselves to chanting and meditation, making a sincere effort to attend to their personal responsibilities. If the master had had more followers, our country might not have had to experience internal difficulties such as disorder and poverty and invasions by foreign powers. We might not have had to suffer the conflicts of the division of South and North. Even so, the master predicted that Korean Buddhism would be purified and known to the world. He referred to the Korean national flower, the rose of Sharon, as a symbol of globalization to indicate "the world is one flower." He also said that the true spirit (true teaching) is latent in the spirit of the Korean people: Just as spring buds grow beneath the unmelted snow, when the time comes that true spirit will shine through to the world. He further said that due to his spiritual influence over the whole of Tŏksung Mountain for more than forty years, the mountain had become the source of Buddhist teachings and would produce many awakened people.

Ordained monks and nuns, as well as lay believers, respect the master as a teacher, or like a father or brother, and are guided by him on the correct path of life. We still feel sorrow at his passing and the departure of his physical body. Countless people mourned his death, not only at the various Sŏn centers and diverse Buddhist schools but throughout the country. Those who had desperately wanted but were unable to meet with the master while he was alive hurriedly came to see him off when he died. They silently listened to the master's teaching and expressed their unending sorrow. If you could have collected the tears shed in mourning at the master's death and put them in a jar, the jar would be full. Buddhism in the world today has yet to go beyond the level of doctrinal Buddhism; given that situation, it is a miracle that an awakened person like the master was born in a small country still unknown to the world.

Tolstoy is respected as an intellectual giant, but he misunderstood the Buddha's teaching of nirvana as a teaching that negates the self in the present in favor of the search for nirvana in the future. Nirvana is the state in which one completely understands and fully utilizes internal and external reality. In that state, whatever one does, one functions in unity and thus attains great comfort in which everything is possible and one never feels insecure. In other words, whenever, in whatever form, and in whichever world we live, we live without being constrained by time or space. Nirvana is the state in which one attains security of body and mind, enjoying the pleasure of non-doing amidst the suffering and pleasure of life and death.

Tolstoy's religion was love, but a love that has hatred as its opposite. A teaching in which love and hatred are one recognizes that there is only the circular logic of the chicken and the egg. The absolute goal of life is to attain comfort. When a thought arises, along with it comes the distinction between the agreeable and disagreeable aspects of the thought. Nirvana, where instead of loving someone the idea of loving itself disappears, is the state where one attains great comfort. In Buddhism everything is one's self; only through one's self do time, space, and life come into existence. Our life is the result of our own mind, and our self and our mind refer to reality-at-this-moment. Everything is absolutely about "right now" and is based on self-affirmation.[29] But Tolstoy interpreted Buddhism the opposite way, and in doing so not only revealed his ignorance but also misled the next generation. Among universally respected thinkers it is rare to find one who has realized that Buddhism teaches how to completely comprehend and fully utilize reality and its inner truth, which is creativity. Very few have recognized that this teaching is essential to fully becoming a human being, understanding that this is the principle of the world. Some of these thinkers have dismissed Buddhism as nihilistic or judged it as a philosophy that suppresses people. They do not realize that such an evaluation merely reveals their own ignorance. Unaware that reality is a shadow of creativity, they have acknowledged only the material mind on which material objects rely for their existence. Buddhism reveals its actions, not its body. It is a secret teaching that can be recognized only by those who have a high level of mental maturity. Mr. Einstein, who explained everything in the material world, declared that "the truth of the universe is Buddhist teaching."

How many among the world's scholars and religious leaders are knowledgeable enough to understand what the Buddhist masters teach? The answer would convey the level of spiritual understanding of people in other parts of the world today. That was why Master Man'gong decided to give up the task of worldwide proselytization to which he had once thought of devoting his body and mind. Shedding painful tears with his compassionate mind, he left this world, delaying his proselytization for a future incarnation. The master always said, "A great number of people come to see me, but if I ask, 'Has anyone seen Man'gong (the master's dharma name)?' how many could respond positively?" That is because there was nobody who actually saw beyond his appearance and actions to his real essence.

The master talked to us about those who studied under him and heard his daily dharma talks: "You see my activities and receive teachings every day, but you know nothing about where your own teacher's daily activities come from, which also means that you do not know the source of your own activities. How, then, are you different from animals?" I at least understood the meaning of the master's words, and sometimes I responded to him with a roar of laughter, but other times I would just smile, thinking to myself, "Everything in the world, each and every sound, are all the source of your daily activities, and they are the essence of our activities."

If the master were reborn in heaven, he would not let himself be enthralled by pleasure, and if he were reborn as a child in this human world, he would devote himself entirely to his practice and quietly walk his path in a state of oneness of self and others. It is nature's law that when the quiet winter passes, the busy spring season arrives. Just as the world passes into quietness, the master entered the quietness of death. I believe he will come back to this confused human world and occupy himself with playing the role of the savior. Among the master's disciples who studied under him while he was alive are those who directly inherited his teachings and activities. I wonder, though, whether any of them perfectly inherited the master's teaching both in their understanding and activities. I only hope that this writing of mine, through which I aspire to transmit the master's teachings, will help generate numerous followers of the master who will reach the discovery (awakening) of the all-capable self and who can accomplish the activities of the universal self.

Wherever Master Man'gong went he brought laughter, and his every movement was a manifestation of his marvelous teachings. When we met the master individually, because we did not yet fully understand the lessons he so sincerely taught us, we often could not answer his questions. So embarrassed and worried by our ignorance were we that we could not sit up straight in front of him. However, since there was no gap in our mind in facing the master, his generosity saturated our hearts and souls, and, just as drizzle eventually dampens clothes, we were nourished by his teaching.

The master had the power to control the life and death of all beings. To have such power means that he had completely mastered the universal principle. That his actions were so flawlessly performed in any situation is evidence that they were part of an inconceivable universal network of cells. He had, that is, completely mastered the eighty-four thousand activities and thus was in harmony with both principle and action. In other words, he had attained the joy of non-action.[30] The goal of this essay has been to present the image of the master as a true human being, but the mirror that reflects the image is not up to the level of the image itself. Because of my clumsy writing, the image portrayed here is blurry, sometimes not fully or correctly reflected. But I believe that I have drawn the master's contour almost true to reality, so that anyone who reads this essay will be able to grasp the idea that a human should live as he did. Anyone encountering this image of the master who does not feel deeply impressed at some point should take that as a signal of a personality flaw that makes him like a doll bound by time. Reality, which is the extension of your mind, as it will be in your next life. If you are not capable of confirming what happens now, you cannot guarantee your next life. If that happens, you will not be in a situation where you can investigate reality, without which you will lose your human status. With this in mind, each individual should weigh his or her value as a human and learn whether he or she would be capable of sustaining the correct frame of mind at the time of death, the ultimate form of suffering for sentient beings. One should prepare oneself for death.

I now know that the way to prepare for death is to continue my practice in the Buddhist society where the master once resided. In so doing, I need to break the boundaries created by ideas, such as that of the relationship between master and disciple or the transmission from the master to student, and make them one. When the flower of the unification of the master (the Buddha) and the disciple (the sentient being) blooms, I trust that the light of the Buddha will brighten the world again.

> October 20, 1956[31]
> Kyŏnsŏng Hermitage, Tŏksung Mountain
> Disciple of Master Man'gong
> Kim Iryŏp

CHAPTER 5

On New Year's Day of the Twenty-Fifth Year after Joining the Monastery

Twenty-four years is a fragment of a moment compared to the innumerable *kalpa*s [eons of time] that existed before and will exist after this life. All the same, the time before I joined the monastery, though only twenty-six years ago, seems to me like the ancient past. I published the following end-of-year poem in the *Chosŏn Daily* newspaper:

> Half of my lifetime has gone by and won't be recovered;
> The time afterward I was to hold on to use it for my benefit;
> This year too was like a galloping horse, though: It once again
>   kicked me and ran away.

This poem reflects what I truly felt at the time. I had made a new resolution the year before that I would make better use of my time to devote it to my own work. But I was not able to keep that promise. I had by then been a Buddhist for about five years. Before that, since the time I was carried on my parents' backs, I was a follower of Jesus Christ. When I was about eight years old, I heard that all those who did not believe in Jesus Christ would go to hell, a very frightening idea to a child. However, I believed that my parents and I would have no problem, since we were believers, and thought how pitiful were all the people who did not believe in Jesus. I imagined that I would become a missionary when I grew up, even proselytizing to cannibals in far-off islands. I believed that God would not let me be eaten, or, if my sinful body became food for cannibals, He would take my soul to heaven. Such thoughts gave me great satisfaction. Nevertheless, proof only by the mind (faith) cannot have strong power (to those who do not have rigorous faith).[1] I did not fully appreciate the value of faith. I believed in Jesus at that time, but I thought that the teachings of Christianity could not be realized in this world or witnessed in this physical body.

78

I absent-mindedly believed in God's grace and protection and that if a person's prayers did not bring visible results it meant that he was not a qualified believer.[2] Because I was unaware at the time that Jesus taught by skillful means to guide ignorant sentient beings, questions and doubts arose in my mind. Eventually I lost faith—that precious treasure. Why, I asked, did God, who is omnipotent and omnipresent, not foresee that Adam and Eve would eat the apple of good and evil? He gave them freedom! Being human beings and full of desire, Adam and Eve were bound to eat the apple in spite of God's command not to. If they had freedom, was it not clear that they would use their freedom to eat the apple? If God was the original creator, the seeds of good and evil must have been part of the design of His creation. Is He therefore not responsible for both good and evil? Being God's creations, humans cannot have the sense of an individual identity "I." Therefore, would they not feel it unfair that they should suffer in hell for their actions? These doubts liberated me from the pressure of believing that God was always watching me, and I fell into a lifestyle that deviated from the teachings of God. I became an apostate, denying even the doctrine of the existence of heaven and hell and putting my soul in danger. For almost ten years I was a non-believer and a woman who flaunted social convention. I claimed that it was a weak and foolish person who hid and put up with her discontent in order to save face and because of the opinion of others.

I also asserted that morality cannot have an absolute value and that chastity cannot be the standard by which to measure the purity or impurity of one's body. I contended that a person who can erase even the shadow of her former partner from her mind can renew herself and become a virgin once again. Such a person is a free individual. Anyone who can regain her virginity has great courage and can overcome whatever difficulties she might face to create a new life. These ideas constituted what I called the new theory of chastity.[3] My commitment to these ideas led me to be extremely faithful to my own partner. At the same time, I was impulsive and determined when I decided to end a relationship. However, I was inexperienced and the freedom that I wielded was like a sharp knife in the hand of a child. What saved me at that time was the Buddha's teachings. Even now, almost forty years later, I can feel even in my dreams the great bliss that I experienced after I entered the world of Buddhism.

Just as I had aspired to proselytize Christianity in the land of cannibals, my conversion to Buddhism gave me a deep, heartfelt desire to spread the teachings of Buddhism, which were profound and insightful and to which Christianity was not even comparable. I tried to proselytize through my writing, employing Buddhist expressions and terminology in my poems and essays, but the result was not very good. I also proclaimed passionately to whomever I met that converting to Buddhism was the solution to all of life's problems. However, not only did nobody listen to what I said, but a close friend openly made fun of me, saying, "You are crazy about Buddhism." Still, I did not give up and continued to ponder how I might spread Buddhism as widely as possible. I came to think that I would be a great writer and produce numerous works to spread the word about Buddhism. I also knew that it would not happen any time soon, given the limits of my talent and knowledge. My rash personality prodded me to think that I could accomplish the goal of being a great writer with the help of supernatural power. It was for that purpose that I went to see Master Yongsŏng, who was known to have special expertise in that area, and asked him how to gain supernatural powers. As a result, I learned to practice loud chanting, calling the name of Avalokiteśvara Bodhisattva repeatedly. Having practiced this for about two years, I came to understand that the works of those thought to be great writers in our time are nothing but empty structures.

I realized that what was known as a great work was not created out of the perfect material for writing, which is no-thought. A work of art that is not a product of the soul, the mind, or the spirit is nothing but an illusion created through a play of colors reflecting habitual energies formulated over time. They were not works produced through the creative power of the original spirit.[4] Writers of such works, then, are nothing but pretenders, incapable of creating a living, active entity. Even on the most superficial level, I could see that these writers could not dare imagine that there existed creativity that could not be expressed in words.

I could only laugh at myself for ever dreaming of setting as my ultimate goal becoming such a writer. My Buddhist teachers, moreover, made me realize how foolish the dream was, how perfectly ignorant I was to be a creator-writer when I was not the owner of my own self and actions, and that Buddhist teachings are not about supernatural powers or this material mind, but rather about the original mind free of all writings, languages, and theories. My teachers also showed me that, so long as I did not fully embody the Buddhist teachings, which means to be a person who is one with all the beings, nothing would subject itself to me, nor could I in any way control time. They also taught me that if I wished to spread Buddhism to others, I must first know Buddhism myself. Only then did I realize that, before I could begin to live as a human being, I had first to be equipped with a human mind. I also realized that becoming a human being had to be my priority if I were to become a creator capable of being fully in charge of my writing.

I came to realize as well that, even though I had done everything I wanted to do and had been afforded the best conditions, I was not satisfied. I vaguely realized that I was not able to attain satisfaction because of my desire to absolutely possess things and experiences, which is impossible. I also began to see, though not clearly, that if I achieved perfection, inside and outside, I would be absolutely free and no longer feel imperfect, no matter what the situation. Moreover, I was aware that to be a person of culture meant to be a direct disciple of the Buddha, who is the "great person of culture," and that was why I joined the monastery. To join a monastery! To my surprise, by joining the monastery I found proper teaching. I felt like a blind person who somehow has found the way to enter the front gate. In that way, I reached the starting point of a path leading directly to discovery of my self and a life as a human being. Once you are situated at the starting point, you can see the goal without obstruction. Joy filled my heart as I visualized my goal! Feeling like a thirsty deer as she smells water, I contacted all my colleagues who I thought might be as thirsty as I was, even though I knew I should hurry to quench my own thirst first. And thus I came to write again, even though that was not in the domain of my responsibilities. I say this because a new year is yet to arrive to me.[5] It would be days yet before I reached a certain level of mental maturity. In terms of secular work, people might question whether someone who had not attained a certain level of expertise after twenty-five years would ever reach it. But I would respond with a question: What would you do about a thirst that lasts for eternity? I was not keen to invite others to accompany me on this journey, but at the same time I could not just take this path alone in silence. By joining the monastery, I completely changed the standards by which I judged the value of life.

It has been said that art is long and life is short, but I would restate that on a universal scale and shout out loud: Because life is long, art will not die. Existence by nature contains contradiction: It is an eternal continuation of the unchanging process of arising and ceasing. The original essence of existence, however, has neither a birth nor a death. It is like the ocean, always there, even though the individual waves, big and small, arise ceaselessly on its surface. Somebody also said that the essence of human beings lies in their thinking, but I would strongly emphasize that the being whose thinking has come to an end is a human. A being who relies on speculation and distinctions is a sentient being whose life is dependent on fragmentary thoughts; such a being cannot overcome the problem of life and death. For a being whose thoughts are unified, life is a whole and so is death. Since this whole is non-being (*mu*), it is not buffeted about by the big and small waves that surround it.[6] A being that is not manipulated by its environment is a being who has completed itself. When one claims "Everything is myself," individual beings disappear and one can become the leader of everything.[7] Only if you complete your self will all problems be resolved. This "I" is the unity of the beginning and end of all beings. That is the time when all the qualifications of our existence cease and we are able to perfectly exercise our own qualities. That is the point at which we experience self-sufficiency, and we are the owner of time and space. Time and space are now our own self, which means we are free and self-reliant. In fact, time and space are of our own making. Our feeling that this life is an endless continuation of discontent is like the experience of being unable to know the ending of a mystery story. We can never satisfy our curiosity. When we see that there is, in fact, no secret to reveal other than our own curiosity, we realize our silliness and laugh. Likewise, only when we realize that we are the very mother of possessions, and that those possessions are in fact nonexistent, can we become a being who does not cry.[8]

Self and other are one, which means that when I am alive, my life is made possible by virtue of limiting the other, which is death. I eventually come to face death, and when the other comes to life, that life is made possible by limiting my own life, so I again return to life as well. Through life and death, which constitutes the fundamental rule of existence, and the dual function of union and dissolution, which is the contradiction of existence, the causal conditions and assembly and disassembly are endlessly repeated. This means that what we call the self is originally exchangeable: Self is the other, and the other is the self. No entity exists independently, and no space is its exclusive possession.

Let us think about time. The past has already gone, the future is yet to come, and the present is a mixture of the past and the future. So which time is the time? Then, which "I" is "I" and which time is the new year? Fixed stars circle around, as do planets; day and night they take their turn as life and death repeat themselves. Good and evil are one, and when we talk about heaven, its opposite hell is sure to exist. Everything turns around; nothing can be trusted and nothing is fixed: everything is illusory. And yet something remains when heaven, houses, life, and even consciousness disappear. What remains is the thought of the thought that thinks about "I." Individual existence is made up of fragments of this thought. To complete one's self means to unify fragments of thoughts that consist of the past, the present, and the future so that we can utilize ourselves at our own discretion.

The original self is that which exists before a thought arises. What I call the new year is the time when I discover "myself," the being before a thought arises, when I come to utilize myself at will, and thus when my life as a human being opens up. Such a new year will surely come. It is in anticipation of that day and in order to reach as many followers as possible that I have decided to write this essay. Our contemporaries, including writers, who say good things and proclaim virtuous ideas are not yet aware of the unsurpassable realm that exists beyond consciousness. I do not know when in my past life I encountered this teaching that I have continued [following] until today, but the joy I feel is as if I were the only one to know and follow this path, and I cannot help but spread this teaching to the ends of the earth and sky

Before we begin any work, we should gather the power of the mind, which is the original body that enables us to carry out that work. Concentration of the mind is the power that makes possible the success of the endeavor. I would like to let people know about this and also let them know that a person of culture should prepare her materials before she plans and draws outlines of a work. During the time when Buddhist teachings were part of people's lives, that is, during the era of culture before humans lost their humanness, a person who wanted to become a painter prepared to study with a great painter by training the unity of mind through the practice of making ink. The aspiring painter made ink until he could put a drop of ink in water and ink and water would not mix together. If a person wanted to study with a great musician, he would prepare himself by concentrating all his mental power on his auditory sense so that he could recognize the song sung in the master's house even from a hundred *li* away.[9] Only when one reaches such a state will a painting come alive and a song move even an insentient being.

A creator is not a special being. Even an insect can be a creator if it recovers its original mind (creativity). People in the secular world talk and write about the absolute equality of existence. But they are not aware that they have original creativity and thus do not know how to use their birthright. As a result, they have lost their capacity to create. Even a grain of sand or a blade of grass contains within itself all the elements of creativity. To devalue yourself with ideas such as, "I have no talent" or "How could I possibly make that happen" is to betray yourself; it is a suicide of the spirit. There is no special seed that generates a genius or a talented person. Talent and genius are functions that accrue by virtue of how we felt and what efforts we made in previous lives. With enough effort anybody can be a genius or a talented person. There is nothing that cannot be accomplished with sufficient effort. You need only keep in mind the principle that because nothing is free you should not waste time. Without paying one's dues, whatever the price, you cannot be a great, free person leading life shaped by your own will.

When I was in the secular world, I tried to control time without making the necessary effort. How was I to control time? I did not know then that, whatever it was, I could not control it unless it became one with me. And yet I pretended I was a human being. How foolish I was. Even a child knows I cannot use something not in my possession. I pretended to be a human ignorant of the fact that there could be no freedom for me until I was fully in control of my own self. How could I not have been aware of that? Because I had lost my self, I could not make plans and calculate how to "budget" for my life. Perhaps I thought that one could just live through it all. But that was a life of wasting time. I wasted my youth, which is, biologically speaking, the most precious time to implement one's ideas! Only when I reached middle age did I realize that one has to catch time to use it fruitfully.

That idea became a bridge leading me to join the monastery. This is what is meant by conditions caused through multiple previous lives. That connection opened a path in this life that will continue in the lives to come. Carrying the heavy baggage called karma, trudging on the weak legs of ideas, I have yet to reach my destination even after twenty-five years, and now I am facing another new year. In my own way, I have given all my body and mind to the effort, walking for dark nights on end without rest, and I do not even now know how much further I will have to go. What would I do if I knew that I would have to endure a thousand years' suffering or ten thousand years of difficulty? This is a path that I cannot not take. I know that if I go through the process, I will definitely arrive at the destination, and, thus, I just try my best. Even this life, which lasts only for a hundred years, needs several decades of preparation. How much more so the preparation for a future that has an infinite life span? Should I not expect to endure the suffering of the moment to earn eternal comfort?

This body is like a garment we wear for this one life. A human being should not have a problem shedding this garment, but since we are like dolls, death is the most difficult thing to deal with. The most urgent task, then, is to prepare ourselves for death. As long as we have this human body, when we hear the teaching of the Buddha we should make sure to attain the mind of the Buddha. Since the extension of this mind is our next life, preparing for death is preparing for life in the next existence. People keep themselves busy, saying that a year has gone by and a new year is coming. This comedy should be a part of the pleasure of human life, but the truth is that the new year will just repeat the year that has just passed. There is only "now." The time called "now" is also a moment in which the old year and the new year change their roles; "now" is only a name, since nothing stays still for a moment. If that is the case, is there such a thing as a human being who owns time? As soon as there is an encounter, there comes a separation; each birth is followed in no time by death. In such a situation, what is the reality of human existence? All that remains is thought.

At this moment, various scenes from the past twenty-five years—remote and recent, this incident and that—and my feelings about them, which are another aspect of the incidents as I remember them, all appear in front of me without a specific time frame, space, or frequency. The future as well, if I would like it to, becomes a part of myself now. Time and space are one thought, and this thought is reality itself, which the current reality proves. When we think about this, that is forgotten; when we see that, the existence of this is obscured. This is phenomenal reality, which tells that all things are nothing but thoughts and others are but my self. This phenomenal reality consists of fragmentary thoughts, which are the thoughts of the "small I." But the "great I," in whom all thoughts are unified, is proof that the entirety of thought is the same as the entirety of time and space. On the vertical level, a thought is extended to three divisions of time (the three lives of past, present, and future) and on the horizontal level to ten directions (the four directions, the four directions in between them, and those above and below), hence, there exists nothing that cannot be seen nor a thing that cannot be heard: there is nothing that one cannot think or do. This is the proof that one thought is the same as ten thousand years.[10]

This one thought has created the sea of suffering of ten thousand ideas below the joyous peaks of a thousand thoughts, and since the beginningless beginning, it has mocked the countless sentient beings. Ignorant sentient beings, having no awareness of these secrets, laugh when they face joyous peaks and shed tears as they face the sea of sorrow. There is no end of the repetition of the life of joy and suffering, of comedy and tragedy. Happiness and misfortune do not exist in and of themselves; they are false feelings created by humans. If we are capable of grasping the thought that is behind thinking and learn how to utilize it, we can control our thoughts.

Only today, twenty-five years since my joining the monastery, did I come to realize that, when I recapture the thought that controls me and the I who is the thought that enables thinking, I will be an independent being able to lead life at my will. My former self discarded the foundational thought, the creator, and the all-capable "me," and became enslaved by the false thought of the created and led the life of a caged being. I had led that life of imprisonment through my numerous previous lives over eons of time. The idea of "sending out the old year and greeting the new year" had no meaning for me other than that time was passing. The time that we sense is not the real time. You should make your own self out of time before it is sensed, and only in that case will time follow your command and keep pace with you, regardless of what you would like to do. By so doing, you will always be able to meet your responsibilities.

Starting from this new year's day of the twenty-fifth year of my life at the monastery, I will diligently follow the path toward the completion of myself. I will forever let go of the past years, which are part of a false history. I promise myself that I will make this new year and this new day [the beginning of] a new history (the new day when the Buddhist teachings newly brighten the world) when I will live as an authentic human being.

The Day of Sending the Old Year and Greeting a New Year
Time originally does not exist, how could the old year go and a new year come?
Being enslaved by thought, one says going or coming.
Only the "I" which becomes one with Time and Space exists, roundly and self-reliant
(Outside the gate of Palace of No Sleep, who is that person who is taking a big step?)

> January 1, the Year of Hen (1957)
> Kyŏnsŏng Hermitage, Tŏksung Mountain

CHAPTER 6

A Proposal to the World Fellowship
of Buddhists Conference

To the Chairperson of the Conference:

I, a Buddhist nun and member of the general conference of Buddhists, the largest gathering of people, wish for the results of this conference to change the history of humanity, which has been lost in currents of confusion, so that a true history can begin to shine. With that prayer, I submit this proposal.

People in the *sahā* world hurt others for their own profit and invade other countries to benefit themselves. In this situation, human nature becomes so cruel that it floats on a sea of poison where people kill their own brothers and sisters. The great scientists have come to play a role in providing the means to commit violence, and superficial peace and freedom exist only at the level of international gatherings that merely provide occasions for those who have power to take advantage. Modern human history, which offers a commendation to murderers, a false record of the activities of human beings, is nothing but tissue paper. With what teaching, then, do we save this cruel world, which we dare not call the world of human beings?

Some might propose compassion and love as an answer. Compassion and love, however, originally do not exist. The Buddha's compassion and God's love exist for the Buddha and God themselves. Since for the Buddha and God, the entire universe is themselves, and since sentient beings are parts of those selves, the Buddha or God [naturally] takes care of other sentient beings.[1] When we talk about sacrifice or dedication, we mean activities done for the sake of one's own self. However sensible and truthful recommendations that come out of this meeting of a universal scale might be, they cannot but be subject to the dualistic nature of this worldly logic (the logic based on thinking) and the world cannot be saved by such teachings. Why do you think the Buddha denied his forty-five years of teaching? It was because his teachings, which he offered until the last moment of his life, consisted of teachings on salvation based on thinking, and he knew that they could not be the fundamental cure for the disease. Teachings for salvation cannot be expressed through thought, in writing, or in words, since they contain unfathomable meanings. Truth cannot be verbalized.

We can say that people should be rehabilitated through compassion and love, that nuclear weapons should be prohibited, that treaties and unbiased views should be maintained, that the solution is right systems, provisions, -isms, or equal distribution of materials or equal rights — but all of these theoretical schemes for peace can never actually benefit humankind. A real cease-fire is possible only when there is an end to the sources of the struggle. A cease-fire on a universal scale will happen when we recognize that the sources of conflict are the six countries within each individual being (the six sense organs of the eyes, ears, nose, tongue, body, and consciousness). That is to say that what is at issue is the recovery of the mind in each individual.

We know that a single match can cause a great fire and a single wave can give rise to ten thousand great waves. We can see that personal emotions provoke group emotions, which influence feelings on a national scale that in turn lead to global-level warfare. This process is based on the contradictory logic that views all beings through the dualism of self and others. By this logic, since two beings cannot co-exist, for the self to stand, it has to push others away. It is a natural principle that conflict occurs as soon as thoughts arise. The sources of conflict are the six senses of each individual, which are a function of the mind of material desire. The six senses are born of delusion. Delusions are the accumulation and extension of one's karma (the nature of which is generated by habitual energy, the spirits).

Each individual's life is a reflection of his or her own karma. The comedy and tragedy of life as well as suffering and pleasure can be compared to a crazy woman being manipulated by the reflection of her own image in a mirror as she laughs or cries. She believes the image in the mirror to be someone else's, not her own. Just so, the fundamental ground of peace lies in the recovery of the minds of individuals living in this world, a group of people who have lost their minds.

If each of us were to become aware that he or she had lost his or her mind, would not that awareness mark the beginning of recovery? To be a human being is the beginning and end of all problems, and once we become human beings we recover the wholeness of the human mind. Recovery of the mind is the priority, and when that happens we will realize that what is reflected in the mirror is our own self and we will try to control our six senses. Desire, resentment, attachment, and affectionate feelings will be reset as we enter into the secure life (nirvana; that is, the unchanging peaceful state) of a normal person. When this happens, the six senses of the normal person, that is, the six senses in their peaceful state, quietly perform their functions. Only then will each individual being in the universe, itself a collection of individuals, be able to attain absolute equality of existence and lead a balanced life, within which each being will enjoy self-sufficiency.

When you reach the state of the unity of self and others, you realize that there exists no being above yourself that humans need to fear and no being below yourself that humans can despise. Your own freedom will help you free others from what constrains them. Assimilated by others' freedom, you will lead a life of great freedom even within a state of great constraints. In that state, you know that suffering and pleasure, fortune and misfortune, are all functions of your mind. The bothersome ideas that heaven is livable and hell is impossible come to an end. The person who understands the imperative of having her own freedom admits the power of other people. She knows that there has to be agreement; without it, she cannot change the direction of a bird's flight, even if she has a knife sharp enough to cut a piece of the sky; she will try to convince others, not force them.[2]

Since we are not separate beings, others are part of our selves. We cannot expect peace unless we recognize this reality. Without attaining the state that self is others and others are the self, there is no way to enjoy one's freedom, nor a way to save others. In what manner, then, does one realize the state of the unity of self and others? This is the problem. The only answer is meditation (meditation means cultivation, and cultivation is a way to recover one's self, which is the original mind of each individual, which is creativity, and which is the self in which the self and others are united). This is the very marrow (the correct teaching) of Buddhism.

The law of the secular world, which is the external aspect of Buddhist law, is the history of the repetition of prosperity and decline. Buddhism today exists in a world that has reached a state of decline (the end period), and I have heard that, even in a country where Buddhism is a national religion, only doctrinal Buddhism is being practiced.[3] That being the case, even for those who claim to be Buddhists, as thoughts arise, the polarization of self and others also arises and conflicts follow. In the original state before thoughts arise, the self and others were one, but since practitioners have forgotten this, conflict is said to have reached a stage of cruelty where brothers and sisters kill each other, a truly sad situation.

Every single being is entirely my reflection and a part of the Buddha, and self and others are all the Buddha. Even if the person is a Buddhist, if she does not fully embody this teaching, real war is inevitable. Followers of the Buddha are responsible for saving both humans and gods and thus, at a time like the present, should devote themselves to that purpose without respite. But, instead, Buddhists today are tainted by the cruel activities of sentient beings and cause turbulence. Truly, Buddhists who have grasped the marrow of the Buddhist teachings cannot find room for apology for such a state of affairs. The marrow of the Buddha's teachings is the truth found in meditation. What is urgent at this point is to build meditation halls everywhere, to provide places to practice.

People say that the song of a Buddhist revival can now clearly be heard. In the East, those who have initiated their believing minds gather together, while in the West the cultural avant-garde is responsive to meditation practice. The first thing to do then is to have a meditation hall in the conference center and select a teacher who would be universally respected as a leader and under whose guidance numerous practitioners could be trained and the wind of practice could contribute to the humanization (that is, buddha-fication) of society. When this happens, human cruelty will become harmony, which will initiate the unification of Korea and of Germany as well as bring world peace. War will be reduced to the level of discord in procedures and on a fundamental level, the whole of humankind will enjoy peace.[4]

World peace and human freedom will be accomplished when each nation makes the effort to see that each individual becomes a true human being. At least Buddhists should know this. Even now, if a great person of awakening were to appear, that person would be the center of the universe. With that person as the head of the universe and all the living beings the various parts of one body, the head would guide the body parts to work in harmony, and the body parts under the guidance of the head would properly perform their respective functions. Would that not be a peaceful universe?

It is said that in ancient times, when the Buddhist teachings were the basis of daily life, a country was evaluated according to whether or not an awakened individual was present there. Whatever the material condition of a country, if an awakened person existed there, no one would dare disrespect or consider that country poor.

Even a child would wonder whether something belonged to her if she could not use it as she wished. And yet people in modern times say "I" and develop attachments to this "I" when they are not capable of utilizing this "I" at their own will. There is an "I" that one can utilize at one's will, but people do not try to find it. That is because they do not understand the meaning of the Buddha, and since they do not know what the Buddha means, they do not know what the "I" means.

The most urgent matter in this situation is to spread Buddhist teachings to all of humankind. There is no better way to propagate Buddhism fully than to help people grasp the marrow of Buddhism, which lies neither in learning Buddhist doctrine nor sustaining Buddhism nor believing in Buddhism, but in practicing meditation. With this in mind, I propose here that the conference issue an emergency declaration so that the work can begin immediately to establish a meditation hall in each Buddhist temple. This is the single special duty of Buddhism at the moment.

The above should make clear that the main purpose of this proposal is to emphasize that for this conference to have any meaning for Buddhism, it should focus on making people whole persons. When this proposal is realized, the history of the human world — which has become an anti-human world — would finally begin to change; the day of the return of the great teacher of the three worlds — that is, the day of the revival of Buddhism — will arrive; and the universe will become a great universe without discrimination where a thousand buddhas and ten thousand sentient beings will gather together. It will be a place of eternal safety (nirvana), a place of absolute equality where not even a fly or a crawling bug would be rejected. This will be the great heaven and earth where the entire world itself becomes the great conference of Buddhism.

This proposal is not based on the ideas of this nun, but on the great teachings of the Buddha. It should therefore be welcomed sincerely by the conference and put into practice. Only then can the correct teachings of the Buddha be realized.

> Bhikṣuṇī Kim Iryŏp
> September, the Year of the Dog (1958)
> Kyŏnsŏng Hermitage, Sudŏk Monastery,
> Tŏksung Mountain, South Ch'ungch'ŏng Province

CHAPTER 7

Why Has Buddhism Launched
a Purification Movement?

The Buddha signifies everything; he is wholeness. To exclude even a turd or a handful of dirt makes the Buddha incomplete. How, then, does purity or impurity come to be an issue in Buddhism?

The Buddha is the unity of phenomena in the universe (after a thought arises) and that which is before the creation of this reality (before a thought arises). The Buddha is the original name of the universe. The Buddha is the unification of this and that, yesterday and today, you and I, the unified self. The Buddha is another name for one's self.

The universe is the original body of one's self, and all the things in the world are one's self. Only the being that is all-capable can exert the full value of its existence. Each of us is entitled to absolute equality, and thus whatever position we might take or in whatever body we have, if we are capable of leading an independent life, we become a being of the highest value.

That being so, how does a human being, considered to be the most precious among beings, come to be incapable of leading his life at his own will? No one can use a thing however he wishes if that thing does not belong to him. People do not even try to see the reasons why they are incapable of controlling their own lives. This is the state of people today. Humans have become betrayers of the universe, which is themselves. Being attached to a fragmented self, they do not know how to move beyond a small-self life, the life of a partial self. In other words, people cannot recover their great selves once they have lost that great self.

This earth is a ghetto of lost selves. But there will be a day when those lost selves will disappear from this earth. It is in order to make that happen that Buddhism as a religious institution came to exist. By teaching people the wholeness of human beings, Buddhism teaches the unity of mundane and supramundane phenomena. Buddhist education clarifies how from the same seed two different types of self, the small self and the great self, have evolved and thus shows how all beings together can become great selves.

A student grows up to be a member of a society in the secular educational system. In the Buddhist system, an ordained person completes her education at a monastery and thus learns how to fully utilize the independent mind (the mind before a thought arises), the mind free from notions of purity and impurity and the susceptibility to manipulation by her circumstances. Having realized the independent mind, she can return to the secular world and live free from the dualities of good and evil, beauty and ugliness, heaven and hell. Only when one reaches this stage is one a liberated being, the highest level of which is the "great free being" (*taejayuin*) liberated from all kinds of constraints.

Nothing is free; success does not come without effort. Just as nothing is gained without sacrifice, the state of great freedom cannot be attained without enduring hardship. This is the principle of the universe. The price of ultimate freedom is not material or quantifiable. It is rather devotion to the goal of no-self, the self after annihilation of the material self. When even one's consciousness is extinguished, one finally attains the universalized self. All tender feelings and sensual desires, the strongest among human desires, must be extinguished. With respect to sensual desire, the Buddha observed that if human beings had two such powerful sorts of desire they would not be able to attain buddhahood.[1] When even an *arhat* is cremated, the seed of [sexual] love remains in the ashes. Only when that seed is completely burned away can one reach the land of purity. A young monk allowing himself to fall for a woman's sweet charms faces graver danger than a child attracted to a leper offering candy. Leprosy damages only the body, not the mind. The object of sensual desire is an ogre that devours one's true life [both body and mind], an effect that survives for lives to come. The Buddha said that it would be better for a monk who has broken a precept regarding sexual desire to drink a bowl of water boiled with iron than continue on as a monk living off the donations of believers. By giving up this one life, he would save ten thousand lives of others.

Monks should strictly observe 250 precepts and nuns, 500. The precepts related to sexual relations between men and women are the most important. Then there are the detailed precepts that cover various concrete aspects of behavior, including how to open one's eyes or how to walk. Having reached the state of perfect observance of the precepts, one should then be mindful (based on causes and conditions) of the 84,000 subtle actions, such as how to treat a piece of shit or handful of dirt. Only when one can perfectly embody these precepts does one become a complete person who is united with the universe without beginning or end.

The precepts are divided into actual observation of precepts (*sagye*) and keeping precepts in principle (*igye*). To actually uphold a precept means to put it into action; observing a precept in principle means that, regardless of whether the precepts are actually practiced, there is no contamination of mind. Śakyamuni Buddha performed a variety of sacrificial actions (in the process of his practice to attain buddhahood): he plucked out his eyes and amputated his arms and legs to donate them to the disabled; he chopped off his bones and sliced off his flesh to treat other people's wounds; he gave his body to hungry animals;[2] and he offered his head a thousand times to those who needed one. As a result of such actions, he earned the complete body that is capable of a trillion different transformations.[3]

By upholding precepts in action, one purifies the physical body; by observing precepts in principle, one purifies the mind while also making the effort to fully observe the precepts in the 84,000 subtle actions. Through the observance of all of these precepts one becomes a complete person who has attained enduring peace and freedom and in whom self and others are one.

At the meditation center here on Tŏksung Mountain, I have witnessed people who have not lain down for three years, who have sat without moving or drinking for seven days and nights, who have remained outdoors throughout the winter practicing standing meditation in icy cold weather, and who have practiced seated meditation for seven days drinking only water. For the first ten years or so I could not endure cold places or hot places, and when the temperature was normal, sleep attacked me; I managed to do walking meditation for seven days at a time, falling occasionally, and to practice in the seated position. In order to fight against sleep, I wore a scarf embedded with needles that would pierce my chin if I drowsed, or I pinched my thigh, which became black and blue as a result. When my practice did not make progress, I wished I could just give up. Knowing the difficulty involved with practice from my own experience, I absolutely admire the way the people I just described concentrated on their practice. People in the secular world have no idea what meditation practice involves, yet they talk and write about it. In the same way, even though they cannot imagine what verbal Sŏn (*kudu* Sŏn) means, they talk and write about it without any hesitation, which is really laughable.

People nowadays speak quite often about Buddhist doctrine or use Buddhist expressions. One cannot but welcome this situation, since there is nothing that is not Buddhist teaching. Moreover, familiarity with Buddhist discourse serves us well as a foundation for the future, when Buddhism once again dominates the world.

For those of us today who believe that ten years is long enough to change even mountains and rivers but who lack mental power, the Buddhist concept of time must be overwhelming. However, since humans live innumerable lives, we should be able to endure ten thousand years' suffering to avoid a billion years of suffering. To accomplish that, the priority is to separate yourself from your body while you are still alive. You must also extinguish the spirit (thoughts), which is the accumulation and extension of your habitual nature, in order to arrive in the land of purification. Once you reach that stage you will not deviate even if you find yourself in the land of non-purification (reality). The world, which is the external aspect of Buddhist teaching, is the history of the repetition of rise and decline. Taking advantage of Buddhism's present state of decline, secular people who have spouses and children can claim to be monks and appropriate the position (both physically and mentally) of real monks, who, though the quality of their practice is high, are weak in power to the point where they must beg to maintain their status.

Practicing Buddhism when you have only yourself to worry about is difficult enough. When you have obligations to a wife and children and must make a living for them, you cannot fully devote yourself to practice. Even if a person could, he should not be accepted into the monastic community. At a time when the purification movement is in its initial phase and as yet lacks human resources, the presence of pseudo-monks and pseudo-nuns merely confuses the situation, causing one to wonder whether the movement is for purification or contamination. The great masters who have completely freed themselves at both the theoretical and practical levels of practice should be in the forefront of the movement. The fact that they have yet to participate might be an indication that the cause and conditions for the movement are not yet ripe (that the general level of people has not reached that state). Secular scholars, having insufficient experience with Buddhist practice, are not up to the task of leading the purification movement; likewise, the masters, who have exclusively devoted themselves to spiritual cultivation, cannot fully take control. Mistakes therefore occur in the process. This being the case, there are those among supporters of the movement who think that married monks, who are the majority, would be in the best position to maintain the current state of the Buddhist order. However, Korean Buddhism as it is now is a secularized Buddhism. With such a Buddhism, it is not possible to maintain even its current state. Moreover, if the time ever comes for Buddhism to flourish, since it is not based on spiritual training, it would be like constructing a building on sand. What we need to do is move forward with our original belief. And the time for that has come. Korea, the first among Eastern countries to do so, boasts an increasing number of intellectuals who support Buddhism; in the West, both avant-garde intellectuals and ordinary people are converting to Buddhism by the tens of thousands each year. World Buddhism, formerly focused on doctrine and scripture, is now returning to the correct teaching (that is, meditation, the training of recovering the original mind).

Moreover, intellectuals who practice Catholicism or the teachings of Jesus Christ have begun to realize that God comprehends and utilizes creativity but is not the actual creator. They realize that were God the actual creator, both good and evil must have come from Him, making Him responsible for their existence. Imagine an evil person who is subjected to the pain of hell challenging God: "Did I ever ask you to be created? Why did you create me and make me suffer this terrible pain?" People have come to understand that this view of God as creator demeans God immensely.

The purification movement has experienced various difficulties, but it is now slowly shaping its path. The Buddha and God originate from the same seed. They are the ones who found and utilized the purified seeds of their selves. Why can't we sentient beings be like them and find the seeds that are our own selves and freely utilize those selves? Once we become aware of this problem, we cannot but practice with all our hearts. The phenomenal world, being a repetition of life and death and pleasure and pain, is impermanent and untrustworthy. However, there is no way we can avoid this life: This is the unchanging law.[4] A being is responsible for endless lives to come and thus should prepare for eternal life. Preparation means recovering one's wholesome mind. Only when we recover the purified human mind does the life of a human being finally begin. The purification movement is like needing to get rice first in order to cook it. It became necessary because of impure reality (and even impurity is purity once it unifies itself).

CHAPTER 8

Is the Mind One or Two?

To Mr. C., Who Has Recently Converted to Catholicism

It has been almost thirty years since we last met. During that long time, we have not had a chance to exchange letters, but an acquaintance of mine from time to time has sent your news to me up on this mountaintop. I was so sorry to hear that you were ill lately.

You were a longtime Buddhist, and the news that you recently converted to Catholicism was quite unexpected. I thought that you knew at least basic Buddhist doctrine: that Buddhism is a teaching that unifies the states of before and after the creation of all beings; that the Buddha is the unity of existence and non-existence; that the Buddha is a pronoun for the universe, or an alias of each individual being; and that the Buddha is a pseudonym of life. The day is coming to a close and still there is an endless way to go, and you have yet to say what "the correct path" of life is...The correct path of life is the eternal life code of one's self. The entire human race is struggling in a maze of confusion, but, whether unconsciously or not, you had entered the source of life. Despite that, you have now turned away from that path, which is truly sad for both you and others.

Life means one's self (the self before a thought arises, the self that one can utilize at will). One's self being one's own, should one not be able to utilize this self at will? If you cannot utilize your self, can you still claim that the self is your own? This is simple logic that even a child can understand. How, then, could you turn away from the teaching that leads you to find your self, the teaching that enables you to utilize freedom and peace at will, and go outside of it, claiming that that is the way for you to survive?

A person's influence on others is exactly in proportion to that person's value. You were a leader of the Korean people and a guide for their future. When such a person changes the direction of his life, how great will be the impact on others? Being confident that you are a great scholar, many people must have thought that you had developed through your own determination solid ideas about life. Believing that you formulated your own ideas about life, how would anyone imagine that you could so easily have changed your mind? Who would ever have suspected that you had not yet established the direction of your ideas about your life? Moreover, I believe that a great scholar should be a complete person, a person who embodies the universe in him or her. How could have anyone have thought that you were a scholar who was yet to be aware that a scholar can be a scholar only when his mind is free?

Even though your confusion as to the direction of your thought is observable, no one could possibly trivialize your contributions to this country when the number of intellectuals is so limited. For almost seventy years, you contributed to the construction of modern Korean culture at its initial stage. Now you have destroyed all of your accomplishments; you have even denied all the support that you had offered to others. I am sure that you are not unaware that this is an act of self-betrayal. This cannot be considered a courageous decision to erase the past in order to take a new path. The religious mind is the entirety of one's mind in life, and your conversion brings me nothing but doubt. You will not understand what this doubt means, much less so all the people in the secular world who do not even know what religion means.

Let me ask you this: Are your mind of the past when you were a Buddhist and your current mind that believes in God the same or different? If they are the same mind, why change your religion when all that has changed is the name of the founder of the religion you believe in? If they are two different minds, which religion will you follow in the future when your mind changes again? You withdraw from Buddhism because you are not aware of the ultimate meaning of religion. All shapes and all activities in time and space are fragments of one's mind. The mind of the object of one's faith and the mind that has faith in that object are not two. The object of your faith is he who has learned to combine all the fragmented minds into one. The mind that has faith in that object is fragmentary. This fragmented mind should unite with the mind of the object of your faith so that you become, yourself, the head of the religion of your belief. This is the very meaning of religion. In other words, the goal of religious practice is to attain an all-capable, non-dual self, such as the heads of religions have attained, and to utilize what we have learned because, originally, we were ourselves head of that religion.

The Buddha is the head of a religion that teaches the absolute quality of existence and helps us to attain it. When we inherit the teachings of the founder of a religion, we become his followers, and we, his disciples, become complete human beings and ourselves head of that religion. Once we become true human beings, all problems are resolved. The beginning and end of the problem is becoming true human beings. By becoming human beings, all problems are removed. If you have retreated from the ultimate religion—which teaches how to put an end to all problems—to take up a preparatory religion based on dependence on the head of a religious school, not only are you far from being a religious practitioner, you are ignorant about the meaning of religious practice. You should fear for yourself now that you have turned your back on religious practice.[1] The ultimate goal of religious practice is to free oneself from the material mind that changes from morning to evening so that one can attain a mind that does not change, be it in favorable or adverse circumstances. That you did not know this and yet have been respected as the greatest leader of this country says something about the level of the Korean people, a not insignificant issue.

Buddhism is the paramount religion among religions, and our ancestors made it a national religion, with everyone from kings to subjects living according to the spirit of Buddhist teachings. The spirit of those Koreans who led a Buddhist life remains with us today, offering hope to the Korean people as they prepare for a future of world peace and focus their full energy on reviving Buddhism. Practitioners offer their spiritual energy and others their physical effort. You were a follower of the Buddha for several decades, and the spiritual benefit of that practice enabled you to reach your current status as a scholar and leader of society. How great will be the impact of your conversion on the entire Korean population! When one is in a low position, there is always the possibility of moving up, but when one is in the highest position, one wrong step leads to the place where there is nowhere to go but down. The character for *"chong"* in *"chong-gyo"* (religion) means the Buddha, and religious education means Buddhist education.[2] By retreating from the comprehensive religion to a derivative religion, you have shown that you do not know what religion means.

God is not the only object of your belief. The mind that has faith is one's own mind. If one fully devotes the mind to something and sincerely believes in that object, even if that object is a tree stump, the stump will act with and respond to one's prayer.

The entire power of one's activities is called the creator; it is the state before the creation of the universe, and the universe is its expression.[3] The reason why most humans fail to behave as true human beings is because they have lost the wholeness of their minds, which is the entirety of this power. The reason that we Koreans failed to be the true descendants of our ancestors, who were true humans, and have remained in an inferior state is because we have been guided by people like you who do not have the spirit of a leader.

At this point, I am even thinking that it would be better for you to add a statement to your will so that as you change your physical body, you can correct your compass, which has been working upside down. This would lead both you and others to salvation. During the Three Kingdoms period, when Buddhism prospered,[4] the value of a state was determined by whether it had as its leader a person of Buddhism. Regardless of how poor a state might have been, if it had a spiritual leader, people far and wide showed their respect. They expressed their concerns about the spiritual leader's well-being and even lent generals to protect the person. The presence of a spiritual person at the head of a state was understood as proof that the people of the state had the proper mindset. If a barbarian state invaded a state headed by a spiritual leader, the barbarians were at least aware of the value of the spiritual leader. They might take the leader hostage, but they would treat him as a universal teacher of wisdom and let him devote himself to teaching others. Buddhist history has recorded many such stories.[5] It is said that war in those days was not truly real [in the spiritual sense] because people back then received a Buddhist education, which taught them that all existence comes from the same seed.

The Buddha is the entirety of the inside and outside of the world; and the reality of life, the external aspect of the Buddha dharma, is the repetition of prosperity and decline. The revival of the current state of the Korean people, which has reached the nadir in the cycle of decline, depends entirely on the recovery of the marrow of Buddhism, which means recovering each individual's original mind, which also means restoring the Buddhist teachings.

Buddhism is in its initial stage of recovery, and the Buddhist monastic order suffers from internal conflict and division, a condition that might have caused you to lose your faith and that may have made you retreat from Buddhism. However, there are ample signs that Buddhist teaching is now on its way to recovery. As the materialism of its culture becomes old, the West, in its self-motivated efforts at rejuvenation, is looking to the East and coming to admire the spiritual culture of Buddhism. The Korean Buddhist order should not lose this opportunity and is in the midst of preparing itself to welcome it.

Not only do believers and thinkers take interest in Buddhism but a number of the cultural avant-garde have converted to Buddhism. We can predict from this that, with the help of Korean Buddhism, it will not be long before Buddhism regains its dominance. Westerners so far are familiar only with the idea of going to heaven, which is nothing but one change of life in our innumerable lives. In this sense, they are myopic, even concerning visible things. Through hypnotism, if not with their physical eyes, they saw evidence of the existence of previous lives and became attracted to Buddhism. It is said that several thousand Westerners convert to Buddhism every year. Awakened people in other cultures are now joining Buddhism; I hope that you are at least aware that you are going against the stream.

I am not publishing this writing with the intention of publicly criticizing you. Neither do I mean to discuss which religion is superior in terms of doctrine. I merely want to let people know how sad it is that you once took up an unsurpassable teaching that is difficult to encounter in innumerable eons and now have let go of that precious opportunity. I want this occasion to be an example to all those who feel lost in their search for how to live this life. Still not wanting to embarrass you, I do not offer detailed comments on this incident, and I ask for your understanding and hope this will bring you some awakening.

Since the origin of the countless number of beings is not known, the ultimate ending of existence also cannot be known. Since the origin and ending are not known, it is also not possible to know who and for what reason all of existence was created.[6] But, whoever the creator might be, there is no way to avoid one's own existence. There is also no way to know how many lives one will live, and no one has ever even tried to count them. Among innumerable existences, it is said that four types of existence are most difficult to attain: It is difficult to be born as a human; it is difficult to be born as a male; it is difficult to leave the secular world and join the monastery; and it is difficult to encounter the Buddhist teachings. Of these four difficulties, [you have accomplished all three] except that you did not join the monastery, and you spent your entire life as a lay practitioner and are now almost at the final stage of becoming a teacher of gods and humans. And yet you have given up this high position, stepped back to the beginner's level, and raised your voice on the radio and in writing to the entire world saying that the place where you are now is the secure realm! The image of such a scholar stuns even the spirits, making them crumble in tears.

It is pointless to discuss all of the people in this world who have lost themselves. But you are a leader of the people; you are the one whom I have trusted all this time! As a Buddhist, for yourself, and for me, who has spent the past nearly thirty years at this mountain monastery with nothing to look back on, what a reliable person you have been!

The more I think about human nature, the more I cannot believe in it.

I have now finally realized that I have lost myself and feel such anguish about it. But other people, including my acquaintances, who are unaware that they have lost themselves, would not understand what I have written here. I am sure that many of them would deride me. If they knew only "one thing," they would know everything, but since they do not know their real selves and have deserted themselves, I do not know what to do.

Allow me to repeat my points. The Buddha is each individual's original self and the owner of the universe. Since the name "the Buddha" differs from our own name, it is understandable that we may have difficulty understanding the Buddha. But we do not even attempt to understand ourselves, who we really are, and yet still claim to be human beings. How pitiful! If an individual uses the expression "I," shouldn't that person be able to control this "I" at will? People do not even think about the implications of this. Even a child understands that something that she cannot use at will in no way belongs to her. However trivial a thing is, if that thing does not belong to her, she cannot use it at will. In the same way, it is vain to talk about an "I" that cannot control the self, which is directly related to the "I," and to believe that everything depends on "me" or on how "I" do. How can such beings ever behave like true human beings?

The value of a being lies in knowing its own self, controlling that self at will, and thus being able to establish its existence based on that capacity. Unaware of this, people boast of holding the highest position among all beings. If individuals really wish to claim to be human, they must ask why human beings live such constrained and uncomfortable lives. If we are capable of asking this of ourselves, we will realize that the source of the problem is that we do not know our own selves because we have lost our selves. Not knowing our own selves, we do not think about inquiring into our real identities. Since we do not think about making inquiries into our own selves, we fail to learn anything from our own thinking, and our thinking comprises our own selves and others, events, names, and images. Having failed to learn from our thinking, we are lost in delusion and thus have no freedom or peace.

Let's think about this: It is a fact that this body exists. Thus, wouldn't it make sense to first clearly understand what happened before and what will happen after this existence—that is to say, before birth and after death—if we are to prepare and plan for life as a human being? If we had only one life, where would the problem lie so long as we could live surrounded by material comfort? Life would simply come to an end and there would be no reason to be concerned about it and feel stressed. Suppose it were possible to go to heaven in the afterlife. But heaven, being part of this reality, is part of an illusionary reality that is subject to the universal principles of arising, staying, ceasing, and emptying. What good is it, then, to have happy dreams of heaven? Awakening from a happy dream is just the same as awakening from a bad dream. Only the void remains. The only issue of concern is to prepare for this life, in which good and bad dreams repeat, one after another, without end.

The price we must pay for this life is solely our individual responsibility. Others cannot share it, not even a hair of it. The structure of the universe is based on an exchange system. We must pay the price of this life in full, if, at the very least, we are to maintain the current state (with this body in this life). If we pay the price of this life and still possess a surplus, we will be able to lead a life in heaven; if we find ourselves with a deficit, we will be demoted to lower levels. However, the law of the world is based on the principle of polarization, which has continued for eons from the beginningless beginning. That being the case, being in heaven or in hell should not be too much of a problem.[7] Isn't it true that for a being that exists for eternity, the ultimate achievement would be to attain unchanging comfort? This state cannot be attained unless we find a way to take control of our lives. The idea that faith in God will lead us to peace and freedom is as dangerous as a patient mistaking the temporary relief brought by a painkiller for a complete cure of his disease. I hope you are aware of this.

The God who is omnipresent and the Buddha who was born into this world are both idols. The omnipresent God will cease to be present, and the Buddha who was born into this world will disappear. Worshipping these idols is only the first stage of discovering our own selves. Reaching the essence of these idols entails the discovery of the self, which means taking refuge in the Buddha (the same as taking refuge within our individual selves) and in God.

All beings exist through the dual functions of cohesion and dissolution, which are based on self-polarization,[8] and the life of any being involves the repetition of coming in and going out of existence. The process of change over inexhaustible eons infinitely recurs. What happens when a traveler of eternity, incapable of finding a day's comfort, is blind?

A couple of days ago, three pastors of the religion of Jesus visited this temple and I had the opportunity to meet them. As we conversed, I told them, "Everybody is blind, but though your job title is 'shepherd (*mok*)-teacher (*sa*),' it seems that even you are not aware of your own blindness. What is happening? The soul is a material entity, and a material entity is a being that eats and that can be seen through physical eyes. But the followers of Jesus do not seem able to see this soul and thus criticize Buddhists who offer deliverance (by guiding the dead soul for the first forty-nine days after death and with memorial services) as performing the work of the devil. You leaders are responsible for such ignorance. In Buddhism, sages provide souls with deliverance in person."

"Please have faith!" religious traditions tell us, because having faith while alive means the soul will have faith after death as well.[9] The soul that has faith will be led to a good womb, and if this is not possible, the soul is revived and advised to return to the path upon which it previously wandered (as in a dream). Upon returning there, the soul realizes that it had not been aware of the reality of existence before and immediately begins the practice of controlling the mind (through meditation or chanting). Or in other cases, the soul is called in, fed the same food consumed by those who are alive (since the soul is also a material entity, it has a consciousness, eats food, and hears things), and dharma talks are offered, all of which should lead the soul to awaken. As a long-term believer in Buddhism, you should have constantly seen these things; or have you been little more than a fool for all of this time?

A sentient being relies on and is guided by a teacher, but when this sentient being comes to realize the nature of the self, which her teacher has learned and passed on to others, the sentient being finds salvation and, in turn, is able to guide others.[10] When an individual is on the road, that person must get through difficult situations such as climbing mountains, crossing rivers, and walking in the wind and rain. Likewise, we, pilgrims on the journey without end, must overcome all types of good and bad situations, and in facing those situations, must not let them drag us down as though we were sinners.[11] When we are in control of where we walk, when we are the director of our own path, we are able to find peace of mind through realization of the reality of existence (nirvana), whether we are dealing with essential or inessential issues, whether we are in action or at rest, whether we find ourselves in safety or in danger.

Religion offers the solution to the secular world and secular people, but all the same it is subject to secular laws. Since God exists, He also eats and acts. And who is suffering from what God has done during his lifetime? If God is the original creator, the seed of good and evil must have been in the original design of creation, and who is responsible for that? In fact, God was only an engineer who used the material at hand. But many of God's followers misunderstand God's role in creation, and now that you have joined that group, I hope you will understand the situation when you read this essay.

You are a historian. Do you plan to study history in the context of Catholicism, which does not recognize the existence of previous lives and which can talk only about a single scene in the future lives to come? Because you didn't have clear ideas, you devoted your time to the records of ignorant people, studying a bunch of false records of life, and claimed to be a historian. Like other beings, you also lived a thousand years ago and ten thousand years ago. Do you not think, if you are to claim to be a real historian, you should say something about those lives? If you cannot tell what you personally have seen and heard, would you not, at least, be obliged to report the record of what really had happened at that time? When I said "See you tomorrow" to my nearsighted friend, my friend retorted, "There is no tomorrow," and wanted to end our friendship, dismissing my idea as absurd. Were you trying to serve this myopic view in our time? Without a real object, a shadow cannot exist; likewise, it should be common sense that behind secretly transmitted tales and legends exist the real stories that are their essence. As for this precious fact that is relevant only to human beings,[12] would you let it be excluded from official history and instead recorded as an unofficial story or a mere myth, as if it were the dream-talk of ignorant people?

It is said that in those days when the Buddhist teachings were part of everyday life, wood-cutters walking on the mountain paths or servants smoking on the paddy fields would talk about the difficulties they suffered in their mothers' wombs or mysterious tales of what they had experienced several eons ago. Swapping such stories was a form of informal conversation among those who lived in a world of constant peace. Even if you never reach the ultimate state of comprehending and utilizing your own self, for the sake of success in your profession, you should stay with Buddhism. In order to accomplish anything, even as a superficial historian, you would probably need at least "the super-knowledge of the past lives of oneself and others" (*sungmyŏngt'ong*), which could be one of the first effects of Buddhist education. I wonder how you could have ignored this. If you had had just a little bit of faith, you could not have forsaken what is related to "the super-knowledge of the past lives of oneself and others," which you see right here and which the people in the world consider impossible.

While you were studying Buddhism as a follower, you must have witnessed those fully in control of the change of this body, which is like a garment we wear, and also you must have heard many stories of those who are capable of exercising unimaginable and inexplicable supernatural powers. Comparing such phenomena to what you see in Catholicism and what is recorded in the Bible, the miracles of the religion of Jesus are like a drop of water, whereas Buddhist super-knowledge is like the great ocean. What were you thinking once you had read, heard, and seen what is possible in Buddhism?

You have thrown away your own invaluable treasure house in exchange for a rented treasury belonging to others. You have given up the fully equipped self and moved to a religion that takes faith as the ultimate and that teaches reliance on other-power. That is because your feeble mind has difficulty comprehending a doctrine that demands that one embody all the requirements of life within oneself and deal with them for oneself. That is why in Buddhism, the followers of the religions of humans and gods, Catholicism, and the religion of Jesus [Protestantism] are compared to lost children.

There is the story of a child who was lost at a young age and lived by begging. The child stole because he was hungry and was beaten and mistreated because he stole. Once, trying to hide from others, the child came by accident upon the front gate of his own home. But the house looked so magnificent and the people inside appeared so absolutely decent that it scared him. He ran away from the house, but someone (Jesus) was sent to attract him, telling him that if he came back to the huge house and did errands, he would have warm clothes and good food. The child-servant stayed at the house for a long time, becoming familiar with it, and as his fear disappeared, he was told that he was in fact the house's owner. He was now ready to live as the proprietor of the house.[13]

Just as those who fall on the ground should rely on the ground to get up, so we, the small idols, rely on great idols like the Buddha or God to stand up. Once we pick ourselves up, we walk on our own. Until we are able to walk on our own, until we reach the state of non-self, we must have absolute faith. While still alive, a person should separate from his physical body and even his soul should disappear. When the small self is extinguished and the person is united with the great self, he has attained the state of absolute salvation. This is the time when he recovers his complete self. This is absolute oneness. This complete self is a complete entity that is at one with even a piece of shit or a handful of dirt.

The expression "oneness" is used in Catholicism as well, but since God is understood as a special being, how is oneness possible? In Buddhism we become the universe itself; each of us is the being in which all the requirements for existence are contained. As a result, we are completely free in our actions as we are in our relations to others who would benefit from compassionate action: If a person asks for food, we give it; if someone feels thirsty, we offer something to drink; we relieve the pain of the sick person and console the lonely.

Both sentient and insentient beings are our other selves, our own body. Even when we act as individuals, the action, which partakes of the entirety of the universal power, has a hundred different effects. Followers of a religion whose god prohibits the worship of other gods do not make obeisance to the statue of the Buddha and claim that such disrespect is an act of religious piety. Their minds fall far below the mental level required of a believer. They would be better off preparing to be virtuous wives or loyal subjects and train themselves to be like Pak P'aengnyŏn, who refused to submit even when tortured with a hot iron.[14]

In Buddhism the mental capacity of person like the loyal Pak is considered to have reached a level at which, minimally, one can maintain the constant state after death; such a person is at least prepared for death. In facing death, if one cannot cut off all aspects of the mind, be it suffering or joy, and unless one unifies all aspects of the mind, be it the mind that believes or one's original mind, one can neither be saved by others nor save oneself. Mr. Ch'oe, your mind waivers even now while you are alive. It will only get weaker as you age, so you should be firm with your mind. You should unify your thought with the being that exists before a thought arises. The thought before you exist creates things and generates situations. In other words, the beginning and end of the universe, the birth and death of a being, is the arising and ceasing of a thought. In the beginning is the arising of a thought; this one wave is followed by ten thousand waves; each fragment of thought generates a different world, like a particle of dust creating different beings and thousands of different functions.

The unity of this world and these beings becomes the basis of one's thoughts. A thought is fragmentary, but it is also the unified material mind.[15] Taken one step further, one can exercise creativity, which means to comprehend and utilize no-self and no-thought (that is, awakening). In doing so, that individual becomes a true human being. Catholicism is not aware of the being before a thought arises, which is the original entity that exists outside of God or the soul. Catholics conceive of God or Jesus as a superhuman being that will save humans only if humans believe in this idol.[16] When these idols fall, believers fall as well. This situation arises because thoughts constitute reality and reality is based on the principle of duality, which entails the repetition of the arising and passing away of an existence that is by its nature impermanent. Buddhist doctrine does not take the statue of the Buddha, which Catholicism criticizes as an idol, as an object of salvation. Polarization is the principle of the secular world, which is only the external shell of the Buddha, and thus cannot go beyond the material realm. However, if a person can at least master the principle of the secular world [the principle of dualism], she will be able to punish spirits, as well as move freely back and forth between this world, heaven, and hell. This ability to move [between different realms] is not reserved only for humans; it extends even to heretics, demons, managers of the underworld, and powerful shamans, whom we may still encounter today.

In ancient times, when people's mental maturity was superior, the utterance of a sage could completely transform people's thinking, and their mental capacity enabled people to perform ten thousand things at the same time. We live on Earth, which is two billion years old. Along with this aging planet, we are beings of declining capacity. Even though we possess mental capacity, the utilization of our full power is absolutely forbidden until we become complete beings again and earn back all of our mental power and thus regain our full capacity. It is as if to attempt to use that power prematurely would disturb its accumulation. It is important for everyone to practice concentrating the mind. But people today do not recognize those who focus on such practices and instead, having only limited mental capacity themselves, believe all human beings to be sinners, incapable of becoming sages or achieving perfection; they say, "We human beings cannot accomplish such things." I thought you were aware that people have lost their minds and would make an effort to gather your mental power. On the contrary, you have left the institution called Buddhism, a superior institution that can guide us in collecting our minds, and instead are attempting to enslave the minds of others.

It should be common knowledge that "religion," "the Dao, "the self" as well as "the Buddha," "the mind," and "one's nature" are interchangeable nouns for what is complete, independent, autonomous, and self-sovereign. Good and evil, beauty and ugliness, pain and pleasure are one. But doesn't Catholicism promote doctrines that focus exclusively on beauty, goodness, and joy? This is a principle born of a demon because it only focuses on the external aspect of the world. Religious education involves attaining nothingness, that is to say, the wholeness that makes up the inner essence of the principle of the secular world. A demon is the external aspect (the entirety of the reality of thought), and the Buddha is its inner aspect (nothingness, which is the inner essence of daily reality), but relying only on the Buddha is demonic as well. The unity of a demon and the Buddha comprises the attainment of buddhahood (wholesome being).

The activities of the Buddha encompass all of the phenomena that are within the scope of thought. What is called Buddhism and the Buddha as well as all of the Buddhist rituals is also the principle and the forms of a demon, whereas the essence of the Buddha is nothingness, which is creativity. The Buddha, who is capable of fully utilizing this creativity, is the supreme person of culture capable of creating all things at will. You are a person of culture, are you not? As a person of culture, you were not aware that the Buddha is the great person of culture and is thus your mentor.

Catholicism teaches that non-culture in the material world is evil, and in order to promote the pleasures of heaven, the supreme life of the material culture, it emphasizes goodness and compassion exclusively. But heaven exists only in opposition to hell. What, then, are you to do?

This world of reality is the history of the repetition of prosperity and decline.[17] But there exists no other world. Even in this reality we should be able to live the life of the unchanging true self, a life where we are the controller of our own mind. This is the meaning of practicing religion. Only the Buddhist person of culture can hold on to his or her proper mind in a life of ups and downs, pain and pleasure, life and death. The concrete realization of culture should be limited to Buddhist culture because Buddhist culture is the unity of culture and non-culture.

Even simply to achieve success in the secular world, we need time for no-thinking. Catholicism offers a teaching that would have us attempt to attain salvation through the mediation of the Virgin Mary, God the Father, His Son, and Holy Spirit, but since they exist within the limits of material reality, they are not the solution. You have no idea of what will happen in the next life, and in this life, you are already old and sick. Are you attempting to retreat and give everything up? Do you want to rely on God so that you can leisurely pass your time? But leisurely passing time is not allowed. A moment's rest results in tragedy for ten thousand eons to come, and I do not think you would want to accept such a deal.

With the mind that led you to convert, it would not be easy to truly believe in God. Unless you rekindle your believing mind, in the face of death your future will look absolutely hopeless. Thus, I want to tell you that now is the time to rekindle your mind and return to Buddhism. Even a journey of a thousand *li* depends on how you take the first step. You should aim to reach ultimate awakening.

The Buddha, who is the compassionate father of beings born out of the four different states, the undifferentiating mentor of the three worlds, facilitates the absolute equality of all existence and never allows this equality to be withdrawn. He does not refuse even a worm if it comes to him, nor shut out a fly. It is not too late even now. I have written this piece in the sincere hope that you and your disciples will together all come to this realm of security.

CHAPTER 9

What Is Faith?

*Contemplation upon Reading a
Letter from My Friend M.*

In the secular world, to study means to increase the quantity of one's knowledge; for monks and nuns, to practice means to dissolve whatever one already has, both in quantity and in quality, so as to grasp and utilize the inner essence of that which exists before a thought arises. As a nun I have yet to fully realize progress in my practice and, thus, there are people in the shadows of feelings that linger in my path. I especially find from time to time the shadow of a friend from my childhood whose name is M. Then I received, for the first time in a long time, a letter from M. She wrote,

> ...Among the friends living at the dormitory at Ewha Hakdang, where our childish dreams flourished, even though you wore a long skirt, K., you were a classy dresser, while I was known as a classic beauty. Maybe that was the reason. Anyway, we two were the most talked about in the dormitory. After graduation, as adults, we became failures at the original job of a Korean woman, which is married life. K, you had a complicated marriage, but perhaps that allowed you to enjoy a relatively free and peaceful life, whereas I led a simple married life with a family but suffered from serious problems. In that situation, K.,[1] you were always there for me to talk to about my problems, showing your concern, which I will never forget. It has already been more than thirty years ago that we had black hair and red cheeks. After we parted, we got gray hair and wrinkles, and I wonder whether we bear any trace of the dandy or the beauty. Can you imagine how hard my heart was pounding when I heard about you in the media? But I realized that my heart was beating not simply because I was happy to hear about you. K., you are the daughter of a faithful Christian pastor and you have left Jesus? How could that possibly be? That was the source of my astonishment....

When I received the letter I was desperately trying to propagate Buddhist teaching, which is the solution to all problems. I once had a dream where I tried to spread the teaching as I walked with friends from the dormitory to a church. I had been looking for an opportunity to give this teaching first to those with whom I was close, and, ironically, I received this letter from my closest childhood friend. I could not but laugh, but my laughter was more like crying without crying.

That was because as I was trying to open myself up to take ownership of the great space of a billion worlds that everyone shares, my friend M.'s letter was deploring my refusal to be confined to a small house called heaven. The "great space" refers to the entire universe, including heaven, the human world, hell, and others realms. This universe contains innumerable beings, and at its center exist the world of planets. Along with the sun, which sends out light to us from the center, there exist planets such as Venus, Jupiter, Mercury, Saturn, Neptune, Earth, and Uranus,[2] a total of eight. In addition, science has discovered a number of similar systems that make up small universes, bringing the total number to 20,008,000. The Buddha mentions about ten billion suns and moons, and science says that there are fixed stars thousands of light-years away. In addition are countless universes above and below the sky.

In modern Asia, this entire universe would be referred to as the Buddha. The Buddhist teachings are comments on one's own self. The Buddha is the universe, and the universe is one's own self. Anyone who does not know the Buddha does not know his or her own self. The people in this world are like a group of puppets who have lost their selves. That is why the Buddhist teachings, which are a way of finding one's own self, are so necessary. The self, which is conscious of itself, and the world, which is the self's reality, are the external aspects of the Buddha; the Buddha that exists before it is named and before the self exists is the inner aspect of the Buddha, the original mind that is my creator.

The world, the external aspect of the Buddha, is bound to come to an end, and the internal aspect of the Buddha, having existed for two billion years, has reached a point of senility. Buddhism for now is returning to a state of respite. Religious education is not about making us do good things. It is intended to help us recover the mind that knows how to erase the discriminating judgment of good and evil—that is, the original mind of human beings—so that we can live not by following fixed rules but by relating to the contexts in which we find ourselves. Good and evil are the creations of humans. Heaven and hell are one stop in the process of existence and will continue without end in future lives.

I attended a Christian church beginning when I was a baby, and at the age of eight I made up my mind that when I grew up I would go to the land of cannibals to propagate Christianity and guide poor savages who would otherwise be destined to suffer in hell. However, because of the narrow-minded teachings of my pastor father, who was unwavering in insisting that belief in Jesus was the only way to get to heaven, I lost my faith, a precious thing and the only path to salvation that sentient beings in this world have. Faith does not lie in its object but in the mind of the faithful. Even if we have faith in a tree stump, if that faith is absolute and we have a complete mind that has become one with the object of our faith, the peace of self-sufficiency will bring eternal comfort. Since the mind that has faith and the mind that is trusted are originally one, we reach our original nature, which is the state of unity.

The mind of believing, that is, the evidence of faith in one's mind, falls far short of guaranteeing absolute faith. When I believed in Jesus, I naïvely thought that things must be the way they are because of God's grace. And yet I did not experience that grace in my life because my faith was not strong enough. I realized this only after I became a Buddhist. In fact, the religion of Jesus does not know how to teach that God is my original essence; that I have separated myself from my own essence; that because God is always taking care of sentient beings, His alter egos, we can connect with Him if we pray to Him with one mind (no-thought); and that, with the help of God, we can realize our full capacity and thus finally become God, which is the ultimate state of our own selves.[3] The mind that searches for God based on desire, the mind that thanks God — all such notions should be eliminated, and in the void created by such an action of emptying out (the state in which all speculation and even consciousness are extinguished), in that state of unity we can be connected with God. In that state, we understand the benefit of prayer and religious practice. But I was searching for God through feelings within the realm of consciousness, emotion, and material things, which made it difficult to see any evidence of prayer.

After I became a follower of Buddhism, I realized for the first time that religion is an education in how to live, and religious teaching should be realized right here in this life. It concerns everything that happens right in front of our eyes, whether it concerns this body that is born and lives again and again or what one searches and wishes for. How can teachings unrelated to what is happening right now — such as whether we go to heaven in the afterlife, whether such things are possible, or even speculation about the Buddhist doctrines or the will of heaven — offer any ultimate solutions to existence? Whatever the Buddha or God may say, only those teachings that I see with my own eyes, hear with my own ears, experience, and thus about which I have no doubt can be described as the real content of religious education, which is comprehensive edification.

Teachings that one simplemindedly believes cannot offer a sense of self-sufficiency. Only when the believing mind is absolutely sincere can one temporally unify one's mind so that one does not feel a void. Also, objects of belief change, change being the principle of the world, and the believing mind that is not grounded in the practical cannot be steady and consistent. When I was a child, I observed missionary ladies of the religion of Jesus. When they were young, they were passionate about propagating the teaching and always smiling, but as they became older, they seemed forlorn and lonely and, thus, shed tears. They lived thousands of miles away in a foreign land, separated from their families. Even though they adopted people of a different land as their own people, they must after all have felt that was not enough. I wondered whether they felt disillusioned about their lives, which they had devoted to Korean people who lacked understanding and love. Thinking about that made me feel ashamed to be a Korean, but at the same time I felt sympathy for them. As I write this essay, images from that time appear in front of me as if they were pictures hanging on a wall.

The religion of Jesus tends to rely on "other-power." Christianity does not teach that happiness and misfortune are both just a function of one's own mind, that the extension of this mind is the afterlife, that one should not try to search for anything outside of oneself, and that establishing one's own mind right here at this moment sets the foundation of eternal life. Since the religion of Jesus lacks this teaching, it is only natural that a Christian feels lonely when his physical state becomes weak. We should not take life for granted but should always prepare for death, and by doing so improve our mental power. However, all but a small number of the followers of Jesus naïvely believe that God's grace and Jesus' guidance will lead them to heaven and, having no mental strength, they lose self-confidence as their physical bodies age. Moreover, because they are not clear about what it means to go to heaven, even among the followers of Jesus, different people believe different things. Although all are followers of God, the meaning of going to heaven varies from denomination to denomination.

Among Buddhists, on the other hand, except for the numerous people who want merely to benefit by making offerings to the Buddha, whether one really believes or not, there is a unified idea of how to attain buddhahood (be a complete person). To be guided by Jesus means that on one's deathbed one should have a unified mind freed of all feelings and attachments and thereby has cut off all suffering. But being constrained by secular life, people practice the teaching of Jesus as if it were their side job, unaware that in that manner they will never reach the ultimate state of a believer. When they pray to God, instead of contacting Him directly, they pray in the name of Jesus. This practice of dependency prevents them from recognizing the principle that only by dedicating everything do we gain everything and that a wish is realized only when a price equivalent to the value of the wish is paid.

Whoever it might be, this body and soul, which are the extension and accumulation of the habitual energy of a sentient being, must be extinguished for resurrection to take place. Christians say that this body will be restored to life after the judgment that follows death. Do they not know about the obvious principle that the body and soul are subject to time and space and therefore cannot avoid the repetition of happiness and misfortune, life and death? How then could they understand the Buddhist principle that transcends body and soul, and how could they even imagine the practices of monks and nuns? Christians teach that one can go to heaven, but because heaven is part of this world, their teaching cannot help one attain the final resolution.[4] That is because the other side of good is evil, and heaven has hell as its opposite. Christians' understanding of heaven is not based on the principle that self and others are one. Even compassion and love, if practiced without the understanding that self and others are one, will play their opposite roles at some point.[5]

Unless we separate from our own body while we live and completely extinguish even consciousness (soul) and are born again, we cannot attain eternal salvation. In the sea of feelings where thought still exists, suffering and pleasure continue to repeat themselves. In Christianity, it is said that only those chosen by God can go to heaven. If that is the case, how is God different from an ordinary man who loves only his family members and subordinates? Since God is omnipotent and omnipresent, can He not make everybody believe in Him? The Buddha declared that because of absolute individual freedom, he cannot save those sentient beings who do not believe.

If a person has faith, even though he is like a doll, he has the mental capacity to eventually attain the wholeness of human nature. Faith is the world's best teacher, and thus the Buddha would save any being, even a venomous serpent or a demon. God must be like the Buddha, but He created a human that is partial and incomplete.[6] By saying that God is the creator, instead of glorifying God, we demean Him. Out of nothing, good and evil were produced, which means that the seeds of good and evil were in the design of God's creation. If an evil man were to challenge

God, asking Him: "I did not have any idea of evil, so why did you create me and make me go through this unendurable pain in hell?" God would have no words to respond.

People say that God gave humans freedom and then tested them, but if God is truly omniscient, there is no reason for God to play such a devilish game. With original creativity, God makes all things in the world, and He is also responsible for destroying all of them. The customs observed in heaven, Jesus' whereabouts at this point, and his methods of teaching human beings are all recorded in the eighty-four thousand teachings found in Buddhist scripture.[7] By attaining the all-capable mental power, one can use this physical body as an airplane and travel between heaven and hell at will. But since time and space depend on one thought and heaven and hell are right here at this very moment, there is in fact no reason to travel back and forth. Even though we are incomplete, even though we possess only the small self, we are still capable of utilizing this original mind, which is creativity.

Think about this! When we remember a person, a place, or an incident, the images appear in front of us. Incidents in the future, as well, appear before our eyes as we imagine them. When we concentrate on one thought, things are here at this very moment, whereas when things are put at a distance, the time becomes the past, the person exists far away, and the place retreats. When we focus on the object of our vision, we see and hear nothing else. Everything depends on one thought, on the mind, which is the beginning and the end. This can be proven in the situations one encounters as a small self. Everything is clear. The seed of all beings is not two, and the original mind, which is equipped with everything, is always one. The religion of Jesus does not teach this; it emphasizes only the love based on dualism and claims that snakes are enemies and evil. The human being is the unity of the demon and the Buddha; the mind of a snake and that of a human are originally the same. A snake is an individual entity that consists of evil habits, and what is called a demon is generally the reality of the universe. The essence of a demon is a phenomenal reality in the world, and the inner essence of the universe is Buddha Nature, which is the existential self of all beings. The demon is this physical body and soul, and the original mind that is our self-nature is the truth that cannot be verbalized.[8]

When a person falls to the ground, he should pick himself up with the support of the ground. Sentient beings are small demons and small idols. They take refuge in the Buddha or in God, who are big demons and big idols, because they want to learn from the Buddha or God, who have already learned the truth of the original mind, or creativity. The teaching that Jesus is the truth and life, if it can be verbalized, must be false. How-ever, since everybody already has truth within themselves, we can sym-pathize and understand the meaning of that statement. Religion makes real the truth that cannot be expressed in language. The religion that ne-gates the reality of life is the religion that has failed to realize ultimate real-ity. Any religious doctrine that fails to exactly reflect the lives of humans is heretical. To believe without knowing the meaning of religious belief is merely superstition or blind faith.

My friend M. says that she is a missionary and happy to be a servant of Jesus. If a person is a child of God, is Jesus not her brother? Is it possible for an average person to volunteer to be a servant of one's brother? More-over, God, Jesus, and I were all the same before thought arose—that is, before birth. My unity with God makes me a complete person. There exist no beings above humans that humans have to fear and no beings below humans that humans can despise. Nowadays, however superficial their commitment, even non-believers are calling for absolute equality. How then can it be said that God claims a special privilege in a religion that teaches equality and non-self? How does a human, who is different from God in terms of quality, unify with God? God is more directly related to me than my own father, since God is my original body. If I believe in God and make no effort to recover my own body, but instead am satisfied with being a servant of God's son, is such a person not out of her mind, rather than practicing a religion? One can claim that God is not one's original body, and one's relationship to God is like that of the relationship with one's parents. Still, is it not common sense that children grow up to be-come parents themselves?

I have been making every effort to return to the life in which self and others become one, from a life in which self is separated from my original essence. That also entails a return to the life in which religion and the secular world become one; yet, my friend deplores this, because I refuse to remain a servant of Jesus. How can I explain this to my ignorant friend, M.? I began to feel tension once again in my tears, to which I had not given much meaning.

The universe is in a state of demolition. It has lost its original mind, and all the beings in the universe are in a state of confusion. Since my friend M is also part of this group of sentient beings, I was not especially surprised to be facing this situation. Non-believers use all of their energies and source materials in consumptive, secular activity, but do not engage in productive religious life. Since their activities focus on an empty enter-prise without any spiritual foundation, when the business fails, the busi-ness owner breaks down as well. I should admit that, passive though it may be, at least my friend M. has accumulated mental resources through her prayers to God, who is doing a good business that benefits her in both her life here and in heaven.

However, to see family members whose minds do not function properly live in a crumbling house is like watching tragic images of ship-wrecked passengers hanging on to fragments of the ship in the immense ocean, being tossed about by the wind. In this sort of situation, which is pervasive, the Buddha is the leader, guiding people toward salvation. As a novice follower of the Buddha, I indulged myself in the joy of walking the untrodden path, and my heart pounded like a deer that has caught the scent of water. Calling out with sincere concern to my follow humans who are suffering from the same disease but who are getting lost on the other side, I cannot help but take up my pen and write this. If my friend M. continues to believe in God and follow Jesus, she will go to heaven. Compared to the non-religious people clinging to the wooden fragments of a shipwreck, living in heaven would be like being securely on board. But she seems unaware of the danger she will face when the waves get rough. Taking a ship as the permanent ground of one's being is as danger-ous as a patient believing that the temporary cessation of pain as an effect of painkillers is a permanent cure for her disease.

Only when one leads a life through the unity of heaven and hell and oneness of suffering and joy, and only when one has firmly secured the mental capacity that is unswayed by external forces, can one reach the other side, which is unchanging, secure territory (nirvana). Be it the Bud-dha or Jesus, they always taught according to the mental capacity of the learners. Because of the situation of the Jewish people at the time, Jesus taught only about going to heaven (which is a turning point) and left out what happens before and after in the reality of existence. That is why people are not aware of the principle of transmigration: that existence goes through birth, aging, sickness, and death and that the universe also evolves through arising, staying, ceasing, and emptiness. When you have the capacity to concentrate, when you are in a state absolutely devoid of attachments, you can make real whatever ideas you might have. You are able to act and thus embody the ideas as well as comprehend them. Those in heaven are people who maintained normal lives, based on the degree of their merits within certain limitations; they do not say odd things like "my mind is reality," "my mind is my destiny," or, "if one eats, one feels full."[9] Yet, a life in heaven is vain, much as is one scene from a happy dream. However happy one may be in a dream, what good comes of it? Once we awaken from the dream, that's it. Hence, one should completely awaken from this unending cycle of good and bad luck, and reach solid ground where one's sleep or waking state does not fluctuate. This is the only way to attain self-satisfaction.

In the midst of the ceaseless repetition of life and death, should a person accumulate sufficient merit through good behavior to get to heaven, the pleasure of living there would prevent her from practicing the mind. Likewise, if life unfolds as we wish, physical effort becomes unnecessary, which naturally leads to a state of non-production. In that case, when the day arrives to tally up our acts of compassion and love, we would find ourselves in a situation like the rich person facing bankruptcy.[10] Instead, it is important to realize that although we may live in a shabby place, eat humble meals, and wear ragged clothes, if our mind is at peace, we are in heaven. In other words, we should be able to be a complete person in whom time and space are embodied; although time and space are widely extended, we should still be able to unify them and recover them in our own self. You should comprehend the reality of life in its entirety, without exception, and then, when you face a hundred, a thousand, or ten thousand different situations in life, you can react to them consistently. The reality of life exists in all different shapes, forms, colors, and smells. Since they are all fragments of your own mind, you should collect them all to make the whole, which completes your self. This is the way to reach the ultimate and essential meaning of religion. Discussion of different states of good and evil, different forms of beauty and ugliness, different feelings of fortune and misfortune, and judgments between right and wrong belongs to the laws of the secular world, not to religious truth. Believers in our time are not aware of this, which is why they cannot have even a day of peace. In recent years, both believers and philosophers take as ultimate reality such limited concepts of God, spirit, or soul. This body is life's clothing, and this soul is the machine that life manipulates. The creator of this body and soul has no physical body; it just acts. It is called the dharma body.

The unity of the physical body, the karma body (soul), and the dharma body is your own self and your own mind. When this unity happens, your organizational structure is complete. This is the time when you forsake external idols like God or the Buddha and when you leave institutions like Christianity or Buddhism; this is the time when you become liberated and take ownership of the entire universe. At that time, all beings that are part of the universe you own will finally occupy the unchanging land of freedom and peace.

In sum, everything depends on the mind. When one concentrates one's mind, there is nothing that one cannot accomplish. There is a story of an ignorant old lady who misunderstood the expression "the mind is the Buddha" (*chŭksim si Pul*). She chanted the phrase "the straw shoes are the Buddha" (*chipsegi Pul*)[11] with a focused mind, and eventually became an all-capable person in whom all things become one.

A living being has no way to end its life. That being the case, should we not prepare ourselves to live? Since to prepare oneself to live means to concentrate one's mind on the principle, should we not return to that principle? Sentient beings call the changing of clothes a death and face it with utmost fear, just as a fish is terrified when the water in the aquarium is changed. If one lives with one's mind still distracted, wasting time on this and that, what will happen when death approaches without warning? With an incapable mind, the future is hopeless. We should first practice chanting or meditation (cultivation of one's mind), which is the best way to focus the mind.

The tick-tock of a clock is the sound of the footsteps of the demon called impermanence rushing after you. This demon of impermanence does not care whether you are young or old. Moreover, there is no guarantee against a surprise attack. There is no being that can guarantee that you will still be alive a minute from now. The extension of this mind is the innumerable lives to come. A mind solidly established, then that is the preparation for death. If one has confidence in the power of one's mind, there is no reason to be bothered—whether the stage for one's next life is to be in heaven or in hell.

Just as all of Śakyamuni Buddha's forty-nine years of dharma talk were the talk of a demon, what I have written so far cannot avoid severe criticism by those intellectuals who understand Buddhism. Just so, I hope to see reactions to this essay from the followers of Jesus.

CHAPTER 10

The Path to No-Mind

A Letter to Mr. R.

Our "romance," which caused quite a scandal both in Seoul and in the countryside, came to an end thirty-six years ago. It floated away like the fallen leaves. Compared to the infinite number of lives we are destined to live, that year or two together was like the shortest dream in a short period in our lives. It is not our relationship that compels me to write this letter now. I have a habit of making decisions without thinking them through and before I'm sure they are actually what I want. When I make a decision, I stick to it passionately, and once I accept something as my own in my life, I'm blindly faithful to it, like a bear; I only ever see the positive side of it and will accept that life as perfectly satisfactory. Then once reason returns and leads me to conclude that I should end that life, I can pack up my stuff without a bit of regret. When that happens, nothing can call me back, no matter how loud those calls might be. Yet it is said that for two people even to brush past each other on the corner of a mountain, a previous relationship of five hundred lives is required. How, then, can we say that the couple of years we spent together meant nothing?

More than the five hundred lives, even five million times the lives we have lived are the reflection of our spirits, which consist of the extension and accumulation of delusive, habitual energy generated from a chain of fragments. I wasn't aware of this thirty-six years ago when I was living in the secular world. It was as if that life was real. Let me repeat: The reason I'm writing this letter is not because of the relationship we had back then.

After I joined the monastery, I came to realize why humans are regarded as the most precious beings in the world and why they set the standard of existence. I learned that only when we have control of ourselves can we realize our potential as the most precious beings among beings. The images of those days I spent with you nearly forty years ago — scenes seen both from a distance and close up and various events and my feelings about those events—all appeared before me. Reality proves that all of those images were the products of my thoughts.[1] They belong to the world of the "small self," the world in which I relied on my molecule-sized mind. As a being of the great self who possesses a complete mind, I would be proof that time—past, present, and future—and the entire world in terms of space are one mind and that this one mind is my own. By attaining and utilizing this state of mind, we show that we are in the state of the "great self." Isn't it amazing that the world's entire population has lost its self and yet is unaware of that fact? I would like to send this message to all people regardless of whether they are close to me or have a beneficial relationship with me. The power of this vow is the sole reason compelling me to write this letter.

Had I meant this letter for you alone, a brief message would have sufficed to let you know this. But I intend this letter to be read by anyone. Children prefer candy that is not good for them, but they hate the medicine that would save their lives. Likewise, sentient beings are attached to transient feelings of affection instead of drinking the eternal water of life. Thus, as one would sweeten medicine for children, I will sugarcoat my message with the story of our romance and thereby convey the message I want to send to people.

We went our separate ways thirty-six years ago, one of us to the south and the other to the north, and since that time we've exchanged no letters. There was, however, someone who kept me informed of your whereabouts, and I heard that you had settled on the northern shore in the province of South Pyŏngan, where you owned an orchard. I also heard that you created a small park inside your orchard and that the park was so exquisite that tourists constantly came to see it. For the next three years I was kept informed about your activities.

I assume that you also have frequently heard about me, as I am still the subject of people's chatter. About three years after our separation, your close friend, the painter, told me for the first time how you felt about us. He said that you deeply regretted our separation. He showed me how you beat your chest, calling yourself silly, like a woman trying to put back together the broken shards of porcelain. He also said that it was love itself you loved, not the person. Judging from what he said, he didn't seem to understand you. So, I told him that it was I who left you because my love was not perfect enough and because you shouldn't remain single; thus, I was the one responsible for our separation.

About five years later I happened to come across your brother-in-law on a streetcar on my way downtown from Sŏngbuk village. I didn't ask about you, but he volunteered that you were into hunting and had met a young woman living in a hut below Tasŏk Mountain. He told me that you lived with her and had a son with her, but that your wife set fire to the hut, which naturally led you to divorce her. I heard no news about you for some time after this encounter.

About ten years after I had joined the monastery, I saw a poem by you in a newspaper wrapped around some incense and candles a visitor had brought to the monastery.[2] Spotting your poem there, I had to read it.

On the Reed Beds
I would not dare try to count
the number of the members of the great reed family.
Facing wind and rain,
they would not let trouble come to their family.
All the same, the exchange of feelings between parents and children
  seems troubled,
A slight touch of the wind would let them reveal
Their heartrending feelings so desperately.
As the lonely soul of a reed
Soaks my heart stealthily,
The sleeping memories of my love
Are once again awakened to the fullest,
My soul in search of my love
is aimlessly wandering.
At the end of the earth, on the border of the sky,
Where would be the traces of my love?
Where the imprints of my love have erased,
Unfamiliar images tell me impermanence;
My longing knows no bounds,
The retreating figure of the love who has left me
I once again retrieve
From my heart battered and bloody;
My lips shiver,
Tears, as if they were my love,
Touch my trembling lips.[3]

If you lived in a city, there would be any number of things to divert you from boredom; you could also meet a woman with whom you would be content having in your life. As it is, your simple life affords nothing for you to see when you go out but abandoned reed beds along the shore and lonely seagulls flying back and forth. When you return home you find a coarse country wife with an expressionless face; your simple food is the same at every meal. I imagine you in such a monotonous life and I can sense, though vaguely, how a sensitive person like you might feel. I would like to share with you the path out of a life of loneliness and suffering, which is why I picked up my pen to write you. This is the path of no-mind. No-mind is not something one learns; rather, it is the original mind of the human being that has, because it is tasteless [i.e., without qualities], been forsaken by its owner. We have therefore voluntarily assumed a possessing mind, which is a reservoir of afflictions, and as a result suffer from the beginningless beginning throughout eons of time. I want you to know that once you learn no-mind, that is, once you achieve wholeness of mind, even in an environment drearier than your current situation, you would be able to create all sorts of tastes.

For now, you are absolutely in need of consolation. Loneliness doesn't comfort you; it makes you search for whatever is available to assuage the loneliness that confines you in a dark and chilly cave. To learn how to achieve the state of no-mind, which cuts off all sense of loneliness as well as mental neediness, is the only way to gain access to all that you need. Once you overcome the possessing mind, or limited mind, you earn no-mind, which encompasses all the elements you want: the mind without limitations. In the no-mind state, there is no "your" mind or "my" mind, nor is there a "this" mind or a "that" mind. In the no-mind state, all of these are unified into one: the all-capable self, which is the creator of everything. The life of each individual is a reflection of her spirit, that is, her mind. A person's life is conditioned by the degree of goodness or evil, bigness or smallness, weakness or strength of his mind. And that's why it is important to attain the state of no-mind, which is the all-capable mind and the creativity of the soul. If you want your soul to live freely according to its own will, you must attain this state of no-mind and let it function. Only then can you maintain the position of a human being, the most superior being among beings. If you're incapable of controlling your soul, isn't that proof that your soul doesn't belong to you? This is why no-mind, which is the true mind, belongs to each of us. Our everyday mind changes one thousand or ten thousand times; its external aspect is a repetition of the process of a ten-thousand-times transformation, and thus it cannot be trusted. What one believes to be the mind is not actually the true mind, and that is why I am telling you to find no-mind. Whatever exists through thought is not the true mind; this is why true mind is called "no"-mind.

This "no" of no-mind isn't the other side of a being; rather, it's non-being, which encompasses everything. Only the soul that has completely mastered this state of non-being can avoid being swindled by circumstance or influenced by emotion. Hence, in this state of non-being the mind that suffers from longing would be able to take a rest. The feeling of loneliness is a material thought. To think that loneliness or sadness is an emotion caused by someone else is a delusion. In a situation where there is no contact with the external world and where consciousness is not aroused, at whose direction other than one's own would thought after thought continue to arise? This reality proves that both the external world and one's consciousness are one's own creations.

When you're in the state of no-mind, you can enjoy both loneliness and pleasure at will. Any time a doubt arises and is not resolved increases curiosity. However, once you realize that there was never actually any mystery to solve and that doubts and curiosity are one's own creation, doubt subsides. This is also the case with loneliness and pleasure.

This means that no-mind is in fact one's own self. Because we've have lost our selves, there arise complex situations like feelings of loneliness or of pleasure and our life is without peace. The "I" that we can find right here and right now is the "I" that is the other side of "I." If each individual in the world finds his or her "I," the self and others would be one and the entire world would be at peace. Peace means one's own self, which is why we shouldn't try to find peace outside ourselves. This is also why you're mistaken in thinking that you feel lonely because you've lost your love.

The principles of the physical world are based on polarization: If you meet your love, you'll be separated from her; if you love someone, the time will come when you hate that person; since you're alive, you will have to face death. Anyone who thinks this life is improved by love is like a leaf that falls from the tree and is caught by the wind to be endlessly buffeted about. Mr. K. said that you were in love with love, but I don't think he knew what he was talking about. I say this because Mr. K., too, has lost his true self, the original identity of his thought.

You have lost your self—the "I" that is the true self and your own self-nature—and having once loved love you now feel the loneliness of loneliness. In the daily lives of human beings, all things, like feelings of loneliness and of affection, good and bad acts, birth and death, are nothing but vanities that flap in the wind, which has neither goal nor meaning. However, it is also reality that when I don't eat, I feel hungry, that when someone hits me, I feel pain. That this reality continues until future worlds come to an end and even afterward is the fundamental principle of the universe. This is the problem.

Moreover, the reality is that all beings should take responsibility for their own lives and cannot relay their responsibilities to others. This means that each being should earn his or her own way in life. But where does one find the ground for making a living? No-mind is the fundamental source of [spiritual] income (that is, the basis for cultivation of the mind), which also means it is the way to learn the original identity of one's own thought. Spiritual income is the basic ingredient and physical effort is what cooks this ingredient. It's absolutely necessary that we make the effort to have a dual practice: The mind should set the direction of one's life; action provides the means to move in that direction.

When mind and action work together in this way, no time is wasted and the universe is healthier. Buddhist groups create educational institutions designed to teach this principle. I encourage you to sign on with such a group as soon as you read this letter. The moment you join the Buddhists, you will learn that without effort there can be no accomplishment, and without paying the proper price nothing can be gained. I've wanted to send you this message several times since joining the monastery, but after the Korean War, I didn't know whether you were still alive. Furthermore, I made every effort not to waste my time so that I could focus on practice, which made me set aside all other matters. About three years ago in the fall, a nun from Kyŏnsŏng Hermitage was doing her begging practice in the South Gate area in Seoul. She told me that as she entered a small tile-roofed house, a good-looking, rather small gentleman of about fifty years of age had hurriedly scooped a bowl of rice for her. Before he handed her the rice, the man asked her where she came from, to which she responded that she came from Kyŏnsŏng Hermitage on Mount Tŏksung. He told her that a nun with the secular surname Kim must be at that hermitage and handed her a name card. The nun gave me that name card, on which was written, "I wish you a long life. Since you have awakened to your mistake, happiness is yours now." It was your name card with these words so clearly written.

I was and am still a human being who desires life [rather than death], and thus it made me very happy to learn that someone I had known before had survived the war — the war that no one had ever imagined or experienced before — and was leading a new life. I asked the nun whether you said anything about visiting me. I looked at your name card from time to time but didn't feel much about our past. You seemed to think that this present physical life is the only one and thus wrote wishing me a long life. As I occasionally returned to the words on your name card, I found myself smiling. When you were young, you were pessimistic about life and demanded I join you in a double suicide, and now that we were old you seemed to have a stronger desire to live. As I was thinking about this, scenes from the past that I had forgotten came back to mind.

At that time, I was yet to realize my dharma body. Not only that, I didn't yet understand my soul, that is, what this physical body — the karma body—means. When I was still in the secular world, if I set my mind on something that I wanted to do, I didn't care what other people said or thought. Was I stupid or naïve? That was me. I would believe what others said without considering the possibility that they might be dishonest, even when I was repeatedly deceived. However, although I might have been deceived throughout my life, I don't remember anyone seriously deceiving me. Perhaps that was one of the reasons why I didn't follow my friends' advice that men weren't to be trusted.

That was also the case with you. You deceived me from the beginning of our relationship when you told me that you weren't married. I trusted you and as a result had to endure various impossibly embarrassing situations. But I believed that you behaved the way you did because of love, and never once did I have a bitter feeling against you. Instead, I blamed myself for not being able to keep our promise of living together forever as husband and wife. The fault was my own imperfect love. Still I decided not to lead a double life and then put my decision into action. I thought that having any remaining feelings about the life with you that I was about to end made me a weakling incapable of creating my own life. Memories from the time when I left you are vague, like scenes from a movie seen of an evening. My life with you has by now been completely cleared from my mind.

At the time we were together, your parents were very traditional, and it was absolutely beyond you to talk to them about a divorce. When your parents learned that their son, who was studying in Japan, was having an affair with a modernized woman, they threatened to stop underwriting the expenses for your study; they also refused to send you even the smallest amount of pocket money. Your parents proposed that if you kept your wife and had me as a concubine, they would support you as before. Both you and I were adamant that that was not acceptable, thus finding ourselves in a situation with no exit. I suggested that we separate and remain as lover-colleagues, the meaning of which would be ambiguous to others. But you were the son of a rich family who had no practical experience and no idea of how to earn your daily bread. You seemed to suffer enormously, and because of my financial difficulties, you proposed that we commit double suicide.

You were a poet and whatever you said sounded so poetic. You told me that even if we could live as we wanted, our lives would last at best seventy years. How much more beautiful it would be if we could face the last moment together, in a state of satisfaction, and take that moment to eternity? I wasn't persuaded, but I also couldn't argue against your proposal. Had I tried to persuade you, you would have misunderstood me and thought that I was looking for a way to break up with you. I remember that at the time, not only was my heart fully devoted to you, but in my daily life as long as I was with you I had never talked to other men or had a cup of tea with another man. I thought that should have been proof enough that I was faithful to you and that there was no gap between us; I don't know why you were always suspicious of me…

Do you remember the day you left me a note saying, "You must still have some beautiful feelings for this world. Enjoy it all by yourself and have a good life"? With this, you ran out of the house threatening to kill yourself on the railroad tracks. I was so shocked at the time that I felt as if I could see you throw yourself from a cliff. I still feel the shock of that moment. I ran out to find you, feeling that I had to promise you that we would commit suicide together.

That day you immediately went to Port Chinnam more than 150 miles away to see your brother, who was a doctor there. You brought back heroin, which would make us sleep forever. From the pink box, I picked up a capsule the size of a thick finger and aimlessly stared at the white powder inside. Two doses of the drug had the power to put an end to the precious lives of two people. I am so dull by nature that I was not overly frightened. I just felt that my ears were blocked. Because I had decided by all means to avoid suicide, I was not too worried or fearful about the situation.

I wasn't then awakened to the principle that both body and soul exist forever and that each being was responsible for her or his own existence. Nor was I fully aware that nothing could be attained without paying the proper price and that no success came without effort. But I asked myself why a healthy young man and woman should put an end to their lives, erasing their existence in society, even though they couldn't make a great contribution to it. I had the kind of temperament that never worried, no matter how difficult a situation I might face; and killing myself was therefore the last thing I would do. I always had a vague hope that there would be another way to get through the situation. Please don't think that I had ever considered you a coward, or that this changed my feelings for you, or that I was disillusioned with you because of it. My memory clearly tells me that this wasn't the case.

In sum, we were confused beings unaware of the responsibilities of being humans. We naïvely thought that to live meant simply to get through each day and were oblivious to the consequences of a life of mindless consumption. It's important that the hands of a small clock keep moving, for if they don't, the clock is like a mechanical corpse to be thrown into a garbage bin while still ticking. Likewise, even though we're unaware of it, we should keep making efforts as long as we are alive.

You were someone without an income, born with a silver spoon in your mouth, who grew up as a precious child, experiencing no difficulties. And then, for the first time, you faced an embarrassing situation because of money, and because of me, a parasite to you, you suffered even more both mentally and materially. This is what led you to such extreme thinking. I fully understood you in that.

In addition, I thought that it was generous of me to try to understand your other behaviors. All in all, because we were unaware at that time of the principle that there was no way to avoid this life for eternity, our lives lacked direction. We created our environment, which made us consider suicide in response to an unavoidably grave situation. At that time, you were about to drive both our lives and the situation we had generated into the pit of self-destruction. The most urgent issue for me, then, was to avoid death and at the same time not cause suspicion in your mind.

Not knowing what I was thinking, once you had my agreement about our double suicide, you looked so lively, as if you were a man facing death who had found a way to survive. The day you secured the drug, we planned to take it at midnight at the boarding house in Toyŏmdong—the house that your father owned and rented out to someone else—where we used to have our rendezvous. You let me hold on to the drug until the time to take it. Holding it in my hand, I was deep in thought, trying to find a way to carry out my scenario. I planned that we would avoid death but would go all the way to the point just before dying, which would make you think that hadn't worked out because of something beyond our control. After some deliberation I came up with a surprisingly marvelous idea.

The drug is a white powder, one among many white powders. I wondered why I hadn't thought of that earlier. Perhaps I was fixated on how dreadfully deadly the drug was and couldn't think outside that box. You would never notice the difference if I filled the capsules with some other white powder. Truthfully, to find in a short time such a fine, shiny white powder would not be easy. And I had to do it without your finding out. I couldn't think of anyone to communicate with about this, and you didn't give me a chance to go out to get something to replace the drug. I didn't know what to do, and as a final resort decided to replace the powder with baking soda, which, far from being similar to the original powder, was thick and brownish; the difference was noticeable. What's worse, the two parts of the capsule fit so tightly that however carefully I replaced the contents inside, there were visible spots that indicated some kind of tampering. What would happen if you noticed that I had changed the contents of the capsule? That greatly worried me. Because the capsules no longer contained the lethal powder, I should have been free from worry, but my anxiety was as severe as if I were facing death. I examined the capsules this way and that way, trying to think of a solution but ended up giving up the idea of fixing them and put them inside a drawer.

The time had come. Kim Tongin, a novelist living in P'yŏngyang, was staying at the boarding house and by coincidence came to our room that evening for a chat. He lingered until late while we waited, embarrassed, for him to leave. Then we sat, awkwardly, without words, checking each other out. I finally brought a glass of water and took out the pills. The front gate, worn out by visitors to the house, seemed to have fallen asleep in silence. Next to us was our bed, a would-be momentary resting place for our two corpses, calmly waiting for us. Had someone asked the wind to be on patrol that night? Until late, the wind moved, making a brushing sound that made you uncomfortable. We wondered whether we heard someone's footsteps. I was nervous as we stared at the pills left there on the floor. You looked deep in thought different from mine. I think we exchanged some final words, but I don't remember what they were. I only remember vaguely that you didn't even notice that the contents of the capsules had been changed. You were sincere about death, which impressed me for long time afterward. Affected by your seriousness, I myself forgot that I had replaced the contents of the capsules.

This being the situation, I wasn't scared of death and was completely purified by your sincerity; ten thousand different feelings became one without distinction within me; I began to cry uncontrollably. I didn't know why, but the tears fell on and on without end. I assume that you shed tears as well, but I didn't have the leisure to check on how you were doing and have no memory of your crying. I don't know how much time passed, but it was a lot, and I vaguely recall that because I knew that the drug wasn't real, I was the one who first swallowed the pill. You looked startled, and I said, "You've demanded my death every day; what are you startled at now? Does death renew your desire to live?"

You responded, "I guess I was startled at seeing the last moment of your life—your life, which is more precious to me than my own." The expression on your face changed. You held the glass of water in your hand and took a deep breath. You said, "I'm taking this pill only to be with you at the end of our lives." You swallowed the pill and with quite a miserable expression on your face said, "I wish I could see my father one more time before I die…When he hears of my death…"

You used to tell me that after you had left your hometown to study in Seoul and then Japan, if you had a cold your mother would know it somehow, would feel her throat becoming clogged. She would then go to the hill through which her son made his journey to Seoul and to Japan, look far away in the direction of her son, and tearfully pray for you to all the deities in heaven and on earth. And you had no thought for your mother; you did, though, think about your father, quite desperately I realized, at the last moment of your life. My parents had passed away more than ten years before, and I had nobody except you to worry about my life. But all the same, I did not want to die. I was only trying to find a way to make you want to live again. And the words that you used to say to me all the time came back to me, and I told you, "You weighed our feelings and you've pestered me every day that yours were far heavier than mine. Now I admit that the weight of your feelings is heavier than mine but that was because you carried your feelings for your father in addition to your feelings for me."

You didn't respond. Instead, you held me in your arms and lay down. You said, "This is the end of all the suffering, and this is the beginning of a free world that belongs only to you and me. Now you and I are one. Cut off all other thoughts."

I pretended to push you away and said, "You tell me to cut off other thoughts? I've accompanied you all the way to death and still you do not trust me. We would brawl even on our journey to the underworld after death…"

You held me tight against you and said, "Don't say that. How can I have any suspicion at this point? It's not suspicion. It's simply an expression that I am too fortunate."

I responded no more. Burying my face in your chest, my mind wandered. I counted the time, and it became clear that the drugs we took were not death pills. Was it because I had cried my fill that I only vaguely thought about what would happen tomorrow? It felt meaningless, like a scene in a play.

You said, "I don't feel sleepy. I rather feel fully awake, isn't that strange?" Awhile later, you repeated the same thing. Not being able to keep silent, I responded, "Maybe the pills were past their expiration date and no longer effective?" My voice sounded natural as long as I believed what I was saying. Following the teachings of my pastor father, I never could tell a lie, but my words and actions that night were influenced by a situation of the most urgent emergency. You objected strongly, saying that the pills were used by your brother for medical purposes and there was no way that the expiration date had passed.

I said, "Could you have mistaken the pills?"

You immediately challenged the idea. "I've been to my brother's office many times since I was a child, and I know all the names of the drugs. I know what is what." I could hear a rather loud knock at the front gate (probably somebody looking for the owner of the house), soft footsteps (probably somebody going to the bathroom), and voices. With all this noise, I became more and more awake. Sleep was far away. I believe you were in the same condition. In this manner, the night had come to an end. The night light, which sleeps only during the day, seemed to tire, having stayed up all night. As it retired, blue lights appeared outside the window, and I felt like sleep was slowly invading me. At that moment, you said in a voice full of relief that you were not dead, "It does not look like we will die. People said that one cannot control one's death. Does this mean that we are destined to suffer a bit more?"

Somebody was shouting, "Open the front door," and I could hear footsteps from the street. The sounds of all the living beings lingering around us close by and from afar forced us to get up. We began our breakfast as usual, as if nothing had happened. It was fortunate that we didn't die at that time. If we had regained our original mind and our ability to move back and forth between life and death, it would not have mattered whether we died then. But we had yet set our life goal. If we had faced death in that state, what would have happened to us in our endless future lives? After I became a Buddhist, I learned that once you set out on the path to a goal, as long as you do not change the goal and persistently advance toward it, you will eventually achieve it (the discovery of one's self). This awareness gave me perspective and helped me understand our situation at the time.

I am only at the starting point on the path of life, and I believe that even God would not deny this fact. I hope that you and the others as well will read this letter with an open mind. Back then, we didn't have even the level of awareness that most people generally have about life's dangers and bloody resolution. Not to mention that we were unprepared for the struggle for survival. We were just fools leading our lives with no thought. I was like a donkey with strong legs but blind eyes, tall but absolutely immature and possessing of grandiose thoughts for a woman. As for you, though a poet, you had great ambition, which made you ignore your talent and disposed you to a life full of material desires.

I was searching for a way to live with authenticity. In the process I came to learn why human beings set the standard of value among beings. It's because the beginning and end of all problems is how to be a real human being. Once we attain that state we will possess the key that answers a hundred or a thousand questions and will be free and at peace, occupying the most precious position among all beings.

A human being has knowledge of her own self, embodies that knowledge, and thus lives freely. The "I" that you consider to be at your command in fact is not at your disposal. How then can you claim to be the owner of your own self? You should find the "I" at your disposal, which is no-mind, and fully utilize that "I." No-mind is the other side of the mind we use in daily life. By turning yourself inside out you will find awakening.

Our love at that time was relatively pure, but at the same time, deep inside, I realize that there existed the mind to take advantage of each other and thus our relationship was based on selfish desire. The benefit of having feelings for others is that they bring consolation, the ability to rely on each other, and so on. Our love was conditional love. Moreover, it was clear that you loved me not as an individual, but because of your sexual desire. I could tell that when you praised me by telling me that under the double eyelid of my eyes were hidden ten thousand different expressions or when you complimented my beauty, praising my voluptuous cheeks, attractive lips, and beautiful hands. When I stayed at a boarding house in Mejiro in Tokyo, you came to visit me. It was only the second time you came to see me and we didn't yet know each other that well. You looked at my hands, which were resting on my knees, and out of blue you said, "I think women's hands are most attractive, even magical. If a woman has beautiful hands, only then could I solely devote my love to her." I still remember that you were checking my reaction as you said these words.

People say that love between a man and a woman is possible through a moment's exchange of glances. Ours was no different. We saw each other for the first time at a meeting. A second meeting followed. At that time, a number of Korean students studying in Japan frequently visited my place, and I usually paid little attention to you. Because of that, even though you came to see me several times and I met you with a smiling face, I kind of ignored you. But how you were anticipating our encounter! When you were finally able to tell me that you loved me, you said that you were even thinking that you would just come to kiss me and leave. I wasn't much different. I loved you conditionally because you were handsome and wealthy, and we had the same interests.

I remember our personalities at that time. You and I had both mind and body, but we tended to privilege the mind. I vaguely preferred the mental world, and you were overwhelmed by making a living, which would change your personality. I didn't mind going through difficulties in terms of the material conditions of our lives as long as we continued to love each other. I was not deeply aware of my responsibilities as a human being, and my desire to write pushed me toward the path of a great writer.

At that time we dared identify ourselves as persons of culture. But a person of culture means someone who is aware of a material and inner essence of being and who is capable of utilizing it. We can't deny that we were like spoiled children who thought that life meant just passing time. We didn't know that one is fully responsible for one's own existence, that one should make every effort to preserve and advance one's own life, and that not even a second can be wasted. The ultimate goal of the person of material culture is to attain the state of the person of mental culture. I do not know what you are doing nowadays, but it was a mistake back then for you to change your career and get involved in business.

Each individual has at least one talent, and this is the result and extension of efforts made through numerous previous lives. If you don't utilize this talent in your work, that is a waste of time and effort. At that time, you turned your back on your talent. I don't know what you are doing for a living now, but a hundred years' worth of effort has disappeared like dust. People in the secular world frequently use the expression "sacred" when they talk about love. But it doesn't seem that there are many people who understand the meaning of the sacred.

The sacred refers to the state in which all of one's individual characteristics have disappeared. It is a state in which even one's soul has disappeared. When one reaches the state of complete extinction, the other and everything else are also extinguished. The world of complete emptiness (the state of oneness, that is, the state of unity) will emerge, and this is called the sacred world. This sacredness is the place of no-mind, which is the concentration of one's mental power — mental concentration, or unity of the universe — be it love, affection, the believing mind, filial piety, the patriotic mind, the humanistic mind, compassion, or even the evil mind. The essence blooming out of this concentration is the completion of one's personality.

Whatever the starting point of our journey, once we reach unity of the mind, or sacredness (the state of nothingness), there is nothing we cannot do. This is the universal principle. Mental concentration is the material for the existence of all the world's beings, but since sentient beings are unaware that such unified mental power enables a being to be all-capable, they live according to a fragmented self. Consequently, their lives lack freedom. Sentient beings with similar karma get together and create their own life-world, sharing it with countless other sentient beings. When you look at the sky, you see a group of shining stars as numerous as the grains of sand on a beach. Each group of stars is a world of beings like that of humans, which is located at the center of the universe. Below the human world exists the non-culture world of non-humans, which includes endless hells. Above the human world exists the realm of desire, the realm of form, and heaven, known as the realm of non-form. These are real worlds that Buddhist scriptures describe in terms of the distances between different realms, the number and characteristics of inhabitants, and the customs of each realm. The state before a thought arises is called creativity, and the state after a thought arises is called reality. Creativity is one's original mind, and how much creativity one has regained decides one's level of mental capacity. Based on that level, numerous people are connected. The realm with the sun at its center is the *sahā* world. Beings that reside in heaven, leading the life of non-beings, are beings of superior culture. This is the realm where people of unimaginably superior capacity reside; goodness is their essence. They are sacred sages, people who are self-sufficient, that is, capable of sustaining themselves with regard to daily necessities. They do not even need the sun or the moon, since they are capable of producing light themselves. What they think and what they say are accepted as they are.

In the heavenly realm of Amitabha, the practice of chanting is necessary. But in all other heavenly realms, there is no need to practice self-improvement. All that is needed is to indulge oneself in pleasure without even practicing meditation.[4] Amitabha Buddha encourages people to practice, but there is no requirement that one go to Amitabha Buddha's realm to practice. All one needs to do is chant the Buddha's name. Anyone who thinks that it is possible to go to heaven or nirvana by simply relying on Jesus or the Buddha without making an effort is a most pitiful individual.

The goal of believing in the Buddha or Jesus is not to go to heaven or to be born in nirvana. The goal of faith is to learn the principle that the Buddha or Jesus practiced; therefore, we must learn about all-capable creativity, which is one's self, so that we can rely on that power. This world is home to people who are capable of visiting different realms of existence at will and whose mental capacity is infinite. They exist somewhere in the world, waiting for other people to mature enough to receive their teachings. The inhabitants of the heavenly realm have infinite mental capacity, but only a small number of them are actually capable of retrieving their original self and fully utilizing that self's mental capacity. Only when one reaches that state can one be said to be a buddha. This is the state of complete mental capacity of the all-capable self, and of the perfect being; only in this state can one live freely, being aware of the causal conditions of one's current state, whether one is in heaven, in the human world, or in hell.[5] Even by the one-sided knowledge attained through secular education we sometimes learn that which we cannot explain or fathom. Grappling with such secular knowledge is difficult enough, so imagine how difficult it can be to harness the all-capable mental capacity that is invisible and beyond thought. Do you prefer the satisfaction you feel by dismissing this capacity as superstition or unscientific thinking? Such a foolish person invites darkness into his or her life. This world is filled with such people, and that is why the world is in its current state of darkness. A person should only be able to deny or accept something without hesitation when the evidence is clear. Only when a person has that capacity for judgment can he trod on the right path as a human being. People in our time are wagging a toad's tail. They trust science as if it were all-capable, even following scientific discoveries that are yet to be substantiated. When someone talks about something unthinkable, people deny it like a cicada that refuses to believe in the coming of winter. Innumerable are the things that humans cannot fathom and that they do not know even exist. Even though people are totally unaware of what they do not know, they still perceive themselves as intellectuals. And when others acknowledge them as such, these so-called intellectuals offer teachings. With pride, they deny that which is essential to understanding life. How pitiful.

The innumerable realms and human beings are shells. There is no shadow without an object and no shell without contents. The contents are not the mind that is subject to pleasure and anger but something beyond that mind; they are the original mind that is the real "I."[6] Since the contents, or the original "I," exist, then one's thinking is real as well. Yet we lead our lives forgetting about this real essence, the real "I," which is why we have lost ourselves. This mind is made up of material; there is not a moment when this mind does not exist. In whatever state the mind might be at each moment, if one can unify the mind, and thus reach the state of no-mind, one can achieve the ultimate result. As I mentioned earlier, even in the case of love, if one is capable of unifying love, one becomes a perfect individual.

Let me tell you a story. There was a man whom Avalokiteśvara Bodhisattva needed to help. The bodhisattva transformed herself into a beautiful woman and waited for the man on a path on Sŏnam Mountain. Encountering this stunning beauty, the man became entranced. The woman gave him a come-hither look. The man followed the woman along the rough mountain paths and through the valleys below, all the while thinking only of her. Finally they reached the edge of a cliff. The woman jumped off the cliff into the ocean and waved to the man from the water. In the trance of love, the man reached out to hold the woman's hand, and by so doing, he fell to the ocean. At that moment, he realized the all-capable self.

Once one discovers one's self and thus becomes a perfect being who embodies time and space, love does not mean just love between one man and one woman. All beings become the objects of one's love.[7] For a man, all females will be his lovers and wives. Over the course of the innumerable lives we have lived, this body repeatedly has gone through the process of coming into and going out of being (or life and death). During that process, many different beings have been our lovers and spouses.

Because there was a meeting, a parting is inevitable, and since there is a parting, another meeting will take place. This is the principle of the universe. Once a person realizes this principle, he becomes a being who would not complain about breaking close ties with someone and would not lament that his lover has left. Such a person must have realized the relative nature of life, death, suffering, and pleasure, and should be able to turn an eternal life of a lonely soul into an eternal life of an awakened spirit. The awakened spirit exists before the existence of the Buddha (or before the existence of all beings). However, since the word "Buddha" is a pronoun to refer to all the things in the world, the existence before the awakened being is called the awakened spirit.[8] This, in turn, has other names, such as "the world of the Buddha," "the realm of emptiness," "no-mind," "the Way [Dao]," "the truth," "I," "the mind-heart," or "thought." The Buddha that manifests in the world bears names such as Śakyamuni Buddha, Amitabha Buddha, and Maitreya Buddha.

Only by attaining buddhahood can one rest assured that he or she has access to the resources for living in the innumerable eons to come. Only when she has the spiritual resources for living can she be the owner of a safe life that is the beginning and the end of the original hometown of a being. The treasure house, called buddhahood, is shared by everybody and therefore cannot be any individual's property. I have managed to enter the treasure house but have yet to learn how to utilize the treasure, although I have witnessed with my own eyes how others do so. Therefore, even if the Buddha or God tells me that I am wrong, I have no doubt that I am on the right track. My assuredness is not about having faith; it is about having evidence. Faith demonstrates one's adherence to the evidence. When I encountered this superior teaching, I felt like a person who was dying of thirst and found a bottomless water fountain. It is impossible not to think of sharing this teaching with those who suffer from the thirst for life as I have. I am now like a deer that has smelled water and is running toward it. I encourage you to follow me.

How fortunate that we didn't commit suicide back then. If we had died at that time with no preparation for death, how could I have encountered this superior teaching and sent it to you? This life extends into innumerable lives in the future. If I hadn't encountered this teaching, how dreadful that future would be! It is said that taking one's own life is a sin worse than taking others' lives. To give up this life, which is the distillation of cosmic beneficence, is the ultimate disrespect of the universe. To do so is to be a traitor whose life is a failure. Since the suicidal person will incarnate downward, that person will not know what kind of evil realm he or she will fall into in future lives. Once he falls into an evil realm, he will not know when he will be born as a human again. It is true that life in this body or as a spirit is like a dream, and to deny dreams is to deny life energy. That is because life energy is a being that dreams. Dreams are expressions of life energy, and the act of dreaming is the function of life energy. That which enables us to have dreams is the source of life energy, which is nothingness. The combination of these three[9] is perfect life energy, or true being. Should we face an untimely death without attaining the state of true being, our spirits will have to be born in the realm of hungry ghosts, and we lovers will wander around rough mountain paths and deep valleys, hand in hand, wailing. In the meantime, the human mind in us will gradually become dim, and life after life, our existence will degrade. Suffering will increase, and as suffering overwhelms us, our hatred will deepen. Our vow that we will not separate even at death will turn to a curse that we will never see each other again in life or after death.

No being can avoid life. However trivial a being might be, it feels love and hatred, since life means to have consciousness. How will a being whose incarnation is downward ever reach the state of true life? Think with common sense. If we were to have had difficulty in maintaining our current state as human beings and were to give up, this would predict what our future would be like. In this life, we need to eat and we desire comfort. All the requirements are there to attain comfort. To eat, we need to work; to feel comfortable, we need mental resources (meditation practice). Once mental resources, that is, the project for mental progress, is set and thus the two directions of material comfort and mental cultivation are established, a balance in life is achieved. Not only will loneliness and suffering disappear, but as we walk on the correct path of life, we will feel safe. I might have already bored you with this story from our youth, a drama from the time when we were in our prime, but I want to tell you one last thing. That is about the four difficult things to attain: It is difficult to be born as a human; difficult to be born as a man; difficult to join the monastery; and difficult to encounter the Buddhist teachings (and thus to grasp the meaning of self).[10]

If you understand this teaching, you have just enrolled in the third grade at the Superior School of Life (superior, but without having an inferior as its opposite) as a lay practitioner. One more grade and you will finish your university education and become a perfect being. A perfect being is a being in which self and others become one, and thus a perfect being attains absolute comfort. I'm a human being like you, but I'm a woman. It's said that, in terms of quality, the difference between men and women is as wide as the distance between the sky and the earth. It's said that for a woman to become a manly woman is as difficult as to attain buddha-hood. What is the good of me learning all the good teachings before you do? If you believe the teaching and cultivate yourself (which means to study controlling your mind), you might be able to jump to the stage of the Tathāgata very quickly and save me. Since we already have ourselves, and we can't deny that, we should learn about the basis of our existence. That is all I am saying. When we have this body, when we hear this teaching, we should understand the teaching and not lose the opportunity to keep it with us. In eternity, which is the extension of this life, we will surely be able to attain buddhahood (and become a perfect being).

Sentient beings know how to read and write, since those skills are fundamental, but sentient beings are ignorant of what they really need to know about their existence, and that is why they experience endless suffering. More than making money, we need to make ends meet where our mental income is concerned. That is the most urgent issue. Making money is for life in this world, but taking care of mental cultivation is a business related to eternal life. If we fail to maintain mental cultivation, we will have difficulty maintaining the current state of the small self as well, and eventually we will lose the status of being a human.

Mental income or mental cultivation means to discover (or to get awakened to) the original state of the mind, and that is possible only when we extinguish the material mind and reach the state of no-mind. Because of the lack of resources called mental capacity, we experience the inconvenience called loneliness and suffering. Once we discover the original state of the mind, everything is resolved. It depends on one's mind whether, even in hell, one enjoys the pleasure of heaven. I repeat: Happiness and misfortune are all dependent on one's mind.

People in the secular world also say that everything depends on one's mind and that one's mind is one's fate. But when they face real situations, people can't control the situation as they want. What's more, when they aren't able to control their own minds, people don't ask why they aren't capable of being fully in charge of the situation; nor do they ask whether they can still consider their mind as their own. Since people do not reflect on these issues, they fail to free themselves from the iron chains of the karma they have created. Those who have lost their minds are leading others who have also lost their minds in endless fields full of danger over endless time. You are one among those wandering the fields. This news I am sending you should be precious to you, but I am not sure you are aware of that.

People say that to live this life that lasts at best a hundred years is a big deal. Since this news offers you a teaching to resolve the problems of the lives to come, even the expression "precious" can't appropriately measure its value. For those who've lost their minds, what can be more urgent than to retrieve their own mind? If you learn from this teaching in which direction you need to proceed, you will already feel full of energy for life (that is, you have resources for life), and you will feel safe. The sense of security will bring you courage, and wherever, whenever, in whatever state you lead your life, you will be well. Even though you claim to be a man of culture based on material things, changing your life in that direction was not a wise decision.

A person of culture should be capable of transcending the realm of the material; she or he should reach the ultimate state of the person of culture in her or his mental state. You were a man of culture but took a different direction. Now that you are in your sixties, have you experienced the satisfaction or happiness that all human beings wish for? Even if you might think you have, that experience is based on the fragmented mind and so is relative and of limited scope and as a result soon disappears. The state of no-mind is infinite; it is the realm of freedom where one plays in between suffering and pleasure.

No-mind is eternity in terms of time and everything in terms of elements. To completely attain no-mind is to be free in one's creative activities and to accomplish something in that field. It was the dream that I always aspired to, and it's also the dream that I have now forgotten. But it was the dream of the time when I believed that dream was the only true reality. You're a special friend with whom I took a path up to the point close to death, willing to give up all and everything. Since you're such a friend, I'm sending you this special message. I invite you to get rid of all the thoughts you've had, and I hope you can think different thoughts. And now I will let go of this pen of no-mind.

August 29, 1958 (The Year of Dog)

CHAPTER 11

Having Burned Away My Youth

A Letter to Mr. B.

The knife of an enemy can only hurt the body, but who could have known that the touch of love could damage both body and mind? Do you know what it's like to suffer, to groan in the midst of the ruins of love holding a heart fatally wounded by the knife of separation, the knife that was the very transformation of the touches that had caressed your body and soul? In one corner of my chilly room sits a lonely desk with a clock on it. The clock, my only friend, has stopped working and is looking at me dispiritedly because, in my sorrow, I failed to wind it. I threw myself on the desk, looked at myself shedding tears as if that were my daily routine, overwhelmed by the urgent feeling that I could deal with this no longer. Shall I send this message through the clouds up above? There is no hope that you will read this letter, but I cannot help but write it. As I write this letter, the characters throw themselves into my tears and become blurred on the page. It seems that they are sending me a message of regret, saying "How could we ever fully express the depth of your remorse?"

Your last letter to me said "...since the causes and conditions for our relationship have come to an end, I should now say good-bye to you...." You once told me "We will be together until death separates us," and you solemnly promised me that we would be one, both in body and mind, through the eternal eons to come. And you abandoned me, leaving behind nothing but a letter containing a couple of cheap words of good-bye without even telling me the reasons for your departure. You didn't even let me know where you were going. You simply ran away, leaving me with the phrase "the causes and conditions for our relationship have come to an end." How could I have ever expected that this miserable day would come? I'm not a woman easily given to emotion, so at least I didn't faint. I know things are impermanent, but faced with such an abrupt change in my circumstances—it was like getting a cut without knowing it—I couldn't even feel despair or anger. There were only tears whose meaning I couldn't understand falling down like a string of pearls.

Just the thought of your letter made my eyes wet, but I couldn't help reading it again and again through my tears. "The causes and conditions of our relationship have come to an end!" What an improbable collection of words these are that have turned my whole world upside down. These heartless words, similar to their ignorant owner, were careless, written without any thought of the pain in my broken heart.

What are these "causes and conditions of our relationship"? Why does he say that they have come to an end? And we cannot see each other again? Never again? Is he dying? Is that why he says that we won't be able to see each other again? Whatever these words mean, isn't it clear that he wants to say good-bye forever? Is it true? Yes, it's true. Still, this paper doesn't change its color; it's deaf. And these characters, like carcasses, do not even pretend to feel pain when I bite them and beat them! Still they are the only things to whom I can let out my complaints. Oh, my poor heart! These ignorant characters, even though they cannot know they are unfeeling, are the only medium that can convey my suffering. I remember a story about the daughter of a gatekeeper of the town of Puyŏ during the Paekche period. The eighteen-year-old girl wrote a letter on an oak leaf with all sincerity to her lover who lived over the mountain. The oak leaf found its way over the mountain and through the valleys and finally delivered the letter to the right recipient. It was the union of feelings and soul that caused the action that made this possible. But my heart, that object of betrayal, has no chance of entering the same state of absolute sincerity as that girl's. I must send my pleas through the medium of others, and where in this vast world can I find your whereabouts so that my words will reach you?

I believe that there is infinite spiritual power, but I am not confident that my spiritual power is strong enough to melt your ignorance. Hence, I have no idea what I should do with this unbearable agony. It is true that the word "cause" conveys a rather strict meaning and its significance in Buddhist teaching is second only to "the mind," "one's nature," and "the Buddha." However, in the expression "causes and conditions," the word "causes" is combined with the word "conditions." Because of the movements of "causes and conditions," changes occur; so doesn't the expression indicate flexibility and that either this or that could happen? You utilized that one expression "causes and conditions," and it became a tyrant that turned love, which is my lifeline, into a toy that you keep when you want it and get rid of as you wish.

I thought that when a man sets foot in the land of love, he becomes a puppet forever controlled by the queen of love. I have never thought I could leave a lover out of any part of my life, nor do I believe in being two-faced. How, then, could I ever suspect that you were the kind of unscrupulous man who would send a letter like the one you sent to a woman like me? I was so completely shocked by this unexpected incident that my mind still has not returned to normal.

You brought, though temporarily, great satisfaction and hope to my life, which had been so lonely; but you also gave me even greater disappointment and sorrow. Like the setting sun that takes with it the shadows of all things as it goes down in the west, you took all things away from me. If somebody stole something that was very important to me, I would harbor a grudge against that person. You have completely swept away from me the very basis of eternal life — the asset that is my mind — so how could I not grind my teeth and resent you? What I have written so far is nothing but a rationalization that my disappointment has created concerning the object of that disappointment. At this point I don't even have resentment. Whatever the rationale, I don't really understand the situation. The only absolute desire I have is that I have to see you. Each morning as I wake up I pray that I will hear from you, and each night as I lie down and admit to myself that no news has come that day, I sigh. That has been the tenor of my days. Sometimes I feel energetic and have the vague hope of thinking "perchance," and then I collapse with despair. Such days of anguish have lasted for four months and nine days![1] How many more days must I endure this?

When I was eleven years old, I would bet with a friend. My friend won three times — but only by cheating — and, proud of herself, she jumped for joy and made fun of me. I was so angry that I didn't know whether I should kill myself or kill my friend. I felt like my heart had lost its sense of direction and stopped beating. Had I simply acted out of my anger, I could have done something terrible, but the thought struck me like lightning that the priority should be to relieve my pain. I was able to calm down, and as my anger somewhat subsided, I reflected on what had happened. I realized that I was upset because I had lost, but also my anger overwhelmed me whenever I thought how hateful it was to have to see that awful friend who had deceived me and boasted of having defeated me. I realized that the state of my mind at that time was nothing but emotion that had arisen out of momentary anger.

The things that ignite anger in fact do not have specific causes. Humans can generate a thousand different conflicting emotions like joy and sorrow, pain and pleasure. Although the differences might be as infinitesimal as a strand of a hair, they can be the cause of situations that become life-and-death serious or make people become enemies for generations to come. Young as I was, I was able to think deeply about this and I told myself, "If that's the case, why don't I try to have peace of mind?" I seem to have come to a realization that all the elements were there to achieve peace of mind!

As I grew somewhat older, I also realized that there were people who felt unhappy even under the best of circumstances, which meant that even in the worst possible situation it was possible to be bighearted. People always say that your mind is your fate, but people are not capable of controlling the fate that they themselves make, all because people lack mental power. These thoughts made me realize that I could create a world of great peace only if I could control my mind. Because of these experiences, whatever situation I faced, I didn't get angry or feel irritated.

One time I saved the proceeds from my writing and amassed the largest sum of money I had ever had in my life. I went shopping at the big department stores like Hirada and Mitsukoshi, but after hours of wandering and seeing the piles of goods at those stores, I discovered that my money fell far short of the price of the items I wanted. I realized then that any amount of money I might have would only generate the thirst for more money. I told myself that having enough food to console one's stomach and clothes to protect oneself from cold and heat should suffice to make one satisfied. That was how I learned not to feel poverty as pain.

When I went back home during vacations, I didn't very much care how my stepmother treated me and tried to maintain peace of mind. My father, seeing me behave in that way, felt sorry for me and, I was told later, privately shed tears. Even when I had to face the break-up of my engagement, I caressed my flushed cheek with my hands and consoled myself saying, "Don't feel hurt. Who knows? There might be a better man for me." That was how I got over it. I tried to live in this manner, not worrying regardless of my situation. And then you brought me a life of endless tears and left. How could I not have resentments, and how could I not hate you? To avoid this suffering, instead of waiting for you to change your mind, which I was not sure would happen, I thought of rejecting you. How foolish I was. I didn't know what kind man you were. I just trusted you and made all kinds of plans! It was humiliating that I wasn't able to forget you even when I knew how foolish that was. I was suffering from a self-generated agony! Come on, let's put an end to it. I clenched my teeth and sat with eyes shut, determined. The tears that gushed from my closed eyes were strong enough to drill a rock, and waves of sorrow swept over me, all of which I transformed into a poem, attempting to turn off the fire of my feelings.

What will I do tomorrow
Now I am all alone?
On this dangerous path of life
How should I make it all alone?
My lover, you have many acquaintances to be with.
What would you know about loneliness?

My feelings, which were like waves in the ocean or burning fire, melted in the passages of the poem and created a sea of loneliness. Now that I am drowning in that sea of loneliness, the instinct to survive makes me struggle to grab whatever I can to get me out of the waves of solitude that drown me. I am like a suckling child who has no choice but to hold on to its mother even though the mother is beating it. Looking around in all four directions, I don't know to whom I should direct my heart and to whom I should cling.

To consider giving you up was nothing but an emotional and psychological reaction of a moment. As the sea of my loneliness became deeper, the mountain I had made of your existence became higher and other people's existence didn't even come to my attention. Nowadays, people in Seoul treat me as a female writer even though I've not published a book of poetry or fiction. When I get all dressed up so that I look good to others, people praise me as a voluptuous beauty. Perhaps this explains why people gather around me, some confessing passionate love, others making efforts to attract me by offering to improve my situation. But I have no room left for any man but you. That's not because I want to be physically faithful to you, but because I'm a woman who practices the "new theory of chastity."[2] Whether a hand has tampered with filthy things or has never touched a particle of dirt, a hand is just a hand regardless of whether something pure or filthy gets on it. Likewise, it's not important whether or not a woman has a physical relationship with a man; what matters is the state of the woman's mind. If a woman has completely closed the books on a relationship and is ready to fully devote her love to a new partner, she can at any time claim to be a virgin. Only such a woman, devoting her new love to a man who understands this idea, can re-create her life. This is the new theory of chastity that I practice.

It's not merely my feelings that make me want to be with you. You have a vision of life that even world-renowned thinkers and respected figures are not capable of having. You continued your self-cultivation without interruption and wholeheartedly dedicated yourself to the benefit of society. I could tell that, with a long period of cultivation and ample experience, an educated person such as you are would definitely become a great person who would benefit human beings. I had wanted you not only as my lover but also as a mentor. I didn't want to lose you, so naturally you became the entirety of my existence.

My father was from Yonggang, South P'yŏngan Province, and a pastor, a faithful believer in Jesus. He practiced Jesus' teaching to love others as you love yourself, exactly the way it should be. He lived his entire life with a mind full of gratitude to God and ended his life with a sense of fulfillment. My mother gave birth to five children including myself, but all except me died young. My mother wasn't able to have more children. My father, who was the fifth generation of the only child in the family, completely embodied the teachings of Jesus and therefore, even if the most beautiful woman in the world tried to seduce him, he would never forget that he was a married man, and his mind would remain untouched by illicit desires. My mother lamented that she preferred to die so that my father could remarry and have a son, but, since she couldn't die, she just cried all the time. She said that she would raise me, her daughter, to be a great person so that she would have no reason to envy someone with ten sons. Because she attended a Christian church, my mother was rather enlightened compared to others. In those days, when most people couldn't even imagine that girls needed schooling, she sent me to school and gave me the experience of feeling pride at being called "girl student"![3]

My mother had promised me that she would support my education all the way up to college, even if she had to sell the house and fields to pay for it. But she passed away the year I graduated from elementary school, and my father died after I graduated from high school. Both of my parents died young.[4] My maternal grandmother, who was over seventy years old at the time, shed tears whenever she saw me and lamented, "If your mother had raised another daughter before she died, you would have someone to call sister, but you are like something springing out of a chasm in between two rocks; you are like a radish uprooted from the soil. How could I bear to see you drifting all alone in this vast world?" With the financial support of my grandfather, I was able to study in Japan for several years.

When my mother was still alive, she did not bother to teach me about womanly virtue or the things a woman ought to take care of. My mother did not treat me like a woman, but, without holding to any specific standard, she wished to raise me into the most excellent, mannish woman in the world so that she would not envy even someone who had ten sons. My maternal grandmother and my aunts disapproved of my mother permitting her daughter to run around without having been taught about womanly things. They asked my mother how she could fail to provide me with clothes and other things for marriage. My mother retorted, "Do you want my girl to pack up a bunch of stuff for marriage and live like a slave?"

Having grown up in a dormitory, which was like a monastery, I was naïve and gloomy. Without much discipline at home, or much experience, I had yet to find a direction in my thinking. Yet I came to be involved in society when Korean society was in a completely confusing state. The way I hung around as I pleased at that time must have looked ridiculous. Moreover, to the eyes of a girl whose loneliness made her thirst for love, the thing I found attractive was cheap, low-grade romance literature. I used to be very alert so as not to commit sin in the eyes of God, but slowly I began to withdraw from that mindset, and faith began to retreat from my consciousness and doubts gradually settled in. I thought:

It is said that God is omnipotent; why, then, did he keep the tree of good and evil in Eden and give freedom to humans? If eating of the apple from the tree of good and evil was the cause of the fall, why didn't the Creator just make Adam and Eve to be good people instead of occupying himself with sending his only child to be crucified? Shouldn't Jesus, if he were a real savior, be able to save both good and evil worlds? Nothing is impossible for Jesus, so why can't he make all the people in the world believe in him? It is said that God exists in the mind. Does he exist, then, in the good mind or in the evil mind? Since God has a mind of equality, he should exist in both the minds of the good and the evil; and if so, why doesn't everyone's mind become the mind of God instead of remaining good and evil minds? How would God respond if an evil man—created by God and at the same time God's victim—who, experiencing unbearable suffering in hell, went to God out of despair and asked, "Why did you create humans and hell and make me go through this suffering?"

It's said that people in heaven can see everything. How, then, can a person enjoy the pleasures of heaven when she sees all the rest of her family suffering in hell? The God who always exists and the Buddha who was born into this world are both images and, thus, idols. Moreover, to create a God who is not visible is to create an idol of the mind. The Christian Bible says that the Buddha is an idol, but isn't it the same whether you make Christian paintings and keep them as sacred objects or create Buddha images and keep them for yourself? If idols are shells, then don't their contents exist as well? Or are God, Jesus, and all the sacred beings nothing but empty shells? Oh, how would I know?

Such were the doubts I experienced at that time. I could not get help in finding answers to these questions from my father or other Christians; they only scolded me for my lack of faith in having such wavering thoughts and advised me to pray with a repentant heart. There was no way to find answers for my doubts.

After I met you, all my thoughts were focused on my feelings for you, so I didn't even think of asking you about these doubts of mine. One day when we hadn't planned to see each other, I was wondering whether you had a lecture scheduled that day and, if so, whether I should go there just to see you. As I was thinking this, sitting in my room as I always did, I looked out through the door. To my surprise, dressed in a white suit and with your face looking even brighter, your eyes quietly shining like dark jade, and with a gentle smile on your face, you entered my room. You said that you had dropped by on your way to Kakhwang Temple.[5] You explained to me that day, in response to my questions, the doctrines of the teachings of Jesus in comparison with those of Buddhism. You said,

> Buddhist teaching in Sanskrit is called dharma, which has a comprehensive meaning. One can interpret it as the mind, which is all-capable, or the "I," which exercises freedom. It includes all the activities, all material, both good and evil, the principle, right and wrong, as well as truth and delusion. This being so, any theories or doctrines are part of what came from this dharma. Everything is dependent upon the functioning of one's mind. The mind — that is, the dharma — is the creator. Even though one does not know the original mind, if one can unify the mind even partially, one can surely accomplish those works that are partial. For practitioners, exercising one's mental power in this manner is an obstacle to one's practice, and, thus, it is prohibited. But there are people who, in the process of practice, have gained supernatural powers, and if necessary can make a human being appear simply by writing the character for "human" on a loose leaf. The religion of Jesus says that God is the creator, and it is true. God has this power, so must have created humans. But that He created all the things in the world means that there existed, before the creation of the world, original nature (the mind, that is, one's original identity). There also existed the original seed of matter,[6] which contains all the elements of anything material, and He created by using these material elements. Even though we cannot tell which beings were made out of which matter, since He created each being based on each being's own material , it is as though one created oneself. Be it an animal or a villain, there is no reason to blame others. If God had actually created all the basic structures of a human being, humans would be nothing but machines, with no functions or consciousness. In order to develop themselves in life, they would always require God, which

means that humans would have no freedom to either obey or betray God, and God would be responsible for both good and evil.

You also said,

God is a creator, that is, a being who has grasped and utilized all-capable self-identity. However, God was also created. For that reason, God cannot take full responsibility for everything.[7] All beings have created themselves. It is not that God is in one's mind; God *is* the mind. This mind that feels happiness and sorrow is one's own mind. It is also the God of God, and it is the Creator that created all things, including God. This is the mind that everybody possesses. Anyone who has not yet found this mind should at least know that he or she has not yet become a complete human being. Heaven is the supreme realm of culture, which includes the realms of desire, of form, and of non-form. The owners of that realm can all be called gods. The religion of Jesus characterizes God with such expressions as "unity" and "perfection," but it would be correct to call Him the Buddha, who is the pronoun for all things. The prohibition against eating the forbidden fruit of the tree of knowledge of good and evil was simply a way to test faith. If one is a believer, one should first be a believer who has faith in the object of one's faith and become a believer who absolutely believes in either God or the Buddha and, thus, reaches the state of no-self. Through that process, one comes to understand what the Buddha or God has also understood. Therefore, one becomes the Buddha or God. To follow one's mentor or the elders who lead one to the correct path is also a part of the religious mind. A person who does not have a religious mind is like a tree without roots; thus, he or she comes to lose the true energy of life. Being ignorant, sentient beings cannot follow the correct path if it is not their goal to do so. Buddhism teaches that one should find one's own Buddha within, which is one's self-nature. It is the source of the historical Buddha as well as the name and image of the Buddha. Likewise, the religion of Jesus teaches that salvation is possible only when one understands the message for oneself, rather than through relying on others.

Jesus' crucifixion is a manifestation of his dedication and the sacrifices he made throughout his life. Even the Buddha has three things that he cannot do (that is, change sentient beings' karma, save sentient beings with whom he does not have causal conditions to guide, and save all sentient beings because their numbers are infinite). Likewise, there is nothing that Jesus can do about the habits that each individual has developed into his or her personal nature in the course of life. Since one's original nature and one's freedom are one's own responsibility, Jesus can teach everybody to believe in him, but he cannot force everyone to do so. The freedom that led men to eat the fruit of the tree of good and evil was given to humans as original freedom, given by God. For that reason, even God cannot change human nature that has, over time, become habitual. All beings are the Buddha; that is, they are their own self. Therefore, to take refuge in the Buddha means to return to one's own self.

The realm of thought-created images is comprised of illusions and idols. All things are created by one's thought, so the question of whether one should worship or not already implies that one worships an idol. Whatever can be thought of is material; thus, thoughts always have objects and an object in reality always goes through changes. Omnipresent God and the historical Buddha are also idols. One who does not believe in statues or idols should also not believe in the Buddha or Jesus. As has been said, when one falls on the ground, one gets up by supporting oneself by the ground: Humans reach the state of truth by standing on the legs of idols. Buddhist doctrines are more profound than those of the teachings of Jesus and make one's belief in Jesus more truthful and one's respect for God completely sincere so that one can eventually become God. Not knowing this, some followers of Jesus, without making any effort to understand Buddhism, think that Buddhism contradicts the teachings they follow merely because Buddhism seems different. This situation is pathetic. All religions and philosophies are paths leading to Buddhism.

You could have spent more time on detailed explanations, but since you were on your way to a lecture, you were running out of time and had to leave. I accompanied you to listen to you lecture on the theme of "self." The content of your talk was similar to what you had told me in our private meeting. My father had not taught me to elevate my thoughts, as you did that day. When I was about to ask a question about God, he stopped me and told me that I should not use such inappropriate words toward God; he advised me that I should repent, pray, and ask for sacred faith. If there had been a fire in our house and our home and all the possessions in it had been destroyed but our family members were all safe, my father would have thanked God for saving his family; if all other family members were killed, he would have thanked God for saving him; and if everybody had been killed, he would have thanked God even more for taking him to heaven. This was my father's faith. Even though he did not know the Buddhist teachings, his faith might have enabled him to experience a complete awakening to his own self. But even on his deathbed he sang gospels with a happy mind, and then he went to heaven. I only hope that he listened to God's dharma talk and achieved liberation. That idea came to me because I remembered your saying that the state of liberation is an unchanging state of peace; insofar as heaven and hell are one, both are the world of equality.[8] My father's family had only one male child in each generation for five successive generations. Since I have neither a brother nor male cousins, there is no one who can offer an ancestral ceremony for my father at a Buddhist temple. When I think of my father, this realization makes me feel deeply sorry for him. The human body decomposes, but the consciousness-soul is eternal. Based on causes and conditions, it will be born again; wherever it will be born in whatever form, it will always desire food to maintain life. As it crosses the boundary between life and death, it feels severe thirst...Such things are proven by reality, but in this human world, which depends on only a small part of the mind, whatever cannot be seen is considered unscientific. When dharma talks are given, the "consciousness," which is now freed from the physical body and thus has a clearer vision, can better understand what it hears. Isn't this why Buddhism teaches that the forty-nine days of rituals or annual rites for the dead should be offered for every deceased soul?

To return to my story, I was at that time completely in a non-believing state of mind to the extent that I denied the idea of heaven and hell. I was not ready to set the direction of either my thoughts or my profession, but I still managed to cross the Korea Strait several times to go to Japan and performed the dual function of being a student and a member of society. I considered myself to be extremely talented at writing and thinking such that I believed I was on my way to becoming a great author...I didn't know what path to take or how to proceed to attain that goal, but I indulged myself in reading literature without questioning its value. I occasionally copied appealing expressions from my readings and created interesting passages of my own and published, in newspapers or in a journal, my essays, memoirs, short stories, and poems written in modern or classical Korean literary style. I even made myself the editor-in-chief of the first women's journal to be published in Korea, entitled *New Women* (*Sinyŏja*).[9] Korean society had yet to adopt the practice of educating women, and so it was natural that there were no women writers in the Korean literary world. I am not saying that I made myself an influential writer within Korean society, but when my writings appeared in newspapers and the journal, the entire population welcomed them unconditionally. Moreover, whenever I was called upon to do so, I unabashedly took to the podium and delivered a talk without thinking what a poor speaker I was. I rapidly earned fame and was even referred to as "professor."[10] At that time, there were numerous such unqualified professors among men in Korean society.

However, whether at home or out with people, I was still wrapped in loneliness and searching for that "one thing": the absolute love of one man to compensate for the lack of love of parents, siblings, and relatives. If only I could attain the absolute love of a man, I was ready to ignore whether my living environment would be fortunate or difficult, what other people might say about me, or even the constraints of morality. I thought that human beings were animals of feeling: They were born out of love and lived for love. How, then, would it be possible to attain inner satisfaction without love? If a person could not have inner satisfaction, with what energy would she perform her services to society? I was a fool who thirsted for love. Surely there were men who tried to take advantage of this, attempting to use me for temporary pleasure or comfort by pretending to love me. Moreover, my strong personality caused me to do as I liked, and had I wanted, I could have chosen any lifestyle. While my father was alive and until sometime after he passed away, I thought that God always watched over and protected us and that He knew each and every move I made. And since my father's words were those of God, I could not free myself from his teaching even for a moment. I was always under strong pressure to remain faithful to my father's teaching, which dictated that if one finds fruits on the ground that has fallen from another's tree, one should not pick it up for oneself because it belongs to another. Further, my father taught me that even an expression like "gal" was a curse word and should not be used. Faithful to that education, when I was in a situation where I was dying to curse, I would say, "I'm sure you're X's daughter," using the name of the father of a friend whom I hated. In those days, I was naïve enough to believe that if a woman had her hand held by a man, if a woman had a husband with whom she made a vow before God, whether the man was a devil or disabled, the woman could not leave the man. Later I came to claim a new theory of chastity. What ugly change had I made?[11]

When I was young, my father had perhaps already noticed my tendency, or he was just commenting on the behavior of those young men and women who were receiving newly introduced Western-style educations. Each time he wrote me a letter while I was in school in Seoul—and thus an object of people's attention in my hometown—he said, "I believe that you've been studying hard in the midst of God's grace. You should always pray to God to help you not deviate from the right path." With the exception of their relationship with God, I must have played the most significant part in my parents' lives. For me as their daughter, except for God, only my parents existed. When my father visited Seoul to attend a pastors' meeting as a representative of Chinnamp'o, he came to see me at my dormitory every three or four days. Whenever I had a chance, I would sit in front of the glass windows on the second floor, watching all day for my father to come see me. I would not retreat to my room until I could no longer distinguish between the road and passengers and when my shadow was consumed by the heartless evening light. When my father finally visited me, I would complain how anxiously I had been waiting for him. My father would reply, "The procedure to see you is so complex. It would be easier to meet a king. If not, I would love to come to see you every day. I think the vacation is close, right? You can stay with me longer then, so don't be so anxious." At that time, even if it was her parents a student was meeting, there was always supposed to be an observer. My father and I were unusually close and we talked about many things, but I would rather not say anything about that, since I do not know which one among them is appropriate to write about here.

When I thought of how much I loved the father whom I had lost...new tears welled up. Perhaps I had done many things in my previous lives that made me shed tears. This thought reminds me of your saying that ripening pleasures call for agonizing sorrow, which also reminds me that I should devote myself to meditation practice, which could dissolve all kinds of sorrow...My father, who was simple and faithful, thought that heaven and hell were opposites and did not know that even heaven was part of the material realm. He thought that if only one entered God's heaven, all problems without exception would be solved. He thus always prayed to God that I would be a faithful follower of Jesus, and my mother prayed to God that her only daughter would grow up to be an important figure in the world so that she would have no envy for people who had sons.

How beneficial my circumstances were at that time! In accomplishing our utmost ideal of completing our own self, if we do not have faith, on what would we construct it? If I had followed my father's teaching and remained a faithful follower of Jesus and not had my self-nature contaminated, and then converted to Buddhism, I might have attained awakening as soon as I heard your dharma talk. However, once things are spoken of, or thought of, they materialize. There might not be a teaching or a way to get hold of these things, but however profound a teaching might be, once it is expressed in words or written in language, it is subject to the principle of dualism and cannot help but create contradictions. Then there will be nothing that is not questionable...As the Bible says, because of my doubts, my faith retreated, and I lost the power of the vow generated by my parents. It turned out that I had destroyed those salutary circumstances and taken a rough road.

I was lucky to meet you at that point in my life and to receive guidance, both mentally and materially. However, more important than any advantageous opportunities or circumstances is each individual's way of thinking, which is what decides the path of good or evil. As always, you taught me well each time we met, but if all I was thinking about was enjoying my feelings for you, I would have been a person who would never be saved. It happened about a month after you began to come to my place to see me. It was around two o'clock in the afternoon on a day when the spring rain drizzled. Since you had never broken an appointment, even if there were a storm, I did not worry about the rain. The time you promised to come had not arrived, but I was already tired of waiting. I sat down and mindlessly looked at the only sliding door in my room, which faces north. I fantasized that I would be joyful when it stealthily opened and you entered through it; then, when it softly closed, to my sorrow it would release you from my room. With that in mind, I was talking to the door: "You open yourself and make me happy by letting in the person I am waiting for; and you cause me sorrow by closing yourself after the person has left. Will there be a time when you will free yourself from these dual responsibilities?" The thought startled me. I chided myself, scared to think that a terrible answer might come out of the mouth of the sliding door. I stayed silent, cautiously watching the sliding door, and then, though I had not heard your footsteps, the door slowly opened and your bright face appeared. Your appearance brought me back to reality. In order to welcome the world of joy and satisfaction, I had to be generous and forgive superstitious thoughts that brought absurd misgivings. I will not try to describe the scenes of that sacred day when I was so filled with contentment that I was not even aware that I was so. I worried that my efforts to render in words my satisfactions of that day might distort them. I will only say that I remember that, since you were not constrained by time that night, you gave me all types of satisfaction.

You placed your hand in my lap—a hand that was white and soft despite all the manual labor you said you had done while studying abroad with no financial support—and you said, "Where and how did our relationship make its way until today, when we have become so close to each other? It is said that for two people to pass by each other at a mountain corner, they would need to have had five hundred years' worth of relationship in their previous lives...It would be interesting if one could read one's fate and know what happened in the past and what would happen in the future." You grasped me with the hand that had been in my lap and let me lean against you and continued, "I've been waiting until today to tell you in detail about Buddhist teachings. They are precious and you should listen very carefully." You had a serious look on your face as you said this, and I remained silent, my face down, preparing myself. You said,

> After Śakyamuni Buddha had finished his practice in the snow mountains,[12] he returned to society and delivered the supreme principles to which he had awakened. But his audience was like the blind and the deaf and could not understand him. Having no other option, he taught at this initial stage the Teaching of God and Men, that is, the teaching in which humans believe in gods. Then, step by step, over the next forty-nine years, he taught all five teachings: the Teaching of the Small Vehicle (Hīnayāna), the Teaching of Awakening, the Sudden Teaching, and the Complete Teaching. At the end of those years, he denied all that he had said and rejected all teachings save one: You should realize and attain the "real identity of the universe," which is also the real image of "your true self," and by doing so, jump out of the suffering of transmigration in the six realms (of heaven, humans, gods, hungry ghosts, animals, and hell) and lead an independent life of your own.

You continued:

> In other words, heaven has hell as its opposite, and next to the world of supreme happiness exists the world of extreme suffering. Even if you are born in the world of heaven or of supreme happiness, the future could be terrifying and dangerous. This medicine [of being born in heaven or in the realm of supreme happiness] is one-sided; only when heaven and hell become unified does one earn eternal peace. To repeat, things that can be thought of and spoken of cannot transcend the material realm and remain in the scope of dualism, which is why they cannot be trusted. Everybody wishes something good will happen to them, but that is because people are not aware of the principle that when good things come to their hands, bad things happen to them too. You should learn about the thought that generates doubts about what makes the separation between good and evil, that is, the thought that unifies heaven and hell, and this thought should be the whole in which the thought before a thought arises and the thoughts after its arousal have all been cut off. This one whole thought, which is free from polarization, is nothingness, in which one should discover one's true self.

Having said this, you changed your position and looked at me, who was listening to you with all sincerity, and said, "So please tell me: Are there any doubts arising in you after you have heard what I've said?"[13]

For no reason, I found myself blushing. I felt like I should have doubts, but I didn't have any yet. You pressed me again, and I said, "I wondered what is this thing that is listening to you?" Hearing this, you laughed loudly, the first time in a long time, and looked at me with a satisfied expression. I assume that you were happy to learn that I was quick to understand. In fact, what I said to you was only an impromptu response. I was just thinking, "What is this thing that is listening to him?" which was not bad as a response goes. But you thought that my question meant that I had actually learned how to express doubt, and you said, "Good, that's good, that's right. If you understand the real identity of this thing, which is so alert to listen to the sounds, you will understand that that thing is the course of all actions — sitting, standing, seeing, or hearing. Anyway, that which sees and that which thinks are one...But the doubts should flow incessantly like flowing water whether you are asleep or awake, and you should also have an absolutely sincere mind. Once the doubts are sincere enough to be one whole, three days is a long period of time and seven days even longer. With one thought, everything will be completely transformed." That is why, you added, there were many people in earlier times who, at hearing one word, attained sudden awakening about life and death and thus attained the all-capable self and were freed from the cycle of life and death.

You also told me,

This work of finding oneself is extremely difficult. Ānanda, a disciple of the Buddha, had the ability to memorize flawlessly, without making a mistake in even an article, all the talks delivered by the Buddha over the period of forty-nine years. In addition, Ānanda had five supernatural powers, but still he could not be the Buddha's successor because he was not able to embody the teaching of finding one's self. He felt so frustrated that he went to see Mahākāśyapa, who was appointed as the Buddha's successor, and asked, "I have heard that you have received from the Buddha a special teaching other than the robe of gold brocade and a jasper bowl.[14] What was that?" Hearing the question, Kāśyapa called his name, "Ānanda?" "Yes," Ānanda automatically responded. Mahākāśyapa said, "Knock down the banner at the front gate." But Ānanda still did not understand and felt irritated. Kāśyapa severely scolded him, "You and I will have to write down the Buddha's teachings, which are like gold and jade, and transmit them for all eternity. But you are so slow in understanding, what are we to do?" Ānanda was so frustrated that he determined that if he failed to be awakened to his own self, he would kill himself. Standing at the edge of Viari Cliff, he sincerely focused on meditation for three days and nights without moving and finally was able to become awakened to his self.

I did not, for my part, have a clear doubt at that time, but I did feel that the teaching you offered was the most valuable one that I had ever heard or seen in my life and that I should become awakened to what it means to be a human and that I would not be sorry to devote all of my life to knowing what I was. As you were leaving and tying your shoes, you said, "The tick-tocking of a clock is the sound of the footsteps of the demon-killer named impermanence, which approaches us to take our lives. We should press ourselves to finish our work while we have the body of a human being, since eternal life is an extension of this life. To make one's mind straight in this life is to prepare for death; if we do not prepare ourselves for death, what will happen in the long future to come?" Having said this, you slowly walked away without a backward glance. As I watched you disappear, I did not even feel sorry about your leaving. I was absorbed in my own thoughts, asking myself whether I was lying or whether I really had that doubt when I responded to you earlier, if I had truly asked myself what this was that was listening to you.

In those days while waiting for our rendezvous all my thoughts were occupied with happy images of what we would do together, and after each meeting I re-lived again and again each moment when we were together, the way you moved, spoke, and the expression on your face. In between I seemed not to have my own time. But still, as I lay down that night, I remembered what you had said about having doubts and contemplated its meaning and thought to myself: seeing, hearing, sleeping, and thinking—these are all part of everything that goes on in the world, as are birth, death, pleasure, suffering, moving, or staying still. If one were to make a list of all the things in the world, there would be no end to it, but since it is said that all things in the world return to one thing, I concluded that it would be simpler to ask what this "one thing" was. I felt that my doubting was somewhat serious at that moment, but it soon disappeared and I had to keep asking myself, "What is this one thing?" till very late that night. The next day and the day after that, the doubt continued; and for the next three or four months I kept doubting, even though there were also many moments when doubt eluded me. I gradually came to pay more attention to my feelings toward you, and since it is a principle that one can't have two lives, rather than focusing on doubt, my mind would want to turn to my feelings for you, and I would gradually become preoccupied with thoughts of you.

However, the doubt was only temporarily held in suspension. I worried that the mind that now followed the teachings of the Buddha might lose its intent just as it had lapsed in following the teachings of Jesus.

I did not forget your saying that we could not give up living and that if we could not complete this practice, there was no way to avoid eternal suffering. I could not forget that not simply because they were your words or my belief but because it had been proven in reality. In order to avoid imminent suffering, I knew I should concentrate on my doubt, but instead of working on that, whether in my dreams at night or in my thoughts during the day, I indulged in picturing the various images of you, who had been so tender to me, even though I did not know where you might be or what you might be doing at that moment and with whom.

The weight of my feelings for you only gets heavier. What should I do? It seems that one's feelings can deceive during times of change. The entire world looks like a manifestation of you. That which is quiet represents you in silence and everything that moves is you moving. I hear the sound of your footsteps, even though you are not coming, and my heart races. I find you where you are not and my heart speeds up again only to find that the person is not you. My eyes, embarrassed by their mistake, soak themselves in futile tears. Does this not mean that I cannot lose you however much I try? But why do I still have these desperate feelings, the desire to see you and no one else? As you told me, this is a human tragedy that occurs because of the existence of the boundary between self and others, a boundary that is the result of not realizing that others are one's own self. Like someone who sees the finger that is pointing at the moon rather than the moon itself, I am a foolish woman who cannot forget the feelings that you once had for me and fails to practice how to unify the self and others as you taught me. Why won't you come to see me to correct this folly of mine?[15]

You are not completely exempt from responsibility for this state of affairs. Why did you teach me about the moon while at the same time showing me in your own person something even brighter than the moon, something that causes ecstatic feelings, that is, the law of nature called love? Why did your words and eyes say different things? My ideas about doubt were actually a gesture because I had received only an intimation of an education. The idea that I should concentrate on the question of doubt easily blew away, like the wind passing over a rock. Be that as it may, there is another reason why the tears I am shedding today are different from other tears I've shed. I think it was on this same day last year that we met alone for the first time.[16]

Before we had our first date, we tried to read each other's minds; we each had the feeling, even though we didn't say so, that we wanted to have time alone together. If I had burned away the desire to meet you at that time I wouldn't have to feel the pain that returns each anniversary, like the recurrence of the pain from a serious wound. It happens because the pleasure receptor shares the same sensory line as the pain receptor. But this is just my reasoning trying to shout what is suppressed under the weight of my fixation and fear that the day will come when even the memories of my feelings toward you will disappear. Even now I feel bad that I don't know whether our anniversary is today or yesterday.

Had I known that we would be separating like this, I wouldn't have allowed myself to forget the date or even the time of our meeting. At that time I couldn't imagine that we would ever separate. I was thinking idly that better and happier days would continue forever. How could I have predicted, even in a dream, that the pleasure of our meetings would turn into the unbearable pain of separation? Even so, my life at the moment consists of replaying memories of that happy past.

You refused an invitation to become president of a university and instead became the president of a Buddhist newspaper company. I went to see you at your office several days after you took up your position. You were alone in your office on the second floor. On the wall behind your desk hung the picture of the Buddha leaving his palace to join practitioners; below it were glass windows through which I could see the light green leaves of a weeping willow swaying in the spring wind.

You gestured toward a chair and I sat down next to you and sipped the green tea that had been given to you by Hwaŏm Monastery in Kurye, Chŏlla Province, where they grow tea. Drinking the steaming tea with its beautiful aroma, I said, "This is really a high-quality tea. It seems that the people from Chŏlla Province, as the saying goes, have a dual personality. I know from my experiences with a couple of them…Chŏlla people seem two-faced, but there are many high-quality products that come from that province, like this tea, mats with flower designs, window blinds, trays, fans, paper, and other things…"

You smiled at my words and said, "I'm also originally from Chŏlla Province. You should really keep an eye on me."

It was totally unexpected to hear that you were from the Chŏlla region because you don't have an accent.

"Oh, really," I said.

Looking at my blushing face, you asked in a low voice, "And your hometown is?"

The suggestive tone in your voice as you asked me that question was divinely mysterious. I wouldn't describe it as soft or affectionate; your voice was like a poem that resonated at the deepest level of my heart and moved me more than any beautiful music could. I could hardly say a word just then because of the beating of my heart but also because I had to leave shortly to make way for others who were there to see you.

Sometime later you came to see me and told me that my reply to your question about my hometown — "I'm from South Pyŏngyang" — was quite insufficient. I was embarrassed because I had talked badly about Chŏlla people, not knowing that you were from that region, and your voice was so enchanting that I didn't know what to say. You said, "Zhang Sheng gave his name and address to Hong Niang even without being asked."[17] I felt more than affection for you; I was sure that what you had just said was a clear confession of your feelings for me. I saw the magnetic expression in your eyes when you asked me, "And your hometown is?" When I realized that you had strong feelings for me and as I sensed in your voice that the attraction was mutual, I felt as if it made up for all the suffering I had endured in my life. I did not even know how to describe the immense beauty and ecstasy I was feeling at that moment. I would just call it "the most beautiful," an expression I would use as a pronoun for all the things in the world.

Who would have ever imagined that the love I thought would erase even the footprints of sorrow in my future lives would one day be the fountain of immeasurable tears? But at that time, as I was walking down the steps of the newspaper office building, I was overwhelmed with strange feelings, and I could not tell if they were sorrow or joy. Rubbing my chest with my two hands, I shouted in my heart, "This must be love! This must be love!" Today those memories and others have become a new source of sorrow for me. But I am still waiting for the future when we will continue our past; this is what makes it possible for me to maintain this life. I survive these days because the memories I have of our past still have meaning for me. Whether these memories bring me pain or sweetness, I could not survive without them. For a moment today, I indulge in idle complaints, praying that this letter, which is the continuation of our past, might renew your feelings for me.[18]

Sometime after the day we met in your office, I returned to see you, bringing with me my manuscript, which I had prepared at your request. When I arrived at your office, everyone, including the office boy, was working diligently, licking envelopes for urgent mailings to be sent to various regions. I volunteered to lend a hand, which other people welcomed, but you said that you would not let a weak woman help, the reason being, you said, that using too much saliva depleted one's level of energy. I was so moved whenever you showed concern for me like that. I gave up the idea of helping out, my heart full of appreciation for your care for me. You, who once worried about me wasting even a drop of saliva, now show no concern about whether I shed a bucket of tears. How futile life is. Whenever we walked down the street, you never allowed me to carry heavy things, not even my own coat. You would not let me cross even a narrow brook alone or climb a high hill by myself. Now that your mind has changed, it seems you want me to carry on my shoulders a burden of sorrow heavier than my weak body and soul can endure. Who would have dreamt that a day like today would come? How should I now climb the high mountains and cross the deep rivers on the path of this endless life?

I can still see your smiles, which had melted my sorrow and pain, and your body, the only thing I felt I could rely on in a rough, changeable world. I still do not believe that you were so fickle; how then should I understand why you handled the situation as you did. Do the words "causes and conditions" justify everything for you, allowing you to ignore whatever suffering the other person might have to go through, so that you can clear yourself of all responsibility? In this world, things have two sides, a subject and an object. Who gave you the right to determine things for our situation all by yourself? Today at least, even though I live on memories of the past, I have the absolute freedom to have my own emotions that even you can't take away from me. I glean whatever I want from past days and create new days from them; and meanwhile I cry, I feel, and I vainly complain.

I was a foolish woman who didn't know the principle that, in planting the seed of love you also sow the fire that consumes the flower of love. I used to dream that I could have both the fruit and the splendid flower of love. You created a beautiful flower garden in the desert of my heart, and from that memory, on the grassy field called disappointment, I've paved a road made of ten thousand different feelings. As I wander down it, I thank you for having enabled me to build this road.

One Sunday my friends came to persuade me to join them in picking chestnuts, but I refused, hoping that you might drop by. After waiting for you all day, sometime in the evening I went out to the end of the alley. You appeared there with a small folding chair made out of a poplar tree with wooden legs. You said, "Since you said you didn't want to sit on the dirt, I've made this for you. It's a bit rough, but it's practical!"

Trying to sit on the chair, I said, "I'm heavy and the legs of the chair look weak. I'm afraid they might collapse."

You reached out your hand in a gesture of support and said, "Do you see these hands and legs? I wouldn't mind cutting them off for your convenience. Don't worry; have a seat and I'll hold and support you."

You must have meant it as a joke, but I was so moved by your words that I couldn't speak. Your voice was soft, but my ears heard it as a strong message that I should believe what you said.

You came on a Monday sometime after you brought me the folding chair. "The wind is a bit chilly, but the sun is warm. Why don't we go to the Han River and take a boat?" you said. You said you came on Monday because Mondays were when the river landing was least crowded. As we were floating along, it seemed as if my feelings for you became deeper on the river than even the firmest love I felt for you on land. Once we reached Ttuksŏm Island you let the boat return, and we walked until we found a cozy spot. We deferred to each other about who would sit on the folding chair you had made for me, and while we were each trying to make the other sit, I fell and got sand in a cut on my hand. It started to bleed. You cleaned the sand off my hand and blew on the wound to ease the pain, saying that, with treatment by such a renowned doctor as yourself, my cut would heal immediately. I can still feel quite vividly your hands, with which you finally led me to sit on the chair, and your breath, which was so warm.

About ten days ago, my foolish heart made me run with that chair to our Mecca, the spot on Ttuksŏm Island where we had spent time together.[19] In my mind I imagined that everything would be as before; but reality betrayed me. Not even a leaf of a tree held your wished-for scent. Only the warmth of the sunshine was the same. I almost collapsed, overwhelmed by ten thousand different feelings as I stood all alone on a hillside. Even the mountain birds that had been singing happy songs when we were there enjoying ourselves now pretended not recognize me and flew away, leaving a cold wind behind. This is a world where even the birds in the air treated me coldheartedly. I, too, should be coldhearted, but a certain warmth remained in my heart and turned even my tears warm.

How could this be my only memory of us and how could I, with a couple of hundred words, describe the unforgettable stories of us together? It's true that for a time you made me extremely happy, but all of those stories are dreams that have disappeared. If they were to end up being dreams, I would rather they had been nightmares. But the dreams were so beautiful they are difficult to forget. If to disappear is the nature of dreams, why can't I forget them? Not only can I not forget them, each scene within the dream comes alive and causes me pain. In the midst of that evasive liminal state, your voice asking me, "And your hometown is?" has turned into a strong charm that caresses my cheek. What should I do?

The echo of that simple question had pierced through my bones and reached my soul so that each time I heard it I experienced extreme joy. When I don't hear it now, I'm miserable. Back then, you were consistently genuine with me, and so the days of joy continued. Why can't you continue to be genuine when it brought such joy to our days? You told me about the principle that affairs of the world are all relative. That means that we cannot be genuine all the time, and because of the mind that seeks joy, the sorrow that we do not seek also arrives. Then, according to that logic, because of the mind that wanted to see you, I couldn't see you. But all I can think of is seeing you again, which is the problem.

I am suffering from a terrible cold that has confined me to my room. The incessant cough batters my heart, which already ails from yearning for you. If so much as a hair on my head were to be blown by the wind, you worried that I might catch cold. Any time I took a deep breath, you searched my face, concerned that some worry had made me sigh. Now that you are gone, all of the other men who used to promise me everything to earn my love have also disappeared. I live on the pittance I earn from my writings in a small rented room without any friend to visit me. Sometimes, like creditors, those pressing me for overdue manuscripts show up, but nobody cares whether I live or die. I am all alone. But why should I feel lonely over whether other people come to see me or whether they care for me? My only anxiety is whether, together with your body, your feelings for me have left forever, like a cloud floating away. Before I met you I was all alone, but that loneliness was not even loneliness. That loneliness was a sweet loneliness that contained an expectation that someone who could console me would come along. I might describe my present loneliness as the misery of a widow who has received the letter informing her of the death of her only son, whose arrival she had been awaiting for days and nights, believing that she would once again see the happy day come when she could hold him. Or should I compare myself to a merchant whose dreams of a family and a good business are lost when his partner absconds, leaving him to face his creditors alone in his empty store?

Don't you think that you made me pay too high a price for the temporary pleasure you offered? But I should place the responsibility more on myself, who cannot forget you, instead of condemning you and accusing you of cruelty. Is this suffering the price I must pay for my own failings? Ah, I don't know. I just want to experience, even for a moment, your voice, which echoes in my soul, and your tender look. If there is a way to avoid suffering like this again, I am fully ready to endure my current agony. In other words, no matter how cruel you have been to me, I do not hold you responsible. Just please come back to me as the man you were before. The night has deepened and I hear only a few footsteps from the street; the gate of the motel next door seems to be taking a rest as well. Only the distant sound of shouting, "Roasted chestnuts, roasted chestnuts," disturbs the empty air. That dim sound coming through the quiet night reaches the harp of my heart, making it play, and I'm reminded of another episode from the time we were together.

It was one of those very cold evenings last winter. You produced a bag of roasted chestnuts from your pocket and said, "They must be all crushed; I held them tightly, as if they were your body…" It was first time you had said something funny like that, with your face all bright as you entered my room. You had been seriously concerned about my always being alone. Feeling that my room was cold—and even worse, that the clothing I was wearing was too thin—you gave me a sad look, took off the coat you had bought abroad, and gave it to me.

You said that women were less resistant to cold than men. I would rather have offered you my coat, but instead you made me take your only coat, which made me unhappy. I put on your coat without any special response and still cannot take it off. I should have kept my room warm and prepared some food when you came to see me, but I did not even have that much common sense. All I did in expectation of you was stay in my room waiting; all my other work was suspended. Even the sound of the footsteps of passersby made my heart pound.

Sometimes I laughed at myself for being so fixated. But even now, in my present situation in which I reflect on my inner self, I still think that no one could surpass me for a mind always bent on you. With that in mind, I wrote a poem.

Beyond control is the flame of love,
Which has burned both body and mind;
After the flame is extinguished, all that is left are cold ashes,
And scattering away is even the last particle of ash;
The mind concentrating on my love would still grow brighter,
Shedding light on the path in front of my lover.

This poem, with which I was unexpectedly inspired, sounds more detached than my feelings were at the time. I repeated it all alone and that somewhat calmed me down. Instead of shedding tears at the sorrow of separation as I usually do, the poem gave me a chance to think more rationally about the reason for the separation.

I have always trusted you unconditionally, so how could I possibly rationally feel any resentment toward you? I just want to understand how this painful separation happened. But what good is it to ask when I do not even know your whereabouts?

Like a foolish woman who tries to put back together the fragments of a broken jar, I can't help returning to a dream of the past that can never be true again. You had emphasized with all sincerity that we should never lose each other. You're the same person as before, living peacefully somewhere. No one who meets you now would see the shadow of my sorrowful soul following behind you.

If the causes and conditions of our relationship are all exhausted, why is it that I have to follow crying behind your shadow? The cause and conditions aren't something that can be dissolved one-sidedly. Thinking of causes and conditions reminds me of a line in a poem I wrote in response to criticism of our relationship in its happy days. I wrote the poem because, at the time, the causes and conditions of our relationship were only too natural. Since I didn't know then that the causes and conditions would exhaust themselves, I wrote,

> Green mountains are numerous, so is blue water,
> Green mountains are reflected in blue water through causes and
>   conditions,
> Who would argue against green mountains and blue water smiling
>   at each other?

You showed no interest when I shared this poem with you. However, you said, "The words flow well, but why should anyone be bothered by what others say? Everybody needs to make the best of their time and enjoy themselves; that is the definition of paradise. Just before I returned to Korea from abroad, I traveled to Sweden with a female classmate. We weren't in a position to get married, so should the plan of some mischievous god of copulation have resulted in a child of mixed blood, my travel partner would have been put in a seriously embarrassing position. But we agreed that we couldn't forgo the opportunity and spent a night of beautiful dreams together. That was the beginning and end, and we parted ways the next day. I was never to meet her again." Was your attitude toward me the same as toward that woman?

I know, though, that you do not choose a woman to love simply according to your mood. I know that because you told me the following story. "In Great Britain there are remains of which the date is unknown. There is such a place on a mountain rarely visited by people; the only traces of life there must have been left by people who worked the slash-and-burn fields under the protection of the sky and safeguarded by mountains and trees, making friends with wild animals. Two lovers must have lived and died there, hidden from the world." As I listened to you telling this romantic story, I imagined a sweet-scented, sad scene in which we would spend happy times under the roof of our thatched cottage in a place where nameless birds flew freely and we stroked the deer and the roe. Nobody would know when we died after such a happy life.

You also said, "How about we go to Manchuria to live by farming millet and cultivate ourselves?" One time you asked me, in all serious-ness, "What if we live in a cave on a mountain and cultivate ourselves? There would be only the two of us. When we ran out of food, I would trav-el dozens of miles to get it, carrying it on my back. As I arrived home, you would bring out something to eat carefully arranged on an old tray and wipe away the sweat from my forehead. Would such a secretive life ap-peal to you?" Whatever you did or said was completely sincere. You were that kind of person. I believed that lovers were like two stones bound together: If one stone leads, the other follows. Thus I responded positively to whatever you suggested. All in all your dealings with the opposite sex were totally kind and at the same time careful. You were passionate and at the same time self-possessed. Moreover, you made it fundamental that our relationship should be based on mutual respect...

If you put all of these factors together, it wasn't wrong for me to trust you. You're not the type of person who would trample on my genuine love...What, then, has caused this separation? Don't I have a right to know why we had to break up? You prioritize your public life over your love life, and in that context, something might have happened, perhaps, that made you leave me. Once you mentioned that a person who devoted himself to public service would have no time to spare for family life. I responded by asking, "What is the distance between the person who has perfectly fulfilled his responsibility as head of a family and one who has succeeded in public life?" You smiled and said, "You're one step ahead." All that you have accomplished in your daily life is evidence of your sac-rifice of your private life to the public good. Your stated goal was to get involved with public projects by first becoming a public figure. What is meant by "a public figure," you said, is not the typical public figure that most people envision. By a public figure you meant a person who has completed his or her self and is therefore capable of leading a self-sov-ereign life and whose activities are guided by universal principles. Now I realize the pressure you felt because of your devotion to the practice of becoming a complete person (the practice of the concentrating mind).

Thinking about your view on life provides me with some explanation for your actions. You told me that all the great actions of the Buddha were performed to save sentient beings of all kinds in the world, including even strengthening the tuberculosis bacterium to do its work of consuming a person's lungs.

You also told me,

> To think means to exist. Thought is the creator of the universe. A bacterium, like the Buddha, has its own thought. Thought means self, and to be faithful to one's own self means to undertake Buddhist activities, and Buddhist activities mean activities of the universal scale. Once the tuberculosis bacterium completely damages a person's lungs, the individual, having lost the use of his lungs, would have to leave his house. With that, the bacterium would be expelled from the cold room and would disappear. The world would be a lonely place, but preparations for a great construction begin with this nothingness. The ultimate stage of the activities of Śakyamuni Buddha is also this state of no-trace (the state of clarity and stillness).

You continued,

> In the world of being that resumes after this nothingness, the activities of the Buddha and of the bacterium would be reversed. But in the real world, there is a great difference in the position of the two. That is because the Buddha possesses the great self that embodies the universe, whereas a bacterium has lost its universal self and relies only on the smallest fragment of mental power. Even a bacterium, however, if it is faithful to life as a bacterium, can recover the universal self. A healthy universe depends on every being's fidelity to its own existence. Being faithful to one's existence means not being distracted even slightly by external conditions such as pain and pleasure, advantage and disadvantage. Further, you should not be preoccupied with what has happened in the past or what will happen in the future, nor should you allow yourself to be distracted by impure things. The past, present, and future should be unified into a single moment, and the space of self and of others should likewise be unified. When this unity is fully accomplished the result will be a successful and complete life in which time and space are completely embodied. This is the life of a human being.

You said,

> If you think about reality in greater detail, it is a mass that exists in space; not only does it include volume, but it also includes temporal phenomena such as birth, aging, sickness, and death, beginnings and ends, prosperity and decline. It also includes that which is generated through sensations such as warmth and coldness, sound, light, and

odor, which do not exist in and of themselves but through our thoughts. In perceiving these illusions, we give them names. Caught in the rainbow net named causes and conditions, we create delusionary forms. They are like shadows, but this shadow-like existence, as it is, is imperishable and continues without end in the future. It is not possible to get rid of a shadow-like existence, which is the cause of endless problems. The imperishable image is the reality itself. The reality and one's own self have the same inner essence. The self makes actions, and the self and actions are not two different things. This means that the self that is a part of reality should first embody reality so that the self is able to keep pace with the universe that is the reality, and thus maintain eternity.[20] It follows that one should first be faithful to one's daily life, which is the reality at hand. That is the price we pay to maintain at least the position of the small self. Further, being faithful to the present reality not only means becoming engaged with projects in daily life but also generating a spiritual income. The latter should surpass the former.

You told me that you were thinking of securing a small property, gathering together colleagues, and creating a retreat center where participants could produce the necessities of life as well as engage in cultivation of mind. That would be a way to perfect one's character through the unity of effort and cultivation. I know you were more concerned about your self-cultivation and were not overly interested in creating a happy family life. I could not imagine that an external event would affect us, nor could I imagine that my mind and yours were separate. I naïvely thought that when the time came, it would be only natural that we would get married and create a family, and I never felt that I should doubt that prospect. That being my understanding, what worries could I have had? The only complaint I had was the frequency of your absences, which prompted me to write a poem.

> On a long winter night,
> I would like to have my stories told,
> Even before the first story is said
> The light of dawn is afresh,
> If I knew this would be my lot,
> I would have stopped myself.

I must have written this during those days when you didn't have much feeling for me and I felt so alone and restless. But if your indifference was really because of your public life... you wouldn't have had time for another woman, would you? I'm positive, though, that you had another woman at that time. You told me that if a person had faith in someone, that faith should be absolute; and if something totally unexpected happened, that person should not be disappointed but instead show faith, which is the very meaning of fidelity to truthfulness. Now I think that you said such things as preparation in case your secret were revealed. When I said that I would come to visit you, you said, "I stay at my friend's place, and my friend is always very hospitable to my guests. I feel sorry for my host that I've decided to receive guests no longer." I had no objection to what you said. However, a friend of yours once told me that he, a woman, and you had studied Buddhist scriptures under a dharma master named Master Hwan at the Sin'gye Monastery on Kŭmgang Mountain, and that he saw the woman at your place. He also told me that your relationship with her seemed more than a friendship. He even told me that she had a mysterious power to attract men. But I had such strong faith that I had your love—as if love was something that could be tied up at one spot— that I wasn't bothered by what I had heard.

You were always prompt in meeting me, but even when we were together, you seemed to feel pressed and frequently checked the time. Now that I think about it, I see it as an indication of your effort to hide my existence from your lover. However, my personality is such that once I set the boundary of my life based on the situation at the time, I don't see or hear anything that happens outside that boundary. So there was no way I was going to sense what was going on with you.

My only regret is that learning about this affair of yours didn't assuage my pain. In the past when we met at a public event, our surreptitiously exchanged looks were such a pleasure. When we had a chance to be alone in a quiet corner, you covered my forehead, nose, cheeks, and hands with your kisses. At these moments, your eyes, which sometimes chilled me, made me feel that your whole body was smiling. You were entirely transformed into a touching regard and seemed completely devoted to me. Your manner toward women was so respectful, even more so than that of any Western man, that when you came to see me, you were like a caring husband, which made me melt. I was so happy that I wasn't aware that seven or eight months had passed since we first met.

Have those happy days gone away forever? I wouldn't ask to have all the happiness back, but I wish I could see you from time to time. I'm desperate to realize this dream, but I don't have any way to let you know about these feelings of mine…In your last letter, you said, "Please don't be disturbed, just keep moving forward. If you can take constructive steps in a world where female figures are rare, I would be more than happy for you. I'm a man so whatever happens to me won't be a big deal." Even though you had left me, you still seemed concerned about what would happen to my life, and this gives me a thin hope that I might see you again. I assume that you must have some situations that forced you to leave me that you couldn't tell me about.

You told me that the practice to recover one's own self could be done in the secular world, that one needn't travel far for the self-cultivation. That's because the practice is to learn about the real nature of the one who sees and speaks in the moment. However, this cultivation involves serious training and relentless struggling with one's habits. When one pursues self-cultivation in the secular world, the power of the demons adds to existing habits new habitual energy created by the back-up troops of what one hears, sees, and feels.

When faced by such allied forces, how could anyone like me, who has weak mental powers, win? That's why it would be better to stop my social activities, which would in any case not be of much help to society, and go to the mountains for a couple of years to focus on practice. You did mention this, but I didn't understand exactly what it meant and thought you were saying it on a whim. Does this mean that I was only concerned with our feelings for each other and didn't understand what you were saying even when you tried to communicate it to me? Was this why you disappeared into the mountains with your colleague, that woman who studied Buddhist scriptures with you? Is this why you don't let me know your whereabouts? I can't deny that I was seriously disappointed at the news of your going off with that woman. But right now, the world without you is dark and stifling and the source of my tears is my longing at the thought that you won't be coming to see me in this empty room.

At the moment I have no intention of distinguishing who was right and who was wrong, nor do I want to try to reason with you. To make you appear before me is the sole desperate issue for me, and I know that even this hope is futile. I have never been a happy woman, but neither have I ever felt this miserable. But I think I've reached the limit of my waiting. I'm someone who tries to make do with the situation I find myself in, and if things don't work out, I try to find a different path. I have to make up my mind. I would rather have another letter from you that would make me permanently give you up. I perhaps can let you go emotionally, but you are my guide on this endless path in life, and I cannot but follow behind you on your path.

You lost your parents early and were raised by your grandmother. You participated in the March First Movement as a young intellectual. While living in exile in a foreign land where you had nobody to turn to, with only your three outstanding qualities of determination, trustworthiness, and talent to rely on, you overcame all kinds of adversity. Through your unceasing efforts, you completed the highest level of academic education, and, degree in hand, you made a glorious return home. Wasn't that evidence that you had in your previous lives cultivated the mental power of thousands? However, people who had lost their country were ungrounded both politically and socially.[21] You had no family to celebrate your return after over ten years abroad, but you couldn't have expected your homecoming to be so lonely.

What's more, there was no institution in which you could work and no colleagues with whom to collaborate. All high-level positions and benefits were already in the hands of Japanese. However strong your heart, the situation must have hurt you. Still, you never let on and no matter whether the work was respected or not or whether the pay was high or low, you dedicated yourself to whatever work was available. And unbeknownst to others, you continued your spiritual practice. I was so touched by the way you carried on in the face of such hardship. I saw that society was not yet able to fully appreciate a person like you, and I deplored the way the world trampled on someone so precious and how people turned their backs on the very kind of individual they most needed. I longed for the day when I could officially declare you to the world as my husband!

You truly brought the spring wind and made flowers bloom on the hill of my mind, which had until then had been like a bleak autumn. You couldn't have imagined the pleasure I felt at anticipating the time when the fruit would be ripening. As I wandered in an enchanted world of recollection, these memories sometimes made me forget the misery of separation. But the momentary pleasure of memories of the past gave way to the cruelty of the long sorrow that was my reality. I couldn't linger in that world for long. If it is, as people say, that a fallen leaf reports the coming of the fall, I realize that it is possible your love will never return. However, you told me that the life and death of this body, as well as meeting and separation, are successive, and thus one can predict that the joy of meeting is inevitably followed by the sorrow of saying good-bye. What you said has now become my reality, but I've yet to fully realize it. I continue to be consoled by the desperate hope that we'll not be separated forever or that we're not destined to be complete strangers.

If ever such a day and time of permanent separation were to come, my misery would be unfathomably deep. What a pitiful state I am in! If polarity is the principle of the universe, then the days when I cannot let you go will be followed by days when I wait for you. How much better it would be if all the energy I put into thinking about what might or might not happen were used for spiritual practice. My desire to see you is so obstinate, like a disease, that no philosophical statement or rational argument can make it go away. There is only one way to get past this pain, and that is through the teaching that supersedes all scholarly theories and breaks down all stubbornness, that is, the principle of practicing to find "myself." To find "myself" so that I can rely on my mental power is an ambiguous concept, but recently I experienced an incident that would have awakened anyone.

I told you once that a friend of mine named Wŏn Chuhŭi had joined a monastery at Kyŏnsŏng Hermitage on Tŏksung Mountain in Yesan.[22] Her husband, whose last name was Im, had been a monk when he was young, but left the monastery to pursue a desire to study. With no help from anyone, he finished his degree in English at Waseda University in Japan and became a middle school teacher. He was like an old bachelor desperately in need of someone's tender love and care. Once married, he was devoted to his wife. When they were at home, he would always be checking on whether his wife was cold or hot and then opening or closing the window to suit her. When they went out, he behaved as though he was willing to carry her in his arms or on his back. There seemed to be no gap between his existence and his wife's: When her clothes got rumpled or her shoestrings untied, he immediately noticed it and fixed it. On school days he missed her so much that if he knew she planned to go downtown, he would wait at the window of his office at school and watch her pass by. He would continue his vigil until she disappeared from sight before returning to his desk. His colleagues made fun of him, saying, "If she were your mistress, catching a glimpse of her might be fun, but you see your wife every day and night, and still…If you miss her so much, we can see about getting her a desk next to yours so that you can work together!" His colleagues mocked him, but he just smiled and without any embarrassment responded, "She is both wife and mistress to me!"

When his wife had to go out alone, he never forgot to say "Be careful at the crosswalks and watch out for automobiles and streetcars." He ordered his guardian spirit to accompany her, which he said would prevent trouble and keep her safe. Whenever he went on a field trip with students, he needed his wife's caresses in his dreams, and only after that was he able to climb a high mountain and take care of his students on the climb. On the way home from the field trip, he so hated the train for moving too slowly that he wanted to jump out and run home. His devotion to his wife was such that you can imagine how painful it must have been for him to let her join the monastery. He remarried, and several years later, a friend asked him about life with his new wife compared to life with his former wife.

His barely audible voice came through a long sigh that sounded like it had been buried in deep memories. "How could you even compare my current marriage with my life with my former wife!" he said, his head drooping.

Having been such a devoted husband, he volunteered to accompany his wife to the monastery on the day she joined. His wife walked with him to the spur of the hill and said, "I should say good-bye now." Her words rang in his ears, and he felt a fire burning in his heart. The heat of the fire reached his eyes and hot tears spilled from them. He couldn't look at his wife. In a state of shock, he was not sure whether he was heading home or going in a different direction. Fortunately, he was able to find a bus heading for his home and got off at his stop. Disheartened, he walked up the hill of Sŏngbuk Tong, where he could see the roof of his house colored by the setting sun. At that moment all the energy drained from his legs, and he crumbled on the spot. He calmed himself down after a while and regained enough energy to walk home. At home he was greeted by a chilly wind and a cleaning girl with eyes wet from weeping. How could he express his feelings at that moment! For twenty years in this lonely world he had endured various difficulties at home and abroad, but the agony he felt just then was as if he had been hit by the hammer of an enemy created out of the most painful experiences possible combined with ten thousand different feelings.

That night his suffering was infinite, and when he awoke the next morning, his eyes felt heavy, as if something were covering them. Thinking that he might have an eye disease, he went to see his eye doctor, who told him that a fever had caused the problem. He remembered the heat he had felt when his wife said good-bye at the crossroads. That heat must have caused his eye disease.

He couldn't bear to be all alone in his room, which felt like an empty station waiting room where trampled papers were scattered about and which was crowded with phantom-like images of his wife. He aimlessly hung around the streets along which his wife used to pass and went to the places she used to visit with the desperate hope that he might be able to hear her voice or smell her scent. One day he decided to go see her at the monastery. Luck was not on his side, though. He had car trouble on the way and had to stop overnight. Thinking that he would rather walk throughout the night with the hope of seeing her than suffer from restless anticipation, he walked along the rough mountain road for twenty miles without resting. When he finally saw his wife, he was more than ready to tell her about the hardship he had just been through, but her chilly reception made it all too clear that she didn't welcome him. She reminded him that she had left the secular world and that he could come to see her only to discuss the Buddha's teachings, not to make an appeal on behalf of his feelings.

The man became enraged as he returned home. He burned all her photos and whatever of her belongings he still had. He got rid of the comforter that he used to hold close to his body as if it were her. Lying down that night, forcing himself to get some sleep, he gritted his teeth. But in his dreams his wife appeared, sweet and gentle as before. He had to return to a reality where he found increasingly that there was no place for his heart to settle. At night he frequented the cinema and during the daytime he wandered the streets wearing a hat. When he taught classes at school, people said that he wasn't his normal self. At home he could sleep only with the help of alcohol. Worried about the situation, his friends made efforts to find a woman for him, and eventually he married a gentle woman named Soon Yang, or something like that, who was educated at Tongdŏk Women's School. Within about five years the couple had three children and led a happy life. Then one day he had a bout of indigestion that turned into dysentery that took his life in less than a week. He was not yet forty.

The death of a human being might not be a big deal, and it might be that I just told you a long boring story about a happy couple. There is nothing special about a husband who loves his wife. But this man's love for his wife was exceptional. And yet despite his great love, which was fundamentally different from that of other husbands, his wife chose a path that few could imagine taking, and her spirit of detachment could be a model for others. More than that, I want to let the world know about his tragic situation so that it might be a mirror to help everyone change the way they think about life. I hope that the example of this couple will help others realize that we have all lost our selves and that we should take refuge in the Buddha, who can cure our disease.

One life that is a hundred years long is said to be a big thing to deal with. How much more grave is it to take the first step (the initial period of one's encounter with the Buddhist teachings) at the crossroads between the path that leads to an infinite life of happiness or the one that leads to misery for immeasurable time in the future? For my part I have yet to complete my spiritual cultivation…The first thing to realize is that we all live a pseudo-life relying on pseudo-mind as a result of habitual energy, and only with this realization will there be any hope that we will try to find our real mind. My friend's ex-husband died three days after my last visit to him. What follows is the description by another friend named Sukhŭi who was with him at his death:

Sukhŭi was his ex-wife's best friend and also a Buddhist. He seemed truly happy to see Sukhŭi and began to talk about his ex-wife as soon as he saw her. He told her that his ex-wife, who had joined the monastery, was like a buried treasure jar. On the outside she was an ordinary housewife, but on the inside there was no woman with a clearer mind. He had joined a monastery as a child and had heard many dharma talks. He dreamt of becoming a renowned monk, a guide for gods and humans, but he fell short of realizing this goal. His ex-wife chose the path of salvation on her own initiative, however. He and his ex-wife lived together for six years and had paid off the mortgage and made monthly payments on other debts, including those for his clothes and pocket watch, and even managed to accumulate some savings. It was at that time that his ex-wife joined the monastery. The pocket watch, which was his ex-wife's wedding gift to him and somewhat beyond their budget, was a symbol of his ex-wife's love. Things change and in each life there is both tragedy and comedy, but a watch doesn't care and just continues to faithfully fulfill its responsibility, keeping time unerringly. A family should adopt the mindset of a watch. Things happened and things were forgotten; the weather could be cold or warm; but all the same, the watch stayed with the husband and faithfully accompanied him even on his path to death. The watch was the proper symbol of his ex-wife's love. It never left the husband; even in the moment before his death, he caressed it as he shed copious tears of farewell. Then the owner of the watch had to leave it...Tears traced a line down his face.

Both he and his ex-wife had suffered from severe poverty and the lack of humane relationships. But with hard work and by living frugally, within six years they were able to create a firm foundation for their family life, which gave him extreme satisfaction. The couple thought that each of them should have a strong grounding in his or her own reality, which would prepare them to work as citizens of the world. Thus, their primary goal had been a settled family life, to which they deferred all other wishes. In the sixth year, for the first time since their marriage, they were able to consider a vacation. They decided to go to the beach in Inchŏn. In a honeymoon-like frame of mind, the couple set off on their outing. On the first day as they walked side by side along the beach, the wife said, "Look." The husband looked up and there on the eastern side of the beach under a rise with several tall, unidentifiable trees was something the size of a fist shining in all the colors of the spectrum. Out of curiosity the couple hurriedly approached the object only to find that it was nothing but an oyster shell. Disappointed, the wife became moody. As they returned to their lodging, she said, "The empty oyster shell still has its splendor, but what was inside the shell must already have been on someone's dinner table and disappeared in a single bite. The shell is still displaying its magnificent colors, but the tide will soon be high and it will be carried away at low tide. It will be smashed against a rock or get stuck in the mud and exist no more on that beach where sea birds fly by aimlessly."

"I am working on something that I expect to be a masterpiece and that might satisfy my desire for fame; I might be successful with that work and become renowned in the world, but even so, I will have to face death in thirty or forty years. That is a settled fact. After death, whatever great fame that might be attached to my name will be nothing, just like the oyster shell that showed off its color but had lost its contents. My work might teach something to my readers about how to live this life, but there are a thousand or ten thousand different paths in life to choose from, and I cannot possibly know that the path I taught to my readers is the right one. The moment I saw that oyster shell, my life changed, and at the same time I lost confidence in my work. Before, I believed that my work should reflect my worldview, which should be a correct understanding of the world. I realized that I should first become a human being and learn which path I should take in life, and only then would I be able to say anything to others about the right path in life. If I don't know whether I'm actually leading life as a human being, how can I dare examine the inner workings of human existence? If I don't know the internal operations of human existence, however great my description of its external aspects, my description would be as useless as a work of art made of ice on which beautiful things are inscribed."

Since the wife had lost interest, the couple cut their vacation short and returned home on the third day. The wife was interested in the Buddhist teachings (which are instructions in unifying the phenomenal and noumenal aspects of the universe) and suggested that they make another trip, this time to see their Buddhist heritage at Pulguk Monastery in Kyŏngju. The buildings at Pulguk Monastery and the Buddha statue in its stone cave were an inheritance from our ancestors during the period when Buddhist teachings were embodied in people's daily lives. Seeing that overpowering spiritual heritage, the wife was strongly moved. At the same time, she became very reflective, raising questions about whether that cultural heritage, which is an immediate reflection of people's lives during the period when Buddhism was in its heyday, was still demonstrating the power of Buddhism; she wondered why Buddhist teachings had become so invisible. As she sighed about the situation, a decent-looking old monk told her,

> Buddhism is a teaching through which one comprehends and realizes the universal creativity that existed before a thought arises. All the man-

ifestations of the teaching are means to save sentient beings, and they exist in the material realm of naming and form; they are creations of the human mind, which arises and ceases. They are part of the historical cycle and thus must be part of the sea of waxing and waning. That is why Buddhism is declining now along with the declining universe.

The historical Buddha has gone and the omnipresent God is no longer here. Those who are known to us as buddhas and bodhisattvas are all creatures created through creativity.[23] So are sentient beings, but sentient beings are in a state of confusion, whereas the buddhas and bodhisattvas have realized their own selves (the essence of one's self) and fully utilize them. However, even the buddhas and bodhisattvas cannot save sentient beings; all they can do is to teach them the way to salvation.

The path to salvation is to find your own self and thus become a free being. Once you become a free being, you go beyond the boundary called Buddhist teaching and also leave behind the idol called the Buddha. That is the same as knowing you do not need a boat once you have crossed the river. Religious doctrines are the principle of the universe. That is why you should avoid being a believer who confines herself to religious doctrine. A doctrine is actually a surface phenomenon, subject to the law of polarization and thus subject to the law of impermanence.[24]

However, a beginner should first become a Buddhist and learn the spirit of the Buddha — that is, the illumination of wisdom — from "good and virtuous teachers." (Buddhist teachers are called by this name because they are the embodiment of all good and virtuous knowledge.) Good and virtuous teachers are those who succeeded the Buddha, who was their predecessor and the first teacher (who realized the principle of the universe ahead of others and thus inaugurated the succession from the first Buddha to the buddhas that followed). From these teachers you should learn the principle of finding yourself, the way to become a free being, which is the practice of meditation.

Currently there is a teacher named Song Man'gong who gives lessons at Sudŏk Monastery in Yesan (which also has a quarter for nuns' practice called Kyŏnsŏng Hermitage).

Having heard such kind and serious advice, the wife began to consider joining the monastery but didn't mention carrying out the idea, much to the husband's relief. As they returned home, the husband hoped that the idea of joining the monastery would gradually fade from his wife's mind. Everything depends on the mind, and another incident occurred that reminded the wife of the impermanence of existence!

The wife loved all types of flowers. Some go on about the beauty of the moon and others like a specific season, spring or autumn, for example. But the wife thought that favoring the moon or a season tended to encourage a blue mood, whereas flowers soften rough mountains and wild fields. They are the lord of peace that offers calm and comfort even to those who have anger or complaints. They are the god of purification that cleanses all things. Therefore, the wife said that flowers could boast of never being enemies of anything.

As the couple made their way home, the wife saw a hundred different flowers, which she imagined decorating her small house and welcoming her with smiles that made her happier than any family member's welcoming words. Flowers, which gave the wife such pleasure and joy, were her best friends. She worried more about flowers freezing than a person suffering from the cold. Time flew by relentlessly and in no time fall had arrived, as it did every year. One night an unexpected frost completely ravaged her flower bed, which was her garden of joy, and all of the charming flowers were turned into skeletons listening to a song of mourning sung by crow-tits sitting at the end of a naked branch. The situation reminded the wife that life was like frost dangling on a plant; it existed in between breaths. With that realization, the wife decided that very morning to join the monastery.

The husband said that during the initial period of their married life the couple considered joining the monastery together. The day the wife decided to join the monastery she told her husband, "You have worked hard for twenty years to master secular knowledge, which is useful only in this life, at this moment, with this body. If you had instead spent that energy learning how to embody the entire universe in your self—a teaching that can be used anytime, anywhere, in whatever form you happen to be born—you could by now have become a great person free from all constraints. Time has already passed and you can't do anything about the past, but even now, before you get too old, you should join the monastery, entirely dedicate yourself to practice, and become a complete person. Shouldn't one become a human first, before engaging in everyday living, before beginning work? What we call business now is a pitiful situation akin to a blind person leading another blind person through the middle of nowhere, holding on to each other, not knowing where to go. There is a proverb that says 'Instead of wishing to catch a fish after having arrived at a pond, go home and first knit a fishnet.'"

The husband, however, confessed to his wife that he had completely left behind the ideas he had had as a monk. And furthermore, because he had not yet satisfied his appetite for human emotion, he could not yet let go of this life of secular desires. He told his wife he would wait for her for three years, begging her to study and practice the teachings and then come back to him. He told Sukhŭi that sometimes when he was alone he imagined he was a monk and also thought a bit about Buddhist teachings, but as he lived in the midst of the secular world with the secular people, he had become a secular person himself and had forgotten even the concepts of the Buddhist teachings of a monk.

The wife asked him to allow her to join the monastery alone, even if he would not want to join himself. He wanted to be understanding, but the idea of separating from her was too much for him to deal with. The wife, however, told him, "The reality in which we live is nothing but a dream. In this dream, the thing most susceptible to change is one's feelings. But people consider these feelings for others to be of utmost importance, and that is because not only human beings but all things in existence in this world were born out of feelings; feelings are the beginning of life. Because of the chimerical transformation of feelings, since beginningless eons of time, all beings have experienced endless suffering, and you know this too well. I believe that even though you are not ready to leave the secular world, you will not interfere with someone who has to break the chains of affection so that she can be a free being." It was clear that his wife wouldn't change her mind, and since his love for her was such that he had to sacrifice his feelings for her and even though he didn't want to let her go, he had no other choice but to allow her join the monastery.

Left alone after his wife joined the monastery, the husband thought that, although it was only natural for a husband to love his wife, nobody in the world could love his wife more than he did. Then he wondered where she found the power to jump beyond his love, a love so dense that there could be no gap and so vast as to cover the entire world. Did her courage come from her betrayal of his love or did it come from her faith? The two ideas fought against each other in his mind, making his life unbearable.

His failure to answer this question caused him such extreme suffering that he couldn't sleep without first drinking. One evening he saw a film in which a young Catholic woman left her lover and took the path of martyrdom by voluntarily declaring her faith. Only then could he confirm for himself that his wife must have joined the monastery because of the power of faith. Having answered the question, he was able to settle down.

At first, even though he could understand his wife's reasons for joining the monastery, the pain of separation was so severe that he didn't have room to think about his own spiritual cultivation. After he saw the film about the Catholic woman, he might have been able to do more than just calm himself down had he not been consumed by lust. His preoc-

cupation with his emotions made it impossible for him to return to the
Buddhist teachings he had practiced early in his life. He sighed that he
alone was responsible for his deplorable situation. He had worked hard
for twenty-some years to master secular studies, which were nothing but
the accumulation of knowledge, and he had naïvely believed there was
some hope in that lifestyle. Now that he was facing the final moment of
his life, which had caught him by surprise, he said that he was more hor-
rified than those who were afraid of death and ignorant of what it meant.
That was because, he said, those who committed a crime with an awareness of its sinfulness should pay a higher price than those who committed
a crime without knowledge of its sinfulness. Like children occupied with
their play while their house is on fire, those who were not aware of the
meaning of death would not be able to prepare themselves. But he had
ignored preparing for death even though he was aware of how grave a
situation it would be. He was the only one to blame for that and wondered
where he would now turn to obtain forgiveness. It was absolutely terrifying, he said, to know what it would be like after death for one who had
not prepared for it. He said that to live this one life was not an easy task,
but to contemplate an unending future and to know that there would be
no way to do anything now about that future...He implored, "Should I
beg the king of the underworld to extend my life so that I can learn about
resurrection?"

He remembered a story of a monk.

Once there was a monk who ignored all monastic duties and instead
indulged himself in mischievous behavior. Finally the time came for his
death, and the messengers of death came to take him, carrying all the
implements for punishment. The monk was oblivious about what he
had done but was aware that he had to avoid the situation. He didn't
know what to do and trembled all over. With extreme politeness he
begged with all his heart, "Please allow me seven days. I would like to
live like a real monk at least for those days before I die." Since the request was to live like a real monk, the messengers of death thought they
should allow him that opportunity. They granted the request and withdrew. The monk practiced with a *hwadu* that he had heard before: "Ten
thousand things return to one. What is this one?"[25] He so concentrated
on this question as to make his doubt become one with the universe. On
the seventh day, the messengers returned. They searched all over but
could not find the monk and returned to their realm empty-handed. The
monk had concentrated on his doubt about this one thing for the seven
days and reached the stage of one mind, wherein even doubt itself was

cut off and thus not discernible to anyone. That was because the being born and dying of a being became self-reliant for him at that stage.

For the great person, being born and dying are of the same world, whereas for a common person, the separate states of being born and dying succeed one another, which is why the ordinary person suffers through ten thousand lives and ten thousand deaths. In front of me lies the sea of ten thousand lives and ten thousand deaths, in which I would drift and suffer for lives to come. Is this not a horrifying reality? If I am able to get into a state of quietness and clarity, undisturbed by my surroundings, as had the monk chased by the messengers of death, I might be able to save myself. But I know too well that having no spiritual cultivation during my lifetime, I cannot expect such power to suddenly come to me at this moment. This makes me give up any thought of even making an appeal to the messengers...

Ahhh...I'm really in serious trouble. The only result of my existence here would be to make my wife a widow and my children fatherless...that would be it. It's said that affection is the cause of suffering. And because of my affections, my current wife and my children have to deal with this suffering with no idea of when it will end. My former wife who joined the monastery overcame this suffering caused by affection and found eternal liberation, and now her path and my own are as separate as that of heaven and earth. I wish now that I'd not known about this...

Was he frowning or was he crying? A rain of tears fell down the dying man's face. But Sukhŭi was rather glad to hear such an unexpected confession from the poor soul. Muting the sound of her breath, she paid attention to his story. At times when the patient seemed to have difficulty speaking, she would withdraw to the hallway to chat with his mother-in-law, or she would leaf through a newspaper in the patient's room and give him time to rest. But the doctor insinuated that it would be better for her to leave the patient alone. Sukhŭi withdrew from the patient's room altogether and went to see his wife, who was, for the time being, staying in a corner room with her children so as to protect the patient from their noise. The wife's face was slimmer than it had been three years prior when Sukhŭi last saw her, but her slender white face still looked young and beautiful. The moment Sukhŭi saw her, the idea that she would be a widow at such a young age brought Sukhŭi keen pain and tears wet her eyes. But the wife seemed rather calm, saying in a somewhat embarrassed voice that the room must smell bad because of the children. She made room for Sukhŭi to sit down and said,

My husband's condition was really serious yesterday. As his final moment was approaching, since he knew that it would be absolutely dark, he said that he regretted stayed away from Buddhism, and for the same reason, he wanted, as his final words, to tell the family he was leaving behind about the Buddhist teachings. He said he would speak with utmost sincerity and begged me to take his words to heart. He said that as time was a succession of day and night, life was a repetition of birth and death, and we could not avoid the fact that we would all die one day, I should not feel sad about his death. He said he felt sorry that he would have to leave me with the care of the children, but that instead of his protection, which after all was only the protection of a human being whose spiritual and material capacities were quite limited, there existed a principle, the absolute power, that would allow us to lead a better and more secure life when it comes to the issue of life and death. He said that I might think it inappropriate to say such things on his deathbed, but because he had neglected to share Buddhist teachings even with his own family, he was facing a desperate situation in his final days. He continued, "People say that what one says on one's deathbed is sincere. What I will talk about from now on is truly precious teachings. If you have a faith in what I say and practice it, even as a widow, no, even though you would die five thousand times, your life would be one of happiness without end. If there were someone who could satisfy all your demands and make you a perfect person, would you not go hundreds of miles to meet that person and give all you have in order to obtain what you want? I would lead you to a teacher you can meet right here who can provide you with special teachings. All you need to obtain these teaching is your faith, as you have it now, and your sincerity."

He continued: "Who is the person who gives us all we need and makes us someone who can give everything we have? That is Avalokiteśvara Bodhisattva. Avalokiteśvara Bodhisattva said that sentient beings are self-indulgent and fail to maintain a focused mind. If sentient beings repeatedly call the name Avalokiteśvara Bodhisattva, like a child calling for its mother, at first the calling might be nothing but a mechanical gesture, but the time would come when the mouth and the heart correspond to each other. That is the time when the person becomes connected with Avalokiteśvara Bodhisattva, who would then grant all the person's wishes. Not only that, but at the ultimate stage, the person who calls the name of Avalokiteśvara Bodhisattva would realize that the person herself is the one in whom everything is provided; she is a complete being; she is herself Avalokiteśvara Bodhisattva. You should completely rely on the Great Compassionate Mother, Avalokiteśvara.

However great the love of your parents, relatives, or your children for you, they are all limited human beings, like me, whose limitations prevent me from satisfying your wishes. But Avalokiteśvara is the Compassionate Mother in whom everything is provided. She has no beginning and no end in responding to your wishes. I thought that telling you about this would be like leaving you with a great treasure, more precious than enlisting people to protect you, or leaving you with great assets. You should keep this in mind: One calls out for Avalokiteśvara when one feels one's capacity falls short or when one feels it necessary to rely on others. But in fact, by calling out to Avalokiteśvara, one comes to realize the identity of the being who is calling out Avalokiteśvara and realize that one is Avalokiteśvara oneself. This is awakening. The food one eats is beneficial only for the body, but calling the name of the Buddha is nutrition that benefits both body and mind."

As she finished the story, a smile spread over the wife's face. She said, "I was deeply impressed by his talk and even wondered why he had not told me about all these valuable teachings before. Yesterday afternoon my husband received various treatments from Dr. Pak, a well-known doctor in the field. It seems that the treatments worked. Before the treatment, my husband was not able to eat or sleep at all, but last night he slept well and this morning he finished an entire bowl of gruel." The wife looked relieved. That could represent the mind of someone who believes in and wishes for something that he desperately needs, however absurd that wish might be. If the wife had prayed to the Buddha sincerely enough to pay for the couple's karma, her wish could have been realized. However, she didn't seem to have such strong faith yet... "What a pathetic hope she had," Sukhŭi thought, feeling an empathetic sadness toward the wife.

At five o'clock in the afternoon, Sukhŭi went back to the patient's ward. He welcomed her as if he had been waiting for her, and his facial muscles moved slightly with excitement. The patient seemed to collect all his energy to talk to Sukhŭi. He continued his story.

My wife knew nothing about Buddhism. From time to time, we went together to the Buddhist center, pretending to learn about Buddhism but also just for entertainment. I also went to Buddhist temples more like I was sightseeing, even though I said I went there to make offerings to the Buddha. Buddhist temples are one's religious home where one's ancestors rest, but when people go to Buddhist temples, they say they go for sightseeing. How ignorant I was! I didn't make time to hear about Buddhist teachings, nor did I spare time to talk about them. While living as a completely secular person, I have almost forgotten even the idea of evoking a religious thought to either to my family or my students. The only responsibilities of which I was aware were those associated with humane feelings. Now my end is close, and I did not have a chance to say anything meaningful. Such was my situation when you came to see me. I was much encouraged that you were moved by my words, and I said much more than I expected. As you know, in Buddhist teachings there are four difficult things to attain: that is, it is difficult to be born as a human, it is difficult to be born as a man, it is difficult to join a monastery, and it is difficult to attain Buddhist teachings (to become a complete being). Among the four difficult things, the first is to attain this body of a human; even though it might have only a fragmented mind, we should make every effort not to lose this body in our next lives. Only in a human body can we rely on the mind to make a correct judgment to study Buddhist teachings and practice how to concentrate one's mind.

The Buddha said that people in heaven indulge themselves in joy and thus fail to cultivate their minds, whereas people in hell are focused solely on the struggle with suffering and animals are too dull for spiritual cultivation. Only humans in the *sahā* world, where there is both joy and pain, are in the proper situation to practice how to find oneself, that is, to find the ultimate truth. I was born as a human being in the *sahā* world, I was born as a man, I joined a monastery, and I encountered the correct teachings of the Buddha. What a beneficial situation I was in! But because of the poison of feelings and attachments, I have given up all of those favorable conditions—which could have taken ten thousand eons of time to obtain—and I am now facing this last moment, an extreme situation that shows no promise of ending...

In the springtime approximately ten years ago, I went to Kyŏnsŏng Hermitage to see my former wife, who had joined the monastery. She told me that I should recover the mind in this life, while I am still a human being...

Sŏn Master Man'gong said to the gathered assembly, "Nothing is more pitiful than losing a human body wearing the robe of a monk." His thunderous voice still echoes in my ears, but...

"The patient made a face," Sukhŭi said. "He seemed to struggle to express what was on his mind. A bluish color suddenly spread like sweat over his forehead and you could hear the sound of him swallowing."

Sukhŭi felt stifled as if the sky, the earth, the patient, and herself were gradually being suffocated. A doctor hurriedly tried an emergency measure against the background of the wailing of the patient's wife, children, and parents—"sadness" doesn't begin to express the scene. But, on second thought, more pitiful even than this hellish situation where one person rushed out to call for doctors while others hurried to contact relatives was the patient himself. He was now the protagonist in a tragedy at its most extreme. The situation at the time was painful enough; however, once the patient passed beyond the boundary between life and death, he would have to suffer in the unfathomable abyss of three hellish realms (of hell, of hungry ghosts, and of animals) for who knows how long.

Sukhŭi said, "What other things could the patient think about at the moment when he was about to plunge into this abyss?" This body is like a garment made of the mind that is called "me." We can change clothes whenever they get torn or wear out. When we change our clothes, the form of the clothes changes according to our state of mind. We have generated a thousand or ten thousand different garments that we wear one after another, each of which is what we call our body. How many times we change our body should not be a big deal, and yet we still call it "death" and take it as a serious matter. How ignorant we are to think like that. Sukhŭi continued her report: We should be able to change our clothes at will, but instead, changing is understood as a death and both the person who is facing death and those around the dying person howl in despair. But fortunately neither has completely lost consciousness. The patient, who was on the verge of passing through the division of life and death, was stunned by the danger he was facing. However, at the same time, through the energy generated by the situation, he overcame the pain of dying and managed to regain his breath and speak again. He said,

> I am now facing misery at its extreme in the exposure of reality. In front of me is my lonely soul, which is about to lose this body and whose path ahead is unknown. My dead body will be drowned in the sea of tears shed by my widowed wife and fatherless children and carried to a burial place amidst the mourning songs of pallbearers. My young widow and my fatherless children, who would now be as far away from me as the distance between heaven and earth, have rice to eat and a house to stay in for today. But in the future, without a husband or a father, they might face a miserable situation of hunger and cold under the eaves of someone else's house. Who can say this could not happen…

The patient was not able to finish, Sukhŭi continued, because the relentless messenger of death rushed toward him and removed from the body his poor soul, which quietly and without resistance followed the messenger. The dead body looked calm and undisturbed, as if the patient's good will had composed it. Sukhŭi continued, "Following the will of her husband, the wife, though deep in sorrow, seemed to believe in the great power and compassion of Bodhisattva Avalokiteśvara, as she constantly moved her lips to call out the bodhisattva's name. She behaved with calmness and, although she did not yet look to be fully mature, she effectively performed her role as head mourner. Her five-year-old child followed her everywhere grumbling for something to eat. Those present could not but shed a tear at the scene."

A dharma teacher who was there for a service gave a dharma talk for the soul. Sukhŭi wrote down parts of the poem that he delivered and showed them to me.

> From where does life come?;
> To where does death go?
> Life is an arising of a fragment of floating clouds,
> Death is a disappearance of a fragment of floating clouds,
> The floating clouds originally do not have their own nature;
> And so do life, death, coming, and going.
> There exists one thing that always exists;
> Settled deep, it does not follow life and death.[26]

The forty-nine days of prayer for the dead took place at Kyŏnsŏng Hermitage, where his former wife, Chuhŭi, was staying.[27] The prayer was performed at Kyŏnsŏng Hermitage because Sŏn Master Man'gong, who was known to have great dharma power in offering guidance for the dead, was there. Sukhŭi, who was at the deathbed of the husband, also attended the first seventh-day prayer, where she met Chuhŭi. Following is a story of Chuhŭi that Sukhŭi told to me as she heard it at the ceremony. The former wife said,

> When I first began our marriage, our priority was to settle the internal and external aspects of our lives. If he were to avoid battling the dusty streets, whether he was going far or staying close by, I had to give my husband streetcar fare of ten cents. I did my part to help the budget with whatever income I made from my writing. We didn't mind wearing worn-out socks and shabby serge suits. I had to buy kitchenware as well. With frugal housekeeping, we were able to pay off all our debts and our family life was finally on track. We also had no problems in our love life. My husband had suffered all his life from the lack of both material resources and sincere human relationships. He completely relied on me and was fully satisfied with our life together. At this moment in my

life, I decided to leave my husband. After my departure, the house was empty except for my husband and a housekeeping girl. Even my belongings were packed and set aside in one corner of the house. Since my husband had lived in a monastery before, he knew what I would need. Like a mother packing for her daughter who is about to go study abroad, he packed for me a knife, a pair of a scissors, a lamp, and even a spoon and chopsticks. He was such a kind person and quietly endured the pain against which he was absolutely powerless. As I was leaving, my husband looked at me with complete helplessness even as he marshaled all his energy to remain calm. Knowing how he felt, my heart was heavy in leaving home, even though my journey was to find the hope of the absolute. Once I arrived at the monastery, I could be more rational in judging the situation. He had asked me to come back after three years to continue our married life. He had also said, completely obsessed with his affection for me, that he had not yet satisfied his desires and thus could not give them up. Before we married we had discussed the possibility of joining a monastery together. More than that, he had made vows before various buddhas and bodhisattvas and received precepts. He became a follower of unsurpassed Buddhist teachings to be a teacher of humans and gods and wear the clothes of the most precious. I couldn't believe that now he could say such horrible things. I came to hear the dharma talk that all sentient beings were trapped by the chains of love and thus destined to endure extreme suffering into infinity. I suffered because of love, but I was also trying to decide if I could possibly remain attached to it. He had lived a life of extreme privation of human affection, and I could understand why, for the time being, he might want to continue on with his life, but I thought that in due time he would find the correct path. However, he never did change his mind, which made the way he ended his life inevitable.

Chuhŭi continued,

He was repentant on his deathbed, but it is clear that he did so simply because he knew about the teaching of causality, which made him realize that his life after death was hopeless, that he would have to face suffering for an infinite period of time. This scared him unbearably, and he howled with fear. I am saying this because, even though he was moved by the sight of a Catholic woman voluntarily sacrificing herself for religion, he still hadn't returned to his religion. That being so, how could there be room for him to teach the greatness of religion while he was facing his own death? Moreover, he demonstrated a lack of knowledge about religion. The believing mind is the mind of absolute sincerity. Absolute sincerity means that all polarization should be removed and even the name and form of absolute sincerity should be forgotten. It is a state in which religion, the believing mind, the Buddha, Jesus Christ, should all be forsaken. Yet he was haranguing about this state in words. The Catholic woman's action was laudable, but it might be that her story was not sincere enough to lead others to a state of absolute sincerity. I once heard a story about a woman named Ilyŏm. Influenced by the Buddha of the Jewel Light, Ilyŏm sold about a pound of her flesh to a sick person every day for a week, and she donated all the money to the Buddha of the Jewel Light. As she heard the simple teaching that this mind is the Buddha, she became awakened. I was greatly impressed by this story.

After I joined the monastery, I had difficulty focusing on my practice, and, in turn, I was confused about my own self. The agony was so strong that I would rather have been extinguished. I thought I wouldn't care if I didn't attain buddhahood because I hadn't realized what it means to be a real human being. I knew that the extinction of the material did not lead to the disappearance of the real life that is the basis of material existence. When I was still in the secular world, when I was in a state of absolute despair, I felt secure because I thought I had a last resort, which was to give up everything, that is, to take my own life. But when I realized the principle that one does not die, my agony reached an extreme point. It was truly a suffocating situation and I cried a great deal. At that time I thought that if only I could come to realize who "I" am I would be willing to jump into a den of lions or into a fire. But still it seemed that I was not capable of bearing the pain of cutting off a pound of my own flesh every day for a week…

The woman's behavior was true evidence that she had acted with ultimate sincerity. That she did not die even after she had cut off more than ten pounds of her flesh is proof that the foundation of life is the mind, that is, independent creativity, that it does not rely on the flesh, that this flesh is a house created and destroyed by the mind. When the material mind and the mindful mind become one in all sincerity, the life and death of this body can be controlled by the mind. Even though one has yet to attain one's self, which is the owner of the wholesome mind, if the believing mind is strong, the power of the mind will enable the person to perform miraculous acts. Jesus also said that with belief as small as a mustard seed a person can move a great mountain and bring it to him. The believing mind is one's own mind, and that is because one's mind is all-capable creativity. That is to say, absolute sincerity has no exceptions…It is devoting oneself without margins; if one devotes oneself without margins, one will, in turn, earn the entire universe without margins and live life on a universal scale. This is the principle that one should give up everything to earn everything. In other words, once one devotes the small self in its entirety, one would earn, in return, the big self.[28]

If he had been able to repent at the last moment of his life to the degree that he could completely give up himself, everything could have been resolved. I am truly sorry that that was not the case. If he had been sincerely penitent, he would not have had a chance to even think about how helpless he would be in his afterlife, and in that case he would be in a state of quietness where all linguistic expression had been eliminated and there would be no sense of regret. Instead, he shed dry tears and ranted pointlessly. Even while he was in an absolute panic, not knowing how to face his own death, he still could not detach himself from worries about his poor wife and children. Since this life is an illusion, a sense of helplessness about the future and the fear of evil outcomes are delusions. All one needs to do is find one's own mind, which is the root of all delusions, and, thus, enter into calmness. He was unable to reach this point, which means that he was unable to get to the bottom of religious consciousness. But he was a conscientious person during his lifetime, and, though belatedly, he did have regrets. Since he returned to the Buddha, if only in his thoughts, and died quietly, scolding himself, he might not lose the Buddha's teachings in his next life. But he had lost his footing on the edge of a cliff and as a result had led a life that could only go downward all the way, and since it is said that being born a human being again is a chance of less than one out of a hundred, one cannot guarantee…At any rate, I hope that the dharma talk given by the great master helped him to liberate himself. It is said that a soul is less dull than a being with a physical body…

During the first seventh-day prayer ceremony for the dead, I prayed to Earth-Store Bodhisattva with a mind that was absolutely empty but still wishing that the poor dead would be well-delivered. For some reason, tears fell from my eyes to the back of my hand, and I could not help smiling.

Saying this, Chuhŭi smiled again, followed by a light sigh. She said, "An act of a comic-tragedy with a person I've had a special relationship with seems to have come to an end now." She looked up at me and said, "Anyway, I learned about this urgent issue too late and belatedly joined the monastery. I need to make the best of every second of my life…" She straightened her position with a face full of strain. "I should take him as an example, be on alert and be more dedicated to my practice." She calmly dropped her head.

As I listened to Chuhŭi's story, I came to understand why and how she could give up the husband she loved and her beautiful family life with him to join the monastery. Even when everything goes well in everyday life such that what is and is not, what one likes and does not like, seems clear, or when one has a great many assets or a business that is prospering, it is not easy to maintain that situation. How much more so when it comes to things related to the mind that one cannot control at will? In this spiritual world, it is easy to go downward, but it is extremely difficult to ameliorate one's status. Thinking that, I could well understand why Chuhŭi worried about her husband's afterlife, based on how he lived during his lifetime.

Though only for a brief period of time, you also sincerely talked to me about improving the state of my spiritual life.[29] But at that time I understood everything about you under one label: love. I was such an incapable person, even now, as I witness the situation of Chuhŭi's husband, which should make me fully alert, I am rather bewildered and my mind is muddled. I was like the person walking on a dark mountain. I momentarily saw a light from the other side of the mountain but was in the darkness again and lost my companion as well. I took a path only to find that the path was blocked by enormous mountains; I took another path, which turned out to be the path toward the mouth of a huge snake. I was hopeless and stifled—that was the state of my mind, which I would like to show you even for a very brief moment. It seems that the string of love is too rough and my mind is too weak.

You told me that the person who is aware of the strong mind that enables her to be the final winner is the person who attains oneness of self and others without any distinction. If that is true, then our lives, wherein one gender misses the other gender and one body burns with desire for another body, are like the tragedy of pheasants in the springtime, which, made to feel moody by their own sounds, chirp until they bleed to death! But all human beings are characters in this tragedy. Isn't this why even Śakyamuni Buddha said that if there had been two loves, he would not have been able to attain buddhahood? The Buddha endured with all his strength the relentless pain of separation from loved ones and attained buddhahood. Like him, I should bear this momentary loneliness so as to overcome the solitude of ten thousand eons of time.

A moth lured by the light will head toward the fire and, unable to see the pile of dead bodies of its moth-friends, will scorch itself to death. Like that moth, I was blinded by my affection and couldn't think about the inexhaustible danger of the three evil paths ahead of me. It's said that, in the eyes of a hen, a diamond is worth less than a grain of barley. At the moment all I can think about is your love; I have no time to think about attaining buddhahood or anything else. I can practice forbearance and suppress material desire, but, like one overwhelmed by sleep, I can do nothing about this mind obsessed with love, however pitiful I think it is. What should I do? If my mind had been fully guarded when you were with me, as it is now that you are gone, you couldn't have found a way to leave me. How did this happen? You are gone now, and the back yard where you are absent overflows with my longing for you. In my restlessness, time sometimes feels too long and sometimes too short such that physical time totally loses its value and the idea of long or short seems meaningless. But still I feel that it has been a long time since you left.

Isn't it true that whatever reaches its extremity should face an end? Standing at the dead-end of waiting, I might leave on a journey with empty baggage and no desire to return. If you then had to come back to this empty yard where I once struggled with despair, even if you came floundering through the bushes with tears in your eyes, you would be but an object of ridicule to the birds in the air. Ah, it is not too late. Please come back before my breath, which is sustained by my waiting, is cut off...

The reality that appears before me after aimless talk of my situation is that my letters have piled up on my desk; these are letters that you should definitely read. There should be a time when these letters find their way to you and are touched by you. When that happens, if only out of sympathy for another human being, you should shed some tears for me. With a desperate hope that those tears might change your mind, I have written about my feelings in detail, as if I could send them through the flow of my tears. I wonder whether there might be a way to send them to you. The day my desperate hope is realized will be the day when all of my sorrow, caused by our separation, comes to an end, and I shed all my tears in advance of the day when I can separate myself from my sorrow.

Would that I could send my letters through my tears, which are running down my face! What a helpless and deplorable idea that is! He didn't even say where he was heading; he ran away to the end of the sky or the bottom of the earth. Still I can't forget this heartless person who disappeared without a trace, gone for months now. With hope of letting him know of my anxious mind, I write down my sad stories, but I don't know where to send these letters. Should I send them via water? There are a hundred, a thousand, no, ten thousand different streams and rivers. By which stream or river should I send my letters? How wretched and hopeless my situation is!

Should I send my letters saddled on the fallen leaves? Shall I drop them from a plane? Whatever way I might try, I still wouldn't know where to send them. Since they don't have the recipient's address, I could call all of the postmen in the world asking them to deliver my letters, but there would still be no way for them to be delivered. My letters that cannot be sent... This is a crazy thing to be doing... My heart, which was rather numb, suddenly heated up and I wanted to shred all of my letters. But I calmed down and I folded them up randomly and threw them away. They fell next to the sliding door where they unfolded, scattering about here and there. The letters were not culpable, nor did they seem to blame me or feel pain. They were lying there quietly, waiting to be picked up. Feeling uneasy about further mistreating those innocent letters, I retrieved them and embraced them to my bosom. I cried wretchedly, and there was no end to it. Even when I lost both of my parents and was left all alone like an orphan, I don't think I felt as miserable as I felt the day I cried with my letters in my arms. I cried and cried with nobody to stop me, nobody to pity me, nobody to chastise me. I cried and cried until I was completely exhausted; then I felt empty, as if sorrow had come to an end and my tears had all dried out.

I sat still for a while, guarding the darkness and gazing at the sliding door, and what I had thought in the spring the year before crept stealthily into my mind. I had asked myself, "Will there be a time when you will free yourself from these dual responsibilities of letting in the person I am waiting for and also of letting him go?" At that time I had asked myself why I played with such an absurd idea, but on this day I thought, "Now you have really fulfilled your responsibilities." I felt a renewed sense of impermanence at that moment and suddenly I experienced a turning point in my thinking. You once told me that all the things in the world are changing, and before the joy of a meeting dies out, the sorrow of separation arrives. We should therefore not indulge in the joy of seeing each other; rather, the only thing to do is practice reaching the state of "oneness." The day we attain the understanding that meeting and separation are one and that love and hatred are not two, we will attain unchanging comfort, free from being disturbed by meeting, separation, love, or hatred.

At the edge of a cliff of despair, drowned in a sea of tears, I remembered your words and came to realize the true meaning of impermanence. I realized, too, that the reality of impermanence was of my own making, that I was the one who created meetings and separations that perpetually alternated with each other. So, why should I feel pain over that? Reality is a process of change; however great a person might be—even a righteous patriot fully committed to saving his own life—if his breath stops, he will be buried. The tomb might turn into rice fields less than a hundred years after the person's death, and those who plough them will in turn face the day when they return to the fields. And again it will not be long before those fields turn into a swamp. Is this not true?

The past has gone, the present is passing and will be combined with the coming future and soon be gone without leaving a trace. With the two wheels of transmigration, our lives are turning and turning around. What reality, then, had I hung onto so desperately, refusing to let you go? Whatever is visible and thinkable is subject to change and passing away, including our affections. For what reason, therefore, did I rely on them, believe in them so firmly? I was not aware of this reality and naïvely relied on you. As a house crumbles when the crossbeams fall down, on the day you left me, all of my hopes were plunged into a sea of despair. However, when the state of disillusionment is exhausted, the state of truth appears. Everyday reality is an illusion, but it is also a principle that this reality is part of the history of eternity, so there is no way to avoid it. As we get attached to reality, suffering occurs. Finding a way to avoid this suffering, that is, finding a secure ground that is also the foundation of everyday reality is the state of truth. This is the state where the past and the present become the same moment and where here and there become the same place.

To find this state of truth does not require much time or exclusively rely on religious doctrines; nor are there fixed principles leading to this state. There is no time when we don't have the mind; the only thing we need to do is master this mind in its entirety. This does not exclude even a single strand of hair; this is the mind that is on the other side of the everyday mind. Standing at the edge of a cliff of despair with no one to rely on, I let myself indulge in shedding a sea of tears, but I managed to move one step further, to where I could unify my mind. In that state I finally decided to withdraw from the attachments of the secular world and devote all of my energy to the teachings to discover myself, which is the true reality of one's mind. Once I decided to follow this path, the universe was one with me. It became so clear at this point that the phenomenal world is my body and that its inner reality, which is not visible in the phenomenal world, is my mind. If I had not realized this marvelous teaching, I would have remained bound by the chains of love, which I had created myself, and would have had to endure untold suffering in lives to come. A maxim has it that a misfortune will transform into a fortune, and my situation was exactly like that.

If I could have formed a happy family with you, not only would I have been unable to realize that all the things in the world are changing, but also it would have been difficult for me to return to the purity of the mind. Without regaining purity of mind, it would have been even more difficult for me to concentrate on spiritual cultivation. Food enriches the body, but cultivation of the mind is the true nutrition of the body and the mind. I don't know how much of what I'm saying now I've put into practice, but at least I know that without the mind, the true life cannot survive. That's why I'm just happy to be in a situation where I can focus on my practice free of distractions. This is the great gift that you have given to me. I will offer you even more profound gratitude when I've completed my practice. I know that I should not be satisfied with a small achievement. What is precious is to plant seeds, take care of them, and eventually earn the reward of your efforts at the harvest, but if you give up in the midst of farming, or even after finishing the year's farming, if you stop short before harvesting, all of your efforts will be for nothing. Likewise, if you are satisfied with your accomplishment and stop before you reach the final state, you will be no different from ignorant, sentient beings in that you will have to face the suffering of life and death. This is why I've decided to follow the path of Chuhŭi and become a nun at Kyŏnsŏng Hermitage. Kyŏnsŏng Hermitage is a place that offers the right environment for practice as well as companions for practice. And it has great teachers. I was told that Great Sŏn Master Man'gong teaches there.

At the moment, the wind, which seems to be the only thing not sleeping, is making a soft sound. Walking all alone on the dark street, even the sound of the roasted chestnut seller has become silent. My eyes are still fully open, and it doesn't seem that I will go to sleep; instead I would prefer to send to the entire world this happiest of news, and I sing a song delivering my great vow as follows:

I sing a song;
At my song, the numbers called time and the limitation called space
     melt down;
In order to give absolute freedom to my song,
I have refused to confine my song to the beautiful bindings of high
     and low of melody and long and short of rhythm;
I sing my song out loud, in whatever manner I like;
My song is not a lyric that embraces sorrow and enriches joy;
Nor is it a didactic phrase that encourages the good and discourages
     the bad;
Nor is it the lofty words of the beings in heaven, nor the screams of
     suffering of the beings in hell;

If there were someone who praised my song or who claimed to understand it, that would do nothing but denigrate it;

Am I trying to explain the principle of the universe, which even
Śakyamuni Buddha could not tell? I wouldn't dare have such
an idea;

I just hum a hundred, or a thousand marvelous phrases that both
sentient and insentient beings speak every day as they are;

That is why even a rotten pile of soil or a dried wood stump would
respond to my song; the pressing sense of empty air makes the
rain stop its cry and the wind its laughter;

Waves unceasingly in motion stop their pressing pace, and even the
flat earth, the idler of the universe, moves its ass;

The joyful music in the heaven that has never ceased day or night
calms down on its own, and the whip in hell that is ceaselessly
flogged against sinners quietly falls from the hand of the dead,
who is enthralled;

But it is at a marketplace where I sing the song;

"It's cheap," "No, it's expensive" — the shouting of people bargain-
ing shakes the earth, which swallows my song, like smoke is
absorbed by a cyclone;

As though I am filling a bottomless pot, I continue to sing my song
with an even louder voice, even though it cannot be sustained;

Even if a pot is bottomless, if one continues to pour water into it
without ending, wouldn't that water fill the earth, and eventually the bottomless pot would be filled as well?

I would sing my song for the lives to come until it would overflow
the entire universe; I would let my song be heard even through
the earmuffs that you wear to turn off my song;

I would do nothing but sing my song in a loud voice.

Behind me a clock is telling me that it is three o'clock. In the secular
world, it's time for everybody to be at rest. Even the sound of the breathing of the empty air has stopped. But you once told me that in all Buddhist
monasteries they get up at three in the morning. Last year I stayed for a
night at P'yoch'ung Monastery. At three in the morning an old master was
chanting in a gentle voice, a sound that deeply moved me. Embarrassed to
listen to the master's chanting while lying in bed, I got myself up despite
the fatigue and sat in a humble position listening to him. This experience
made me imagine you sitting in meditation in the quietness of early morning; it is as though I could actually see the scene. (I imagined you sitting
with a woman.)

I thought that your feelings for me were deep, but if you were with another woman, how much deeper must your feelings have been for her to desert me? I'm only worried that being with a woman might create an obstacle to your spiritual cultivation. Please understand that my worries are not like some pathetic flower bouquet sent, along with miserable feelings, as a gift to an ex-lover on his wedding day. I'm a different person from yesterday when I wrote in tears. This experience has made me realize that, depending on your state of mind, you can control life, death, suffering, and joy at will. Because I didn't know about the principle that I am the only one who is fully responsible for my existence, I didn't have clear standards for my life. Nor was I aware of the violent force of life, its determination, and its bloody rules. What great danger I was in in those childish days! In a very short period, my attitude about my feelings completely changed, and now I want to offer my story to all the men and women who suffer from failed love affairs.

To put it simply, as one thought arises, the separation between life and death, suffering and pleasure, self and others, man and woman, occurs. When a border between self and others is drawn, one's sense organs perceive polarization; once a boundary between man and woman is made, everything is understood through this distinction. We have all lived multiple lives, and in the course of these multiple lives we must have had relationships with many different people and have been married to some of them. Meeting a person creates the relationship; turning away from another creates separation. If one would accept this without disturbance to the mind, there would be no need to fight over "your wife" or "my husband," nor would there be any need to struggle to forget those whom you have loved. One would lead a free life, and how peaceful it would be.

It's said that because beings in heaven do not have attachments, the exchange of feelings is complete at each moment and feelings don't stagnate. However, in the world of sentient beings, the desire for love, possessions, and fame has a strong hold; there is no end of suffering and struggle caused by love. We should realize that love and hatred are not two different concepts, and different genders were originally one in oneself. If a person reaches this state of understanding of the nature of self, whether he loves or hates, whether he is a being in heaven or a sentient being on earth, he leads an independent life without being derailed. To lead such a life is what is meant by the life of the "great self." In order to achieve it, the "small self" must be extinguished, leaving not even a remnant as infinitesimal as the tip of a hair. Is this not true? Isn't it the case that while we are still alive, we should be able to separate from our own physical body? However disappointing this world might be, we have lived this reality repeatedly for an eternal period of time, and it would not be easy to get rid of the habitual energy that was soaked in the complexity of that life. That gives us all the more reason to be more dedicated to our cultivation of mind.

The night has now gone. The eyes of the lamp light that so courageously dominated and defeated even the darkest night have now gone dim. The sounds of all the moving things in the world begin to reach me. I, too, should put down my pen and welcome the new day. Today is my new day, which I encounter only once in a thousand years. This is the day when my resurrected life starts. In the innumerable lives I have lived, I do not know how many comedies and tragedies and how much suffering and pleasure, all of my own making, I have gone through. But today is the day all of them are cremated. Together with them, I will today have a ceremony to say good-bye forever to the two extreme lives you offered me: the extreme happiness that I had had with you and the extreme sorrow that I had to deal with after you left me. And yet again, today is the day of my departure to explore the eternal future life. I feel satisfied and happy because I think I have prepared myself well before my departure (having cultivated myself through calm meditation).

In the secular world, when a person does things with a slightly concentrated mind, they call it spiritual cultivation. What I call spiritual cultivation is no such a thing. For me, spiritual cultivation is an effort to discover one's self-nature in the clear state of no-thought in which thoughts are cut off, language is blocked, and conjunctions are not allowed. The entire universe is my self without an exterior. We should stop living as if we are an extra pound of flesh (the life of one who has lost herself). We must turn it around and make the blood vessels and nerves of the real body — the universe — circulate so that we can laugh and cry together with the earth, trees, and even a piece of tile or a stone. Isn't this the truth? Isn't this the way to lead the life of an awakened being? Whoever it might be, if the person engages in self-reflection and examines the other side of her thoughts, she will eventually discover the real self.

You may leave me now. I wouldn't dislike it if you wanted me back, but it wouldn't fill me with ecstasy if you came back. If you don't come back at all, that's fine too, because I've grown up and will cry no more. All of these alternatives are possible now because I have confidence that I am qualified to be your lover or your colleague. And that is because I have realized that meeting and parting are not two different things. I am also determined to dedicate myself to bringing about a hopeful future when I'm the teacher of humans and gods as well as of you. I've decided to be an "early person," a being before the existence of the Buddha or God: I've decided to become a nun.

The Chinese character for "nun" (*sŭng*) is a combination of a radical indicating a human and the main character signifying "early" or "already." This must mean that a nun is a human being before the existence of all beings, before the creation, and that this being would be the teacher of humans and gods. The "early person" is a sincere being who is equipped with the mind before the creation. Even a human who is not able to be a nun can be a real human once she has discovered her own mind and once real life begins.

I shout out loud once again, "One hundred years' education is worth less than a moment of change in one's thinking!"

Thinking is everything, and if a person turns around his way of thinking without leaving even an infinitesimal remnant of old ideas, on the spot he will achieve the "great self." A small bit of awakening of this reality has brought me this much joy!

By changing the way I think, I realize that my world has become more spacious. When I unite with time and space, if I wanted the sky to become the earth, the sky would become the flat earth. If I were to tell the earth to turn itself into the sky, the earth would immediately resolve itself into energy and slowly ascend to the sky. I would also be capable of giving a twist to the directions, making east into west or making north into south. Right here where I am I would be able to construct either heaven or earth. Regardless of my gender, heaven and the empty sky would respond to me, and there would be correspondence between the yin force and yang force. In the places yet to be considered, all material that enables the accomplishment of desire exists. Once one can control one's thoughts at will, all things can be utilized to create one's own reality. Within the limit of my own imagination, I have the right to say things, however absurd those things might be, and because words are reality, I have the capacity to generate reality, however enormous that reality might be.

I was told that a lie exists only in this world. In heaven, because there is no gap between language, time, and space, and because the universe is one's own self, a lie cannot exist. Since all the beings in the world are aspects of me, there cannot be anything outside of my self and thus there can be no betrayal. Sentient beings are beaten by punishing instruments that they have themselves created. All the same, they howl in rancor against the sky, which they think punishes them. I have finally come to realize that I was one of those women.

I have made a harangue of this rather plain story. I just want to point out that because we sentient beings are so used to thinking that it is beyond our human capacity to accomplish something, however trivial, we don't even try. Instead we live enslaved within self-imposed constraints. Only when we discover our self and lead a life of our own can we find the meaning of human life. The small self must be completely extinguished so that we can attain the great self (the all-capable self, that is, the entire universe). We have to give up everything to earn everything. This is the very principle of the universe.

What a person thinks is her actuality, her reality, and her own being. That is why humans possess the capacity to be all-powerful. I am free and all-powerful, but I abandoned myself as a free and capable being and made myself a woman, forcing myself into a blind alley, calling for you, the man, until my voice broke. How crazy that was! How silly!

I am you, and you are me. I was struggling, calling for my own self. How pitiful that was, the image of a person who has lost her own self! If there were no way to change her way of thinking, she wouldn't know that even this partially functioning mind could be derailed as well.

When things go wrong with this physical body that lives only this one life, we know we can't dismiss the problem. How much more so when it comes to the unimaginably long extension of this one-time life. It would be impossible to measure the danger if something were to go wrong at the beginning of this life.

The path of happiness and that of misfortune are at the two ends of a gap in one's thought whose distance is as infinitesimal as the tip of a hair and will be fixed eternally. How frightening! There is nothing that does not disappear. Just moving around doesn't mean we are alive. The value of being here is powerful, and being alive means the movement of the mind, which is free from life and death. I was a living doll that was visible to people and capable of moving. It was because of you that I was able to change my thinking. How can I ever thank you enough? I must become the kind of person who can make it up to you. Only someone capable of repaying an obligation would make your work worthwhile. That would also be a person who accepts responsibility as a parent, child, and citizen. This is the way to become the complete person who fully accomplishes the mission of a human being.

To be a complete person who deserves your favor, a free being who has recovered her own self (resurrection) until the future worlds come to an end and afterward, I will devote myself to the dual path of concentrating on self-cultivation and discipline. I will pursue only this path, this authentic path of life.

> 28th April, the Year of the Monkey (1956)
> Kyŏnsŏng Hermitage (Remembering things
>   that had happened about thirty years ago)
> Kim Iryŏp

CHAPTER 12

With a Returned Gift in My Hand

It was more than thirty years ago, and yet it feels so recent, like something that happened just today. On the other hand, it also feels like a thing that happened a long while ago. When we met, you and I were adults who had already experienced married life, but we were purer and more passionate in our love than any boy and girl could be! Our love was like a universe.

There are only memories now. You've become a religious woman who has transcended the secular world, whereas I'm just an ordinary man occupied with secular affairs. However, because of my wish to attain buddhahood (to be a perfect being) in the future, I would like to tell you my story, and I offer it to you with my two palms together, like a prayer.

The past thirty years that we have been separated comprise but a brief time compared to eternity, but to a short-sighted person like me, it feels like quite a long period. All this time, and known only to me, I've lived without really ever separating from you. Now that what I've been doing secretly has been discovered, I'll tell you everything. It was me who twenty-four years ago had a small, cozy hermitage built outside of Pusan City and sent a person to invite you to be the head nun in charge of the meditation hall there. It was also me who three years later sent a lay Buddhist named Chŏngsimhaeng to ask you to come to Iryŏn Monastery to get treated by a doctor whom I'd arranged with to care for you. I promised the lay Buddhist that if she could manage to get you there, I would pay all the expenses of the monastery. Four or five years after that I was in Taechŏn in a business trip and thought to visit Kyŏnsŏng Hermitage, which I was told was in Sudŏk Monastery in Yesan, but I decided not to and instead sent 300,000 wŏn anonymously by mail.

I heard that you said you had received a command from your teacher, Zen Master Man'gong: "Until your nature becomes like a white lotus that will not be tainted by the secular world, you may not leave Tŏksung Mountain."[1] I heard as well that you said that while you could not be fully in charge of the workings of your mind because the mind is already influenced by one's karma, if you refused to obey your teacher's edict, which you could control, you could not claim to be his disciple. Having heard that, I realized that my behavior, which was based on my feelings, could have no influence on you. I couldn't forget you, but I silently tried to repress my thoughts, and in that way twenty years have passed. Twenty years is not a short period of time, but my business kept me busy so that the days and nights have gone by quickly. Even though a nun leads a life of seclusion, your life has been a topic of people's talk. That means that I hear about your life and pray that you will one day be able to help people save themselves.

Last month some people in our Taegu branch office were on a business trip and went all the way to Kyŏnsŏng Hermitage to see you. They said that the Zen center there had no permanent funding and seemed to be suffering from financial difficulty. When I heard that, I thought that if I could be connected with you, I would be willing to offer financial aid of some kind. And in the meantime I mailed you a bit of money. I was aware in doing so that the money might be returned.

As I suspected, it was returned. Even that was welcome news compared to the time when I was completely disconnected from you. Moreover, you sent me teachings of the Buddha. I will keep your letter and continue to receive pleasure from it. I greatly appreciate and will store away deep in my heart your intention in sending me that teaching. You wrote,

My hands are shaking as I read your letter; I'm trying hard not to lose my composure. It was unexpected, but as I held your letter in my hand, the former self of this nun, which was terribly devastated by the separation from you thirty-some years ago, appeared before my eyes like an image of a tragic woman in an old movie. The image scared me.

How great it would be if your check for a hundred thousand wŏn were a donation offered from your believing mind. This Zen center is desperately in need of ten thousand or even a thousand wŏn, not to mention a hundred thousand wŏn, because Buddhist practitioners live by begging. Even though we live by begging, in our minds we are the rich who have attained self-sufficiency.

I've heard that you have inherited a great many assets and have been very successful in increasing them. I've also heard that you use your wealth for a variety of charitable causes, establishing schools, orphanages, and hermitages, and personally manage diverse works in and outside of various institutions. But such works, seen from the eyes of the universe, are only a tiny part of what constitutes the world. A small brook cannot be compared to the great ocean. Moreover, business conducted without a foundation in spirituality will only meet a destructive, tragic end. That, too, is what happens to the rich man who spends without producing. In all cases, the spiritual ground should be solidified before any material business begins. What should be done first should be done before moving onto the next stage.

The business that human beings do has a cosmic dimension. That is because we own the universe (in fact, the universe is ourselves), and the universe is where we do business. Where would you ground your business now that you have lost all the grounds for business...? You have to prepare the rice in order to cook it. Likewise, you first have to regain what you own in order to carry out your business.

The universe is shared by all; in that regard even a warm or empty space has property rights. The value of our existence depends on how much we realize what we possess. That's why human beings are considered the most valuable of all beings. But even though we are humans we operate at the level of puppets. We eventually must regain what we originally possess and live as mindful human beings.

This Zen center is a place for studying how to become human, which is to say for engaging in the practice of regaining one's mind. When I say the mind, I do not mean the physical mind that feels pleasure or anger. The owner of this body and mind is creativity.[2] This creativity is a being without form or language or a mind with a direction in which to channel itself. That is why it is called emptiness or nothingness.

As a member of this Zen center, together with other practitioners I am in the process of confirming and declaring that the universe belongs to me. We have created a community in order to go through that process, a process that requires neither paper to write on nor language to write with. The process generates a document without a statement or a signature. The document represents non-thought and non-image and uses neither paper nor words. The process is completed when we reach the state where the flow of thought ceases and time becomes quiet and clear, the state where we are no longer constrained by time and space and thus can control time at will.

If we can maintain for a week a state of universalized non-thought, that is, a state of mind without even an infinitesimal distraction and thus without even an idea of thought, and if in that state of mind there arises one thought (arousal of a thought or awakening), the universe becomes ours.[3] This is a state in which a person reaches the level of the Great Vehicle. At this stage—in whatever body he is in, leading whatever life, doing whatever action— following his path without deviation, the person is complete and leads an independent life. At this point he finally becomes a human being, and his life as a human being can begin. In sum, we should learn and attain the foundation of all thoughts that occur before a thought arises.

The thought before a thought arises (activities before physical form) does not have a form; it does not get wet nor does it get burned. It is not disturbed by either pain and pleasure or life and death. Even when the entire universe is destroyed, it alone remains; it is the unsecured and infinite foundation. Anyone may take from it whatever portion he wants and it will never be diminished. This inexhaustible source belongs to each of us. Even the distance between ourselves and the concept of "belonging" needs to be removed. It *is* each of us. But misled by our delusions, we wander out there, searching for it outside ourselves, straying far away from it on a dangerous road.

Once we realize that we have lost our minds, that we have been wandering around perilous mountains and fields crowded with creatures trying to harm us, wouldn't it make sense to turn around? When I realized this reality twenty-seven years ago, I made up my mind to join the monastery and took the path back.

Just like a deer that smells water and heads directly toward that water, I know in which direction I should proceed. But my eyes are yet to be opened. Like a blind person who needs other people's confirmation that she is blind as well as the confirmation of her own experience, I finally became convinced that I am blind. How would I live life after life in endless repetition as a blind person? How would a pilgrim navigate the endless path without knowing the way?

To regain one's eyesight and to know one's path means to find the creativity of the universe that is our selves. This creativity is the other side of the idea of self or the universe; this thought does not require knowledge, nor does one need to search for it, nor to go nor to come. The other side of this thought, however, is not separate from this thought: Here and now cannot be separated from it.

Relying on our delusion, we pursued knowledge and proceeded on our path for numerous lives until we have now reached the point where we need to turn around, take the unknown path, and learn anew. This is what I call the "process." We need to calm ourselves and find some respite from the onslaught of thought after thought until we arrive at the point of no-ideas. We should learn not to learn and reach a state where we search no more.

Once you enter the maze, until you realize its inner structure, the troubling mind does not stop; until you come to the end of doubt, the mind cannot find peace. When you reach the state of no-thought, the state in which you learn how not to know, you will know the very essence of everything, which is momentary and all-inclusive. This is the state where you experience nothingness. At this stage you are able to function as a being unified with environments in a hundred or a thousand different situations; you are absolutely self-reliant. The reality [of the ability to do whatever you want] will suddenly dawn on you. Unless you experience it in your daily life, you cannot be said to have found the complete solution. You know without a doubt when you are leading the life you have realized in the state of no-thought; not even the Buddha can deny that. Therefore, you need to carry on with this practice until you experience it for yourself.

We feel self-sufficient and therefore rich when we learn that what we thought was reality was the work of our delusions. We here at this Zen center realize our self-sufficiency and thus feel wealthy. You're the one who is constrained by depravity, and yet you try to offer your sympathy to us, the affluent?

I would rather sacrifice my money, a million wŏn, and wait for you to reflect on this. I appreciate your offer and hope that you understand my intentions in returning this money.

Bhikṣuṇī Iryŏp
From Kyŏnsŏng Hermitage

I read your letter to the end without stopping but in a rather confused state of mind. As I read the expression at the beginning of the letter about your being a woman "who was terribly devastated by the separation from you," I could see once again the tears falling from your eyes, bluish-black like lakes. I could feel my tears, in sympathy with yours, beginning to surge in my heart, and I was not able to catch the meaning of your dharma talk.

And now you're saying that that sad woman was your former self? You mean that the later self of that woman, dear venerable one, has nothing to do with me? But the fact that you remember having seen me before means that there is still a connection between us. I wish more than ever that you would return to that woman, your former self, the woman who felt such pain at losing me that she would forever hold a grudge. I wouldn't mind if you thought me a hopeless jerk. I would willingly take the role of an unforgivable sinner if it meant that I would be tied up and taken to the court of your highness, where I could kneel before you and ask for forgiveness.

At this point I wish you were an old woman who would rest your head, with hair turned all silver, on my bosom, and not a pious nun sitting high on a dharma chair. The image of your former self all soaked in sorrow might look pathetic, but it also has a certain dramatic elegance to it. Your image now doesn't allow for secular expressions of pathos or loneliness; instead, it's mysterious and solitary, and for me a source of tears.

During our long separation I've been thinking about my behavior, which was a betrayal to you. Once while we were still together my parents tried to marry me off to another woman, and because of that I wasn't able to contact you for two weeks. When I came to see you after that, you told me how, thinking me sick, you had prayed to Avalokiteśvara Bodhisattva all those days. You also said that someone told you I had become engaged and you told them it was impossible. You trusted me without a bit of doubt and considered my love to be your exclusive treasure, even though feelings are something that can change as fast as morning and evening. You were a woman of such extreme innocence and I betrayed you. The remorse of the sinner has remained unresolved in my heart for more than twenty years. Whenever I met you in a dream I looked into your eyes with the intention of asking for forgiveness, but you just passed by, ignoring me. Perhaps that meant that we had had long ties in our previous lives.

And then I read in your recent letter, "the woman who felt such pain at losing you"! The passage shook the mind of a person unable to forget you. However, my conscience tells me that I should not fail a nun who is an intelligent woman in the process of mastering the supreme teaching. I remember the teaching that says that the sin of failing a celibate nun is as big as the size of Mount Sumi.

Even before you joined the monastery you were a generous woman, and you are even more compassionate now. For thirty years you concentrated on your spiritual practice, purifying your mind and body. Even if I tried to pollute your practice now, you wouldn't be distracted, but still I want to ask for your forgiveness and to vent my secular feelings for you who now occupies a high religious position. That such passionate feelings were hidden inside of this worthless old man surprises even me.

When my wife died five years ago, some people encouraged me to remarry and there were also some women who tried to flirt with me. But I'm aware that the sun in my life's journey has already set and that I need to prepare myself for returning (for the next life). I've been practicing chanting aloud, calling out the name Avalokiteśvara Bodhisattva, the mother of great compassion. I know that my effort to accumulate mental power through chanting has failed and I have deviated from my practice. I assume that it will take a while to treat this deviation. I've heard that there is a meditation hall for men on the mountain where you stay. Although I would love to make a dash for it, I control the impulse. I plan to stay in a quiet place for the rest of my life, preparing myself for death. I've learned that if I want to reach a state where I can be with you forever, I must be on the same path as you are.

Dear venerable, would you please choose a place where I can do my practice? I would consider that place a space imbued with your spirit, an extension of where you are. If I go there and do my practice, it would be as if I were practicing in the same place as you. It makes no difference whether I chant "Venerable Iryŏp, Venerable Iryŏp" or "Avalokiteśvara Bodhisattva, Avalokiteśvara Bodhisattva"; when the mind and the mouth correspond with each other, Avalokiteśvara Bodhisattva, Iryŏp Bodhisattva, this bodhisattva and that bodhisattva become one in the state of non-thought. When that happens, the "process" to recover the universe will have been completed. My preparation for eternal life will be done and I will be content and lead an inexhaustible life.

You have sent me a knife of life and death.

From your old friend B.

CHAPTER 13

Having Prepared a Clean Copy
of My Master's Manuscript
(*by* Yi Wŏlsong)

The reason to give up the relationships and responsibilities of the secular world and join a monastery is to find the original mind that has been lost and thus become a human being with a clear mind. It has been more than thirty years since my master vowed to remind those who have forgotten their original mind about this loss. Even without reading or writing, life at the meditation center is busy, and to pursue reading and writing, which are forbidden, is not easy. The master spent what little time she had in the writing of eloquent dharma talks, which have finally been put together into a book here in the effort to spread the Buddhist teachings. As a novice nun who has only recently joined the monastery to become a member of the Buddhist world, and as one whose understanding of Buddhism is not deep, this is an occasion of great joy.

Before, I knew nothing about Buddhism, and like most young girls I had a rainbow-colored dream and fantasized about a coach decorated with flowers and such. Once I came to admire the Buddha's teaching, such fantasies looked as frail as fallen leaves, which easily become crushed. I was told that however bright they might be, one's dreams in the secular world are all vain. I let go of them and set my mind to join the monastery and cultivate myself. Nevertheless, as a young adult, my determination to give up dreaming is limited by my level of mental maturity.

The image of a young "*bhikṣuṇī*" (Buddhist nun) who sheds tears at her tragic destiny; a nun's ink-colored robe and pale shaved head under a newly-made white peaked hood...the smooth, sorrow-evoking movements of a Buddhist dance where the white sleeves of the dancer wave like two wings under the blue moonlight;...As a wind-bell hanging at an angle rafter makes its sound, the sound of a wooden block breaks the silence of the green mountains as if to forget the troubles of the secular world; and the sound of the chanting of a Buddhist nun who looks like an elegant, beautiful boy! In the autumn, with quiet eyes bright like candles, a nun walks on fallen leaves under the pines and picks mushrooms and deep in summer picks bellflower roots…For a young woman about to join the monastery, all these images are not just fantasies that quickly disappear but the very objects of endless admiration. Many people in the secular world feel some attraction to being a Buddhist nun, which must have to do with these preconceived images.

It has been already more than a year since I joined the monastery under my master, Venerable Iryŏp. I now have a shaved head, wear clothes like a man's, and listen to my teacher's profound dharma talks. She tried to teach me and make me realize the vanity of girlish sentimentality, including the tears that fall on the robe of a nun who has practiced Buddhism for over ten years. I will never forget that. There are people in the secular world who feel pity for nuns, but I feel sorry for those people. My mother wailed when she learned that her daughter was to become a nun. My father, brother, and even my younger sibling felt pity for me, and tears fell from their eyes. My friends also pitied me. But the images of them shedding tears all seem futile to me. If there were feelings hidden deep down inside me, even they stir no longer, for which I can only thank my teacher's powerful and great teachings. It was not a matter of getting rid of feelings that are considered human but more to do with making myself a disciple of the Buddha.

My teacher, Venerable Iryŏp, would have me sit on my knees in front of her to give me a powerful dharma talk. On one such occasion she said,

Wŏlsong, we humans have innumerable lives, and it is an immutable fact that we cannot avoid our lives. If life is unavoidable, you should by all means try to find comfort in life. When you are hungry, you need to eat in order to feel comfortable; if there is something you want to do, you should do it in order to feel at ease. If life is that which you cannot avoid, you should definitely try to find the comfort that is the ground of life. The price for this comfort, that is, the price for one's life, is totally up to each being to pay. Others cannot give you for free even a thing as infinitesimal as a particle of a strand of hair. Everything is subject to the law of exchange. The price for comfort is not material; nor is it mental, as in the experience of pleasure or anger. Only non-thought, which is the joyfulness beyond time and space, is the answer. Humans have an infinite number of lives, and if you are not able to find your original mind in non-thought, which is time free from the constraints of time, you will never be able to find the great comfort of mind and body (nirvana).

My teacher also said,

A sentient being's habitual energy accumulated through many lives for numerous eons of time has enormous power. The seed of mental disturbance is especially caused by love. It is said that love still remains in the ashes after an *arhat* is cremated. It never gets destroyed. In order to forget the love that cannot even be burned away, to suppress all the affection that refuses to be suppressed, and thus to attain the maximum level of freedom, we must overcome the maximum level of constraint. This is the fundamental principle of things. Since this is something that can be done, there is no excuse for not doing it. This means putting up with momentary inconvenience in order to attain comfort for ten thousand years to come. If this much detailed teaching cannot move you from the center of yourself, you won't be able to be born as a human being in your next life. To live this life that lasts at best a hundred years is not an easy task. How then would you deal with the endless lives to come?

Each time I heard my master's dharma talk I reinvigorated my vow to practice, and I also reminded myself how happy I was to be in this position. Each talk Master Iryŏp delivered to us was the very words of the Buddha. I felt honored to have the opportunity to prepare a clean copy of my master's manuscript and took special care to make sure there were no errors.

Śakyamuni Buddha gave up the wealth of a prince in Kavilvastu, which he had enjoyed for almost thirty years before he left his kingdom to attain his great awakening. He said that life is a sea of suffering, a fact that I suspect no one would deny. If no one can deny this fact, we should prepare ourselves to get out of this suffering. As a thinking human being, I believe this reasoning to be only natural. At school, students study and put into practice what they learn because they trust their teacher. In society, a person is truly respected if that person is trustworthy. Likewise, a faithful and affectionate father does not lie to his children.

Not only is it a known fact that the Buddha is one of the world's religious leaders, we also know that he has been considered one of three great sages for the past three thousand years. His great words of compassion have been on record all this time. Śakyamuni is a great sage and a spiritual guide. Given that, it is impossible to think that he created the ideas of hell or nirvana and delivered dharma talks for forty-nine years just to deceive us ignorant beings. If that were the case, we would be saying that all the people in Asia who regarded him as a leader, all our ancestors were fools incapable of telling the truth from a lie.

In order to save the sentient beings who transmigrate through the six realms and endure a sea of suffering full of greed, anger, and ignorance, the Buddha delivered dharma talks for forty-nine years. But during his lifetime, and even today, the number of people who attain awakening is very few; the problem of human existence remains unresolved, as people still struggle in this inexhaustible suffering.

It has been more than thirty years since Venerable Iryŏp began devoting herself to studying the Buddha's teachings. Even though she is now more than sixty years old, with her compassionate mind she has decided to publish this book, *Reflections of a Zen Buddhist Nun,* in order to spread Buddhism and offer a lamp to guide sentient beings. This is an occasion everybody should celebrate. If the numerous sentient beings in the world who read this book enter the world of Buddhism and make efforts to find their original minds, that would be the very realization of my master's vow. I pray with all sincerity that everybody will attain awakening. In concluding, I pray with palms together that all the sentient beings in the world receive the compassion of Avalokiteśvara Bodhisattva.

Yi Wŏlsong
Primary Disciple

Part Two

CHAPTER 14

Return to Emptiness

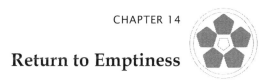

You should keep in mind Śakyamuni Buddha's declaration, made for all of us, that "In the entire world, only I am precious." This "I" is the head, tail, and center of the universe. The universal "I" travels through eternity and eventually inherits that eternity. The mind is the basis of human existence because the mind does not lose the "I." Everything begins from the "I." This "I" exists closest to "me" but can also travel to the end of the world without taking the "I" with "me." The "I" who cannot lose "me" cannot meet the other who is not "me," but since the "I" is related to "others," the "I" shares the life, death, suffering, and joy of others. By so doing, "I" becomes the person in charge of all the things and maintains the position of the most precious being in one's life.

The real "I" is the "I" before "I" begins to think about the "I." The "I" that thinks creates "you." This "you" creates another "you" and division begins. The "I" before a thought arises does not divide; since the "I" and the "non-I" work together, there can be no division. This "I" is one, and this one does not belong to any system of numbering; it is the one before numbering begins. The number "one" is the beginning of division into two, three, and so on.

The "I" and the mind are not two. We are all fragmented, but we still rely on those fragments of the mind. When the self and mind correspond to each other, we lead a life of which we are master. A true being is one whose activities reflect the unity of self and mind. This is a being of oneness. To reflect on the unity of the "I" and the mind in one's activities, one should see through and utilize the original state of this mind. On surface the mind looks like it is based on the material. If you understand life only through the lens of its materiality, human beings become just one more piece of material garbage and lose their humanity. It is not that man is the master of the universe; man is the universe itself. The creator of the universe is the non-self, and what is created by non-self is one's own self, which is the universe. The non-self is one's true self. The true self is not the object of the other but the very unity of self and other. If you only think about "self" or "I," then this self ("I") is an incomplete self that has lost its other half, which is "you" or "not-I." Self creates its own self and this created self, in turn, creates its object, the other that is "you."

The complete "I" before the "I" thinks about the "I" is life in its entirety. The functioning of life creates the "I" who thinks of the "I"; this I creates "you," and the "you" creates the idea that all the actualities in the world are the real "I." The universe, human beings, "I," the mind, thought, the heart, the path, self-nature, Buddha Nature, and the soul—these are all synonyms. What appear in letters are shells of various original spirits; the "I" that is conscious of the "I" only announces the existence of the "I," and the mind that is sensed is only a materialized fragment of the mind.

The self always functions through contradictory polarizations. When "I" think I am hungry, the "I" functions to get something to eat. The next thought is digestion, which is the activity involved in getting rid of that which the "I" has obtained through eating: a contradictory action. The next stage is to think about how to rid the body of what remains inside after digestion. I go through the painful labor of seeding, mending, and harvesting because of my own thoughts, which belong to me but also rebel against me.[1] That is because one has to feed oneself to survive. This silly "I" eats in compliance with my rebellious thought that thinks "I am hungry" and then waits while what I eat rots inside the body, is defecated, and creates again material for food based on that defecation. This endless labor continues and the "I" is its servant.

Am I the enemy of my own thought, or is it my thought that is my enemy? I live or die according to my thoughts, and thoughts arise and cease because of my existence. My existence and suffering continue because of my thought, and my thought experiences trouble because of my existence. Me and my thoughts are tied together head to tail and travel like that through the wheel of life and death for eternity: This is a human being's life. Like me, this universe and the lives in it continue to go through the process of life and death, arising and ceasing, with no end in the future. I am that life. Life is eternal. Everyday life, which is the function of life, does not draw closer to an end either. I comply with my own thoughts, and my thoughts labor for me; my thoughts and I exchange benefits and harm each other. Those who offer their lives to me will also want my life. If you look for benefit, give first. To gain is to lose. By letting go of everything, you earn everything. Those who help you will be those who harm you. Thoughts belong to me. Dreams are my own thoughts and only I can make them come true.

Love is a synonym for enemy. Over the shoulder of sorrow, I can see joy smiling. On the heels of joy, there is sorrow. One's enemy is one's beneficiary. My own self-contradictory activities are my own compliance with life. Irrationality is rationality. One's life is a repetition of transmigration, change, collection, and dispersion—and there is no end of it. Day and night; spring, summer, fall, and winter; last year and this year; birth, aging, sickness, and death; change through formation, staying, destruction, and cessation—these are the two sides of a double-headed carriage that the life-spirit (*saengryŏng*) rides from one eternity to another. The life-spirit is an eternal wayfarer who cannot stay away from the two-sided carriage of life and death, pleasure and suffering.

It is said that the universe is one's own self. It is a dried kernel inside and a dried shell outside; it is a shadow. It is an essence of the universe whose inside is dried and the reality of life whose outside is dried.[2] If we are destined to exist in a reality in which life is followed by death and joy alternates with suffering, we need the will and strength to maintain our mental balance. We should be like a horseback rider who is always balancing himself on the back of a horse. We get the mental strength to keep us in balance from realizing that both the self and others are dependent on the same source of life. When a country, a society, and a family maintain oneness between government and people, when there is one mind between parents and children and one will between husband and wife and among colleagues, there is freedom and peace. Everybody is a life-spirit riding a double-headed chariot. When one realizes that the two sides of light and darkness, of day and night, of pleasure and pain are inseparable and that life is a repetition of this dual nature, one lives free of suffering.

Human beings in our time have lost their minds. We have all lost our own selves. We have all lost our memories. We rely on a fragment of our mind, which is only the smallest piece of a mind that is itself broken into ten thousand pieces. When a person's body takes a rest, she accumulates energy for bodily activities; when her spirit takes a rest, she accumulates strength of the mind. The totality of mental strength is omnipotence. People know that it is not possible to live apart from one's own mind, but just like the individual who does not know how to use her money, people do not know how to use their minds. When one's spirit takes a perfect rest, in the place where all of the spirits gather, one finds the greatest peacefulness.

This place of greatest peacefulness is a place of oneness that you reach after your spirit takes complete rest. Not knowing the meaning of this oneness is the greatest ignorance there is on a universal scale. People have complaints and feel unsatisfied because they fail to unite and unify their individual self and what belongs to that self. It is very important for communal living that everyone have one mind. People in that situation must share space with one another and must unify views regarding what each one hears and listens to; they should divide profits equally and share pleasure and suffering. Only then can each individual in the community reach his or her goal without any problem. When this one thing is accomplished, all of the conflicts, differences, and confusions will eventually be resolved peacefully. The secret of making this oneness lies not in attempting to suppress others, but in trying to be one with others.

This "one" is the original nature of life. During the daytime, one's spirit relies on a body and exists only as thoughts; at night, however, the spirit reveals itself as separate from the body and freely pursues its own course of action. When it finally casts off the body, which is like a set of clothes for that life, depending on the karma it accumulated during its lifetime, the spirit will get a set of new clothes in each of the realms—heaven, human, animal, or hell—and resume its life. The heaven realm is an actual world, which is the utmost material cultural reality. In heaven, based on one's karma, one's life is like a good dream, be it for a thousand years or for ten thousand years. But once it is over, even life in heaven will bring the feeling of emptiness. Only when the spirit reaches the place of greatest peacefulness does it gain its full mental strength. The place of greatest peacefulness is the place where all of the spirits become unified, the place where all thoughts become united and thus become no-thought. Nothingness, wherein no-thought arises, is the original identity of the self; once one regains one's original identity, everything will become realized as one wishes. All problems are resolved only in this nothingness. Nothingness is the original identity of the universe and the original source of life. Thoughts mean "my" thoughts, which in turn indicates that "I" am the one who does the thinking. However, since we are not aware that thinking is our own activity, even though everybody does the thinking, we are not capable of making thoughts come true in real life. A thought is an expression of the individual self. A thought is reality in itself. If a person firmly proceeds with his own thoughts, there is nothing he cannot accomplish. If we say faith is like ground space, reality is like the buildings on the ground. Nothing can be accomplished if you separate yourself from the mind; neither can you do two things or deal with two minds at the same time. To accomplish anything you should concentrate on one mind and dedicate yourself exclusively to one thing.

The concept of "I" has meaning only when one is fully in charge of oneself. We are, on the contrary, far from being in charge of our selves, which is proof that we have lost ourselves. To attain one's mental capacity means to recover this lost self. The "I" in its origin means the "I" before

I am conscious of myself. The original "I" is not a being that can be understood through consciousness. The alter ego of this original "I" is one with the "I" who is thinking. A being who has recovered the entirety of the original "I" deserves to be called the highest being among beings. As Śakyamuni Buddha once said, this is the "I" who is solely precious. The universe is the self and all that exists in the universe are fragments of my spirit. This transformational function of all the things in the world creates a universe of its own, which generates individual entities that lead lives. The unification of the original "I" and this transformational function creates a concrete mind that then creates concrete reality. The spirit, which is the transforming function, is part of my thinking and is unmoving. The entire universe is the unmovable identity of my self, from which all the beings in the world disseminate. When you collect all the dissemination of your self up to the last fragment, and the unmoving identity of your self is completely calm, you arrive at the place of great peacefulness, the place of thinking that enables you to think. This great peacefulness is the original nature of both sentience and insentience. This life is not destructible; nor do the daily activities of this life come to an end.[3]

Life energy is omnipotent and exists before things exist; it does not have a visible shape and yet is all-capable. The existential value of a living organism lies in its capacity to attain life energy and utilize that energy at its will. One's thought is one's mind: the mind creates all the thoughts. Nothing exists separate from the mind—and the mind changes from morning to evening. The original nature of this mind creates all the things in the world. Once all the pieces of this fragmented and broken mind are collected into one, this "one" is the creator. Only when the mind has recovered its original oneness does the all-capable power of the creator begin to function. The original identity of this mind is equipped with all of the elements and thus is completely full: This is the unmovable being that no one dare bother. This is a state that sensations cannot reach, but it is also the seed of all life-beings. The only real life-beings are those capable of giving life to my own seed. Mere existence does not constitute a being, nor do mere movements make up the activities of life.

Only the organism that utilizes its life energy and whose existence is based on life energy has value. Human beings in modern society have lost their life energy, and they live barely hanging on to whatever small piece of it remains. Since these humans rely on a mere scrap of their life energy, they cannot exercise their full capacity, and yet they are not aware of this. Humans are naturally all powerful, but when all of that power is brought to bear, the resulting action is regarded as a miracle or the work of some supernatural power. In this secular world only a few people recognize those beings who exercise fully their life energy. Life has only one thread. All lives are fruit stemming from the same root; life has only one main trunk, but its stems and branches are innumerable. The original trunk of life has no physical form, but its branches have physical characteristics, and a group of sentient beings whose karma is similar in nature comprise a stem and live in the same universe or within the same ethnic group. The branches created by sentient beings who share similar karma disappear one after another as the time for one universe or one ethnic group comes to an end. This type of arising and ceasing continues into eternity.

Because other creatures and I constitute a single organism growing from a single trunk, when another being dies I realize that I am sure to face death too. But because people in this *sahā* world are not aware of this fact, they are unafraid of becoming involved in killing other beings. My mind is my disciple, and it will do whatever I tell it to do. It originally knows neither compassion nor love. Since I am already connected with others, helping others is equal to helping myself. My life is uncomfortable only when I am not capable of controlling my mind. If I am in charge of my mind, then I can live comfortably even in hell. Do not try to find happiness or comfort outside yourself; instead, you should try to become the commander of your own mind and utilize it at will. The entire universe is in your possession, as is your mind. The richest individuals are those who can lead their minds to their full universal capacity. Happiness or sorrow, wealth or poverty, are all dependent on the mind. Anyone incapable of fully controlling her own mind will experience unfulfilled desires even if she possesses everything in the universe.

The mind is the original source of life: it is its hometown. Sentient beings feel homesick from eternity to eternity because they have lost their minds. You should be seriously aware that anyone incapable of fully controlling his mind cannot claim to be a human being. The term "human being" means a being that is awakened to and fully utilizes its mind. There is no way to live in the world while being separated from one's mind. You should reject the idea that heaven is a comfortable place and that hell is unendurable. Instead, you should try to live without being manipulated by your environment. Even the stump of a tree will answer your prayer if you believe without reservation that the stump is an all-powerful being and if you pray to it with all sincerity. A prayer is a method of retrieving that which originally belonged to you.

The mind (spirit) thinks and perceives objects through its eyes. Since an object is a visible entity, one feels the object through one's body, hears it through one's ears, and eats it through one's mouth. It is said that the spirit is an intelligent being separate from the body, which is befuddled; for that reason, the spirit better appreciates tasty food and better understands important lessons. When the spirit is called upon through ancestral or deliverance ceremonies, it eats well, properly hears the dharma talk, and is more receptive to the teaching. When they exist individually, two separate spirits cannot co-exist in the same place. A spirit cannot think about two different things at the same time. At the resting place of spirits, all the fragmented spirits (that is, all thoughts) join together and become one.[4] A friend or a lover should be the one who is capable of singing a lullaby to one's spirit. If a spirit stays in a resting place and makes quiet and orderly movements, it will not deviate from its path or do anything unexpected.

The place where spirits rest is the realm of emptiness, where feelings are cut off and the mind and thoughts are all exhausted. Emptiness is absolute and includes everything. It is justice, truth, and authenticity. Action taken in emptiness is rightness; eyes that see through emptiness are correct; ears that hear through emptiness never comprehend inaccurately. Emptiness is seamless, without the slightest gap; it is filled with all things, including even the unimaginable. Once you attain emptiness, you own all beings. All lives share in emptiness. Even a worm owns emptiness. A being that has lost emptiness is like a water bug caught out of the water that is its body, world, and life. If you wish to earn something, do something, eat something, meet someone, see something, or go somewhere, then you must first return to the emptiness that is your hometown. Emptiness is one's own self. There is nothing that the self cannot do or cannot possess.

Emptiness is nature in its original state. Having no opportunity to encounter the idea of emptiness, Jean-Jacques Rousseau merely exclaimed his admiration, "Nature, Nature!" But his life ended before he accomplished any significant result. By now, Rousseau might have moved beyond the boundary of nature, which is merely felt, and discovered an entrance into nature.

Emptiness is the essence of all existence; it is the original nature of living organisms, the great resting place for spirits. Emptiness is the "I" that makes us think and the creator of the universe. A human who has lost emptiness can be a human no more. Emptiness is the mind of the mind and the seed from which all life grows. If a living organism separates itself from emptiness, it experiences an endless urge to search for something. It is because humans separate themselves from emptiness that they are not content. Their perpetual feelings of dissatisfaction are because they are homesick for their original hometown, which is emptiness. If you wish to lead the most satisfactory life, do not separate yourself from emptiness. Return to emptiness if you want a life that is the most decent, most valuable, wealthiest, freest, and most comfortable. Life itself cannot be separated from emptiness, but we still suffer from desire. This is like feeling hungry within a container filled with cooked rice. This occurs when one is ignorant of the fact that emptiness is fullness. Once one attains emptiness, one possesses all the things in the world. Emptiness is the very storehouse of all that is valuable. The worst kind of ignorance is to be unaware of the fact that we are the owners of emptiness. We believe that this body is what is most valuable, when in fact it is the least valuable. This body is nothing but a shell that will soon decompose.

In emptiness there is neither beginning nor end, neither birth nor death, neither suffering nor pleasure, but our sensations transform situations and create birth and death, pleasure and pain. A lump of gold is valuable, but it has its use-value only when it is molded into something. Emptiness is the foundation of all things; hence, once you attain emptiness, there is nothing you cannot do. A being is more properly called a beast when it does not know that emptiness is the self of the self and the original mind and thus fails to utilize this emptiness. A great artisan knows how to mold things by using the whole lump of gold; likewise, the Buddha or God refers to the being that is capable of fully grasping emptiness and utilizing it to its utmost.[5] To take refuge in the Buddha or God, our teacher, is to learn to take care of the entirety of one's mind, which is emptiness, and thus to live as the artist-creator of the universe. The Buddha and God penetrate the meaning of emptiness and create a universe using emptiness as its material. Christianity teaches "Blessed are the poor in spirit"; Buddhism teaches that one should use both body and mind to their utmost so that not even a remnant of sensation remains. These lessons teach us that we should learn about emptiness. The lord of Christianity does not seem to have fully penetrated the meaning of emptiness, since the Bible contains no clear discussion of it. Emptiness cannot be mastered by using theory, language, words, or expressions. Instead, each individual must be able to live in emptiness free from the constraints of time and space. In this state, even sensations are cut off; that is the state of calmness and clarity.

In the state described above, when one thought arises, the entire universe is created, and when a thought ceases, an entire universe disappears. Birth and death, creation and destruction, all take place through one's thoughts. A person who has attained this state is the universe itself and is in full command of its expansion and contraction. We are human beings but not fully aware of what that means. Only when we attain emptiness will all the things in the world belong to us.

Anyone who attains this emptiness commands all beings and becomes someone who has accomplished the highest values of human beings. Once emptiness is attained, the person takes ownership of both heaven and hell and does not deviate from either good or evil. Emptiness performs the dual activities of construction and dissolution from eternity to eternity without end. Negation is affirmation and affirmation is negation. The greatest truth is the greatest contradiction, and the ultimate good is the ultimate evil. The Buddha and the devil are one, and sentient beings and the Buddha are not dual. "You" and "I," birth and death, pleasure and suffering are also one. Eternal life is a state of eternal death because everything is inside and outside of the same thing; thus, nothing can be separated from anything.

There is nothing that is not emptiness; the body, spirit, and self are all empty. But emptiness is not voidness; it makes one raise the thought of self and creates all the spirits that are accumulations of one's thoughts. Since bodies and spirits are material, they are subject to change. When dissolved, they return to the four great elements of earth, water, fire, and wind, and will be born again based on the nature of their spirit. In whatever form one is reborn, the body is the shadow of the spirit, which is the carrier of life energy.[6] Human beings in our time see this in reverse and thus live as if the body is the spirit's prison and life energy the carrier of the spirit.

The divinity, the soul, God, and the Buddha are all idols created by our thoughts. True faith is to believe in the mind of the mind rather than the mind of these idols. Reality is what is thought of; the original body of reality is what comes before thought. Because the original body has no visible shape, it is called empty; all things in the body of reality exist within emptiness. Furthermore, because this emptiness encompasses all things, it oversees all happenings. A suckling infant does not know how to deal with its own excretion, but once it grows up, that same individual is fully in charge of his or her activities. Likewise, when a person attains and fully utilizes emptiness, his or her normal actions are viewed by other sentient beings as miracles or as the acts of a supernatural power. One's thoughts are expressions, shadows. The true body of thoughts, endowed with the capacity for full-fledged freedom and omnipotence, is emptiness.

Emptiness is the principle that governs the eternal life of humans. In order to lead a free and authentic life, a person should first prepare the foundation of her mental life and let that life begin. She who has lost the power of the mind betrays herself and acts against her own interest. One who has not yet established a life based on his mind is not able to trust his mind; such a person cannot rely on his own spirit and is therefore always restless, searching for something. Because we are not resolute in the knowledge that the mind is the only foundation of life, our efforts are fruitless, like a farmer trying to cultivate without land. In order to weave a fabric, threads must be combined in horizontal and vertical patterns.

Likewise, material things and the mind are the essential horizontal and vertical elements of life. That which does the thinking is the mind, but this mind does not have a shape, and therefore is nothingness. Nothingness is not existence; the mind, which is the internal, original nature of material, and which does not have a visible shape, is like a seed: It does not show itself directly, but reveals its functions through all things visible. There are only existence (*chonjae*) and actuality (*hyŏnsil*); and outside of this actual reality, there is no existence.[7] The only thing that can be affirmed is this actual reality, but it is not trustworthy because it is impermanent. When day breaks, night follows; as soon as night falls, day breaks again. A farewell follows a meeting; and after one bids good-bye, another encounter follows. As soon as one feels unhappy, happiness is imminent, and sorrow eventually follows. Death follows birth, but is succeeded by a new life.

Within impermanence exists permanence. On the other side of voidness lays true reality. Inside the unreliable self is an all-powerful self that is stronger than all the armies in the universe. This powerful self is the self that existed in emptiness before the universe was created, before the names of the Buddha or God appeared and before the blood of life energy became concentrated (into a human being). This self is void inside, yet it is filled with everything in the world. It is the unchanging body of life energy; it is not controlled by life, nor can it be destroyed by death. Complete emptiness is fullness without a gap; only empty hands can hold everything.

One needs to be free from thought in order to find the leader of thought that is in charge of all thoughts. Even without knowing how to read a single character, one can be awakened to all truths, theories, and the original nature of the universe encompassed within that one character. Scholarly activity should set as its goal awakening to that one character rather than merely learning it. To study means to learn to be a human being. The purpose of study is to investigate truth. But the truth that is felt, thought of, and written about is no longer truth — it is non-truth. Real truth cannot be verbalized.

Through secular education, one attains knowledge, and through religious education, one attains awakening. Being awake means that you have established the foundation of your thought and are not manipulated by your circumstances. You form clear decisions on your projects and make consistent efforts to accomplish them. This is the way to lead the life of a human being. You do not attain knowledge through education. Rather, education is a means to recover what you have already been given and to become awakened to what has been lost. The same applies to religious learning: You learn from the founder of a religion how to recover the mind that has been lost and to retrieve activities that have been forgotten. What we believe to be actualities are in fact dreams. The truth is that our daily lives, in which happiness and misfortune alternate, is a dream in which good and bad luck also alternate. We humans become attached to these dreams and, unaware that that is what they are, we cry over them as if they were real. Daydreams are more realistic; because we are more attached to them, they appear clearer. Sleeping dreams, which mix past dreams and those of the future, feel obscure even though they are like daydreams in their unreality. What happens in dreams is rarely remembered, despite being repeated innumerable times.

We tend to relate death with pain, but we forget the pain related to birth. This is evidence that we must have completely lost some of our memories. As a fetus passes through the narrow gate of its mother's womb, sometimes damaging her pelvis, it experiences extreme pain, but no one feels pity for it. This life is a dream, and, like changing scenes in a movie, different episodes continuously occur throughout one's life. Because this actuality is reality in which one lives, one cannot help accepting life and death and feeling pleasure and pain. Although they are dreams, they are "my" dreams and therefore cannot be avoided; nor can I avoid responsibilities related to them. Another reason that dreams cannot simply be ignored is that they are the activities of one's life energy and to deny them would be to deny life energy. I am the one who dreams and that which makes me dream must be inside of me. I need to fully grasp my true identity and be in command of my dreams; only then can I be fully in charge of my mind. Dreams originate within each of us, and if we can find the original source in which all the elements of our dreams coalesce, we can fully utilize these elements and make them real. In dream or imagination, we have infinite freedom, and no one can interfere with that freedom. However absurd a dream might appear, we have the capacity to make it real. Just as we exercise freedom in our dreams, we can act with unlimited freedom and power in real life.

Absolute equality is as true in real life as it is in the dream world because dreams are reality. We have a tendency to distrust our capacity and lose self-confidence when we are faced with a difficult situation. We feel inferior and we doubt our ability to handle a serious situation. But we should remember that it is ourselves who play the leading role in the unlimited possibilities of the world of dreams. If we are to regain the capacity to lead all beings in the world, we must make efforts to live in a way that dreams and realities are not separated into two worlds but are unified into one.[8] To be human means that there is nothing we cannot know or do; by the same token, it is our responsibility as human beings to give to others all that they ask for.

CHAPTER 15

Meditation and the Attainment of the Mind

People always have desires in life, and since their desires are not always satisfied, they become lost in their own complaints. This happens because they fail to attain the foundation of life, the state of mind that is endowed with all the required elements. To live without attaining this state of mind is like trying to cook rice with no rice at hand. Meditation is the way to attain the foundation of life. Meditation (that is, to control one's mind) is all one needs to know in life. Various religious leaders, or leaders of life, tell people that if they believe in Jesus or the Buddha they will be able to reach heaven or nirvana, and that heaven or nirvana is the ultimate place to attain what they desire, which is beyond the imagination in this world. People say such things because they are ignorant of the fact that only when we are awakened through meditation to the boundless no-thought and when no-thought becomes universalized can our desires and security of body and mind (or nirvana) can be attained. In other words, they have failed to learn how to objectify and thus to reflect on themselves. This is the teaching of attaining a state of mind that is the all-capable unity of the self. Once you reach such a state, wherever you live, in whatever form, you will be secure. This is the teaching of Buddhism.

This is why Buddhist teachings are not intended for Buddhists but rather to help each individual attain this state of mind. Buddhism rises and falls with the happiness or misfortune of each individual; the prosperity or decline of Buddhism corresponds to the prosperity or decline of a country and also of the world. Buddhism provides a way to control the mind of the entire universe. As evidence of this, the culture of our world-renowned Buddhist ancestors left behind marvelous works of Buddhist art with which the craftsmanship of our time cannot compete. Even now when only its legacy remains, our ancestral Buddhist culture leads both our bodies and souls into a world where we are relieved of all egoism. This is clear evidence that our ancestors led a comfortable life at the time when Buddhism prospered. What about our lives now that Buddhist teaching has declined? We realize that to be ignorant of Buddhism is the same as not knowing one's own self, and that ours is a time of the worst ignorance. Our lives are proof of this state of affairs.

The only way to learn Buddhism, that is, to learn one's own self, is through meditation. Sages have proven that meditation is the solution to problems ranging from those of an individual, a nation, a society, to those of animals and insentient beings. Although meditation is the treasure that resolves all problems and leads to the ultimate goal of life, it is not difficult to do. Any being that has senses and feelings can do it. Everybody has all that is required: time until infinity and a mind that is equipped with all the necessary elements, so long as they have received and thus earned the teachings of the Buddha, who experienced awakening before us. However, in order to believe in our teacher, the Buddha, we need to reach a state where we are capable of cutting off our own consciousness. The mind must overcome its great enemy (called habitual energy), which we have inherited from previous lives, and the illusions of our senses, which have been generated during this lifetime. If we can do this, no matter where our practice starts from, we can attain the goal.

Preparation for meditation is simple: One needs to forget one's self (*mola'gyŏng*) and cut off all emotions and stay in a pure, transparent, and calm state of mind. By preparing in this manner, whether be it at a monastery or in the secular world, anyone can do meditation. Professional training makes it easier to reach such an independent state of mind. Usually the bondage called a monastic life is the price of great freedom for lives to come. This is why people join monasteries. If a person is very successful as a lay practitioner, he must have already experienced monasticism in a previous life. It is important to maintain a pure state of mind and not to backslide. The goal of meditation is to move beyond the believing mind in which one is forgotten and reach the state of unity. The body is the dharma hall, the meditation hall. Since the mind is the subject of study, in all states of walking, staying, sitting, and lying down, whether one talks, remains silent, moves, or stays still, one can continue to focus on meditation. It is important to remember that without a teacher it is impossible to travel the journey of faith, which has ten thousand different paths.

A beginner should practice in a quiet place—facing a wall with back straight, head up, eyes half closed, in a lotus position—and concentrate on a *hwadu* (Ch. *huatou*) to resolve doubts. Ancient teachers had one thousand and seven hundred *gongan* (J. *kōan*), but anything that can be encountered in daily life can function as a *hwadu*. For example, one may ask, "What is it that enables me to walk?" or, since everybody is always thinking, one may ask, "What is it that does the thinking?" Whatever the situation allows can function as a *hwadu*. When doubts arise, cut down all the groves of thought and do not fall into sleep or confusion; all the series of thoughts should be cut off until the idea of having doubt disappears.

Once this unbounded state of no-thought becomes the universe, at the latest within a week, the true identity of thought, the "I," will emerge. If a person is in charge of his or her own transmigration through the six realms in four different forms of birth,[1] the problems of life for that person are resolved. Reading essays like this and practicing meditation by oneself can lead one down the wrong path, so one should make sure to find a teacher and practice meditation under guidance. A change in the mode of thinking is all that is required; by applying yourself, you should not find it too difficult to accomplish what you desire. Make sure that you practice every day and be patient. Warn yourself against becoming too casual, since that will create unexpected obstacles. Remember that this is not something that can be attained through what you see, hear, learn, or sense.

September 5, the Year of Sheep (1955)
Written by remembering Great Master Venerable Man'gong's
    Dharma Talk

CHAPTER 16

Prayer and Chanting

Meditation is a way of finding oneself through self-reflection. Prayer, on the other hand, is an endeavor with a goal, thus there exists an object to whom one prays. If the object of the prayer is Bodhisattva Kuanyin [Avalokiteśvara], the name Kuanyin means that by listening to the sound (the mind) of the world, the bodhisattva makes happen what is being prayed for. Those of us who live in the weakest and most myopic way tend to identify as "material" whatever is visible to the eye and to name whatever is invisible as "the soul," even though the soul is also material. If the soul finds its owner it will be able to fully exercise its capacity and to make both what is material and spiritual become reality.[1]

Since we sentient beings have befuddled souls, we pray to Bodhisattva Kuanyin because we believe that she can make happen what we cannot accomplish. We do so because we do not believe what we cannot see with our own eyes. However, whether we wish for longevity, talent, a son, a higher social position, material fortune, or whatever else, the difficulty or ease with which our wish is fulfilled depends on the fundamental quality of our existence, which we call karma. Nothing we wish for can be attained without paying a price for it.

When you pray you should first prepare money, rice, incense, or a candle as an offering to the Buddha (obviously everything is the Buddha, but for a sentient being the Buddha has a different meaning). You should then pray with great sincerity and in accordance with the proper ceremony. This is how a prayer should be done. But if you are not able to follow that procedure, you should remember that Bodhisattva Kuanyin is on the same level as the Buddha. The entire universe in its current state is the seat of Bodhisattva Kuanyin. Wherever you are, you should chant with a single and devoted mind, without distraction and in a loud voice, "Bodhisattva Kuanyin, Bodhisattva Kuanyin." If you are able to reach *samādhi* through this chanting, then you will be connected with Bodhisattva Kuanyin. This is the moment of true chanting, when the mind and mouth correspond with each other; this is the place where one reaches one's self, a place in which the distinction between self and other disappears. This is the moment also when the praying person pays the price and, because of the improvement in her mental maturity, her wish will be accomplished. This is the secret of success.

It is easy, when your wish comes true through chanting, to forget the mind of chanting as soon as the give-and-take in the process takes place. You should not be satisfied with the little that you have attained because even though it is good to get what you wish for in life, a favorable situation brings with it what is unfavorable. Hence, what is satisfactory also means what is not satisfactory. Only later will you realize that what you prayed for has eventually turned out to be unsatisfactory, and then you just have to laugh at yourself.

Existence (reality, or demon) and non-existence (the foundation or original quality) together mean the Buddha. But even the term "the Buddha" belongs to the state of demon. What more can we say about what can be attained through one's own pursuits? Residing in the state of demon, the state of delusion, will only result in the eternal suffering of birth and death. We should be able to go beyond the wishful mind, continue to practice the *samādhi* of chanting, and become one with the universe so that we can realize that the original identity of that which chants (that is, the "I" who is all-capable, one's own self) is Bodhisattva Kuanyin herself. Only then will the life of the all-capable self finally begin.

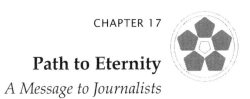

CHAPTER 17

Path to Eternity

A Message to Journalists

The Real Meaning of Life Energy

Before I joined the monastery I came to realize that people have difficulty in life because they fail to secure the "foundation" of life. This realization convinced me that I should find the very foundation of life for myself. It is the same as needing first to prepare fields in order to cultivate crops, to have rice to make cooked rice, or to build railroad tracks for the operation of a train. What I mean by "the foundation of life" is nothing special. It is also called the Dao (path), or life energy (*saengmyŏng*), or the mind, or thought. When we put them all together, we call it the "I." This is the "I" of which one is completely in charge. If I am not the commander of this "I," it cannot be called the "I." This is the "I" Śakyamuni Buddha meant when, three thousand years ago, he declared, "In the entire world, only I am precious." This "I" is not the relative "I" that assumes the existence of I and the existence of you; rather, it is the communal "I," the absolute "I." This "I" indicates all beings that have life energy.

Even a worm can say "In the entire world, only I am precious." That is because a worm and human beings share life energy that is the same in its original form. A worm, however, became a worm because it has just the smallest piece of life energy when life energy is divided into ten million or a hundred million pieces. Because a worm relies on the smallest and thus weakest piece of life energy, it becomes a worm. After the Buddha declared that "In the entire world, only I am precious," he also mentioned that "I am the compassionate father of all beings born through four ways." The four ways refer to creatures born from the womb, from eggs, from moisture, and through transformation. Humans are born out of their mothers' wombs and thus are called "beings born from the womb." A chicken is born from an egg, and thus is a "being born from an egg." Creatures born from moisture include maggots and germs, both of which are generated through decomposition. An example of a creature born through transformation is a cicada. A nymph lives underground for about eight years and then sheds its skin to emerge as a cicada. This means that the Buddha is the father of maggots, which also means that we humans are siblings of maggots. This is because, be it the Buddha, God, humans, spirits, demons, serpents, or insects, all are the same when it comes to original life energy. This is why people talk about absolute equality with reference to life energy. But how can we say that a worm is equal to a human? A worm does not know how to exercise its rights for life and therefore becomes a worm. As I mentioned earlier, it has lost its self to such a degree and its sense of self is so vague that it remains a trivial being. We humans sometimes face a situation similar to that of the worm. The meaning of the life energy called "I" needs to be clearly established, but there are people who are not aware of this. To establish the meaning of life energy means having a life in which the "I" is commander of "I," or a life in which the "I" fully utilizes its own life energy.

Nature Is the Mind

I mentioned earlier the "foundation" of life. To be a living organism means to have the right to live, and this right to live means the mind. Animals have only a vague sense of their mental life: They eat when they feel hungry; when their stomach is full, everything is good. When male and female animals meet, they mate, which generates pleasure; they do not think about love or hatred or whether they share the same ideas. Humans, on the other hand, crave meaning. No matter how obscure an individual human's mind may be, she or he still possesses more life energy than an insect or an animal. All humans do. That also makes them complain when their desires are not fulfilled. Complaints about unfulfilled desires arise because of the failure of humans to grasp their own minds, their life energy. Since a human being is unaware that she has a mind that is the boundless source for all things, she struggles to catch her own mind. The thought of an unsatisfied desire means that this unsatisfied desire must have an origin, which is desire, and this thought or desire belongs to someone.[1] Have you ever thought that your thoughts are your own? A person who does not know how to use what he owns is obviously a fool. The same can be said of individuals who do not know how to deal with their own thoughts.

Let's think about it again. My being comes from me. I am the origin of my being, so who else could have told me about or demonstrated to me my own existence? Since I do the thinking, there must be life energy underlying my own being. The life energy that is the mother of all my thoughts is me. This is what the Buddha meant when he said, "In this entire world, only I am precious." What would it mean to lose "me" or to lose my life energy? The "I" — both the "I" in appearance and the "I" that has appeared before — this "I" is thought, or the mind. Let's say that the "I" is thought. Thought is the spirit and it is because we have a spirit that we feel hunger, thirst, pleasure, anger, sorrow, and joy. It is not because of our body that we experience these things; nevertheless, we tend to think that our body is our life. How can we call a person who believes that his body is his life a human being? Life energy can become revitalized, whereas thoughts are absolute. Thoughts have boundaries. If one enters into the main hall before a thought arises, that is life energy. This life energy is the creator. Christianity needs a more sacred aspect.[2] The original goal of creation is for each of us to find our own mind so that we can lead an independent life through being united with the universe. It is possible to be free; but people do not understand that the self is the unlimited source of life. That being the case, people do not think about finding the source within but instead say that some absolute being exists, or that some external entity takes care of them, or that the problems of their lives are caused by others. In this manner, people try to reach outside themselves to a divine power, God, or the Buddha.

People believe in a religion because of the object of the religion on which they rely. Such people do not know the meaning of religion. Religion is an educational system. It teaches that one should recover one's own, original life and thus live that eternal life for oneself. The mind soon becomes matter. It is not something called God but one's original mind that is endowed with all the necessary elements. Nature, which is finite, is also all mind. It is life energy. The creator is another name for life energy. Since it is life energy, it is ineffable. The Buddha gave sermons for forty-nine years, out of which were created eighty thousand Buddhist scriptures. When the Buddha's sermons were manifested in words, and thus materialized, it was inevitable that those manifested teachings became relative. The written words show only one side of the Buddha's teachings; they are only knowledge. Hence, what is called the Bible or the Buddhist scriptures, God's teachings or the Buddha's sermons, are nothing but milestones. If that is the case, why did the Buddha talk at all? He did so because, since each individual is already endowed with what the Buddha taught, when she hears the Buddha's sermon, she is capable of responding to the teaching.

The Buddhist Law Means the Universe Itself

Life energy is the state of the absolute. Hence, it cannot be shaken. If it is shaken, it is already relativized and becomes matter. Life energy is none other than the creator. What is called God or the Buddha is nothing but the necessities of life energy. Sentient beings, all trees and all animals, co-exist, but they cannot exercise their rights because they have lost their life energy. God and the Buddha knew how to acquire and utilize that energy. Children should be educated and need to learn what they do not know, which is why they should have complete faith in their parents and their teachers. In an ultimate sense, the religion of Jesus cannot be called a religion. If there are Christians among you, please do not misunderstand me. I am not someone who would claim that Buddhism is the best merely because I am a Buddhist nun and I practice Buddhism.

What you need to know about Buddhist teachings is that it is a pronoun for "everything." Everything that can be sensed is called matter. The inner essence of matter is life energy. When life energy and reality are combined, that combination is called the Buddhist law. The Buddhist law then means the universe itself, and attaining buddhahood means to be a complete human being, of which the Buddha is one representative. You must have heard a number of times how the Buddha suddenly acquired his full life energy. That is Buddhism. All religions, theories, and beings are included in the Buddhist teachings. What then could be excluded from Buddhism? At the initial stage of practicing Buddhism, you rely on an object.[3] There exist a fortune-wishing Buddhism (*subok Pulgyo*) and a journalism Buddhism (*ŏllon Pulgyo*). However, institutions that teach how to become a human being are very rare, and those who become Buddhists in order to be fully human and live with that spirit are also rare.[4] The rise and fall of Buddhism is the rise and fall of the universe.

Buddhism is the last resort for those seeking to resolve the problems of the universe and their own lives. Scholars try to rely on scholarly theories and religious people try to rely on religious doctrines. The result is that the issues at hand fail to find a permanent resolution and conflicts arise from people claiming that this doctrine or that school is the way to attain buddhahood. This is not the correct way to practice Buddhism. The fundamental Buddhist practice is to attain the unity in one's mind, one-ness of thought, one mind. Concentration of one's thoughts and unity of one's will, as well as the oneness of life, are essential. When this state is achieved, one's mind has returned to its origin, its hometown. We must return to the origin of our life energy and move one step further from there. Only then will we be capable of managing our life energy at will. I spent a long time as a novice in a monastery and have practiced for about forty years now. I know from personal experience that it is very difficult to change one's habits and mode of thinking. I may look exactly like "me," but I have been away from my original self and have become accustomed to the division of the self and others for eons of time.

The Most Important Factor Is Mental Transcendence

We are so estranged from our original selves that it does not seem natural to be our natural selves; but there exists a silent voice. References to time or space are side-talks. The only thing that matters is this one thought, which is the function of life energy. Thinking does not naturally translate into life energy. Life is an absolute state, and it is difficult to deal with the domination of this absolute; but there is no way to give up this life. Moreover, one is responsible for one's own life. Whether it is a strand of hair or a drop of water, there is nothing that is free in life. A price must be paid.

But look at us today. We have fallen low and live like animals. Our value comes from the fact that humans are the highest among beings. Human beings are the universe itself. Humans are pieces of the universe. Human responsibilities are what we humans have already attained. The word "responsibility" fits its meaning very well. But the idea of responsibility has become common, worn out, and coarse. People just let it float around and are not aware of how precious it is. People do not know that they are false or that they are leading fake lives; they are not even aware that they have lost their selves. Since they do not know that they have lost their selves, they do not try to recover what has been lost. Surprisingly enough, this earth is filled with such people.

As you sit there, you see the natural law. I am not trying to praise you for the process that you have been through, but at least you were born as males. You do have a way to save yourselves. Life energy is one, and that includes insects and plants. They are, however, not human beings. It is difficult to be born as a human; it is difficult to be born as a male; and it is difficult to be a nun or a monk.

Joining a monastery on a mountain or leaving the secular world does not automatically make one a monk or a nun. Being a monk or a nun means attaining mental transcendence. If a lay practitioner is working to attain mental transcendence so that she can recover the mind, and if she makes a great effort to train her mind in that path, she is like any ordained practitioner. It is difficult to attain buddhahood; it is also difficult to be born a human being. Once one becomes a human being, all problems will be resolved. If we humans realize that our goal is to become human beings, we can just live this life and follow the person who has accomplished the goal of being a human. Such people do exist today. What I try to emphasize is that nothing can be accomplished unless you can control your own mind. People in our time become more and more myopic and rely on a fragmented mind. One should become a human being. What people call supernatural powers or miracles are activities of those who have attained true humanhood and thus utilize their full capacities. Once we attain humanhood, we are free to do anything at will. This is not just a theory. In order to have everything at one's disposal, one should first remove oneself. This is what I meant when I said, "having burned away my youth."[5] I meant by that exhausting both my body and soul. But it was hard to change my habits and to alter my habitual mode of thinking. And then I learned that everything depends on me, on the way I deal with things. But it was really difficult, so even though I wanted to exhaust all the habits of youth, I don't think I actually did completely. I cannot tell you much about it, but it is reality, something I can prove.

The Way to Live an Authentic Life

Some people in the audience might think that what I have said is unrealistic or unscientific. In my opinion it is truly irresponsible to level such a criticism, without fully investigate the facts. People say that ours is the time of all-powerful science. But this is like trying to wag the tail of a toad, impossible since a toad does not have a tail. Since people talk about one day visiting the moon, some might argue against me. But I joined a monastery because I wanted to follow the path of recovering the life energy that I had lost. Whether I meet a tinker or a well-dressed person on the street, I feel an urge to follow him and share with him the path to life. Some might think that I should offer my advice only when asked and not volunteer it unbidden. But since I am confident that I have found the authentic way of living, I want to share that path with others. I told you earlier that it is difficult to be born as a male. I know that to be born as a man is as difficult as attaining buddhahood. Even though you are listening to me giving a sermon, your intellectual level is higher than mine. So try to understand what I say and think about it when you go home. If there is someone among you who is capable of answering questions about life, that person should immediately be my teacher. I always want to let others know about what I have discovered, whoever they might be.

Since you are journalists, I assure you I speak with all my heart, so please do not misunderstand me. If I were you, I would pay close attention to what I say. This is a story about me and it is true that I am trying to make my own case. But at the same time, since I had lost myself, I also had lost everything.[6] People in the West talk about going to heaven. Followers of Jesus talk about the Gospels and, truly believing in Jesus, they try to work together in this sea of suffering. The idea is that working together diligently will result in shared success. What we Buddhists try to do is regain our life energy and live our reality. Heaven is the real world, and so is hell. When we talk about Hwanhŭidae on Tŏksung Mountain, it does not matter whether it is here or on Tobong Mountain. I met a person who had been to heaven. It is a vague story, but still real and provable. Strange as it might sound, it is not just an idea made up by people: God exists, the Buddha exists, and one's way of thinking can become deepened.

We arrive at the origin, the hometown, of living organisms by unifying the "small I" and the "great I."[7] You should at least know about this concept. In other words, you should understand the foundation of your life, which is life energy. You should also build a smooth path. You will have to climb high mountains and cross the deep ocean. In order to do so, you should pave a road, build a bridge, and create a spiritual path utilizing your life energy. How can we call someone a human being who has the type of life energy to think that a good life is possible in heaven and not in hell? The original goal is to attain the great peace. This is all that matters. The goal of human beings is to attain peace and calm. If you have not yet attained peace and a state of calm, what difference does it make whether you are in heaven or in hell? Whenever and whatever kind of life one leads, one should be able to attain peace and calm, exert an independent mind, and attain life energy. That is all that matters.

You journalists should be pioneers and let people know about this. Once words exist, reality also exists. Words are like shells. Shells exist for their contents. Because there is an object, its shadow also exists. Likewise, because reality exists, words exist. If you are not aware of this and if you move on as leaders without knowing who you are, how will you lead the people? You have responsibilities to lead the general public, society, and all human kind on the correct path. Your actions give consolation to the people. Your role is to teach people the correct path. If you are merely debating who is right or who is wrong, or if you think your job is done by merely reporting the facts, you cannot say that you have fulfilled your responsibilities. Wherever you are, you should keep in mind that you are leaders. You should first be aware of this fact.

(May 5 [lunar calendar], 1966)

Notes

Introduction

1. See Sung Rak-Hi, "Kim Iryŏp munhangnon"; Chŏng Yŏngja, "Kim Iryŏp munhak yŏn'gu."

2. See No Mirim, "Higutchi Itchiyo."

3. For a discussion of the increasing interest in women's issues during the 1980s and 1990s in Korea, see Cho, "Politics of Gender Identity."

4. Among works published since the 1990s, see Kim Kyŏngil, *Yŏsŏng ŭi kŭndae*, on Kim Iryŏp as a new woman and on her Buddhism (76–78), on Kim Iryŏp's new theory of chastity (125), on the modernization of women's clothing (256); Chŏn Kyŏnggok, et al., *Han'guk yŏsŏng munhwasa*, on Kim Iryŏp's views on chastity (303–304), on Kim Iryŏp's ideas about parenting (340). Mun Okp'yo, *Sinyŏsŏng*, mentions Kim Iryŏp's views on chastity (11), her influence on the formation of the identity of the new women (21), the modernization of women's clothing (46–47), the importance of the journal *New Women* in the history of the new women (55), Kim Iryŏp's views on women's chastity, marriage, and divorce in connection with Ellen Key (165–166), Kim Iryŏp's life and thought (170–174), the evaluation of the new women in the 1920s (271). Ch'oe Hyesil, *Sinyŏsŏngdŭl ŭn muŏt ŭl kkum kkuŏnnŭn'ga*, offers a discussion of Kim Iryŏp's *New Women* in some depth (194–212); Kwŏn Podŭrae, *Yŏnae ŭi sidae*, mentions Kim Iryŏp's short story "Chagak" in the context of the role of the newly introduced education of woman in the formation of the new women (76); Im Okhŭi, "Sinyŏsŏng ŭi pŏmjuhwa rŭl wihan siron," discusses Kim Iryŏp's view on chastity and female sexuality in the section dealing with the identity of the new women (87). Individual essays on Kim Iryŏp and *New Women* also appear in Yi Hwahyŏng and Yu Chinwŏl, "Sinyŏja wa kŭndae yŏsŏng tamnon ŭi hyŏngsŏng," and Yu Chinwŏl, *Kim Iryŏp ŭi Sinyŏja yŏn'gu.*

5. Kim Miyŏng, "1920 yŏndae sinyŏsŏng kwa kitoggyo e kwanhan koch'al"; Yoo, "Study of the Relationship between Christianity and Modern Korean Female Writers."

6. The first publication in English to discuss Kim Iryŏp's Buddhism is Park, "Gendered Response to Modernity." Also see Kwŏngwan, "Iryŏp sŏnsa ŭi ch'ulga wa suhaeng."

7. Oh, "Kim Iryŏp's Conflicting Worlds."

8. Jin Y. Park, "Gendered Response to Modernity"; Pang Minho, "Kim Iryŏp munhak ŭi sasangjŏk pyŏnmo"

9. Pang Minho, a Korean professor of modern Korean Buddhism, evaluates Kim Iryŏp as someone comparable to Yi Kwangsu. In his essay, "Kim Iryŏp munhak ŭi sasangjŏk pyŏnmo," Pang describes Kim Iryŏp as a writer who cannot be overlooked if we are to shed new light on modern Korean literature, which has heretofore been interpreted through a patriarchal lens (357–358).

10. Kim Iryŏp, "Chilli rŭl morŭm nida," 269. This essay was originally published in *Yŏsŏng tonga,* December 1971–June 1972.

11. Kim Iryŏp, "B ssi ege," 89.

12. My interview with Wŏlsong was conducted on June 29, 2007, in Seoul, Korea.

13. Kim Iryŏp, "Abŏnim yŏngjŏn e," 407.

14. Kim Iryŏp, "Ipsan yisip o chunyŏn saehae rŭl majŭmyŏ," 44.

15. Although the correct romanization is "Ehwa," following the official English title Ewha Womans University, I have romanized the term as Ewha throughout this book. Also, Ewha Womans University uses "womans" instead of "women's," in order to emphasize the individual identity of each woman, instead of a collective identity of "women."

16. *Maeil sinbo,* 13 May 1930, 2.

17. For the life and works of Higuchi Ichiyō in English, see Danly, *In the Shade of Spring Leaves.* For a comparative study of Kim Iryŏp and Higuchi Ichiyō, see No Mirim, "Higutchi Itchiyo."

18. *Nyŏjagye* (Women's world) was first published in 1917 and preceded *Sinyŏja,* whose first issue was published in 1920. *Sinyŏja,* however, was the first publication by women for the promotion of the liberation of women. Yu Chinwŏl, *Kim Iryŏp ŭi Sinyŏja yŏn'gu,* 30; Yŏn'gu Konggan Suyu + Nŏmŏ Kŭndae Maech'e Yŏn'gu Tim, *Sinyŏsŏng,* app. 1.

19. The Japanese word for "bluestockings" (J. *seitō*) consists of two Chinese characters: the character for "blue" (J. *sei*) and that for "boots" (J. *tō*); together they mean "bluestockings." The reference is to the expression used to indicate educated intellectual women in Europe during the eighteenth century. The Korean pronunciation of the same Chinese characters is *ch'ŏngtap.* Iryŏp replaced the second Chinese character with a character that means "tower" instead of "boots." The pronunciation of the "blue tower" is the same as that of "bluestockings," that is, *seitō* in Japanese, *ch'ŏngt'ap* in Korea. Given the numerous typographical errors that appeared in Iryŏp's books, this change might have occurred merely by a typographical error in the process of publication. Another possibility is that Iryŏp might not have been aware of the meaning of "bluestockings," and thus intentionally replaced the second Chinese character so that the expression means "blue tower." I have not found any material that explains this issue. On Hiratsuka Raichō's discussion on *Seitō* in English, see her *In the Beginning, Woman Was the Sun,* 140–200.

20. For the complete collection of the journal *New Women* with translation into modern Korean, see Yu Chinwŏl, *Kim Iryŏp ŭi Sinyŏja yŏn'gu.*

21. See ibid. and Ch'oe Hyesil, *Sinyŏsongdŭl ŭn muŏt ŭl kkum kkuŏnnŭn'ga,*

269. It is not clear, though, where the idea comes from that Iryŏp's husband was the sole financial source for the journal.

22. Yi Paeyong, "Ilche sigi sinyŏsŏng ŭi yŏksajŏk sŏnggyŏk," 21.

23. The official founding of Ewha Hakdang is given as 1886. The reality of how the school opened, however, illustrates just how different women's education was in those days. The founder of the school, Mary F. Scranton (1832–1909), a Methodist Episcopal Church missionary, had prepared for the opening of the school for some time but had difficulty attracting Korean women to the idea of an education. Finally, in May 1886 a Mrs. Kim came to see Ms. Scranton and expressed her desire to learn English to become an interpreter for the queen. This Mrs. Kim became the first student at Ewha Hakdang (Ewha Paengnyŏn Sa P'yŏnch'an Wiwŏnhoe, *Ewha paengnyŏn sa*, 50). For the next twenty-some years, the educational structure of Ewha Hakdang was in the process of being developed, and it was not until 1910 that higher education equivalent to a university education began at Ewha Hakdang (ibid., 66).

24. Kim, *Women of Korea*, 219; also see Ewha Paengnyŏn Sa P'yŏnch'an Wiwŏnhoe, *Ewha paengnyŏn sa*, 57–59.

25. Yŏn'gu Konggan Suyu + Nŏmŏ Kŭndae Maech'e Yŏn'gu Tim, *Sinyŏsŏng*, 13.

26. Yi Paeyong, "Ilche sigi sinyŏsŏng ŭi yŏksajŏk sŏnggyŏk," 23.

27. Chŏn Kyŏngok et al., *Han'guk yŏsŏng munhwa sa*, vol. 1, states, "The identity or nature of the new women was quite ambiguous. Female students were called new women, as were those women who had new types of jobs. As time passed, those who had neither received a modern education nor worked in modern jobs but who had short hair and wore short skirts and high heels also called themselves new women. Even so, it has generally been accepted that the term new women referred to those who received a modern education" (71).

28. Im Okhŭi, "Sinyŏsŏng ŭi pŏmjuhwa rŭl wihan siron," 84–91.

29. Kim Iryŏp, "Sinyŏja ŭi sahoe e taehan ch'aegim ŭl nonham," 107–108.

30. Ibid.

31. In "Uri ŭi isang," Kim Iryŏp states, "Without love, there cannot be chastity. Chastity does not mean morality toward one's lover that can be imposed from outside; it is the passion representing the maximum harmony of affection and imagination for one's lover.... Chastity ... is that which is fluid and that which can always be renewed. Chastity can never be identified with morality; it is the optimum state of one's sense of affection" (82).

32. Kim Iryŏp, "Na ŭi chŏngjo kwan," 119.

33. Hiratsuka Raichō writes, "Conventional wisdom has it that virginity is something to be cherished, that purity and innocence are precious, and that girls must not throw away their virginity lightly.... For a woman to forfeit her virginity for security in life, as a temporary escape, out of simple vanity, or for the sake of her parents or family is a crime. Even in a romance, if a woman gives herself to her beloved without feeling sexual desire herself but only in order to be loved, this, too, is a crime, albeit a romantic one. Of course, we cannot be blind to the reality of

women who are forced by poverty to barter their virginity. But what makes their actions more sinful than that of women losing their virginity in a loveless marriage?" (Hiratsuka Raichō, "Hiratsuka Raichō," 1157–1158).

34. The first time Ellen Key was introduced to Korea was in 1921, as we read in No Chayŏng, "Yŏsŏng undong ŭi che 1-inja ellen kei." For an English translation, see No Chayŏng, "No Chayŏng." The connection between Key and Hiratsuka Raichō has been explored (see Lowy, "Love and Marriage"). Ellen Key's major works were translated into English in the early 1910s: see Key, *The Century of the Child* (1909), *The Education of the Child* (1910), *Love and Marriage* (1911), *Love and Ethics* (1912), and *The Woman Movement* (1912). And Raichō and the members of the Seitōsha translated some of Key's works into Japanese and published them in the journal. In that context, Jan Bradsley, in "New Woman of Japan and the Intimate Bonds of Translation," discusses how translation itself turns into a way of bonding.

35. Kim Iryŏp, "Cha'gak," 173; for an English translation, see Kim Iryŏp, "Awakening," in Young-Hee Kim's *Questioning Minds*, 65.

36. Kim Iryŏp, "B ssi ege," 89.

37. In an interview in the journal *Opening of the World* that took place in November 1934, Iryŏp was asked when she began practicing Buddhism. She answered that her involvement with Buddhism dated from the beginning of her association with the journal *Buddhism* about eight years earlier (Reporter B, "Sakpal hago changsam ibŭn Kim Iryŏp,"15).

38. Kim Iryŏp, *Miraese ka tahago namdorok,* 1:497.

39. Kim Iryŏp, "Pulmun t'ujok i chunyŏn e," 154.

40. See Pang Minho, "Kim Iryŏp munhak ŭi sasangjŏk pyŏnmo."

41. Ibid., 155.

42. For a detailed discussion on these two trends, see Jin Y. Park, *Makers of Modern Korean Buddhism,* 1–8.

43. Pang Minho submits that Buddhist reformist efforts to popularize Buddhism opened the way for someone like Kim Iryŏp with no background in Buddhism to practice meditation and eventually join the monastery. See Pang Minho, "Kim Iryŏp munhak ŭi sasangjŏk pyŏnmo."

44. Kim Iryŏp, "Pulmun t'ujok i chunyŏn e," 157.

45. In "To Yonggang Hot Spring" (Yonggang onch'ŏn haeng), published in *Buddhism* in the October 1931 issue, Iryŏp describes the trip as "Going home two years after marriage" and compares her feeling at the time with that she felt when she went to Taegu, her husband's hometown, two years earlier for their wedding. This means that her marriage to Ha Yunsil took place in 1929 (417).

46. Kim Iryŏp, "Sin Pul kwa na ŭi kajŏng," 430.

47. Ibid.

48. Ibid., 431.

49. Kim Iryŏp's essay "Kaŭl sori rŭl tŭru myŏnsŏ" appeared in 1937 in *Hakhae,* and one might consider that Iryŏp still published her works in 1937. However, the

content of the essay is questionable. The essay begins with Iryŏp's reflection on her feelings about the autumn of the year 1937, the third year of her life as a nun. After the initial reflection, Iryŏp states that she was in her hometown Yonggang for summer vacation with her husband and that the couple was hoping that the hot spring would help to strength her husband's health (480). This cannot be the case, since she was at the monastery in 1937. The trip to Yonggang took place in 1931, as described in her essay "Yonggang onch'ŏn haeng."

50. Kim Iryŏp, "Puldo rŭl taggŭmyŏ," 212.

51. Kim Iryŏp, "Man'gong taehwasang ŭl ch'umohayŏ," 33.

52. Ibid.

53. Ibid., 258.

54. The original letter by Man'gong is preserved at Hwanhŭidae.

55. The dates are based on "The Revised Chronology of Master Iryŏp" (Iryŏp sŭnim yŏnbo) put together by Iryŏp's disciples at Hwanhŭidae and provided to me by Kyŏngwan Sŭnim on September 15, 2012. Kyŏnsŏng Hermitage is a Zen meditation hall for nuns, and Iryŏp's direct disciples stay in Hwanhŭidae.

56. Kim Iryŏp, "Sakpal hago changsam ibŭn Kim Iryŏp," 15.

57. Kim Irypo, "The Revised Chronology of Master Iryŏp."

58. The opening date of Kyŏnsŏng Hermitage as a nun's meditation hall varies depending on at which stage it is considered a meditation hall. Haeju states that it might have existed around 1913 when the hermitage itself was built, but still she marks the beginning of Kyŏnsŏng Hermitage as a nun's meditation hall as 1916. See Haeju, "Han'guk kŭnhyŏndae piguni ŭi suhaeng," 132. Kyŏnsŏng Hermitage was a small straw house when it was first used for a nun's meditation place, and thus has the name "hermitage." The current Kyŏnsŏng Hermitage is not a hermitage but a two-story Western-style building.

59. The description of the daily routine is based on an interview with bhikṣuṇīs Tanho and Kyŏngwan at Hwanhŭidae conducted by me on July 29, 2011.

60. Reporter B, "Sakpal hago changsam ibŭn Kim Iryŏp," 16.

61. For an informative discussion in English on Dahui Zonggao's Kanhua Chan, see Schlütter, *How Zen Became Zen*, chap. 5, "A Dog Has No Buddha-Nature: Kanhua Chan and Dahui Zonggao's Attacks on Silent Illumination."

62. For Pojo Chinul's Kanhua Chan, see Buswell, "The 'Short-cut' Approach of K'an-hua Meditation," and Buswell, "Chinul's Systematization of Chinese Meditative." For the translation of Chinul's works, see Buswell, *The Collected Works of Chinul*. Sung Bae Park's *Buddhist Faith and Sudden Enlightenment* also offers a good discussion on how *hwadu* meditation functions.

63. To read Hyesim's contribution to Korean Kanhua Chan in English, see Hyesim, *Gongan Collections I* and *Gongan Collections II*. See Kim Young-wook's "Introduction," translated by Juhn Y. Ann, and edited by John Jorgensen, in vol. 1 for a discussion of Hyesim's take on Kanhua Chan.

64. Kim Iryŏp, "Man'gong taehwasang ŭl ch'umo hayŏ," 34. The *hwadu* is based on the dialogue between Chan Master Zhaozhou and a student. The dia-

logue is recorded in various Chinese sources. In the context of Korean Buddhism, Hyesim included it in his *Sŏnmun yŏmsong chip* as case number 408. (Sŏnmun yŏmsong yŏmsong sŏlhwa happon, 332a). The dialogue goes as follows:

A monk asked to Zhaozhou: "Ten thousand things return to one. Where does the one return to?

Zhaozhou replied: "When I was in Qīng zhōu, I made a shirt and it weighed seven *jin* (approximately 4,200 g.).

65. Kim Iryŏp, "Chilli rŭl morŭm nida," 321–322.
66. Kim Iryŏp, "Chonggyo ŭi mokchŏk," 79.
67. Kim Iryŏp, "Ipsan yisip o chunyŏn saehae rŭl majŭmyŏ," 45.
68. Kim Iryŏp, "Pulgyo esŏ nŭn woe chŏnghwa undong ŭl irŭk'yŏnna?," 159.
69. Ibid.
70. Kim Iryŏp, "Mŏrimal," 3.
71. Kyŏngwan, "Iryŏp sŏnsa ŭi ch'ulga wa suhaeng," 247.
72. Kim Iryŏp, "Puldo rŭl taggŭmyŏ," 212.
73. This definition of Zen Buddhism has been attributed to the alleged founder of the school, Bodhidharma. Scholars now agree that in fact it was not Bodhidharma who coined this definition, but that it evolved over time into its current form. The passage consisting of sixteen Chinese characters was not put together until after Zen Buddhism had been established as an independent school. According to Peter Gregory, "These different lines were not subsumed together into a unified vision of the tradition as a whole until the end of the period with the writings of Tsung-mi (780–841)—but even that remained only another contending claim when it was put forth" (Gregory and Getz, *Buddhism in the Sung,* 4). According to Griffith T. Foulk, it was not until 1108 that all four lines appeared together (Foulk, "Myth, Ritual, and Monastic Practice," 199n16).
74. Reporter B, "Sakpal hago changsam ibŭn Kim Iryŏp," 15.
75. For example, Yi Sanggyŏng, a scholar of Na Hyesŏk, interprets Iryŏp's tonsure as her way of escaping from her failure to realize her feminist agenda. Yi thus criticizes Iryŏp as the one who

without fully realizing the reality of Korean women, vainly followed theories from abroad and was boosted by the praise that she was a courageous practitioner of those theories. But when she realized how strong the suppression against women in her society was, she stepped back without even trying to fight against it. Retreating even, Kim Iryŏp justified herself with the fresh idea that she was pursuing the path to Buddhahood. (Yi Sanggyŏng, *Na nŭn in'gan ŭro salgo sipta,* 455)

Yi Sanggyŏng's criticism here does not seem persuasive; it seems more a reflection of a negative view on the part of Korean society of joining monastic order than an interpretation of Iryŏp's position on women's issues after she joined the monastery. Lee Tae-Suk also evaluates Iryŏp's tonsure as a limitation of her idea of women's liberation and states that by joining the monastery, Kim Iryŏp retreated to a private realm. Lee points out that in Kim Iryŏp's Buddhism, Buddhist philosophy dealt only with individual salvation and failed to offer solutions for real-world problems (Lee Tae-Suk, "'Yŏsŏng haebangnon' ŭi nangmanjŏk chip'yŏng").

76. See Jin Y. Park, "Gendered Response to Modernity."

77. In the first issue of *Journal of Buddhist Ethics,* James Whitehill writes that "Buddhism must begin to demonstrate a far clearer *moral form* and a more sophisticated, appropriate *ethical strategy* than can be found among its contemporary Western interpreters and representatives, if it is to flourish in the West" ("Buddhist Ethics in Western Context," 2; reprinted as "Buddhism and the Virtues," 17; emphasis in the original). Several years later, Daniel Palmer expressed a similar position on the meaning of Buddhist ethics, especially in the context of Zen Buddhism: "If Buddhists cannot develop dialogical responses to these concerns [for social issues], then Buddhism in all likelihood will remain on the periphery of Western cultural practices, representing only an exotic curiosity and not a vital resource" ("Masao Abe, Zen Buddhism, and Social Ethics," 133–134). Publications on socially engaged Buddhism from the late 1990s onward demonstrate Western Buddhist scholars' concerns about the relationship between religious practice and its social dimension. See, for example, Queen and King, *Engaged Buddhism;* Harvey, *Introduction to Buddhist Ethics;* Keown, *Contemporary Buddhist Ethics;* King, *Being Benevolence;* King, *Socially Engaged Buddhism.*

78. Minjung Buddhism is a type of socially engaged Buddhism that was most active during the 1970s and 1980s in response to Korea's military dictatorship. Minjung Buddhists claimed that Buddhist teaching aims to save sentient beings from suffering and that this should also include saving sentient beings from the various forms of suffering generated by their environments, including political suppression and economic exploitation. For a discussion of Minjung Buddhism in English, see Jorgensen, "Minjung Buddhism."

79. Kim Iryŏp, "Sinyŏja ŭi sahoe e taehan ch'aegim ŭl nonham," 106.

80. Kim Iryŏp, "Pulgyo wa munhwa," 19.

81. Ibid., 22.

82. Although the title states "the fifteenth" anniversary of the death of Man'gong, it should be the tenth, since Man'gong died in 1946 and the essay was written in 1956.

83. Ch'oe Namsŏn. "Chosŏn Pulgyo."

84. These dates are debatable. Iryŏp's whereabouts between 1921 and 1925 are not clearly confirmed. Pang Minho, a professor of Korean literature, suggests that Iryŏp began her relationship with Im in the summer of 1923 and ended it around the fall of 1925 (Pang Minho, "Kim Iryŏp munhak ŭi sasangjŏk pyŏnmo," 368–369).

85. A collection of Im Nowŏl's writings, *Angma ŭi sarang,* was recently published. Pang Minho's essay in the volume offers a new evaluation of Im's work in the context of modern Korean literature. See Pang, "Sarang kwa chŏlmang kwa

top'i ŭi romangs"; also see Yi Hŭijŏng, "1920 yŏndae ch'ogi ŭi yŏnae tamnon kwa Im Nowŏl munhak"; Yu Munsŏn, "Im Nowŏl munhak pip'yŏng yŏn'gu"; Park Jeong-sou, "Im Nowŏl, 20 yŏndae angmajŏk modŏnisŭtŭ."

86. Paek Sŏnguk's essays published in *Pulgyo* together with his other philosophical writings were published in 1960 under the title *Paek Sŏnguk paksa munjip*.

87. Kim Iryŏp, *Miraese ka tahago namdorok*, 2:47.

Chapter 1

1. Iryŏp repeatedly states that human existence serves as the standard of values against which the values of all other existence can be measured. The idea seems to reflect the Buddhist theory that the human realm is the only realm in which one can attain enlightenment. The fact that one is being born as a human being itself indicates that the person has the maximum capacity to lead a life in freedom. As will become clear, the fact of being a human, however, does not guarantee freedom and satisfaction in life, since individuals tend to be blind to their own capacity and lead lives of dissatisfaction, failing to utilize their capacity to be the superbeings among all beings.

2. In arguing that "unless everything becomes one's self" one cannot have freedom and peace, Iryŏp's logic runs counter to the modernist self-centered worldview. The idea that all that exists in the world is one's own self is not the same as the subjective idealism frequently encountered in the dualist mode of thinking. Dualism proposes that the human subject as a rational being constructs the world and the subject and objects are related only as subject and object. In Iryŏp's worldview, to identify the world with one's own self becomes possible only when the subject realizes that the boundary between the subject and other is provisional. In subject-object dualism, the subject's world is inevitably limited by the existence of others. The limitation makes the subject feel constrained, and out of this sense of constraint arise complaints and discontentment. The familiar way of dealing with this problem is to expand one's space by "invading" the space of others. War and conflict are inevitable elements of this mode of existence. Iryŏp, following Buddhist logic, reflects that the only way to resolve this dilemma is to realize the true relationship between the subject and object, a relationship from the Buddhist perspective characterized by non-duality.

Chapter 2

This essay was originally published in the *Chosŏn Daily News* (*Chosŏn ilbo*) during the 1950s, according to *Miraese ka tahago namdorok* (47). It also appears in the posthumous publications *Miraese ka tahago namdorok* (32–47) and *Iryŏp Sŏnmun* (54–77), published by Kim Iryŏp's disciples at Sudŏk Monastery with minor editorial revisions to make Iryŏp's writing more accessible. The version that appears in *Iryŏp*

Sŏnmun is divided into eight short essays and three new sections are added: "All the Solutions are One" (60–61), "I Can be a Human Being" (69), and "The 'I' Who Is Thinking and the 'I' Who Actually Is" (73–75). These insertions do not appear in the original essay "Life." Among the three insertions, "All the Solutions Are One" appears in *Miraese ka tahago namdorok,* 2:126–128.

1. Kim Iryŏp considers both body and mind to be material. Mind-body dualism, in which the two are correlated with spiritual and material dimensions, respectively, does not hold in Iryŏp's thought.

2. The heaven referred to here is not the Christian heaven; rather, it refers to one part of the "great emptiness" (*taegong*) that is the universe for Kim Iryŏp. Iryŏp goes into more detail when she discusses her cosmology in "What Is Faith?" (Chap. 9).

3. The Korean word that means literally "root" (*ppuri*) implies basis, ground or foundation, and Iryŏp uses it to imply the ground of existence.

4. For example, a frequently cited passage from the *Laṅkāvatāra Sūtra* claims that the Buddha said nothing in his forty-nine years of teaching: "It is said by the Blessed One that from the night of the Enlightenment till the night of the Parinirvana, the Tathāgata in the meantime has not uttered even a word, nor will he ever utter; for not speaking is the Buddha's speaking" (Suzuki, *Laṅkāvatāra Sūtra,* 123–124). The *Sūtra* addresses the issue again with the following statement: "From the night of enlightenment till that of Nirvana, I have not in the meantime made any proclamation whatever" (ibid., 125).

5. "The secular world" is the translation of the *sahā* world in which we live; this is the world in which Śakyamuni Buddha taught and in which sentient beings are subject to transmigration.

6. The six realms of transmigration include the realm of hungry ghosts and demigods in addition to the four realms Iryŏp mentions here.

7. The employment of the expression and conception of "culture" here is uniquely Kim Iryŏp's. In this cosmology, Iryŏp identifies the non-human world below this earth as the realm of non-culture and the realm of gods as the realm of utmost culture. The concept of culture Iryŏp refers to here becomes clearer in her essay "Buddhism and Culture" (Chap. 3).

8. It is not clear what Iryŏp means by the expression "religions of humans and gods." The ninth-century Chinese Buddhist thinker Zongmi (780–841), in his *Inquiry into the Origin of Humanity* (*Yuanren lun*), describes a fivefold taxonomy, the first of which is "the teaching of humans and gods" (*inch'ŏn kyo;* Ch. *rentian jiao*). The complete list is as follows: (1) humans and gods, (2) the lesser vehicle, (3) the great vehicle's teaching of phenomenal appearances, (4) the great vehicle's refutation of phenomenal appearances, (5) the direct revelation of nature. For an English translation of Zongmi's *Yuanren lun,* see Gregory, *Inquiry into the Origin of Humanity.*

9. The desire realm (*yokkye*) is one of the three realms (or the threefold world) of Buddhism: the desire realm, the form realm, and the formless realm.

10. The reference in this passage is to the Huayan notion that a particle of dust contains the entire universe. At the phenomenal level, a particle of dust looks like an insignificantly small thing, but when the mode of its existence is examined from the Buddhist perspective, a particle of dust is also a part of the entire process of the dependently co-arising universe. Ŭisang (625–702), the founder of the Korean Huayan school, thus states in his "Hwaŏm ilsŭng pŏpkye to," "one is all, all is one, a particle of dust contains the entire universe" (1a). For an English translation of the treatise, see Odin, *Process Metaphysics and Hua-yen Buddhism,* xix-xx, 189–213. For discussions of Huayan thought in this context, see Chang, *The Buddhist Teaching of Totality;* Cleary, *Entry into the Inconceivable;* Cook, *Hua-yen Buddhism;* Haeju sŭnim, *Hwaŏm ŭi segye;* Jin Y. Park, *Buddhism and Postmodernity.*

11. In other words, the present is a combination of the memory of what happened in the past, what one thinks at present, and what one speculates about the future; there is no one distinctive temporal or spatial point that can be identified as past, present, or future.

12. Thoughts are our realities, but since both thoughts and realities constantly change, we do not know how to act in the midst of changing reality. Iryŏp proposes that this incapacity for action happens because we see only the changing surface and fail to realize what is behind or below. This unchanging source of all things is what Iryŏp repeatedly calls "the thought before a thought arises." Action in Iryŏp's conception is "the other side of thought," which is also the expression of the "I," the original source of all beings in the world. Mere movement is not action; an action is when a willful and definite measure is taken in reference to one's reality. Action is possible, according to Iryŏp, only when one realizes what is underneath the surface of constantly changing phenomenal reality.

13. In Buddhism the theory of *trikāya,* or three bodies, refers to the three bodies of the Buddha: (1) *dharmakāya (pŏpsin),* a reference to the transcendence of form and the realization of true thusness; (2) *saṃbhogakāya (posin),* the buddha-body that is called "reward body" or "body of enjoyment of the merits attained as a bodhisattva"; (3) *nirmāṇakāya (hwasin),* the body manifested in response to the need to teach sentient beings. (Muller, *Digital Dictionary of Buddhism,* accessed April 8, 2009). Kim Iryŏp uses the expression "three bodies" (*samsin*) to refer to the physical body (*yuk*), karma (*ŏp*), and Buddhist dharma (*pŏp*).

14. This thought is very much reminiscent of the thirteenth-century Japanese Zen master Dōgen's (1200–1253) idea of "Being-time" (*uji*). In the essay "Uji" in his *Shōbogenzō,* Dōgen writes:

> An old buddha said:
> For the time being, I stand astride the highest mountains peaks.
> For the time being, I move on the deepest depths of the ocean floor.
> For the time being, I'm three heads and eight arms.
> For the time being, I'm eight feet or sixteen feet tall.
> For the time being, I'm a staff or a whisk.
> For the time being, I'm a pillar or a lantern.

For the time being, I'm Mr. Chang or Mr. Li.
For the time being, I'm the great earth and heavens above.

…

We set the self out in an array and make that the whole world. We must see all the various things of the whole world as so many times. These things do not get in each other's way any more than various times get in each other's way. Because of this, there is an arising of the religious mind at the same time, and it is the arising of the time of the same mind. So it is with practice and attainment of the Way. We set ourselves out in an array, and we see that. Such is the fundamental of the Way — that our self is time. (Dōgen, *Heart of Dōgen's Shōbōgenzo*, 48–49)

In this essay, Dōgen philosophically interprets the expression *"uji"* (*yusi*), which in the above is translated as "for the time being"; it can also be translated as "at times" or "sometimes," but the literal meaning is "being and time." That is, being is time. A being is not free from the passing of time; but neither does a being change over time. In both of these situations a being is assumed to be separate from time, and the impact of time is either denied or considered. The idea that being is time indicates that a being does not and cannot exist separate from the diverse factors that constitute being; a being is all of them, which Dōgen identifies as time.

15. In other words, Tolstoy's understanding of Buddhism is like reading a compass upside down. This passage as it is in the Korean original is not clear. It is perhaps for that reason that there are modifications in the reprint in *Iryŏp Sŏnmun*. The passage in the original edition reads "Buddhism is a teaching that completely sees through the reality and its inner essence, and by doing so it fully puts that realization into use. In Tolstoy's understanding of Buddhism, the compass that directs one to the correct path is turned upside down"; the revised edition reads as follows: "Buddhist teaching is a union of reality and its inner essence. It is a complete teaching of inner essence; when sentience and insentience utilize nirvana, which is the only law for them to attain salvation, the unity of being and non-being generates great power (*taeryŏk*), and when they are not in use, mutual negation of being and non-being create great rest. Tolstoy misunderstood such an inexplicably profound meaning of Buddhist teaching and set a compass upside down. How does one explain such a great error?" (Kim Iryŏp, *Iryŏp Sŏnmun*, 65).

16. It is not clear which scripture Iryŏp is referring to when she says that the idea of transforming fire into water is justified in a scripture. The message is that a scripture can theorize and justify any idea rationally but that merely studying Buddhist scriptures with such contents does not help one realize one's true nature and thus attain awakening.

17. The reference here is obviously to Iryŏp's earlier criticism of Tolstoy for his misunderstanding of Buddhism, which Iryŏp compared to reading a compass upside down.

18. The "eight kinds of beings" (*p'albu*) refer to the eight beings in Indian cosmology. "Formerly they were evil, but now having been enlightened by the Buddha, they protect his dharma. They are: (1) *deva*s (*ch'ŏn*) [gods]; (2) *nāga*s (*yong*) [snake kings]; (3) *yakṣa*s (*yach'a*) [spirits of the dead who fly about in the night]; (4) *ghandharva*s (*kŏndalp'a*) [half-ghost music masters]; (5) *asura*s (*asura*) [demigods of evil disposition]; (6) *garuḍa* (*karura*) [golden-winged birds which eat dragons]; (7) *kiṃnara* (*kinnara*) [heavenly music masters who are neither human nor non-human]; and (8) *mahoraga* (*mahuraga*) [snake spirits]" (Muller, *Digital Dictionary of Buddhism*, accessed April 10, 2009).

19. The five supernatural powers (*o sint'ong*) include: "(1) *ch'ŏn'an t'ong*, (*ch'ŏnan chijŭng t'ong*) *divya-cakṣus*, deva-vision, instantaneous view of anything anywhere in the form-realm; (2) *ch'ŏn'yi t'ong*, *divya-śrotra*, ability to hear any sound anywhere; (3) *t'asim t'ong*, *paracitta-jñāna*, ability to know the thoughts of all other minds; (4) *sungmyŏng t'ong*, *pūrvanivāsānusmṛti-jñāna*, knowledge of all formed existences of self and others; (5) *sint'ong* (*sinjokt'ong*; *sinyŏŭit'ong*) *ṛddhi-sākṣātkriyā*, power to be anywhere or do anything at will" (Muller, *Digital Dictionary of Buddhism*, accessed April 10, 2009).

20. In other words, "I" am "I" to myself, but for others, they are also "I's" to themselves.

21. The meaning of the Korean original translated here as "time and space are all 'me'" is not clear.

22. Iryŏp's logic seems to be that since we managed to be born as a human beings, we should lead a lives that pay back the good fortune of such a birth.

Chapter 3

1. "This self is the truth, which cannot be verbalized" can also be translated as "This self is the truth, which does not have an exit." An exit exists when there is a division between inside and outside. But truth cannot have an exit since truth does not have an external realm. If truth has an external realm, the realm which is excluded from truth, such a truth can only be partial and thus cannot be truth. Truth should be all-inclusive without an outside. This is also Iryŏp's concept of self in that the self is the same as the universe in the ultimate sense, since the self from Iryŏp's perspective is absolute openness.

2. In this passage, Iryŏp challenges the biblical story that Adam and Eve ate the fruit of knowledge out of their own free choice and thus are responsible for violating God's prohibition. From Iryŏp's perspective there is a conflict between the idea of God's omnipotence and God's decision to allow Adam and Eve to exercise choice. If God is omnipotent, he should have known that Adam and Eve would use their free will to violate his rule. If so, it is God's responsibility that Adam and Eve, and thus human beings, fail. In this essay and several of other essays in this book, Iryŏp repeatedly mentions the problem of the Christian concept of free will. Her argument evolves to the idea that we should understand God, and

any ultimate being in that sense, and humans—limited beings—from a perspective different from that described in the story of Adam and Eve.

3. The meaning in the original Korean of this passage, starting from "Phenomenal reality" to the end of this paragraph, is unclear. I interpret it as follows: Once we realize that this life is a dream and not ultimate reality, killing other beings for food is simply part of life's activity; we realize that both the killer and the killed are subject to birth and death, and neither the killer nor the killed is a winner. A war that inflicts violence on others might be inevitable, but if one understands that this reality is a dream, even when waging a war (in an inevitable situation), one will not have hatred or evil intent toward the enemy. Iryŏp does not promise a world where war or conflict completely disappears. She seems to think that, like a food chain, in order to exist in this world, a certain amount of conflict is inevitable. The promise of enlightenment is not a complete elimination of conflict; rather it is a promise that one will not be manipulated by the various situations that come up in life. The point is to exercise compassion in the face of conflict and suffering.

4. As can be seen in the subsequent discussion in this essay, the term "culture" has a special philosophical meaning in Iryŏp's thought. It is much more than the usual meaning of a totality of social activities of human beings. To put it simple, to Iryŏp, "culture" represents the totality of the creativity of the human mind.

5. Kim Iryŏp employs the expressions "culture" and "cultural assets" for several different purposes. On the one hand, "culture" is used to refer to material cultural objects, such as Buddhist architecture and art. In this context, cultural objects are referred to as "cultural assets." But the expression "cultural assets" is also used to refer to an individual's mental state, and the "assets" in this case refer to the Zen Buddhist idea that every sentient being is already fully equipped with Buddha Nature and thus has "cultural assets." On the next layer, culture indicates the utmost state of the human mind, which she identifies with Buddhist teachings. There are also authentic and inauthentic expressions and worlds of culture. Critical of the cultural environment of her time, Iryŏp states that in many cases those considered to be persons of culture in her time do not even understand the meaning of culture. Iryŏp claims, as we read in this last passage, that instead of being satisfied with the mere name, one should find culture within oneself, which means to be aware of the fundamental existential reality that she identifies with "life," the very unavoidable, indispensable reality of all existing beings. Later in this essay I translate the same expression "cultural assets" (*munhwajae*) also as "cultural capability and cultural products."

6. Pure sound (or Brahma's voice), or *chitsori,* is part of Buddhist music generally known as *pŏmpae.*

7. The identity of the mason who built the pagoda is not clear; sometimes, the mason Asadal is identified as a person from the Kingdom of Paekche and sometimes from Tang China.

8. In the four examples of training of a singer, a painter, a mason testing his own product, and a scholar's reading of a text, Iryŏp demonstrates the meaning

of what she considers true culture — both cultural capability and products — as opposed to superficial artifacts. A true cultural creation is possible when the creator's cultural capacity is fully exercised and when that cultural capacity is embodied in a cultural product. The process of creation includes a range of training from the seemingly trivial act of making perfect ink out of an ink stick; continuous efforts, such as reading the same text for ten years, until the creator becomes one with the soul of one's creation, as exemplified by a singer recognizing the voice of the teacher from afar; and finally the spirit of perfection as in the case of the mason testing his own product. Throughout this book, Iryŏp repeatedly emphasizes the importance of realizing one's capacity, which is infinite. Iryŏp also identifies this capacity as "creativity." Culture or "cultural asset" in her expression represents the incident in which the inner capacity of creativity (cultural capability) is expressed in concrete reality as a cultural product.

9. Iryŏp does not identify this source.

10. Iryŏp is referring to a publication entitled *Hŭllŏgan yŏinsang: Kŭdŭl ŭi yesul kwa insaeng* (*Images of the women of the past: Their arts and lives*) by Yi Myŏngon. In this book Yi discusses four female intellectuals: Kim Iryŏp, Na Hyesŏk, Yun Simdŏk (1897–1926), and Kim Myŏngsun (1896–1951).

11. The idea that the real self does not have an outside is in accordance with Iryŏp's idea that truth does not have an exit and cannot be verbalized. The concepts of inside and outside exist only when one perceives beings through the prism of boundaries that divide self from others. An exit exists only when there is an inside and an outside. That there is no exit, in this case, does not indicate a sense of confinement with no outlet. Instead, the idea of having no exit means that there exists no boundary dividing the self and others. Understood in this manner, truth, and thus the self, indicates infinite openness.

12. It seems that Iryŏp tried to make a distinction between the concept of "ownership," which is possible only when there is the subject-object dualism, and the idea of non-dual relationship between the creator (or artist), i.e., the subject, and a work of art, i.e., the object. A work of art is not something that is created by the creator but that which is the creator himself or herself. This accords with the idea that Iryŏp tries to explain through the four examples of the training of a singer, a painter, a mason testing his own product, and a scholar's reading of a text. See n. 8 above.

13. In other words, even a great architectural work like the great dharma hall at Sudŏk Monastery is the work of a human being who was in charge of his or her own creativity, and in this sense, the artist (or the mason) and the work of art (the great dharma hall) are not two different entities, but a concrete reality and a representation of the artist's mind.

14. Iryŏp mentions Halley's Comet (Hyesŏng) as one of the eight planets, but it must be Neptune (Haewangsŏng) as translated here.

15. Iryŏp's discussion of the planetary system and its relation to the concepts of culture and non-culture here is far from being fully developed. It is not clear why Iryŏp considers that the eight planets belongs to non-culture or in what sense

clusters of stars other than the eight planets are closer to culture than those eight planets. Iryŏp seems to have developed her own cosmology, combining some of the scientific knowledge available at the time with Buddhist cosmology. She also discusses this in Chapter 2, "Life." Broadly put, the cosmology takes the following format: At the lower realm (which she here also describes as being located at the center) exists the realm of form; this is the realm of non-culture and of non-humans. Above this realm of form comes the realm of both form and non-form. At the highest level is the realm of heaven, which Iryŏp characterizes as the most cultural realm. Ironically, this highest realm is not the most beneficial for one for attaining enlightenment. Since this highest realm contains only the good and the beautiful, it also creates attachments to the good that distinguish it from the bad and the ugly. Iryŏp's cosmology, either from a Buddhist perspective or as scientific fact, cannot attain much validity. Since Iryŏp does not identify the sources of her ideas, we do not know how she came to this cosmology and its value system in terms of culture and non-culture. It seems, though, as Iryŏp claims in the passage following this paragraph, her main point is to underline the importance of the true life of culture, which to her consists of being aware of the non-duality of binary opposites. Mahāyāna Buddhism has a long history of emphasizing the importance of the non-duality of opposites as the fundamental ground of the Buddhist worldview. One representative text that deals with the issue is the *Vimalakīrti Sūtra*. In this scripture, a lay Buddhist practitioner, Vimalakīrti (Yuma kŏsa in Korean), represents the epitome of non-duality: he is a non-monastic practitioner whose knowledge of the Buddha's teaching outwits the Buddha's most advanced disciples; he frequents brothels but without being influenced by their environment. For an English translation, see *The Holy Teaching of Vimalakīrti*, trans. Robert A. F. Thurman.

16. Iryŏp claims that people in her time are confined to the "small I." The "small I" refers to the idea of the self that one attains and maintains by making a distinction between the self and others. Iryŏp reasons that to generate the identity of the self by distinguishing the self from others ironically limits the capacity of the self, since such a self is confined by the boundary created by the self. The goal of Buddhist training for Iryŏp is to help people realize that constraints on the self are created by the self and that the original self, which she calls the "great self" (*taea*), has infinite capacity.

17. Kim Iryŏp here makes a distinction between a true person of culture and a secular person of culture, which I translate as a person of secular culture. There are then three types of people with regard to culture. The first is a person of culture, in whom culture indicates the external embodiment of one's creativity, when creativity is understood as a being's infinite capacity, which Iryŏp considers as an innate capacity of all beings. The second type is a person of secular culture or a secular person of culture, in whom "culture" means a mere presentation of secular knowledge. This is a person of non-culture who is ignorant of his or her infinite capacity for creativity.

18. The expression *"simgwang,"* translated here as "inner light," is a Buddhist

term referring to the light from the Buddha's mind and, in this case, especially from Amitabha Buddha. Here, based on the context, the expression is translated without explicit Buddhist implications.

Chapter 4

This translation is based on "Man'gong taehwasang ŭl ch'umohayŏ," in *Ŏnŭ sudoin ŭi hoesang,* 24–43. The same essay is also included in *Ch'ŏngch'un ŭl pulsarŭgo.* A number of errors exist in the version in *Ŏnŭ sudoin ŭi hoesang.* I have referred to the *Ch'ŏngch'un ŭl pulsarŭgo* version to correct typos but have not adopted any revisions made in that version other than for corrective purposes.

1. Kim Iryŏp considers transmigration to be an unavoidable reality of all that exists. There is no end point in transmigration. In other words, life is not something that comes to an end with death. Because suicide cannot put an end to one's existence, it is important to find a way to survive so that one does not suffer even more in future lives.

2. In other words, one can try to remove oneself from reality, standing on high mountains, cleansing eyes and feet in clean mountain streams. Suffering, however, is not separate from this seemingly heavenly environment. One cannot hide from suffering by trying to avoid reality.

3. The most well-known purification movement in Korean Buddhism took place in the 1960s. The purification movement Iryŏp refers to here is the one during the colonial period.

4. "[T]he eons of time of nothingness" refers to one of the four stages in the repeated process of construction and destruction of the universe. That is to say, the entire universe goes through eons (*kalpas*) where things are constructed (*sŏnggŏp*), where there is stability (*chugŏp*), where things are destroyed (*koegŏp*), and eons of time of nothingness (Kilsang, *Pulgyo taesachŏn,* 1:1042).

5. The phrase "to change the dharma body" means to die.

6. *Ot'ak akse* is a Buddhist theory about the end of the world in which the world is contaminated by the five impurities: (1) the impurity of time (*kŏp t'ak*) refers to various disasters of the epoch such as disease, hunger, and war; (2) the impurity of view (*kyŏn t'ak*) encompasses the incorrect and biased views of people; (3) the impurity of afflictions (*pŏnnoe t'ak*) refers to the mind that is filled with evil thoughts; (4) the impurity of the sentient being (*chungsaeng t'ak*) describes the deteriorating state of sentient beings; and (5) the impurity of life span (*myŏng t'ak*) implies that the human life span becomes shorter (Kilsang, *Pulgyo taesachŏn,* 1:1837–1838).

7. Iryŏp is here referring to her theory of chastity, which is one of the most well-known of her ideas as a new woman during her pre-monastic life. Two of her essays well describe her thoughts on the issue: "Uri ŭi isang" (1924) and "Na ŭi chŏngjo kwan" (1927).

8. Even though I have treated as direct quotes the following speeches of Iryŏp and Master Man'gong, what appears here is actually Iryŏp's recollection of what was said. The 1960 version of the text treats the exchange as a paraphrase, but in the 1962 version Iryŏp treats her and her master's words as if they were direct quotes. I assume she did this for the sake of convenience, and for the same reason I follow the 1962 version.

9. The 1962 version does not include this sentence.

10. Iryŏp seems to think that the spirit is in the same category as the body. In another essay she states that both spirit and body are material.

11. At this point in the 1962 version the following passage has been added: "Everybody has Buddha Nature (which is complete nothingness). We should first ask ourselves why we live this life of suffering and practice hard with faith in no-self."

12. In the 1962 version the following passage has been added: "And this happens because people do not know that only when a person learns and utilizes the body that does not get wet in water and does not burn in fire (that is, the self-nature that does not have life or death), will he avoid the suffering of life and death."

13. "*Chitsori*" is a Korean expression referring to "pure sound" or "Brahma's voice" (*pŏmŭm*; Ch. *fayin*).

14. For the 1962 version of this essay Iryŏp changed "for ten-some years" into "for eighteen years" (358). It is not clear how she came up with this figure. As I discussed in the introduction, it seems that "Practicing Buddhism" (Puldo rŭl taggŭmyŏ), which appeared in the journal *Three Thousand Li* (*Samch'ŏlli*) in January 1935, was her last publication until Iryŏp resumed her writings in the late 1950s. Another of her essays, "Listening to the Sound of Autumn" (Kaŭl sori rŭl tŭru myŏnsŏ), appeared in 1937 in *The Sea of Knowledge* (*Hakhae*).

15. The idea is that since everybody—both the Buddha (the enlightened being) and sentient beings (the unenlightened people)—has the same quality, which Buddhism calls Buddha Nature, awakening should take place immediately. This is the idea known as "sudden enlightenment." Seen from this perspective, even three days or seven days are a long period of time for an awakening to take place. Buddhist tradition explains this idea of "sudden enlightenment" by using a simile of the sun and clouds. Everybody already has Buddha Nature, like the sun, which is always up in the sky. When there are clouds, we don't see the sun, which, however, does not mean that the sun does not exist. As soon as the clouds disperse, the sun will "immediately" appear. Likewise, as soon as the sentient being realizes his or her Buddha Nature, awakening will "suddenly" take place; it will not take three days or seven days. Even though in theory awakening occurs "suddenly" in this manner, in order for this sudden awakening to take place, there must be a fundamental change in one's mode of thinking. This is known as the "transformation of the basis" (*āśraya-parivartana*). The concept is originally from Yogâcāra Buddhism. Buddhist scholar Sung Bae Park explains the concept as follows: "*Āśraya-parivartana* or revolution of the basis [or transformation of the basis] indicates a sudden revulsion, turning, or re-turning of the *ālaya vijñāna* [the eighth conscious-

ness] back into its original state of purity. That is to say, through *āśraya-parivartana* the seven lower consciousnesses which create the egoistic discrimination of an external world based on the dualism of subject and object are eliminated, as are the habit-energies (*vāsanās*) or habitual perfuming of the storehouse consciousness, so that the Mind returns to its original condition of non-attachment, non-discrimination and non-duality" (Park, *Buddhist Faith and Sudden Enlightenment*, 127).

16. That is, the master said that awakening should take place immediately and that even three days is a long period of time as far as enlightenment is concerned. In the story as well, the lecturer attained an awakening as soon as he heard the question "What is it that has turned around?" Iryŏp thus thought that since she was not a smart person, it would take at least three months for her to attain awakening. Three months, she must have considered, should suffice for a "sudden" awakening for a dull person like her.

17. "*Samadhi* of the doubting mind" (*ŭisim sammae*) means to get into deep meditation (*samadhi*) with the questioning mind (or doubting mind). The question, or the doubt, is initiated by a *gongan* or *hwadu*, with which a practitioner meditates. In the case of Iryŏp, as she mentions here, the *hwadu* she worked with was "All things return to one, what is this one?" A *hwadu*, however, is only an initiator or a catalyst that further triggers in the practitioner the existential question of "Who am I?" The transformation of the seemingly illogical question into a question regarding one's existential reality demonstrates the process of how the ground for the "transformation of the basis" discussed above in n. 16 takes place.

18. Iryŏp repeatedly emphasizes this idea that even though one dies, and this body decomposes, in fact life is endless and there is no way for us to put an end to it. That is so because one goes through endless transmigrations.

19. "The master always gave dharma talks with Buddhist meanings of this presupposition. I have a long life, and it is inevitable that practice should take long and that I should complete a long practice." This passage is in the 1960 version (35), but omitted in the 1962 version (260). Given that the meaning in Korean is unclear, I have omitted it as well.

20. In the 1962 version Iryŏp changes the "three realities" into "the two realities of body and spirit" (261). She seems to have made this modification because the same Chinese character compound for three bodies (*samch'e*), which I have translated here as three realities, is used several lines down to refer to the three bodies of physical body, karma body, and dharma body. Here, I have translated the first instance as "three realities" and the second as "three bodies," since, even though the Korean expressions are the same, they refer to two different trinities.

21. A number of elements of Iryŏp's Buddhism represent the uniqueness of her thought. Faith is one such element. The position of faith in the Buddhist tradition is different from that in theistic religions. Religious traditions that are based on "other-power" emphasize faith, whereas those based on self-power, such as Buddhism, have to address some issues related to faith before employing it as a basis of religious practice. One question that needs to be answered is the subject-object structure related to faith. Faith means faith in something. This inevitably

introduces subject-object dualism, whereas Buddhism is based on the rejection of such dualism. A question then arises regarding to whom this faith is addressed, if we discuss faith in the context of Buddhism as Iryŏp does in this passage. It is well known that the Buddha himself declared at his death that each individual should be his or her own lamp. But Mahāyāna Buddhism went on to develop various figures to act as guides to sentient beings. Such guidance is interpreted through the concept of "skillful means" (*pangp'yŏn*). Faith in the Buddha, or faith in bodhisattvas, can be interpreted according to this idea. In Zen Buddhist tradition, faith takes an important position, as discussed in Sung Bae Park's *Buddhist Faith and Sudden Enlightenment*. Iryŏp's concept of faith includes an idea similar to what is known as "faith in the teacher" (*chosin*). This is faith in the fact that one's teacher is living evidence of enlightenment that functions as an inspiration for one's practice. Iryŏp's emphasis on faith is ironic, however. As she has already expressed and will further discuss in other essays appearing later in this book, one of her objections to Christianity is that it demands blind faith in God. Iryŏp argues that Christianity's emphasis on faith in God relegates human beings to the status of robots, whereas each individual is a free being in Buddhism. How, then, is the faith that she emphasizes here different from Christian faith? In Zen Buddhist practice, as fundamental as the faith in the teacher is the faith that "I am the Buddha." Without an awareness of this reality, one would not engage in practice or would merely pray to the Buddha or bodhisattvas asking for help, which turns one's practice into purely devotional Buddhism. Faith, Iryŏp emphasizes here, is the faith in one's capacity for enlightenment. A sentient being is an unenlightened being. The Buddhist teaching that each and every sentient being has Buddha Nature and thus is a buddha inevitably contradicts one's reality as an unenlightened being. Faith is the only bridge that connects the reality of unenlightened state of the sentient being and the Zen Buddhist premise that a sentient being is a buddha. In "On the New Year's Day of the Twenty-Fifth Year after Joining the Monastery," Iryŏp confirms once again the importance of faith in Christianity. She confesses that it was her incomplete understanding of the teachings of Christianity that caused her eventually to lose her faith, which she defines as "the most precious treasure."

22. That is, he died and moved on to the next world.

23. In other worlds, only when the self completely empties itself and accepts the world's diverse phenomena can it become a whole. The passage might be read as a confirmation of an egocentric individualism in which everything is understood through the lens of the self. But the message of this passage is actually exactly the opposite. A self is a whole in Iryŏp's Buddhist world. In order for a seemingly fragmented self to recover its wholeness, it must shed the self-defining boundary that it has created. When that boundary is removed, the openness of the self accepts all things. Hence, it is described as the "quintessence of nothingness." Having an identity means creating a boundary; without a boundary there is no identity. Although a boundary confers a certain identity, it also imposes constraints by virtue of creating a fixed identity. Nothingness or non-being, as opposed to being, is pure openness and thus freedom. Iryŏp claims that a being's

true identity, from Buddhism's perspective, is this openness. Further, a realization of this openness is possible only when the self-created boundary is eliminated.

24. The meaning of the passage "As far as we grasp the meaning of the idea that time and space are the beginning and the end, this would allow us to control all of our thoughts" is not clear in the Korean original.

25. The Korean original of this entire paragraph is unclear. Iryŏp herself must have realized this, because in the 1962 version only the last sentence of this paragraph appears and the rest of the paragraph is condensed into one sentence: "If one completely attains nothingness (non-beings), one can naturally earn all the beings" (264).

26. Oseam is a hermitage at Paektam Monastery on Mount Sŏrak. The hermitage has a story related to its name, but it is different from the story that Iryŏp narrates here. No information is available about the source of Iryŏp's narrative.

27. In the 1962 version, after this is added: "This is why one should continue to practice without cessation."

28. This is the teaching that Man'gong gave to Iryŏp in 1936.

29. From "In Buddhism everything is one's self " up to here I have followed the 1962 version, since the 1960 version is not clear.

30. Eighty-four thousand means countless or an infinite number in Buddhism (Kilsang, *Pulgyo taesachŏn,* 2:2668).

31. There seems to be an error in the title of this essay, which indicates that it was written on the fifteenth anniversary of the death of Man'gong. He died in 1946 and this essay was signed in 1956, so the title should say "tenth anniversary." If it were written on the fifteenth anniversary, the date would be 1961. The Korean version of the book in which this essay is included was published in 1960.

Chapter 5

1. Kim Iryŏp's major criticism of Christianity is its dualistic standard with regard to the issues of good and evil, creator and created. Iryŏp discusses this issue in detail in this chapter. The discussion is also found in Chapter 13, "Letter to Mr. B." Another of her criticisms is about the nature of Christian promise. Iryŏp contends that the rewards promised to the good people by Christianity can be confirmed only in the afterlife. During this life, the only confirmation that God exists and thus the only proof of all the rewards that Christianity promises is in one's mind, which Iryŏp identifies with one's faith. Since there is no tangible proof of God's promise actualized in this life, if one's faith is not rigorous enough, doubts arise and eventually one loses faith. Iryŏp considers this having been the case with her when her Christian faith faltered and she eventually declared herself a nonbeliever. As opposed to the postmortem realization of the promises in Christianity, Iryŏp claims that Buddhist teachings become one's reality in everyday life, if only one tries to practice.

2. Here, I have followed the 1962 edition.

3. The new theory of chastity came to be known as a trademark of Kim Iryŏp as a new woman during her pre-monastic life. In relation to this idea, Iryŏp published two essays. The first essay, "Uri ŭi isang" (Our ideals), was published in 1924 in *Punyŏjigwang,* and the second essay, "Na ŭi chŏngjo kwan" (My view on chastity), which was an expanded version of "Uri ŭi isang," appeared in the January 8, 1927, issue of *Chosun ilbo.* Iryŏp claims that she discussed this idea about the new theory of chastity as early as 1920 when she organized a forum known as the Blue Tower Society (Ch'ŏngt'aphoe), a gathering to promote women's position in a society. No record of this meeting exists except in Iryŏp's autobiographical essays.

4. Creativity or creative power for Iryŏp refers to the original energy of the universe, which is also the source of all existence and which is also referred to as "the original spirit."

5. In other words, a new year as an enlightened being is yet to arrive. According to the calendar, a year comes and a year goes by, but as Iryŏp states at the end of this essay, a real new year should be the time when a new horizon of life arrives, and that occurs for a Buddhist practitioner when she reaches a new level in her practice.

6. I have followed the 1962 edition for this sentence.

7. In other words, once one realizes the unity of all beings at their deeper level, one is the owner of oneself and thus the leader of all beings. When one realizes that "everything is myself," the division between self and others is removed, and a being as an individual disappears. This is, for Iryŏp, a way to overcome the limitations of individuality, of a being understood as a fragmented individual. A fragmented being is characterized by its boundaries, which are its limitations. As one realizes the Buddhist worldview, in which a being exists through causes and conditions, one realizes that the boundaries of individual existence are only provisional. Awakening to this reality of one's existence, for Iryŏp, is characterized by the state of absolute freedom.

8. The 1962 version of this essay bears the title "A Being Who Does Not Cry," with a subtitle "On the New Year's Day of the Twenty-Fifth Year after Joining the Monastery."

9. One *li* is equivalent to 0.244 miles.

10. Here one hears again the Huayan adage that one particle of dust contains the entire universe.

Chapter 6

The full title of this chapter is "A Proposal Sent to the Fifth General Conference of the World Fellowship of Buddhists Held in Bangkok."

1. When one thinks about compassion or love, a commonsense approach is to understand it through a dualistic structure: The subject exercises compassion

or love upon the object. The same idea applies to the Buddha's compassion or God's love: The Buddha has compassion for sentient beings, or God loves human beings. Iryŏp contends that the Buddha or God is not the being who relies on this dualistic logic. The Buddha has compassion for sentient beings, not because the Buddha is a being higher than sentient beings, but because the Buddha is a being that has realized the non-duality of the Buddha and sentient beings. When the Buddha exercises compassion for sentient beings, the Buddha does so because the sentient being is his own self. God loves human beings, not because human beings are God's creatures, Iryŏp argues, but because God is the being that realized the oneness of all beings.

The realization of non-duality between the Buddha (the enlightened one) and the sentient being (the unenlightened one) is the very ground of bodhisattva activities in Mahāyāna Buddhism, as is articulated in the *Diamond Sūtra*. In this *sūtra*, the Buddha teaches Subhūti, one of his disciples, that even though the bodhisattva saves innumerable sentient beings, there are no sentient beings to be liberated because if a bodhisattva helps sentient beings attain awakening with the idea that "I" am helping a sentient being, that cannot be a bodhisattva act (see Price, *The Diamond Sūtra*, 37). That is so because insofar as one has the idea of "I," an independent self, from the Buddhist perspective, such a person cannot be free from the egoist distortion of the situation that one is involved with.

2. Freedom is the fundamental condition of existence for Iryŏp. Freedom allows an individual to realize her power over her own life. This realization of the imperative of freedom in one's existence, in turn, requires the acceptance that others also have the same existential right to freedom. A bird flying in the sky has its right to move in the direction it chooses, and unless there is an agreement with the bird, nobody can make the bird change its direction. This indicates the absolute nature of freedom, and realization of this freedom is possible only when one is aware of the communal nature of this freedom. An individual has absolute freedom and so do others, and both one's own freedom and that of others need to be respected. What happens when different claims for freedom collide one another? Iryŏp does not ask this question and that is the limitation of her thought where social application is concerned. The same problem occurs when Iryŏp discusses concrete realities such as war (see n. 5 below).

3. Iryŏp is faithful to the Sŏn Buddhist tradition that considers the study of Buddhist doctrine to be a false practice, since doctrinal study constrains the practitioner within the limits of language, whereas truth, as Iryŏp repeatedly emphasizes, cannot be verbalized.

4. In accordance with the Mahāyāna Buddhist worldview, Iryŏp explains that there are two different layers of the world: the phenomenal and the noumenal. The Buddhist emphasis on non-conflict and the unity of self and others, which Iryŏp repeatedly emphasizes in this essay, is the vision of the world from the perspective of the noumenal level. The inner reality of existence is basically pacific from the Buddhist perspective. This, however, does not mean that there are no conflicts on the phenomenal level. Since beings exist in a physical reality,

which by nature separates one body from another, conflicts are inevitable on the phenomenal level. Iryŏp seems to further minimize such conflicts and redefines war as discord or difference in the process of putting ideas into action. As briefly mentioned in the introduction, Buddhist social theory is not Iryŏp's strong point. In general, Iryŏp's Buddhist thought heavily relies on the noumenal aspect of the teachings, and when it comes to consideration of the impact of the noumenal reality on the phenomenal world in which conflicts are part of daily existence, Iryŏp's Buddhist thought leaves much to be desired.

Chapter 7

1. The story appears in the *Sūtra of the Forty-Two Sections* (*Sishierzhang jing*, 723a–b). In the *sūtra*, the Buddha says, "Among the desires, there exists nothing as strong as sexual desire. Fortunate that there is only one; if there were two of the same sort, there would be no human beings who could attain awakening."

2. I have skipped one line of the Korean original text here because it does not make much sense as it is.

3. The text refers to trillions of different transformation bodies (*ch'ŏn-paek-ŏk kujok hwasin*) of the Buddha, which means that the Buddha can take innumerable forms as he teaches sentient beings.

4. Iryŏp repeatedly emphasizes this fact in her writing. That is, death is not the end of one's existence, and existence is eternal because that is the law of the universe. The universe exists through constant change, endlessly going through the process of arising, sustaining, and ceasing. An individual is a part of this unending process, and for that reason there is no way for us to put an end to our lives even if we wished to do so. This is important for Iryŏp, since ignorance of this fact leads to eternal suffering. The goal of Buddhist practice is to help us awaken to the nature of the eternity of existence so that we can free ourselves from suffering in the eternity of lives to come.

Chapter 8

The original title of the 1960 version of this essay is "C. sŏnsaeng ege" (To Mr. C.), with a subtitle "C. sŏnsaeng ŭn sahakcha ro Pulgyo esŏ ch'ŏnjugyo ro kaejongham" (Mr. C. is a historian and has converted from Buddhism to Catholicism). In the 1962 version Iryŏp modified the title to "Is the Mind One or Two? To Mr. C., Who Has Recently Converted to Catholicism." I have adopted the 1962 title, which I think gives a better sense of the essay's content. For the background of this essay and more about Ch'oe Namsŏn, see my introduction.

1. Interesting to note in this essay is that Iryŏp is taking a clear dualistic stance about right and wrong ways of practicing religion.

2. There is no such reference to this idea of *"chong"* in *"chonggyo,"* the Korean word for religion. Iryŏp seems here to be rather stretching her logic.

3. In Iryŏp's universe, the creator of the world is not a personified supreme being. The universe for Iryŏp is not static but consists of an endless series of movements. The totality of these movements is the creator. Beings like human beings are the results of these activities. Individual beings in this case are likened to waves on the ocean. Waves are not separate from the ocean but at the same time they have their own identity as waves. Individual humans are like waves, but these human waves, before awakened to the ontological reality that they are part of the ocean, see waves as distinct from the ocean, the critical result of which is for each individual to create his own fragmented identity, reducing his all-capable capacity to the fragmented capacity of the individual wave.

4. In the Korean text Iryŏp uses the name "Samhan," which in Korean history refers to the three confederated kingdoms—Mahan, Chinhan, and Pyŏnhan—that existed in the southern part of the Korean peninsula before the third century CE. However, given that Buddhism did not arrive in Korea until at least the fourth century, I interpret "Samhan" as referring to the Three Kingdoms period (Samguk Sidae), when Buddhism arrived and immediately gained influence in the Korean peninsula, then occupied by the three kingdoms of Koguryŏ (37 BCE–668 CE), Paekche (18 BCE–660 CE), and Silla (57 BCE–935 CE).

5. There is no reference to the sources Iryŏp used for this idea.

6. Unlike major Western religious traditions, which offer a creation myth, Buddhism and other major Asian religions such as Hinduism, Confucianism, and Daoism do not claim to know how and by whom the world was created. Hence Buddhism uses the expression "from the beginningless beginning." If the beginning point is not known, can Buddhism tell its followers about the end of existence? Buddhism changes the nature of such a question and instead of telling us the end point of existence, it focuses on the ultimate state of one's existence. Nirvana in this sense is understood to be the ultimate goal of Buddhist practice. Through the attainment of nirvana, the Buddhist practitioner achieves the ultimate state of existence. But this is rather deceptive, since nirvana is not fully described in any of the Buddhist texts. In Zen Buddhist traditions, the treatment of nirvana is even more ambiguous, since the tradition teaches that nirvana is samsara and samsara is nirvana. If this world is nirvana, the logic holds that there is no other temporal or special realm that could be counted as the ultimate realm of existence. Ironically, however, Buddhists, including Zen-ists, do not clearly articulate either that nirvana is not the goal or that one cannot know the end of existence. Iryŏp in this passage unequivocally states that the origin and end of existence are not known.

7. At the phenomenal level, the world and existence are based on the self-contradictory rule of dualism: When there is heaven, there is hell. Polarization is the mode of existence because one extreme cannot exist without the other. Arising is followed by ceasing, birth by death, cold by warmth, and heaven by hell. That heaven is followed by hell does not indicate a temporal movement from heaven to hell or vice versa. Rather, it indicates that, without the concept of hell, heaven

cannot exist; without the concept of light, darkness cannot exist either. If we understand this logic — which is the logic of the phenomenal world — our major concern in life, Iryŏp contends, cannot be whether one is in hell or in heaven. Hell is not desirable, since we know that one suffers in hell; but heaven is not completely desirable either, since we become attached to pleasure in heaven. Since heaven and goodness cannot exist without their counterpart — hell and evil — there is no way that one can experience only one side of the duality. The Buddhist training of the mind is meant to enable us to maintain our free self in whatever environment we find ourselves, which also means to lead a comfortable life, as Iryŏp states in the following passage.

8. As discussed in the previous note, existence for Iryŏp is fundamentally self-contradictory in the sense that a being is subject to the polarizing movements of arising and ceasing, birth and death, cohesion and disintegration. The universe is a continuation of these self-contradictory movements of which humans are only a part. Life continues in eternity in this sense, since the universe makes circular movements through the self-contradictory polarization of birth and death. There is no end to it; just so, the individual's existence.

9. In her criticism of Christianity, Iryŏp rejects the notion of blind faith as the object of religion. However, she does not deny the importance of faith in practicing religion. As she discusses later in this essay, what Iryŏp objects to is a faith based on "other-power," the faith that exclusively relies on the object of belief. Iryŏp acknowledges the importance of faith in Buddhist practice but maintains that it should be faith in the Buddha or God as the model for achieving the state of full utilization of one's creative capacity. Faith based on the dualism of a subject who has faith in an object is rejected, but faith that leads to the realization that the practitioner has the same capacity as the object of faith is the requisite medium leading the practitioner to awakening. Sung Bae Park offers a good discussion on the nature of faith in Buddhism in his book *Buddhist Faith and Sudden Enlightenment.*

10. To discover and learn the true nature of oneself, or of "I," is the beginning and end of Iryŏp's Buddhist philosophy. For Iryŏp, to learn the nature of one's own self, which also means to realize the condition of one's existential reality, is the only path to salvation.

11. As Iryŏp mentions several times in other essays, she does not promise or project a heavenly world after awakening. As we read in her discussion of the nature of heaven, heaven, which is generally characterized as having only positive attributes, is in fact imperfect from her perspective because it represents only one side of the dualistic reality. Heaven is dangerous, moreover, because it makes one attached to this one aspect of existence, whereas existence itself, like the nature of the universe, contains both good and evil in the sense that evil is the other side of good and good does not exist without evil. To exist means to exist in the midst of good and evil, regardless of one's spiritual status. One might wonder why anyone would try to attain enlightenment, or salvation, if in fact it cannot save them from this dual nature of the world. This passage would be Iryŏp's answer to the question. The condition of existence is polarization of opposites, birth and death,

arising and ceasing, prosperity and decline. To awaken is to realize this nature of existence, which is the way to escape the suffering caused by one's attachment to certain fragmentary aspects of existence. In this sense, Iryŏp is faithful to the very core of Buddhist teaching, which is to save the individual from suffering.

12. From the sentence beginning with the phrase "Without a real object" up to this sentence, I have followed the 1962 version. It is not clear what Iryŏp is referring to by "this precious fact that exists only for human beings." Judging from the context, it could refer to the capacity to remember one's past lives. But in general in Buddhism, remembering past lives is not considered an exclusively human phenomenon.

13. This story appears in the *Lotus Sūtra*, which teaches the innate Buddha Nature of all beings. The part of the story where the person sent to call on the child is Jesus does not appear in the sūtra and is obviously Iryŏp's own invention. See *The Threefold Lotus Sūtra,* Chap. 3.

14. Pak P'aengnyŏn (1417–1456) was a scholar-official during the Chosŏn dynasty (1392–1910) who maintained his loyalty to the young King Tanjong (1441–1457, r. 1452–1455). Tanjong was overthrown by his uncle, who later became King Sejo (1417–1468, r. 1455–1468), but Pak refused to acknowledge the legitimacy of Sejo, for which he was tortured to death.

15. In Iryŏp's Buddhist thought, the traditional mind-matter dualism does not hold. Iryŏp thinks that the mind, the soul, and even God have material existence. This means that in Iryŏp's thought system, the concept "material" is not characterized, as it conventionally is, by visible, tangible reality. This seems related to the idea that what cannot be seen by normal people can be seen by those who are awakened. The past lives of those who have attained awakening, for example, are visible to them, as is the soul, or the spirits. Qualifications like visibility and invisibility or tangibility and intangibility are not the property of an entity, but reflect the capacity of the person who deals with an object.

16. From this sentence to the end of the paragraph, I have followed the 1962 version.

17. I have followed the 1962 version for this entire paragraph.

Chapter 9

The 1960 version of this essay has the title "Contemplating with a Letter from My Friend M." In the 1962 version, Kim modified it to "What Is Faith? Having Read a Letter from My Friend M." I took from both versions for the present translation, which I believe gives a better sense of the content of the essay than the original title in the 1960 version.

1. The 1960 version has it as "R.," undoubtedly a typographical error. The 1962 version is corrected to "K." There is another such typo in this paragraph, for which I followed the 1962 version.

2. Instead of "Uranus," Iryŏp repeats "Venus," calling it by its another name in Korean, meaning a morning star (*hyosŏng*, but with a typo in the Chinese character, *hyo*). I have translated it as "Uranus," since that makes the eight planets in the solar system. The 1962 version completely omits from this passage on the solar system everything from "This universe contains" to "above and below the sky."

3. As in several other places in this volume, Iryŏp again deals with the issue of Christianity, explaining the concerns that caused her to withdraw from Christianity and how Christianity should be understood. Iryŏp's understanding of Christianity at this point demonstrates the influence of Buddhism. Mahāyāna Buddhism claims that we are already the Buddha just as we are; by the same token, Iryŏp conflates the idea of God with that of the Buddha. When an individual realizes the true ontological reality of oneself, one becomes God, as one becomes/ is the Buddha in the Mahāyāna Buddhist tradition.

4. For Iryŏp heaven is not the final resolution but merely part of reality, because as she says in the next sentence, heaven is possible within a dualist paradigm, upon which reality of the secular world is based.

5. When reality is based on the dualism of self and others, even seemingly positive concepts like compassion and love can play a negative role, since when others exist as objects of self, compassion or love exercised from the position of the self might not always be perceived as compassion and love by others. As briefly mentioned in an earlier note, the *Diamond Sūtra* in Mahāyāna Buddhism especially elaborates on this issue by explaining the meaning of "bodhisattva activities." In the sūtra, the Buddha teaches Subhūti how a bodhisattva should help sentient beings and practice compassion. When a bodhisattva practices compassion, if the bodhisattva has a sense that he is helping sentient beings, the bodhisattva is already essentializing the idea of bodhisattva and sentient beings, or the self and others. Therefore, the Buddha says, "when vast, uncountable, immeasurable numbers of sentient beings have thus been liberated, verily no sentient being has been liberated" (*Jingang banruo buloumi jing*, 235, 749a; Price and Wong, *The Diamond Sūtra*, 19). What would this paradox mean? The Buddha explains that a bodhisattva who has the idea of a separate ego, a personality, a sentient being, or a life span is not a bodhisattva.

6. In the 1962 version this passage is modified: "God must be a human like the Buddha, but he was partially deified" (Kim Iryŏp, *Ch'ŏngch'un ŭl pulsarŭgo*, 218). That is, God's deified quality contains only goodness, lacking its opposite evil, which is inevitably part of goodness.

7. Eighty-four thousand in Buddhism is not to be taken literally; rather it signifies an innumerable amount or implies all the things in the world. Buddhism says that sentient beings have eighty-four thousand defilements, and thus the Buddha gave eighty-four thousand dharma talks to cure those defilements. The Buddha's teachings are recorded in Buddhist scriptures, but how Iryŏp makes a connection between the activities of Jesus and life in Christian heaven with the teachings of Buddhism is not clear, since there is no mention of the Christian God or Jesus in Buddhist scripture.

8. Iryŏp's Buddhist thought is characterized by an absolute non-duality. This non-duality includes not only the non-duality of self and others, but that of good and evil and the Buddha and a demon. Here Iryŏp explains this idea in connection with phenomenal and noumenal realities of the world. Iryŏp identifies phenomenal reality with the demonic, whereas noumenal reality, which is before a thought arises and conceptualization takes place, is related to the Buddha. The phenomenal world is inevitably dualistic. Individual distinctions and characterizations of individual beings as well as distinctions made through linguistic expressions are all inevitable aspects of the phenomenal world. Because individual identity exists, and because verbalization is always a part of the phenomenal world, the phenomenal world is dualistic, which accounts for the existence, though relative, of distinctions between good and evil. For this reason Iryŏp identifies the phenomenal world as the world of a demon, not in the sense of good versus evil, but in the sense of the existence of separation. In this case, the word "demon" does not imply the existence of the essence of evil. Instead, it indicates the existence of the dualism between a demon and the Buddha, good and evil. On the other hand, the noumenal reality of the world is the Buddha in the sense that no dualistic distinction exits at this level. Conventional societal morality that characterizes a demon and the Buddha to be evil and good, respectively, does not hold in Iryŏp's Buddhist world.

9. The meaning of the passage from "When you have the capacity to concentrate" up to here is not clear in Korean. For that reason I have given a literal rendering based on both the 1960 and 1962 versions. The ideas behind these passages nevertheless remain ambiguous.

10. Iryŏp's Buddhist thought claims a unity of heaven and hell, and thus heaven for her offers only provisional convenience and comfort. Seen from the perspective of the ultimate goal of existence, however, heaven does more harm than good to its inhabitants because, as she explains here, heaven provides a comfortable life without the need for mental cultivation or physical effort for improvement, so when the time comes for its inhabitants to be judged, they face the reality that even though they have not committed sin, they have not practiced compassion either. This places heaven in an inferior position to earth and explains why Buddhism teaches that enlightenment can be attained only in the realm of humans, not in the realm of heaven, which is where those who will attain enlightenment wait before their final birth on earth. Heaven for Iryŏp cannot be the final resting place because it is merely one side of a dualistic polarization—good, happiness, etc.—when the reality of the universe is the unity of all polarizations. Iryŏp's concept of heaven and hell is reminiscent of William Blake, a pioneer of British romanticism, who called for the unity of heaven and hell in his well-known poem "The Marriage of Heaven and Hell" (1790–1793).

11. The expression "the mind is the Buddha" (*chŭksim si Pul*) is a phrase in classical Chinese that the ignorant woman did not understand. But the passage's pronunciation in Korean, *"chŭksim si Pul,"* is similar to *"chipsegi Pul,"* which means "the straw shoes are the Buddha."

Chapter 10

This letter was sent to Im Nowŏl (Rim Nowŏl, act. 1920–1925), with whom Kim Iryŏp had an affair during her stay in Japan in 1920. The affair eventually led to a divorce from her first husband. At the time when Kim Iryŏp and Im Nowŏl met he was a well-known figure among Korean intellectuals in Japan. He was known as "a poet of the devil" who followed the literary movement of art for art's sake.

1. I have followed the 1962 version in the translation of this passage.

2. Scholars think that Im Nowŏl (the recipient of this letter) ended his literary career in 1925. If Iryŏp's memory is correct and given that Iryŏp joined the monastery in 1933, this statement indicates that Im Nowŏl was publishing as late as the mid-1940s. The original publication information of the poem Iryŏp refers to here has not yet been identified.

3. I have followed the line divisions of this poem as they appear in the 1962 version.

4. Here, I adopt the wording of the 1962 version.

5. The Buddhist world is a world of causality, and the same cause can produce innumerable different results based on the conditions in which the cause functions. This is the conditional causality of the Buddhist worldview. If a person lives in heaven, for example, there are causes and conditions that have led the person to that state; and so is the case with those living in the human realm or in hell. If a person reaches the state that Iryŏp identifies here as that of the perfect being, she understands through which causes and conditions she is in the current situation, and that awareness enables her to lead a free life, regardless of her circumstances.

6. I have adopted the 1962 version for this passage.

7. In this essay, Iryŏp's concept of love as something beyond heterosexual love is only touched upon. In her final book, *In Between Happiness and Misfortune*, Iryŏp fully develops her philosophy of love, in which heterosexual love gives way to love as a religious concept.

8. The awakened spirit (*kagyŏng*) in general refers to the spirits of the dead. It is an honorific expression showing respect for the deceased; therefore, "awakened" in this case does not mean "awakened" as in the case of the Buddha's awakening (see Muller, *Digital Dictionary of Buddhism*, accessed May 9, 2011). Iryŏp instead uses the expression "awakened spirit" to indicate the state before that awakening, in which the Buddha takes a physical form as, for example, Śakyamuni Buddha or Maitreya Buddha. She does not identify the source for this interpretation.

9. "These three" then consist of dreams, that which is dreaming, and that which makes us dream, each of which is explained as expressions, movements, and the source of life energy. On the one hand, one can interpret this as referring to dreams, the subject who dreams, and the source that makes the subject dream. It is not clear, though, how the expressions of life energy are different from its movements, i.e, that which is dreaming.

10. Iryŏp mentions the four difficult things to attain in the path to buddha-hood more than once in this volume. In contemporary Buddhist scholarship, that one of the difficulties is related to gender has been an issue in understanding women's position in Buddhist tradition, since this could indicate that woman cannot attain enlightenment. It is noteworthy that Iryŏp never approaches from a feminist perspective the idea that one has to be born as a male to attain buddha-hood. As we read the discussion that comes later, it seems that Iryŏp separates the attainment of buddhahood from the four difficult things to attain. She thus states that it might be as difficult for a woman to be a man as to attain buddhahood.

Chapter 11

This essay also appears in *Ch'ŏngch'un ŭl pulsarŭgo* (1962), 10–109, under the title "Ch'ŏngch'un ŭl pulsarŭgo: B ssi ege, che ilsin." I have adapted the title from the 1962 version.

1. According to the date at the end, this essay was completed in the Year of the Monkey (1956). Iryŏp added, "In retrospection of what happened about thirty years ago." There are several passages that indicate that Iryŏp worked on this essay over a period of about thirty years. The passage "four months and nine days" is the first indicator that Iryŏp began writing the essay sometime in 1928, four months and nine days after Paek Sŏnguk left her with the letter stating "causes and conditions of our relationship have come to an end." One difficulty caused to the translation by this prolonged period of writing is the tense. Up to this point in the essay Iryŏp used the present tense, indicating that it was her state of mind in 1928. If the essay was written in the 1950s, for the description of what happened in 1928, Iryŏp should have used the past tense, but she left it in the present tense. In Korean language the mixture of the present and past tenses in describing past events does not cause much of a problem. In English, however, it can be confusing to the reader or can be considered incorrect. I have alternated the present and past tenses following the Korean original, not just to be faithful to the original text but also to preserve the process of the writing of this essay, which I believe to have taken place over a long period of time. The present tense therefore does not necessarily indicate Iryŏp's state of mind at the time of the publication of the essay, but rather at several different time periods, including that of "four months and nine days after Paek left" and, later in the essay, describing her state of mind in 1956, when she completed the essay.

2. The "new theory of chastity" (*sin chŏngjo ron*), as discussed in the introduction, is a representative idea of Kim Iryŏp as a new woman in her pre-monastic period. Iryŏp published two articles directly related to this idea: "Uri ŭi isang" (1924) and "Na ŭi chŏngjo kwan" (1927). In these essays Iryŏp challenges the traditional double standard on chastity and claims that liberation of women from the gendered standard of chastity is key to the liberation of women in Korean society.

3. Iryŏp's description of her family situation here is a bit different from her description in other writings. Here she says that her mother had five children, but in all other of her writings she mentions only four children. Iryŏp was the eldest; when she was about six, a baby sister was born and then another baby sister. One of her baby sisters died in 1907, when she allegedly wrote a poem "Death of My Sister." In 1909 her mother died several days after giving birth to a baby boy, who died several days later. It seems that sometime in between the death of one of her sisters in 1907 and of her mother in 1909, the other baby sister died, but none of her writings mentions this death.

4. Kim Iryŏp's father died in 1915, the year Iryŏp graduated from Ewha Hakdang and the year she moved to Ewha Hakdang Chungdungbu.

5. Kakhwang Temple (Kakhwangsa) is the former name of Chogye Temple (Jogyesa).

6. In the 1960 version, after "the original seed" Iryŏp writes, "which is the *ālaya* consciousness"; this phrase has been eliminated in the 1962 version, which is the one I have followed.

7. Here Kim Iryŏp's concept of the creator changes from the Christian concept of a creator God to a being who fully understands the nature of its self and utilizes that self. God is the creator only in the sense that God is a being who is creatively controlling his or her life. In Iryŏp's view, since God exists, God is also a part of the created. The concept of creator as the one who fully grasps and utilizes one's self-identity is related to her concept of creativity, which is the original energy of the universe and the source of all existence. Iryŏp discusses this issue in detail in Chapter 2 ("Life") and Chapter 3 ("Buddhism and Culture"). By understanding God as both a creator (versus *the* Creator) and a creature, God is exempt from full responsibility for the existence of good and evil. Iryŏp tried in this manner to solve one of her theological questions, but at the same time she causes God to be dethroned from the position of the sole omnipotent Being in the world.

8. The logic behind these passages with regard to the relationship between eternal peace, oneness of heaven and hell, and equality is not clear. What Iryŏp seems to be trying to say is that since heaven and hell are one and they are a world of equality and eternal peace, wherever her father might be, he would be in a state of peace.

9. The first issue of *Sinyŏja* appeared in March 1920. The journal continued until its fourth issue in June 1920. It likely ceased production for financial reasons.

10. "*Sŏnsaengnim,*" which I translate here as "professor," does not indicate a professor at a university. It is, rather, an honorific form of address in the Korean language.

11. This passage seems another indication that this essay was written over a long period of time. In the earlier part of the essay, Iryŏp claims that she practiced the "new theory of chastity" and thus her faithfulness to Paek was not based on the traditional idea of exclusive female sexual fidelity to one man. But here she evaluates the time of her life when she claimed and practiced the new theory of chastity

as an "ugly change" from her earlier life as a faithful Christian. In her writings published after she joined the monastery, Iryŏp almost never reflects upon those ideas regarding gender equality that she supported during her pre-monastic life. This passage might indicate a negative evaluation of her time as a new woman. On the other hand, we can also read the expression "ugly change" as an ironic expression saying that in other people's eyes her change can be viewed negatively.

12. "The snow mountains" refer to the Himalayas. The Buddha, however, attained enlightenment not on a snow mountain but in Lumbini in Nepal.

13. The doubts that are discussed here are not the sort of questions that come up in daily life. The doubt expressed here is an important part of training known as *hwadu* meditation. Sung Bae Park explains the doubts the practitioner experiences in the process of *hwadu* meditation in connection with the structure of faith in Buddhism (*Buddhist Faith and Sudden Enlightenment*, 67–77).

14. Buddhists are traditionally those who voluntarily renounce worldly possessions. In theory the only thing a Buddhist practitioner possesses is the robe he or she is wearing and a bowl out of which he or she eats. In Zen Buddhist tradition, "a bowl and robe" symbolize the transmission of the teachings. When a patriarch recognizes his successor, the patriarch gives his robe and bowl to his successor as a symbol of the transmission of the teaching.

15. Even though Iryŏp uses the present tense in this paragraph, I don't believe that the state of mind described here refers to her state of mind at the time of publishing this essay. Here Iryŏp is still in 1928, "four months and nine days" after Paek left her. See also n. 1 above.

16. Here is another passage that shows that the composition of this essay was not actually 1956, as is indicated at the end of the essay, but rather over a long period of time beginning "four months and eight days after" the day she received a letter of farewell from Paek Sŏnguk.

17. Zhang Sheng and Hong Niang are characters in *Romance of the Western Chamber* (*Xixiangji*), a thirteenth-century Chinese dramatic work.

18. Again, it is clear that "this letter" here does not refer to the letter written thirty years after their relationship ended, but the letter Iryŏp wrote "four months and nine days" after Paek left her.

19. This is another passage that suggests that this essay was written over a period of time, not in 1956.

20. The beings in Buddhism exist as the result of conditions and causes, which means that they do not have an independent essence as such. Since beings do not have an essence with which to obtain independent identity, beings are illusions. This does not mean that beings do not exist on the phenomenal level. However, it should be noted that existence on the phenomenal level is always provisional, subject to constant change as causes and conditions change. The universe consists of all of these beings, which means that the universe also does not have any essence of its own. This is an absolutely non-substantial view of the world whereby the world exists through multi-layered causation. This causation, for Iryŏp, is also subject to the cyclical changes of arising, staying, changing, and ceasing.

21. Paek Sŏnguk returned to Korea in 1925, after having completed his degree in Germany and at a time when Korea was under Japanese colonial rule (1910–1945); hence Iryŏp's expression "people who had lost their country."

22. From here until just before the end of this essay Iryŏp tells the story of a couple. The story occupies about the half of this essay, and one wonders whether it is an actual story told to Iryŏp by a friend or whether it is one she created in order to explain her situation. In her preface to this book Iryŏp mentions that her motivation in writing was to proselytize, and for the sake of that goal she mixed personal stories with Buddhist teachings. This story seems to reflect Iryŏp's intention to disseminate Buddhist teachings through the power of narrative.

23. Iryŏp uses "creativity" in several different senses. Creativity, for her, is one's capacity to create oneself when one is in the state of complete self-reliance. Creativity is also the movements of the universe. In the Buddhist world, there is no unmoved mover who started the world or a creator God who created the world. Constant activity, characterized by the polarization of arising and ceasing, going and coming, constitutes the universe and at the same time existence of individual beings. A being, in this sense, is a product of universal creativity, that is, the movement of the universe, and a being produced in that process also possesses the capacity to exercise creativity without being bound by external forces.

24. Whatever is manifested in the world, to Iryŏp, is subject to the principle of the universe. The principle of the universe is impermanence, because all things in the universe are subject to the law of change; that is, they arise, stay, change, and cease. This fundamental principle of existence in Buddhism is characterized by the Buddha's four stages of life: birth, sickness, aging, and death. Religious doctrine is not exempt from this law, and it is especially so since religious doctrines are expressed in language and supplemented by various rituals and diverse manners of practice. These are all, as Iryŏp points out here, means to salvation, not the goal.

25. "*Hwadu*" (C. *huatou*; J. *watō*), literally meaning a "critical phrase," is a word or phrase practitioners employ in their meditation. *Hwadu* meditation has been a dominant meditation practice in Korea since the thirteenth century, when it was introduced by Zen Master Pojo Chinul (1158–1210), until today. For a discussion on *hwadu* meditation, see the introduction.

26. This is a poem that frequently appears in Korean as a poem about the impermanence of things. One source of the original in classical Chinese is Kihwa Hamhŏ Tŭt'ong (1376–1433). See Kihwa Hamhŏdang Tŭt'ong hwasang ŏrok, 228a.

27. The forty-nine days of prayer is a ritual to guide the dead. During the forty-nine days, the dead are judged based on their life in this world and their next life decided. The prayer ceremony is performed every seventh day after the death for seven weeks, which makes the total of forty-nine days. "The first seventh-day prayer" mentioned later in this paragraph refers to this.

28. This represents Iryŏp's Buddhist world of absolute oneness. The world, the self, or sincerity without margins, without exception is the world in which the polarization of dualism ceases to function. The outside exists only when there is a border between the inside and outside. A margin exists only when one creates

a boundary between the margins and the contents they contain. Dualism, which is an inevitable aspect of the phenomenal world, needs to be overcome in the absolute world of religion. That is the world in which the fragmentary existence of each being is understood not as an individual but in relation to the entire universe.

29. One notices that from here on the narrator's tone changes from that in the previous section, where the narrator is retelling the story of Chuhǔi. In telling the story of Chuhǔi, the narrator is in a different mental state from this next passage, where Iryǒp returns to the situation in 1928 immediately after Mr. B. left her.

Chapter 12

This is a letter written not by Kim Iryǒp but to her from Paek Sǒnguk [Baek Sǒnguk], whose abandonment Iryǒp describes in Chapter 11. It includes Iryǒp's lengthy response to a donation that Paek has made to the meditation center where she was practicing. It is not clear when the letter was sent. Iryǒp first met Paek Sǒnguk in 1927, when she began to contribute her writings to the journal *Pulgyo*, and Paek briefly served as president of the company that published the journal. At the beginning of this letter, Paek says that "it was more than thirty years ago." This would suggest that the letter was written in the late 1950s. The Korean edition of *Reflections of a Zen Buddhist Nun* was published in 1960, about thirty-three years after their encounter.

1. Tǒksung Mountain is the mountain on which Sudǒk Monastery is located.

2. Throughout this book Iryǒp maintains the idea that the mind is also material. In this passage she makes a distinction between the material mind that perceives sense impressions and the mind that is emptiness, nothingness, or creativity. The Korean word for these two types of mind, *"chǒngsin,"* can also be translated as "spirit," but in the context of Iryǒp's philosophy it would be better translated as "mind" (*maǔm*). In other essays as well, Iryǒp uses the expression mind (*maǔm*) and spirit (*chǒngsin*) interchangeably.

3. Iryǒp's discussion of "thought" here might be confusing. Iryǒp mentions in this passage three types of thought: non-thought, cutting off thought, and arousal of thought. Non-thought and the arousal of thought that occurs after one has cut off thought are the same state. The thought that needs to be cut off is the thought based on distinctions and a dualistic way of thinking. It is also thought that arises when we, as the subject, look at the object in the subject-object dualism. Iryǒp is saying that when thought that arises in the dualistic mode calms down, and when one maintains a state of concentration, one comes to the realization that an individual is not a fragmented entity but a being with unlimited capacity, a being that is completely free and fully capable of controlling his or her thought. Non-thought, or cutting off thoughts, does not mean that one does not think or makes efforts to reach a state of not thinking. Only a specific way of thinking needs to be guarded against. The sixth patriarch of Zen Buddhism, Huineng, thus explains

that the core of his teaching is "no-thought" (Ch. *wunien*) and no-thought does not mean that one does not think, but is a combination of "no" (or without) dualistic thinking and "thought" arising from a creative way of thinking.

Chapter 13

Yi Wŏlsong was one of Kim Iryŏp's primary disciples. She served Iryŏp during the last years of Iryŏp's life for about ten years until her death in January 1971. As she mentions in this essay, Wŏlsong helped Iryŏp in preparing a final clean copy of the manuscript for the book *Reflections of a Zen Buddhist Nun*. This essay serves the function of an afterword to the book, but Iryŏp kept it as the final chapter.

Chapter 14

This chapter is a translation of "Kong ŭro toragara" (Return to emptiness) in *Haengbok kwa pulhaeng ŭi kalp'i esŏ* (In between happiness and misfortune 1964), 183–198. *In Between Happiness and Misfortune* is Iryŏp's third and last book. This essay is also included in *Miraese ka tahago namdorok*, 78–95. Parts of this essay, with some modifications and divided into small sections, also appear in *Iryŏp Sŏnmun*, 95–111.

1. One's own thinking is a rebellion against oneself because each activity contains that which contradicts earlier activities, as Iryŏp exemplifies here through the activities of eating and then ridding oneself through excretion of what has been consumed.

2. The meaning of this passage is not clear. I would read it as: the "self" is dried out both internally and externally, even though it claims to be one with the universe. However, in Korean, the passage is ambiguous.

3. Kim Iryŏp's emphasis on "life energy" (*saengmyŏng*) in this essay is worthy of our attention if we want to understand the evolution of her thought. In her pre-monastic life Iryŏp raised her voice against social injustice, especially against gender discrimination in her society. After she joined the monastery she wanted to resolve the problem in a more fundamental manner, which leads her to her meditation on existence itself. At this stage her social criticism gives way to her existential philosophy, especially in the way she thinks about what it means to be a human being. *Reflections of a Zen Buddhist Nun* begins with the essay on "life" (*insaeng*). From the life of a human being, Iryŏp moves one step further into a more fundamental form of existence, that is, what she refers to as "life energy" (*saengmyŏng*), which she sees as the essence of both sentient and insentient beings. Her discussion of "life energy" also appears in the 1966 essay "Path to Eternity," which appears as Chapter 17 of this volume.

4. It seems that Iryŏp's use of the word "spirit" (*hon*) in this passage has sev-

eral meanings. First, it refers to the "mind" when she uses the expression literally, writing *"maŭm"* in Korean with the Chinese character signifying "spirit" (*hon*) in parenthesis. She also identifies spirit with "thought" (*saenggak*). When she uses the expression to indicate "the mind," it generally conforms to the Zen Buddhist understanding of mind. In Iryŏp's philosophy the mind is also related to universal life energy, as we see in the earlier section of this essay, where the mind and spirit seem to refer to life energy. In the passage in this paragraph, the word is also used in its conventional sense of otherworldly beings, as when Iryŏp mentions spirits coming to ancestral ceremonies or deliverance ceremonies (*ch'ŏndojae*).

5. In other chapters Iryŏp used the expression "creativity" in lieu of "emptiness" in explaining the nature of the Buddha or God. "Creativity" gives the impression of more positive activities, whereas "emptiness," a Buddhist concept referring to the non-substantiality of things, could be understood as being similar to nihilistic nothingness. Combining emptiness with creativity, we can get a better understanding of both Iryŏp's concept of creativity and the Buddhist concept of emptiness.

6. Iryŏp's idea of body and spirit is different from body-mind dualism, which in Buddhism is obviously not tenable. As can be seen in this passage and as she discusses it in several other places, Iryŏp believes both body and spirit to be material; "body" refers to a tangible, physical reality with form, whereas "spirit" is the content of the body but is also subject to change according to changes in material reality.

7. One might find a Merleau-Pontean phenomenological approach to phenomena and noumenon relevant here. In this approach, noumenon is assumed, but it does not exist in separation from phenomena. For a comparative philosophy of Merleau-Ponty and Korean Sŏn Buddhism (especially that of Pojo Chinul), see Jin Y. Park, "The Double."

8. I have omitted one sentence that follows this one in the original Korean. The omitted sentence translates as "Reality is that which is imagined and theorized outside emptiness, hence, it is common sense to know that there is nothing one cannot do or cannot know" (*Iryŏp Sŏnmun*, 111). The passage seems erroneous in that Iryŏp has emphasized that there is no "outside" of emptiness, in which case daily reality cannot be something that exists outside emptiness. Rather, I consider that the passage should be read in the negative: "Reality is not something that is imagined or theorized outside emptiness." This is followed by the passage that refers to the fact that one is capable of doing and knowing anything.

Chapter 15

This essay is a translation of "Ch'amsŏn kwa simdŭk" (Meditation and the attainment of the mind), included in *Miraese ka tahago namdorok*, 2, 99–103. I have removed subsection titles. This essay also appears without subsection titles in *Iryŏp Sŏnmun*, 116–119.

1. The six realms are the realm of humans, semi-gods, heaven, animals, hungry ghosts, and hell. The four forms of birth are birth through womb, through an egg, through moisture, and through transformation.

Chapter 16

This essay is a translation of "Kido wa yŏmbul" (Prayer and chanting) from *Miraese ka tahago namdorok*, 2, 96–98. The essay also appears in *Iryŏp Sŏnmun*, 114–115.

1. In other essays, Iryŏp repeatedly states that the mind is material and contends that the dualism of mind and body (spiritual and material) or of visible and invisible realities does not hold since this dualism is tenable only when one fails to see the fundamental oneness of the seeming opposites in the binary paradigm.

Chapter 17

This chapter is a translation of "Yŏngsaeng ŭl sanŭn kil: Ŏllonindŭl ege" (To live the life of eternity: To the journalists) from *Miraese ka tahago namdorok*, 2, 134–144. It also appears in *Iryŏp Sŏnmun*, 124–134. It was originally a transcript of one of Iryŏp's dharma talks, not something she wrote for publication.

1. In other words, one's complaints have a basis in one's desire; one's desire is caused by one's thinking; and one's thinking is one's own because one is the subject or agent of one's thinking. If one is the subject of one's thinking, one should be able to control one's thoughts, and thus be able to manage one's complaints, which means complaints should disappear because, if not, it is like complaining about one's own thinking, like complaining about having one's own arms or legs.
2. In other words, Christianity needs to focus more on teaching people that each individual is sacred, instead of letting them worship God as an object to rely on.
3. I omit the second half of this sentence. The omitted section translates: "there are different objects with different names to rely on; even though not on Buddhism, one should rely on the Buddha." The meaning of this phrase is obscure.
4. Iryŏp is contrasting what she considers real religious education with popular versions of practicing Buddhism: religion as worshipping the founder of a religious tradition, practicing religion for material benefit, or using religion to attain worldly fame through mass media.
5. *Having Burned Away My Youth* (*Ch'ŏngch'un ŭl pulsarŭgo*) is my translation of the title of her second book, published in 1962. It is also the title of the essay included as Chapter 11 in this volume.
6. Following this sentence are two more sentences that I have omitted because their meaning in the context is unclear. The following is a literal translation

of the sentences: "So, what happened in the past—when we think about death at this point, we say, I was at the verge of death—I pointed out how big we have become since we were born from our mother's womb. Since we forget what happened when we were young, we are truly suffering from amnesia."

7. In the version of this lecture that appears in *Miraese ka tahago namdorok*, "small I" (*sosŭng in na*) and "great I" (*taesŭng in na*) literally mean "the I who is a small nun" and "the I who is a big nun" (143). In the version in *Iryŏp Sŏnmun*, the Chinese characters are different (but the Korean pronunciations are the same). In that version, the two expressions literally mean, "the I as Hīnayāna" and "the I as Mahāyāna" (133).

Character Glossary

asura	阿修羅
Chaega ch'ulga	在家出家
Chagak	自覺
Ch'amsŏn kwa simdŭk	參禪과 心得
Chan	禪
ch'angjosŏng	創造性
Chikchisa	直指寺
Chinhan	辰韓
chipsegi Pul	집세기佛
chitsori	짓소리
Ch'oe Namsŏn	崔南善
Chogye	曹溪
ch'ŏn	天
ch'ŏnan chijŭng t'ong	天眼智證通
ch'ŏn'an t'ong	天眼通
ch'ŏndojae	遷度齋
chong	宗
chong-gyo (chonggyo)	宗敎
chŏngsin	精神
Ch'ŏngt'ap	靑塔
Ch'ŏngt'aphoe	靑搭會
chonjae	存在
ch'ŏn-paek-ŏk kujok hwasin	千百億其足化身
ch'ŏn'yi t'ong	天耳通
chosin	祖信
"Chosŏn Pulgyo kaehyŏngnon"	朝鮮佛敎改革論
"Chosŏn Pulgyo yusillon"	朝鮮佛敎維新論
chugŏp	住劫
chŭksim si Pul	卽心是佛
ch'ulga	出家
chungsaeng t'ak	衆生濁
Dao	道
Dōgen	道元
Ewha Hakdang	梨花學堂
fayin	梵音
gongan	公案
"Hae ege sŏ sonyŏn ege"	海에게서 少年에게
Haewangsŏng	海王星
Hakhae	學海
hanmun	漢文
Hayŏp	荷葉
Higuchi Ichiyō	樋口一葉
Hiratsuka Raichō	平塚らいてう
hon	魂
Hong Niang	紅娘
huatou	話頭
Huayan	華嚴
hwadu	話頭
Hwanhŭidae	歡喜臺
hwasin	化身
Hyesim	慧諶
Hyesŏng	彗星
hyŏnsil	現實
hyosŏng	曉星, 爻星
igye	理戒
Im Nowŏl	林盧月
inch'ŏn kyo	人天敎
insaeng	人生
ipsŭng	立繩
Jogyesa	曹溪寺
kagyŏng	覺靈

Kakhwangsa	覺皇寺	*ŏp*	業
kangwŏn	講院	Oseam	五歲庵
Kanhwa Zen	看話禪	*o sint'ong*	五神通
karura	迦樓羅	*ot'ak akse*	五濁惡世
Kido wa yŏmbul	祈禱와 念佛	Paek Sŏnguk	白性郁
Kim Iryŏp	金一葉	Paekche	白濟
Kim Myŏngsun	金明淳	Pak P'aengnyŏn	朴彭年
Kim Wŏnju	金元周	*p'albu*	八部
Kimch'ŏn	金泉	*pangp'yŏn*	方便
kinnara	緊那羅	Pojo Chinul	普照知訥
kōan	公案	*pŏmp'ae*	梵唄
koegŏp	壞劫	*pŏmŭm*	梵音
Koguryŏ	高句麗	*pon chŏngsin*	本精神
kŏndalp'a	乾闥婆	*pon maŭm*	본마음
konggŏp	空劫	*pŏnnoe t'ak*	煩惱濁
kŏp t'ak	劫濁	*pŏp*	法
kudu Sŏn	口頭禪	*pŏpsin*	法身
Kwŏn Sangno	權相老	*posin*	報身
Kyesi	啓示	Pul	佛
Kyŏngbuk	慶北	Pulgyo	佛教
Kyŏnsŏngam	見性菴	"Pulgyo sunjŏn	佛教純全哲學
kyŏn t'ak	見濁	ch'ŏrhak"	
Mahan	馬韓	Pyŏnhan	弁韓
Mahayŏn	摩訶衍	*rentian jiao*	人天教
mahuraga	摩睺羅迦	*sa*	師
Man'gong	滿空	*saenggak*	생각
Manhae Han	萬海韓龍雲	*saengmyŏng*	生命
Yongun		*saengryŏng*	生靈
maŭm	마음	*sagŏp*	四劫
mok	牧	*sagye*	事戒
moksa	牧師	*samch'e*	三體
mu	無	Samguk Sidae	三國時代
mua	無我	Samhan	三韓
mujŏk chŏngsin	無的精神	*samsin*	三身
mujŏk chonjae	無的存在	*sanggi*	想起
mujŏk ppuri	無的뿌리	*sasi maji*	巳時麻旨
mujungyu	無中有	*Seitō*	青鞜
munhwain	文化人	Sejo	世祖
myŏng t'ak	命濁	Silla	新羅
Na Hyesŏk	羅蕙錫	*simgwang*	心光
Nyŏjagye	女子界	*sin chŏngjo ron*	新情操論
ŏllon Pulgyo	言論佛教	*Sindonga*	新東亞

sinjok t'ong	神足通	Tahui Zonggao	大慧宗杲
sin kaein juŭi	新個人主義	Tanjong	端宗
sinsŏn	神仙	*t'asim t'ong*	他心通
sint'ong	神通	*toin*	道人
Sinyŏja	新女子	*t'ong Pulgyo*	通佛敎
sinyŏŭi t'ong	神如意通	Ŭisang	義湘
soa	小我	*uji*	有時
Sŏbongam	瑞鳳庵	*wanchŏn*	完全
Sŏn	禪	*wanin*	完人
sŏnggŏp	成劫	Wŏlsong	月松
Sŏnhakwŏn	禪學院	Wŏnhyo	元曉
sŏnwŏn	禪院	*Xixiangji*	西廂記
Sonyŏn	少年	*yach'a*	夜叉
sosŭng in na	小乘인 나, 小僧인	Yi Kwangsu	李光洙
	나	Yi Wŏlsong	李月松
Su Dongpo	蘇東坡	*yokkye*	欲界
Su Shi	蘇軾	*yŏmbul sammae*	念佛三昧
subok Pulgyo	修福佛敎	*yong*	龍
Sudŏksa	修德寺	*yŏn'gi*	緣起
sŭng (nun)	僧	*Yuanren lun*	原人論
sungmyŏng t'ong	宿命通	*yuk*	肉
taea	大我	Yun Simdŏk	尹心悳
taegong	大空	*yusi*	有時
taejayuin	大自由人	Zen	禪
tae munhwain	大文化人	Zhang Sheng	張生
taeryŏk	大力		
taesŭng in na	大乘인 나, 大僧인		
	나		

Bibliography

Works by Kim Iryŏp

Kim Iryŏp 金一葉 (Kim Wŏnju 金元周). "Abŏnim yŏngjŏn e" 아버님 靈前에 (Before my father's soul). *Tonga ilbo* 1 (January 1925). Reprinted in Kim Iryŏp, *Miraese ka tahago namdorok,* vol. 1, 406–409.

———. "Awakening." In Yong-Hee Kim, *Questioning Minds,* 55–67.

———. "B ssi ege" B 氏에게. In Kim Iryŏp, *Ŏnŭ sudoin ŭi hoesang,* 53–71.

———. "Chagak" 自覺 (Awakening). *Tonga ilbo,* June 1926, 19–26. Reprinted in Kim Iryŏp, *Miraese ka tahago namdorok,* vol. 1, 160–173.

———. "Chilli rŭl morŭm nida" 진리를 모릅니다 (I do not know the truth). In Kim Iryŏp, *Miraese ka tahago namdorok,* vol. 1, 266–384.

———. *Ch'ŏngch'un ŭl pulsarŭgo* 青春을 불사르고 (Having burned away my youth). Seoul: Munsŏn'gak, 1962.

———. "Chonggyo ŭi mokchŏk" 종교의 목적 (The goal of religion). In Kim Iryŏp, *Iryŏp Sŏnmun,* 78–79.

———. *Haengbok kwa pulhaeng ŭi kalp'i esŏ* 幸福과 不幸의 갈피에서 (In between happiness and misfortune). Seoul: Whimun ch'ulp'ansa, 1964.

———. "Ipsan yisip o chunyŏn saehae rŭl majŭmyŏ" 入山二十五周年 새해를 맞으며 (On New Year's Day of the twenty-fifth year after joining the monastery). In Kim Iryŏp, *Ŏnŭ sudoin ŭi hoesang,* 44–52.

———. *Iryŏp Sŏnmun* 一葉禪文 (Zen writings by Iryŏp). Seoul: Munhwa sarang, 2001.

———. "Kaŭl sori rŭl tŭrŭ myŏnsŏ" 가을 소리를 들으면서 (As I hear the sound of autumn). *Hakhae,* December 1937. Reprinted in Kim Iryŏp, *Miraese ka tahago namdorok* , vol. 1, 478–482.

———. *Kim Iryŏp sŏnjip* 김일엽선집 (Selected writings by Kim Iryŏp). Compiled by Kim Uyŏng. Seoul: Hyŏndae munhak, 2012.

———. "Kim Wŏnju: My View on Chastity." In Choi, *New Women in Colonial Korea,* 141–142.

———. "Kim Wŏnju: The Necessity of Women's Education." In Choi, *New Women in Colonial Korea,* 50–52.

———. "Kim Wŏnju: The Self-Awakening of Women." In Choi, *New Women in Colonial Korea,* 30–32.

———. "Kim Wŏnju: Women's Demands and Arguments." In Choi, *New Women in Colonial Korea,* 197–199.

——. *Kkot i chimyŏn nun i siryŏra* 꽃이 지면 눈이 시려라 (When the flowers wither, tears well up). Seoul: Osangsa, 1985.

——. "Kyesi" 啓示 (Revelation). *Sinyŏja* 1 (March 1920). Reprinted in Yu, *Kim Iryŏp ŭi Sinyŏja yŏn'gu,* 168–172, 535–539.

——. "Man'gong taehwasang ŭl ch'umo hayŏ (sibo chu kiil e)" 滿空大和尙을 追慕하여 十五周忌日에 (In memory of Great Master Man'gong: At the fifteenth anniversary of his death). In Kim Iryŏp, *Ŏnŭ sudoin ŭi hoesang,* 24–43.

——. *Miraese ka tahago namdorok* 未來世가 다하고 남도록 (Until future life comes to an end and even afterward), 2 vols. Seoul: Inmul yŏn'guso, 1974.

——. "Mŏrimal" 머리 말 (Preface). In Kim Iryŏp, *Ŏnŭ sudoin ŭi hoesang,* 1–3.

——. "Na ŭi chŏngjo kwan" 나의 情操觀 (My view on chastity). *Chosŏn ilbo,* January 8, 1927. Reprinted in Kim Iryŏp, *Miraese ka tahago namdorok,* vol. 2, 156–159.

——. "Ŏmŏni ŭi mudŏm" 어머니의 무덤 (My mother's graveyard). *Sinyŏja* 1 (March 1920). Reprinted in Yu, *Kim Iryŏp ŭi Sinyŏja yŏn'gu,* 129–132, 498–501.

——. *Ŏnŭ sudoin ŭi hoesang* 어느 修道人의 回想 (Reflections of a Zen Buddhist nun). Yesan, Ch'ungnam, Korea: Sudŏksa, 1960.

——. "Puldo rŭl taggŭmyŏ" 佛道를 닦으며 (Practicing Buddhism). *Samch'ŏlli* 三千里, January 1935. Reprinted in Kim Iryŏp, *Kkot i chimyŏn nun i siryŏra,* 209–213.

——. "Pulgyo esŏ nŭn woe chŏnghwa undong ŭl irŭk'yŏnna?" 佛敎에서는 왜 淨化運動을 일으켰나? (Why has Buddhism launched a purification movement?). In Kim Iryŏp, *Ŏnŭ sudoin ŭi hoesang,* 156–160.

——. "Pulgyo wa munhwa" 佛敎와 文化 (Buddhism and culture). In Kim Iryŏp, *Ŏnŭ sudoin ŭi hoesang,* 15–23.

——. "Pulmun t'ujok i chunyŏn e" 佛門 投足二周年에 (At the second anniversary of being a Buddhist). *Pulgyo,* February 1930. Reprinted in Kim Iryŏp, *Kkot i chimyŏn nun i siryŏra,* 54–157.

——. "Sin Pul kwa na ŭi kajŏng" 信佛과 나의 家庭 (Buddhist practice and my family). *Sindonga* 新東亞, December 1931. Reprinted in Kim Iryŏp, *Miraese ka tahago namdorok,* vol. 1, 429–431.

——. "Sinyŏja ŭi sahoe e taehan ch'aegim ŭl nonham" 新女子의 社會에 對한 責任을 논함 (On the new women's social responsibilities). *Sinyŏja* 新女子1 (March 1920). Reprinted in Yu, *Kim Iryŏp ŭi Sinyŏja yŏn'gu,* 105–108, 475–478.

——. *Sudŏksa ŭi noŭl* 수덕사의 노을 (Sunset at the Sudŏk Monastery). Seoul: Pŏmusa, 1976.

——. "Tongsaeng mŭdŭn twit tongsan: Pomnal i omyŏn kŭriun kŭ kot" 동생 묻은 뒷동산-봄날이 오면 그리운 그곳 (Hometown hill where my siblings were buried: The place that I miss when spring comes). *Sin'gajŏng* 新家庭, March 1933. Reprinted in Kim Iryŏp, *Miraese ka tahago namdorok,* vol. 1, 404–405.

——. "Tongsaeng ŭi chugŭm" 동생의 죽음 (Death of my sister). *Sinyŏja* 3 (May 1920). Reprinted in Yu, *Kim Iryŏp ŭi Sinyŏja yŏn'gu,* 310–317, 672–769.

——. "Uri sinyŏja ŭi yogu wa chujang" 우리 新女子의 要求와 主張 (We new

women's demands and claims) *Sinyŏja* 2 (April 1920). Reprinted in Yu, *Kim Iryŏp ŭi Sinyŏja yŏn'gu*, 187–199, 565–567.

———. "Uri ŭi isang" 우리의 理想 (Our ideals). *Punyŏjigwang* 婦女之光, July 1924. Reprinted in Kim Iryŏp, *Kkot i chimyŏn nun i siryŏra*, 81–86.

———. "Yŏja kyoyuk ŭi p'iryo" 여자 교육의 필요 (The necessity of women's education). *Tonga ilbo* 東亞日報, April 6, 1920. Reprinted in Kim Iryŏp, *Kkot i chimyŏn nun i shiryŏra*, 29–32.

———. "Yŏja ŭi chagak" 女子의 自覺 (The self-awakening of women). *Sinyŏja* 3 (May 1920). Reprinted in Yu, *Kim Iryŏp ŭi Sinyŏja yŏn'gu*, 285–287, 649–651.

———. "Yonggang onch'ŏn haeng" 龍岡溫泉行 (To Yonggang hot spring). *Pulgyo* 佛敎, October 1931. Reprinted in Kim Iryŏp, *Miraese ka tahago namdorok*, vol. 1, 416–423.

Other Sources

Blake, William. "The Marriage of Heaven and Hell." In *William Blake: The Complete Poems*, edited by Alicia Ostricker, 180–194. New York: Penguin Books, 1983.

Bradsley, Jan. "The New Woman in Japan and the Intimate Bonds of Translation." In *Translation in Modern Japan*, edited by Indra Levy, 213–233. New York: Routledge, 2011.

Buswell, Robert E., Jr. "Chinul's Systematization of Chinese Meditative Techniques in Korean Sŏn Buddhism." In *Traditions of Meditation in Chinese Buddhism*, edited by Peter N. Gregory, 199–242. Honolulu: University of Hawai'i Press, 1987.

———. "The 'Short-cut' Approach of K'an-hua Meditation: The Evolution of a Practical Subitism in Chinese Zen Buddhism." In *Sudden and Gradual: Approaches to Enlightenment in Chinese Thought*, edited by Peter N. Gregory, 321–377. Honolulu: University of Hawai'i Press, 1991.

———, trans. *The Collected Works of Chinul.* Honolulu: University of Hawai'i Press, 1983.

Chang, Garma C. C. *The Buddhist Teaching of Totality: The Philosophy of Hwa Yen Buddhism*. University Park: Pennsylvania State University Press, 1971/1991.

Cho, Joo-hyun. "The Politics of Gender Identity: The Women's Movement in Korea in the 1980s and 1990s." In *Women's Experiences and Feminist Practices in South Korea*, edited by Chang Pilhwa and Kim Eun-Shil, 229–258. Seoul: Ewha Womans University Press, 2005.

Ch'oe Hyesil 최혜실. *Sinyŏsŏngdŭl ŭn muŏt ŭl kkum kkuŏnnŭn'ga?* 신여성들은 무엇을 꿈꾸었는가? (What were the new women dreaming of?). Seoul: Saenggak ŭi namu, 2000.

Ch'oe Namsŏn 崔南善. "Chosŏn Pulgyo: Tongbang munhwasa sang e innŭn kŭ chiwi" 朝鮮佛敎: 東方 文化 史上에 있는 그 地位 (Chosŏn Buddhism: Its place in oriental cultural history). *Pulgyo* 74 (1930): 1–51.

————. "Insaeng kwa chonggyo: Na nŭn oe k'at'orik ero kaejong haennŭn'ga?" 人生과 宗敎: 나는 왜 카토릭에로 改宗했는가? (Life and religion: Why I have converted to Catholicism). *Han'guk ilbo,* November 17, 1955.

Choi, Hyaeweol. *New Women in Colonial Korea: A Sourcebook.* New York: Routledge, 2013.

Chŏn Kyŏngok, Pyŏn Chinwŏn, Pak Chinsŏk, and Kim Ŭnjŏng 전경옥, 변지원, 박진석, 김은정. *Han'guk yŏsŏng kŭnhyŏndaesa 1: Kaehwagi–1945* 한국여성근현대사 1:개화기-1945 (Modern and contemporary history of Korean women 1: The opening period–1945). *Han'guk yŏsŏng muhwasa* 한국 여성문화사 (Cultural history of Korean women, vol. 1). Seoul: Sungmyŏng yŏja taehak ch'ulp'an'guk, 2004.

Chŏng Kyuung 정규웅. *Na Hyesŏk p'yŏngjŏn: Nae mudŏm e kkŏt han songi kkoja chuo* 내 무덤에 꽃 한송이 꽂아주오 (A critical biography of Na Hyesŏk: Please place a flower on my grave). Seoul: Chungang M&B, 2003.

Chŏng Yŏngja 정영자. "Kim Iryŏp munhak yŏn'gu" 金一葉 文學硏究 (Study on Kim Iryŏp's literature). *Suryŏn ŏmunhakjip* 14 (1987): 1–26.

Chŏn'guk Pigunihoe 전국비구니회, ed. *Han'guk piguni ŭi suhaeng kwa salm* 한국 비구니의 수행과 삶 (The practice and life of Korean Buddhist nuns). 2 vols. Seoul: Yŏmun sŏwŏn, 2007–2009.

Cleary, Thomas, trans. *Entry into the Inconceivable: An Introduction to Hua-yen Buddhism.* Honolulu: University of Hawai'i Press, 1983.

Cook, Francis. *Hua-yen Buddhism: The Jewel Net of Indra.* University Park: Pennsylvania State University Press, 1977.

Danly, Robert Lyons. *In the Shade of Spring Leaves: The Life of Higuchi Ichiyō with Nine of Her Best Short Stories.* New York: W. W. Norton & Company, 1981.

Dōgen. *The Heart of Dōgen's Shōbōgenzo.* Translated by Norman Waddell and Masao Abe. Albany: State University of New York Press, 2002.

Ewha Pangnyŏn Sa P'yŏnch'an Wiwŏnhoe 이화백년사편찬위원회, ed. *Ewha paengnyŏn sa* 이화백년사 (One-hundred-year history of Ewha). Seoul: Ewha yŏja taehakkyo ch'ulp'anbu, 1994.

Foulk, Griffith T. "Myth, Ritual, and Monastic Practice in Sung Ch'an Buddhism." In *Religion and Society in T'ang and Sung China,* edited by Patricia Buckley Ebrey and Peter N. Gregory, 147–208. Honolulu: University of Hawai'i Press, 1995.

Freedman, Estelle B. "The New Woman: Changing Views of Women in the 1920s." *Journal of American History* 61, no. 2 (September 1974): 372–393.

Gregory, Peter N., trans. *Inquiry into the Origin of Humanity: An Annotated Translation of Tsung-mi's Yüan jen lun with a Modern Commentary.* Honolulu: University of Hawai'i Press, 1995.

Gregory, Peter N., and Daniel A. Getz Jr., eds. *Buddhism in the Sung.* Honolulu: University of Hawai'i Press, 1999.

Ha Ch'unsaeng 하춘생. *Kkadarŭm ŭi kkot: Han'guk kŭnse rŭl pinnaen kŭnse piguni* 깨달음의 꽃: 한국 근세를 빛낸 근세 비구니 (The flowers of enlightenment: Buddhist nuns in modern times who have lightened up Korean Buddhism), 2 vols. Seoul: Yŏrae, 1998–2001.

Haeju 해주 (Chŏn Haeju 전해주). "Han'guk kŭnhyŏndae piguni ŭi suhaeng" 한국
　근현대비구니의 수행 (Buddhist nuns' practice in modern and contemporary
　Korea). In Chŏn'guk Pigunihoe, Han'guk piguni ŭi suhaeng kwa salm, vol. 1,
　129–164.
———. Hwaŏm ŭi segye 華嚴의 世界 (The world of Huayan). Seoul: Minjoksa, 1998.
Han'guk Pulgyo chŏnsŏ 韓國佛敎全書 (Collected works of Korean Buddhism).
　Seoul: Tongguk taehakkyo ch'ulp'anbu. 1979.
Harvey, Peter. An Introduction to Buddhist Ethics. Cambridge: Cambridge Univer-
　sity Press, 2000.
Hiratsuka, Raichō. "Hiratsuka Raichō." In Japanese Philosophy: A Sourcebook, edited
　by James W. Heisig, Thomas P. Kasulis, and John C. Maraldo, 1148–1164.
　Honolulu: University of Hawai'i Press, 2011.
———. In the Beginning, Woman Was the Sun: The Autobiography of a Japanese Femi-
　nist. Translated by Teruko Craig. New York: Columbia University Press,
　2006.
———. "Shojo no shinka" 処女の真価 (The true value of virginity). In Hiratsu-
　ka Raichō chosaku-shū 平塚らいちう著作集 (Collected writings of Hiratsuka
　Raichō), vol. 2, 53–60. Tokyo: Ōtsuki shoten, 1983.
Hyesim 慧諶. Gongan Collections I. Collected Works of Korean Buddhism, vol. 7-1.
　Translated by Juhn Y. Ann, edited by John Jorgensen. Seoul: Jogye Order
　of Korean Buddhism, 2012. http://www.acmuller.net/kor-bud/collected_
　works.html
———. Gongan Collections II. Collected Works of Korean Buddhism, vol. 7-2. Trans-
　lated and Edited by John Jorgensen. Seoul: The Jogye Order of Korean Bud-
　dhism, 2012.
Im Chŏngyŏn 임정연, ed. Im Nowŏl chakp'umjip 임노월 작품집 (Collected works by
　Im Nowŏl). Seoul: Chimanji kojŏn sŏnjip, 2008.
Im Nowŏl 임노월. Angma ŭi sarang 악마의 사랑 (A devil's love), edited by Pang
　Minho. Seoul: Hyangyŏn, 2005.
Im Okhŭi 임옥희. "Sinyŏsŏng ŭi pŏmjuhwa rŭl wihan siron" 신여성의 범주화를
　위한 시론 (Essay on the categorization of the new women). In T'ae, Han'uk ŭi
　singminji kŭndae wa yŏsŏng konggan, 78–106.
Jingang banruo buloumi jing 金剛般若波羅密經. Taishō shinshū daizōkyō 大正新脩大
　藏經. 8.235.748c-752c.
Jorgensen, John. "Minjung Buddhism: A Buddhist Critique of the Status Quo—Its
　History, Philosophy, and Critique." In Jin Y. Park, Makers of Modern Korean
　Buddhism, 275–313.
Keown, Damien. Contemporary Buddhist Ethics. Richmond, Surrey: Curzon, 2000.
Key, Ellen. The Century of the Child (1900). New York: G. P. Putnam's Sons, 1909.
———. The Education of the Child. New York: G. P. Putnam's Sons, Knickerbocker
　Press. 1910.
———. Love and Ethics. New York: B. W. Huesch. 1912.
———. Love and Marriage. Translated by Authur G. Chater. New York: G. P. Put-
　nam's Sons, Knickerbocker Press, 1911.

———. *Woman Movement* (1909). Translated by Mamah Bouton Borthwick. New York: G. P. Putnam's Sons, 1912.

Kilsang 吉詳, comp. *Pulgyo taesachŏn* 佛敎人辭典 (Encylopedia of Buddhism), 2 vols. Seoul: Hongbŏbwŏn, 2003.

Kim Hangmyŏng, O Chaeho, and Han Unsa 김항명, 오재호, 한운사. *Yŏngwŏnhan salm ŭl ch'aja: Kim Iryŏp* 영원한 삶을 찾아: 金一葉 (In search of eternal life: Kim Iryŏp). Seoul: Sŏngdo munhwasa, 1993.

Kim Jongmyŏng 김종명. "Man'gong ŭi Sŏn sasang: t'ŭkching kwa yŏkhal" 만공의 선사상: 특징과 역할 (Man'gong's approach to Zen: Its characteristics and role). *Chonggyo yŏn'gu* 34 (Spring 2004): 203–32.

Kim Kyŏngil 김경일. *Yŏsŏng ŭi kŭndae, kŭndae ŭi yŏsŏng: 20 segi chŏnban'gi sinyŏsŏng kwa kŭndaesŏng* 여성의 근대, 근대의 여성: 20세기 전반기 신여성과 근대성 (Women's modernity, modern women: The new women and modernity at the first half of the 20th century). Seoul: P'urŭn yŏksa, 2004.

Kim Miyŏng 김미영. "1920 yŏndae sinyŏsŏng kwa kitoggyo e kwanhan koch'al: Na Hyesŏk, Kim Iryŏp, Kim Myŏngsun ŭi salm kwa munhak ŭl chungsim ŭro" 1920년대 신여성과 기독교에 관한 고찰: 나혜석, 김일엽, 김명순의 삶과 문학을 중심으로 (A Study on the relationship between the new women in the 1920s and Christianity: Focusing on the life and literature of Na Hyesŏk, Kim Iryŏp, and Kim Myŏnogsun). *Hyŏndae sosŏl yŏn'gu* 21 (2004): 67–96.

Kim, Yong-Hee, trans. *Questioning Minds: Short Stories by Modern Korean Women Writers*. Honolulu: University of Hawai'i Press, 2010.

Kim, Yung-Chung, ed. and trans. *Women of Korea: A History from Ancient Times to 1945*. Seoul: Ewha Womans University Press, 1975.

King, Sallie B. *Being Benevolence: The Social Ethics of Engaged Buddhism*. Honolulu: University of Hawai'i Press, 2005.

———. *Socially Engaged Buddhism*. Honolulu: University of Hawai'i Press, 2009.

Kwŏn Podŭrae 보드래. *Yŏnae ŭi sidae-1920 yŏndae ch'oban ŭi munhwa wa yuhaeng* 연애의 시대-1920년대 초반의 문화와 유행 (The age of love affairs: Culture and trends of the mid-1920s). Seoul: Hyŏnsil munhwa yŏn'gu, 2003.

Kyŏngwan 경완. "Iryŏp sŏnsa ŭi ch'ulga wa suhaeng" 일엽선사의 출가와 수행 (Zen Master Iryŏp's joining the monastery and Buddhist practice"). In Chŏn'guk Pigunihoe, *Han'guk piguni ŭi suhaeng kwa salm*, 221–251.

Lee Tae-Suk (Yi T'aesuk) 이태숙. "Yŏsŏng haebangnon ŭi nangmanjŏk chip'yŏng: Kim Iryŏp non" 여성해방론의 낭만적 지평: 김일엽론 (The romantic horizon of the theory of women's liberation: The case of Kim Iryŏp). *Yŏsŏng munhak yŏn'gu* 4 (2002): 177–201.

Lowy, Dina. *The Japanese "New Woman": Images of Gender and Modernity*. New Brunswick, NJ: Rutgers University Press, 2007.

———. "Love and Marriage: Ellen Key and Hiratsuka Raichō Explore Alternatives." *Women Studies* 33, no. 4 (January 2004): 361–380.

Maeil Sinbo 每日申報. "Insŭp kwa chŏnt'ong e panhang sonyŏn ch'ulkahan Kim Iryŏp" 因習과 傳統에 反抗 少年出家한 金一葉 (Kim Iryŏp, who joined the monastery as a revolt against conventions and traditions). May 13, 1930, 2.

Muller, A. Charles, ed. *Digital Dictionary of Buddhism*. http://buddhism-dict.net/ddb/ (accessed May 9, 2011).

Mun Okp'yo 문옥표, ed. *Sinyŏsŏng: Han'guk kwa Ilbon ŭi kŭndae yŏsŏngsang* 신여성: 한국과 일본의 근대 여성상 (New women: Images of the modern women in Korea and Japan). Seoul: Ch'ŏngnyŏnsa, 2003.

Na Hyesŏk 나혜석. "The ideal woman." In Choi, *New Women in Colonial Korea*, 28–29.

———. "Isangjŏk puin" 理想的 婦人 (The ideal woman). *Hakchigwang* 學之光 3 (December 1914): 13–14. Reprinted in Yi Sanggyŏng, *Na Hyesŏk chŏnjip*, 183–185.

———. "Na rŭl itchi annŭn haengbok" 나를 잊지 않는 행복 (The happiness of not forgetting oneself). *Sinyŏsŏng*, August 1924. Reprinted Yi Sanggyŏng, *Na Hyesŏk chŏnjip*, 263.

No Chayŏng 盧子泳 "No Chayŏng: The Forerunner of the Women's Movement, Ellen Key." In Choi, *New Women in Colonial Korea*, 96–99.

———. "Yŏsŏng undong ŭi che 1-inja ellen kei" 女性運動의 제 1人者 엘렌케이 (Ellen Key: The forerunner of the women's movement). *Kaebyŏk* 8 (February 1921): 46–53.

No Mirim 盧美林. "Higutchi Itchiyo wa Kim Iryŏp ŭi yŏsŏngsŏng taejo" 通口 一葉와 金一葉의 여성성 연구 (Comparison of femininity between Higuchi Ichiyō and Kim Iryŏp). *Ilŏ ilmunhak yŏn'gu* 40 (2002): 141–165.

Odin, Steve. *Process Metaphysics and Hua-yen Buddhism: A Critical Study of Cumulative Penetration vs. Interpenetration*. Albany: State University of New York Press, 1982.

Oh, Bonnie B. C. "Kim Iryŏp's Conflicting Worlds." In *Creative Women of Korea: The Fifteenth through the Twentieth Centuries*, edited by Young-Key Kim-Renaud, 174–191. Armonk, NY: M. E. Sharpe, 2004.

Paek Sŏnguk 白性郁. Paek Sŏnguk paksa songsu kinyŏm saŏp wiwŏnhoe 白性郁博士頌壽記念事業委員會, ed. *Paek Sŏnguk paksa munjip* 白性郁博士文集 (Collected writings by Dr. Paek Sŏnguk). Seoul: Tongguk taehak ch'ulp'anbu, 1960.

Palmer, Daniel. "Masao Abe, Zen Buddhism, and Social Ethics." *Journal of Buddhist Ethics* 4 (1997): 112–137.

Pang Minho 방민호. "Kim Iryŏp munhak ŭi sasangjŏk pyŏnmo kwajŏng kwa Pulgyo sŏnt'aek ŭi ŭimi" 김일엽 문학의 사상적 변모과정과 불교 선택의 의미 (Evolution of Kim Iryŏp's literary thought and the significance of her engagement with Buddhism). *Han'guk hyŏndae munhak yŏn'gu* 20 (2006): 357–403.

———. "Sarang kwa chŏlmang kwa top'i ŭi romangs: Han'guk ch'oech'o ŭi yesul chisang chuŭija Im Nowŏl sosŏljip" 사랑과 절망과 도피의 로망스: 한국최초 의 예술지상주의자 임노월 소설집 (Romance of love, despair, and exile: Collected writings of Im Nowŏl, the first Korean writer of art for art's sake). In Im Nowŏl, *Angma ŭi sarang*, 156–183.

Park Jeong-sou (Pak Chŏngsu) 박정수. "Im Nowŏl, 20 yŏndae angmajŏk modŏnisŭtŭ" 임노월, 20년대 악마적 모더니스트 (Im Nowŏl: A diabolic modernist in the 1920s). *Sihak kwa ŏnŏhak* 10 (2005): 161–186.

Park, Jin Y. *Buddhism and Postmodernity: Zen, Huayan, and the Possibility of Buddhist-Postmodern Ethics.* Lanham, MD: Lexington Books, 2008.

———. "The Double: Merleau-Ponty and Chinul on Thinking and Questioning." In *Merleau-Ponty and Buddhism,* edited by Jin Y. Park and Gereon Kopf, 97–112. Lanham, MD: Lexington Books, 2009.

———. "Gendered Response to Modernity: Kim Iryŏp and Buddhism." In Jin Y. Park, *Makers of Modern Korean Buddhism,* 109–127.

———, ed. *Makers of Modern Korean Buddhism.* Albany: State University of New York Press, 2010.

Park, Sung Bae. *Buddhist Faith and Sudden Enlightenment.* Albany: State University of New York Press, 1983.

Price, A. F., and Wong Mou-lam, trans. *The Diamond Sūtra and the Sūtra of Hui-Neng.* Boston: Shambhala, 1990.

Queen, Christopher, and Sallie B. King. *Engaged Buddhism: Buddhist Liberation Movements in Asia.* Albany: State University of New York Press, 1996.

Reporter B, B 記者. "Sakpal hago changsam ibŭn Kim Iryŏp yŏsa ŭi hoegyŏn'gi" 削髮하고 長衫입은 金一葉 女史의 會見記 (An interview with tonsured Ms. Kim Iryŏp in a nun's robe). *Kaebyŏk,* January 1935: 12–17.

Sato, Barbara. *The New Japanese Woman: Modernity, Media, and Women in Interwar Japan.* Durham, NC: Duke University Press, 2003.

Schlütter, Morten. *How Zen Became Zen: The Dispute over Enlightenment and the Formation of Chan Buddhism in Song-Dynasty China.* Honolulu: University of Hawai'i Press, 2010.

Sugyŏng 수경. "Han'guk piguni kangwŏn paldalsa" 한국비구니 강원 발달사 (History of the evolution of *bhikṣuṇī* seminaries in Korea). In Ch'ŏn'guk piguni-hoe, *Han'guk piguni ŭi suhaeng kwa salm,* 15–51.

Sung Rak-Hi 成樂喜. "Kim Iryŏp munhangnon" 김일엽 문학론 (On Kim Iryŏp's literature). *Asea yŏsŏng yŏn'gu,* December 1978, 307–326.

Suzuki, Daisetz Teitaro, trans. *The Laṅkāvatāra Sūtra: A Mahāyāna Text.* Delhi: Motilal Banarsidass Publishers, 2003.

T'ae Hyesuk 태혜숙, ed. *Han'guk ŭi singminji kŭndae wa yŏsŏng konggan* 한국의 식민지 근대와 여성 공간 (Colonial modernity in Korea and women's space). Seoul: Yŏiyŏn, 2004.

Taishō shinshū daizōkyō 大正新脩大藏經. Tokyo: Taishō issaikyō kankōkai, 1924–1932.

Threefold Lotus Sutra. Translated by Bunno Kato. Kyoto: Kosei Publishing Company, 2005.

Thurman, Robert A. F., trans. *The Holy Teaching of Vimalakīrti: A Mahāyāna Scripture.* University Park: Pennsylvania State University Press, 1976.

Tomida, Hiroko. *Hiratsuka Raicho and Early Japanese Feminism.* Boston: Brill, 2004.

Tomida, Hiroko, and Gordon Daniels. *Japanese Women: Emerging from Subservience, 1868–1945.* Folkestone, Kent: Global Oriental, 2005.

Ŭisang 義湘. "Hwaŏm ilsŭng pŏpkye to" 華嚴一乘法界圖 (Diagram of the realm of reality of Huayan one vehicle). In *Han'guk Pulgyo chŏnsŏ,* vol. 2, 1a–8c.

Whitehill, James. "Buddhism and the Virtues." In *Contemporary Buddhist Ethics*, edited by Damien Keown, 17–36. Richmond, Surrey: Curzon, 2000.

———. "Buddhist Ethics in Western Context: The 'Virtues' Approach." *Journal of Buddhist Ethics* 1 (1994):1–22.

Yi Chisuk 이지숙. "1910 yŏndae ilbon sinyŏsŏng munhak: Seit'o rŭl chungsim ŭro" 1910년대 일본 신여성 문학: 세이토를 중심으로 (Japanese new women's literature in the 1910s: With a focus on the *Seitō*). *Inmunhak yŏn'gu* 34, no. 1 (2007): 157–175

Yi Hŭijŏng 이희정. "1920 yŏndae ch'ogi ŭi yŏnae tamnon kwa Im Nowŏl munhak: maeil sinbo rŭl chungsim ŭiro" 1920년대 초기의 연애담론과 임노월 문학: 매일신보를 중심으로 (Discourse on love affairs in the early 1920s and Im Nowŏl's literature: With a focus on the *Maeil Sinbo*). *Hyŏndae sosŏl yŏn'gu* 37 (2008): 151–172.

Yi Hwahyŏng and Yu Chinwŏl 이화형, 유진월. "Sinyŏja wa kŭndae yŏsŏng tamnon ŭi hyŏngsŏng" <新女子>와 근대 여성 談論의 形成 (*The New Women* and the formation of modern discourse on women). *Ŏmun yŏn'gu* 31, no. 2 (Summer 2003): 223–243.

Yi Myŏngon 李明溫. *Hŭllŏ kan yŏinsang: Kŭdŭl ŭi yesul kwa insaeng* 흘러간 女人像, 그들의 藝術과 人生 (Images of the women of the past: Their arts and life). Seoul: In'gansa, 1956.

Yi Paeyong 이배용. "Ilche sigi sinyŏsŏng ŭi yŏksajŏk sŏnggyŏk" 일제시기 신여성의 역사적 성격 (Historical implications of the new women during the Japanese colonial period). In Mun Okp'yo, *Sinyŏsŏng: Han'guk kwa Ilbon ŭi kŭndae yŏsŏngsang*, 21–50.

Yi Sanggyŏng 이상경, ed. *Na Hyesŏk chŏnjip* 나혜석 전집 (Complete works of Na Hyesŏk). Seoul: T'aehaksa, 2002.

———. *Na nŭn in'gan ŭro salgo sipta: Yŏngwŏnhan sinyŏsong Na Hyesŏk* 나는 인간으로 살고 싶다: 영원한 신여성 나혜석 (I would like to live as a human being: Na Hyesŏk, an eternal new woman). Seoul: Han'gilsa, 2002.

Yŏn'gu Konggan Suyu and Nŏmŏ Kŭndae Maech'e Yŏn'gu Tim 연구공간 수유+넘어 근대매체연구팀, ed. *Sinyŏsŏng: Maech'e ro pon kŭndae yŏsŏng p'ungsoksa* 신여성: 매체로 본 근대여성풍속사 (The new women: A cultural history of images of modern women seen through media). Seoul: Han'gyŏre Sinmunsa, 2005.

Yoo, Jung Suk. "A Study of the Relationship between Christianity and Modern Korean Female Writers, with a Focus on Na Hye-seoki, Kim Il-yeop, and Kim Myeong-sun." PhD diss., Korea University. Seoul, Korea, 2011.

Yu Chinwŏl 유진월. *Kim Iryŏp ŭi Sinyŏja yŏn'gu* 김일엽의 <신여자> 연구 (The study of Kim Iryŏp's *New Women*). Seoul: P'urŭn Sasang, 2006.

Yu Munsŏ 유문선. "Im Nowŏl munhak pip'yŏng yŏn'gu" 임노월문학비평 연구 (Study on Im Nowŏl's literary theory). *Hansin inmunhak yŏn'gu* 2 (December 2001): 103–127.

Zongmi 宗密. *Yuanren lun* 原人論 (Inquiry into the origin of humanity). *Taishō shinshū daizōkyō*. 45.1886.707c–710c.

Index

Page numbers in **bold** indicate complete chapters

237n4, 252n7, 257n3, 266n2, 267n11; and social responsibility, 6. *See also* chastity; Hiratsuka Raichō; *New Women*; social engagement; women; women's movements

New Women (Sinyŏja), 1, 4–6, 7, 21, 150, 237n4, 238nn18,21, 267n10

new year(s): and the discovery of true self, 81–83, 85–86, 257n5; and the passing of time, 84–85. *See also* "On the New Year's Day of the Twenty-Fifth Year after Joining the Monastery"

nirvana (attaining spiritual peace): and Buddhist practice, 134, 224, 260n6; as a chapter of eternal life, 31; and nothingness, 34, 39, 74–75, 247n15; and peace, 45, 48, 89, 91, 104, 117, 208, 215–217; as samsara, 260n6; Tolstoy's misunderstanding of, 39. *See also* birth and rebirth

no-exit, and the cessation of dualism, 250n11

no-mind/no-thought, 120–139; and creativity, 53, 80, 270n3; as the fundamental source of [spiritual] income, 124–125, 138; and meditation, **224–226**; and peacefulness, 216, 224; and wholeness of mind, 123–125, 132–133, 135, 138, 139, 196, 202–203

non-being/non-existence (*mu*): and the end of suffering, 56, 123–124; power of, 134, 247n15; and the root of non-being (*mujŏk ppuri*), 35–36; and unity, 81–82, 255n23

non-duality: of the Buddhist worldview, 114, 250n15; self and other as one, 82, 89. *See also* Buddha Nature

non-self (*mua*): and dependent co-arising (*yŏn'gi*), 13–14, 24, 246n10; faith of non-self, 69–70, 106; and unification with God, 116, 214–215. *See also* becoming human; "great I"; great self; "I"; non-self; no-self; nothingness; self; "small I"; small self

non-sentient beings, and Buddha Nature, 15, 45–46, 53–54, 196

no-self, 36–37, 57, 70, 93, 107, 148, 253n11. *See also* becoming human; "great I";

great self; "I"; non-self; no-self; nothingness; self; "small I"; small self

nothingness: eons of times of (*konggŏp*), 31, 57, 123, 252n4; existence of nothingness (*mujŏk chonjae*), 34; and life energy, 137; and the sacredness of no-mind, 24, 133, 216. *See also* non-being/non-existence; non-self; no-self

noumenal reality, and the absolute non-duality of the Buddha, 264n8

nuns (*sŭng*): "early person" as a term for, 196–197; Iryŏp's position as head nun of a meditation hall, 20–21; Iryŏp's twenty-five years as, 22–23, **78–86**; Man'gong's dedication to the training of, 12, 176; negative views toward, 50, 207, 242n75; and the path of practice, 59–60, 233–234; pseudo-nuns, 95; and social engagement, 20–21; young women about to become, 206–207; and Zen meditation practice, 12. *See also* monasticism; precepts

oneness: and freedom, 17, 51, 131–132, 215–217, 220; misapprehension of, 17, 106; and the root of non-being (*mujŏk ppuri*), 35–36; world as one flower, 74

"On the New Year's Day of the Twenty-Fifth Year after Joining the Monastery," 22–23, 26, 78–86, 254n21, 257n8

Opening of the World (journal), Iryŏp's interview for, 19–20, 240n37

original existence, 36–37, 45; and life energy, 34, 217–218, 229–230, 232–235; of sentient beings, 116, 217–218. *See also* Buddha Nature; creativity; equality; "great I"

original heart (*pon maŭm*), 36

original mind (*pon chŏngsin/pon maŭm*): and complete being (*wanin*), 15, 38, 116, 118; and creativity (*ch'angjosŏng*), 15, 34, 80, 83, 89, 115, 175–176; loss of, 31; and original existence, 34, 36, 83, 89, 123; and true humanity, 30–32, 33–34, 99–100

Oseam (hermitage at Paektam Monastery), 71, 256n26

About the Translator

Jin Y. Park is an associate professor in the Department of Philosophy and Religion at American University. She received her Ph.D. at the State University of New York at Stony Brook. Her book-length publications include *Buddhism and Postmodernity: Zen, Huayan, and the Possibility of Buddhist-Postmodern Ethics; Makers of Modern Korean Buddhism; Merleau-Ponty and Buddhism;* and *Buddhisms and Deconstructions.*

Production Notes for Kim/*Reflections of a Zen Buddhist Nun*
Jacket design by Guy Horton
Composition by Wanda China with display type in Lucida Sans and Scala
Sans Pro and text in Book Antiqua
Printing and binding by Integrated Book Technology, Inc.
Printed on 60 lb. House White, 444 ppi